New Town
Pages 68–79

Around the Alster
Pages 120–131

AROUND
THE ALSTER

Old Town
Pages 54–67

NEW TOWN

OLD TOWN

PORT AND
SPEICHERSTADT

0 kilometres   1
0 miles   1

**Port and
Speicherstadt**
Pages 80–99

HAMBURG

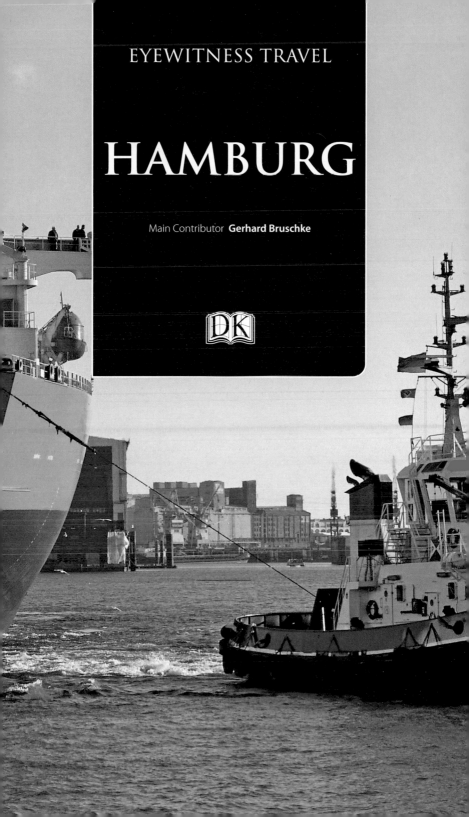

EYEWITNESS TRAVEL

HAMBURG

Main Contributor **Gerhard Bruschke**

LONDON, NEW YORK,
MELBOURNE, MUNICH AND DELHI
www.dk.com

Publisher Douglas Amrine

Produced by Dorling Kindersley Verlag GmbH, Munich

Publishing Director Dr. Jörg Theilacker

Project Manager Stefanie Franz

Art Director and Designer Anja Richter

Editor Brigitte Maier

Picture Editor Stefanie Franz

Cartography Anja Richter, Mare e Monte Kartografie

ProofReader Philip Anton

Contributor Gerhard Bruschke

Photographers Felix Fiedler, Susanne Gilges, Olaf Kalugin

Illustrators Branimir Georgiev, Maria-Magdalena Renker, Eva Sixt, Dr. Bernhard Springer

English Translation Barbara Hopkinson, International Book Productions Inc.

Editor Helen Townsend

Proofreader Susan Thompson

Printed and bound in Malaysia by Vivar Printing Sdn Bhd.

First published in Germany in 2008 by Dorling Kindersley Verlag GmbH, Munich Published in
Great Britain in 2010 by Dorling Kindersley Ltd., 80 Strand, London WC2R 0RL

14 15 16 17 10 9 8 7 6 5 4 3 2 1

Printed with revisions 2010, 2011, 2012, 2014

Copyright © 2008, 2014 Dorling Kindersley Verlag GmbH, Munich © 2009, 2012 Dorling
Kindersley Limited, London A Penguin Random House Company

MIX
Paper from
responsible sources
FSC
www.fsc.org   FSC™ C018179

**The information in this
DK Eyewitness Travel Guide is checked regularly.**
Every effort has been made to ensure that this book is as up-to-date as possible at
the time of going to press. Some details, however, such as telephone numbers,
opening hours, prices, gallery hanging arrangements and travel information are
liable to change. The publishers cannot accept responsibility for any consequences
arising from the use of this book, nor for any material on third party websites, and
cannot guarantee that any website address in this book will be a suitable source of
travel information. We value the views and suggestions of our readers very highly.
Please write to: Publisher, DK Eyewitness Travel Guides, Dorling Kindersley, 80
Strand, London, WC2R 0RL, or email: travelguides@dk.com.

Front cover main image: Clock tower at St Pauli with a cruise ship in the dry dock, Hamburg

◀ Tugs hauling a vessel in Hamburg Port

Contents

How to use this Guide **6**

Bishop Ansgar I. (801 – 865)

Introducing Hamburg

Great Days
in Hamburg **10**

Putting Hamburg
on the Map **14**

The History
of Hamburg **20**

Hamburg at a Glance **28**

Hamburg Through
the Year **44**

A River View
of Hamburg **48**

Vessel in a dry dock opposite the
Landungsbrücken

The Alster Arcades (Alsterarkaden) – a popular place for ambling

Survival Guide

Practical Information **220**

Getting to Hamburg **230**

Getting Around Hamburg **234**

Hamburg Street Finder **242**

General Index **258**

Hamburg Area by Area

Old Town **54**

New Town **68**

Travellers' Needs

Where to Stay **172**

Where to Eat and Drink **182**

Shopping in Hamburg **198**

Entertainment in Hamburg **202**

Children's Hamburg **216**

Snack bar sign at Hamburg Port ("Sandwiches and a river view")

Acknowledgments **269**

Phrase Book **271**

Hamburg Public Transport Map *Inside back cover*

Fountain on the Binnenalster near Neuer Jungfernstieg

Port and Speicherstadt **80**

St Pauli **100**

Altona **112**

Around the Alster **120**

Further Afield **132**

Three Guided Walks **142**

Beyond Hamburg **150**

Hamburg's Rathaus (city hall)

HOW TO USE THIS GUIDE

This guide helps you get the most from your visit to the world-class city of Hamburg. It provides detailed practical information and expert recommendations. *Introducing Hamburg* maps the region and sets modern Hamburg in its historical context. It showcases the city's architectural and cultural attractions, including festivals and events throughout the year. It also provides an overview of the river. *Hamburg Area by Area* describes all the main sights, using maps, photographs and illustrations. In addition, special attractions outside Hamburg are also covered. Information about hotels, restaurants, shopping, entertainment and children's activities is found in *Travellers' Needs*. The *Survival Guide* offers tips on everything from using Hamburg's medical services, telephones and post offices to the public transport system. Handy *Street Finder* maps on pages 242 – 257 help you locate everything you need in this fascinating city.

Finding Your Way Around Hamburg

The city has been divided into six sightseeing areas, each with its own chapter, colour-coded for easy reference. Every chapter opens with an to the area of the city it covers, describing its history and character, and has a Street-by-Street map illustrating typical parts of that area. Finding your way around the chapter is made simple by the numbering system used throughout. The most important sights are covered in detail in two or more full pages.

Colour-coding on each page makes the area easy to find in the book.

A locator map shows you where you are in relation to surrounding areas. The area of the *Street-by-Street Map* is highlighted.

Numbered circles pinpoint all the listed sights on the area map. The Conciergerie, for example, is ❽

Recommended restaurants in the area are listed and plotted on the map.

1 Area Map
For easy reference, the sights in each area are numbered and located on an area map. To help the visitor, the map also shows U-Bahn and S-Bahn stations.

Rathaus ❶ is shown on this map as well.

A suggested route for a walk takes in the most attractive and interesting streets in the area.

Stars indicate the sights that no visitor should miss.

2 Street-by-a Map
This gives a bird's-eye view of the heart of each sightseeing area. The numbering of the sights ties in with the area map and the fuller descriptions on the pages that follow.

Hamburg Area Map

The colour-coded areas shown on this map (*see inside front cover*) correspond to the six main sightseeing areas of the city. Each is covered by its own full chapter in Hamburg Area by Area (*see pp52–169*). Throughout this book, the colour codes serve as your guide. The city's most important sights are described in Hamburg at a Glance (*see pp28–43*). For those who love walking tours, Three Guided Walks (*see pp142–149*) lead you not only to the main attractions but also to some of the city's less-known but no less interesting buildings.

Each sightseeing area is colour-coded.

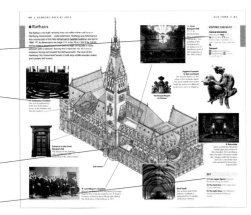

Practical Information lists all the information you need to visit every sight, including a map reference to the Street Finder at the back of the book.

Numbers refer to each sight's position on the area map and its place in the chapter.

3 Detailed information on each sight

All important sights in each area are described in depth in this section. They are listed in order, following the numbering on the *Area Map*. Opening hours, telephone numbers, websites, admission charges and facilities available is given for each sight. The key to the symbols used can be found on the back flap.

The Visitors' Checklist provides the practical information you will need to plan your visit.

Stars indicate the most interesting architectural details of the building, and the most important works of art or exhibits on view inside.

The façade of each major sight is shown to help you spot it quickly.

Numbered circles point out key features of the sight listed in a key.

4 Hamburg's major sights

These are given two or more full pages in the sightseeing area in which they are found. Historic buildings are dissected to reveal their interiors; and museums and galleries have colour-coded floor plans to help you find important exhibits.

INTRODUCING HAMBURG

Great Days in Hamburg   10–13

Putting Hamburg
on the Map   14–19

The History of Hamburg   20–27

Hamburg at a Glance   28–43

Hamburg Through the Year   44–47

A River View of Hamburg   48–51

GREAT DAYS IN HAMBURG

Hamburg, the "Doorway to the World" and one of the most fascinating cities in Europe, draws visitors with its international port and numerous attractions. The itineraries here will help you experience all that this city has to offer from its historic streets to its bustling harbour and bold new developments. Some of the itineraries revolve around particular interests or activities, including history, shopping and travelling with kids (prices cover transport, food and admission). On pp12–13, the itineraries of varying lengths ensure you catch the highlights if your time is short, or if you're in Hamburg for longer, will help you plan your days.

The dome of Hamburg's Kunsthalle (see pp64–5)

History and Culture

Two adults
allow at least €80

- **Time travel at the hamburgmuseum**
- **Views from St Michaelis**
- **Art on museum mile**
- **The ruins of St Nikolai**

Morning
The **hamburgmuseum** (see p73) at Holstenwall (U-Bahn station St Pauli) provides a fascinating overview of the city's history. After your trip through time, head southeast to **St Michaelis** (see pp74–5), Hamburg's most recognizable landmark. Take in the fabulous view from the platform at the top of "Michel", the church's 132-m (433-ft) tower. In a cul-de-sac steps from the church are the **Krameramtswohnungen** (see p72), courtyard apartment dwellings dating from the 17th century. The renowned restaurant Zu den Alten Krameramtsstuben (see p189) is housed in one of the period apartments.

Afternoon
Museum mile runs north and south of the the main railway station (Hauptbahnhof) at the eastern edge of the Old Town. Here, the **Hamburger Kunsthalle** (see pp64–5) displays famous works from Old Masters to Modern Classics, as well as fascinating special exhibitions. In the **Museum für Kunst und Gewerbe** (see pp130–31), applied arts from around the world are brought together under one roof. The **Deichtorhallen** (see pp62–3) covers the history of photography and much more. Heading west past the impressive 1920s office buildings of the Kontorhaus district (see p63), you will end up at the ruined church **St Nikolai** (see p66), a busy tourist attraction and poignant memorial. In Deichstraße (see p67), you can admire the oldest merchant's houses in the city. Continuing along Rödingsmarkt and Großer Burstah, one of the city's oldest streets, you will finally reach the **Rathaus** (see pp60–61), the Neo-Renaissance seat of Hamburg's government.

Shopping in Style

Two adults
allow at least €50

- **Hitting the Neuer Wall shops**
- **Exclusive Jungfernstieg**
- **Lunch in the Passages**
- **Browsing in St Pauli**

Morning
Start at the Stadthausbrücke S-Bahn station where the **Neuer Wall** begins, one of the best shopping streets in the city. Fashion trendsetters have set up shop on both sides of the street, and flagship stores of international labels are located here as well. At the end of Neuer Wall, turn left into **Jungfernstieg** and promenade along the Binnenalster. You'll find the most exclusive boutiques and designer labels along here, as well as the glamorous Alsterhaus (see p198), a well-stocked, high-end department store. "Luxury mile" continues on into **Große Bleichen** where the covered passages are an ideal place to stop for lunch.

Bridge leading to stilwerk, a centre for interior design (see p119)

Afternoon
From Reeperbahn S-Bahn station, walk south along Pepermölenbek street and turn right into the Fischmarkt. Housed in an old warehouse, the impressive **stilwerk** (see p119) offers seven floors of gift items and interior design pieces for those with discriminating taste. For an entirely different experience head east to St Pauli, where numerous stores offer a wide range of goods. The little shops are perfect for browsing, filled with curiosities and great for gift finding.

Rickmer Rickmers museum ship in Hamburg's harbour (see pp94 – 5)

A Day on the Water

Two adults
allow at least €100

- **Sailing the Alster**
- **Tall ship *Rickmer Rickmers***
- **The Landungsbrüken and a harbour tour**

Morning
Head to **Binnenalster** (the Inner Alster; see p124) to enjoy a morning of "Alsterschippern" – boating on the Alster. Boats depart throughout the day from Jungfernstieg dock to sail around the Binnenalster and the adjoining **Außenalster** (see p128). You can get off the boat anywhere and as often as you like, allowing you to combine your tour of the lake with a walk through Pöseldorf or Winterhude. By the time you get back to Jungfernstieg you will have built up an appetite, so head to the **Alsterpavillon** (see p124).

Afternoon
In Hamburg all roads seem to lead to the **Landungsbrücken** (see p93). Here you can enjoy the sea air and the port's hustle and bustle. Visit the three-masted freighter *Rickmer Rickmers* (see pp94 –5) for an insight into shipping during the early 20th century. Afterwards, take the opportunity to discover the harbour on a boat tour – there are many companies offering numerous variations (see pp48 –9). On most of these circular tours, you'll sail through the warehouse-lined canals of the **Speicherstadt** (see pp82–3), and explore the massive development **HafenCity** (see pp90 91). If you decide to disembark here, head to the **View Point** (see p88) for great views of this ambitious project.

A Family Day

Family of Four
allow at least €150 (without Hamburger Dom)

- **Delightful model railways and horrible history**
- **Feeding time at the zoo**
- **A city park with stargazing**

Morning
The harbour-side Speicherstadt area offers attractions for the whole family. More than eight million people have visited the world's largest digitally operated model railway, **Miniatur Wunderland** (see p84), and children's eyes will open wide trying to take it all in. The **Hamburg Dungeon** (see p85) takes visitors back to the bad

The computerized railway and model cities of Miniatur Wunderland (see p84)

old days, highlighting Hamburg's most gruesome moments – not for the very young or the faint of heart. Children are also fascinated by the model city in the **HafenCity InfoCenter** (see pp90 – 91), in Kesselhaus. A multimedia show traces the development of HafenCity, a dynamic new section of Hamburg. The bistro at the InfoCenter is a good choice for lunch too.

Afternoon
Take the U-Bahn to **Tierpark Hagenbeck** (see p136 –7); the city's zoo has many outdoor enclosures and a tropical aquarium. A highlight though is feeding time – try to catch the giraffes having their lunch. After the zoo, head for the **Stadtpark** (see p134), an extensive public green space with plenty going on. The **Planetarium** in the western section of the park is especially fascinating – look into space or attend one of the highly informative star shows. The **Hamburger Dom** (see p44 –6) is held three times a year on the Heiligengeistfeld and is great fun for young and old alike. The festival offers all kinds of fairground rides and numerous food stalls.

The Jugendstil entrance to Tierpark Hagenbeck (see p136 –7)

48 hours in Hamburg

- Sail from Landungs-brücken around the port
- HafenCity & Speicherstadt: Hamburg now and then
- Architectural landmarks "Michel" and the Rathaus

Day 1

Morning To gain your first impression of the harbour and the Elbe, head to the **Landungs-brücken** *(see p93)* to stroll along the quays and enjoy the view. A boat trip of the harbour *(see pp48–9)* allows you to admire large cruise ships close up. A visit to the 100-m (328-ft) long museum ship *Rickmer Rickmers (see pp94–5)* is a worthwhile experience.

Afternoon Head east to the **Speicherstadt** *(see pp82–3)* with its red-brick façades, and **HafenCity** *(see pp90–91)*, a new development designed to "bridge the Elbe". The **Maritime Museum** *(see pp86–7)* documents shipping in all its guises, and **Miniatur Wunderland** *(see p84)* immerses visitors in a scaled-down world.

Day 2

Morning If you're here on a Sunday, the **St Pauli Fish Market** *(see p108)* is a must. Afterwards, walk along the famous **Reeperbahn** *(see p102)*, the centre of the old red light district, until you reach **St Michaelis** *(see pp74–5)* with its 132-m (433-ft) high tower and viewing platform. Another architectural landmark, the **Rathaus** *(see pp60–61)*, is located in the Old Town.

Afternoon The **Hamburger Kunsthalle** *(see pp64–5)* is Hamburg's most prestigious art gallery. At the **Binnenalster** *(see p124)* you can enjoy the sea air, and from Monday to Saturday, wander down the **Jungfernstieg** *(see p124)* and through the **Passages** *(see p76)* for some high-end shopping. **Planten un Blomen** *(see pp78–9)* offers plenty of green space.

Traditionsschiffhafen (Traditional Ship Harbour) at the Sandtorhafen in HafenCity *(see p91)*

3 days in Hamburg

- North Sea ambience from Altona to HafenCity
- Fascinating museums
- Stroll through the gardens at Planten un Blomen

Day 1

Morning Start at the **Rathaus** *(see pp60–61)* and walk along the **Alster Arcades** *(see p58)* to the **Binnenalster** *(see p124)*. The **Jungfernstieg** *(see pp124–5)* and its side streets are a popular shopping area. The **Hamburger Kunsthalle** *(see pp64–5)* showcases excellent art exhibitions.

Afternoon Stroll through the colourful district **St Georg** *(see p129)*. If you want more art after visiting the **Museum für Kunst und Gewerbe** *(see p130)*, head to the **Deichtorhallen** *(see p62)*. The **HighFlyer Hamburg** *(see p63)* rises 150 m (490 ft) into

the sky, offering breath-taking views – especially on sunny afternoons.

Day 2

Morning Take the **Hafen-Hochbahn** *(see p92)* from the **Hauptbahnhof** *(see p62)* to the **Landungsbrücken** *(see p93)*. After a round trip of the harbour *(see pp48–9)*, walk to **St Michaelis** *(see pp74–5)* to climb the tower and then wander through **Planten un Blomen** *(see pp78–9)*.

Afternoon Brush up on your Hanseatic history at the **hamburgmuseum** *(see p73)*, then head to St Pauli. The **Reeperbahn** *(see p102)* with the Spielbudenplatz is well worth visiting – at night as well as during the day. The **Panoptikum** *(see p104)* exhibits waxworks of celebrities.

Day 3

Morning On Sundays, the **St Pauli Fish Market** *(see p108)* is a top attraction. Take a ferry to **Dockland** *(see p34)*. Here in Altona, magnificent boulevards like the **Elbchaussee** and the **Palmaille** *(see p118)* are ideal for leisurely walks.

Afternoon The ship *Rickmer Rickmers (see p94–5)* is a perfect starting point for the exploration of Hamburg's maritime attractions. Nearby are the **Speicherstadt** *(see pp82–3)*, **HafenCity** *(see pp90–91)* with the **Elbphilharmonie** *(see pp88–9)*, **Miniatur Wunderland** *(see p84)* and the **Maritime Museum** *(see pp86–7)*.

Façade of the Maritime Museum, which opened in 2008 *(see pp86–7)*

5 days in Hamburg

- Great views from the View Point or the HighFlyer
- Boulevards in Altona and alleys in the stair district
- Greet ocean liners at Wilkomm-Höft

Day 1

Morning Start at the **Rathaus** (see pp60 – 61), an uncharacteristically flamboyant building for Hamburg. Cross the channels, or "Fleete", to reach the church **St Michaelis** (see pp74 – 5). The **hamburgmuseum** (see p73) provides insight into the eventful history of the city. Then head north to the lively neighbourhood of **Schanzenviertel**, "Schanze", for shopping and eating, and a wander through **Sternschanzenpark** (see p109), with its unusual water tower.

The HighFlyer hovering over the rooftops of Hamburg (see p63).

Afternoon The U-Bahn takes you from the Sternschanzenpark to the **Tierpark Hagenbeck** (see p136). You could easily spend an afternoon or longer here – there's even a hotel (see p178).

Day 2

Morning The **HighFlyer Hamburg** (see p63) at the **Deichtorhallen** (see p62) takes you high into the sky. Here, on the edge of the **Speicherstadt** (see pp82 –3), many museums can be found – among them the **Maritime Museum** (see pp86 –7), **Miniatur**

Synchronized fountains at Planten und Blomen (see pp78 – 9)

Wunderland (see p84), the **Speicherstadtmusem** (see p85) and the **Deutsches Zollmuseum** (see p88).

Afternoon The **View Point** (see p88) observation platform provides the best perspective on the massive building project at **HafenCity** (see pp90 – 91). Here, you can also survey the progress being made on the **Elbphilharmonie** (see pp88 –9) with its spectacular pavilion roof. Do not miss the **HafenCity InfoCenter** (see p90) and the Traditional Ship Harbour in the **Sandtorhafen** (see p91).

Day 3

Morning Embark on a round trip of the harbour (see pp48 –9) at the **Landungsbrücken** (see p93). After this cruise, a visit to a museum ship – the *Rickmer Rickmers* (see pp94 – 5) or the *Cap San Diego* (see pp98 –9) – provides further insight into Hamburg's seafaring history. Take the S-Bahn (S1, S11) to the **Jenischpark** (see p138), an English-style landscape park with two museums.

Afternoon By taking the S1 or the S11 you reach the elegant Hamburg suburb **Blankenese** (see p138) with the **Treppenviertel** (stair district). Move on to the **Willkomm-Höft** (Welcome Point; see p139), where large ships that sail into the port of Hamburg are greeted by a rendition of their national anthem.

Day 4

Morning On Sundays, visit the **St Pauli Fish Market** (see p108). The U-Boat **U-434** (see p108) is anchored behind the Fish Auction Hall. Then, stroll along the **Reeperbahn** (see p102), and have a look at the waxworks at the **Panoptikum** (see p104).

Afternoon Altona offers a tranquil atmosphere. The **Platz der Republik** (see p116), the **Elbchaussee** and the **Palmaille** (see p118) are lined with wonderful buildings. The views from **Altonaer Balkon** (see p117) and from the roof of the office building **Dockland** (see p34) are fantastic. From here, ferries take you to the **Museumshafen Övelgönne** (see p165).

Day 5

Morning The **Hamburger Kunsthalle** (see pp64 –5) and the **Museum für Kunst und Gewerbe** (see p130) are very popular amongst art lovers. Shopping areas such as **Jungfernstieg** (see pp124 –5), the **Neuer Wall** and the **Passages** (see p76) lie within easy reach of the **Binnenalster** (see p124).

Afternoon After a leisurely stroll through **Planten un Blomen** (see pp78 –9), continue to walk along the **Außenalster** (see pp128 –9). The **Museum für Völkerkunde** (see p128), a museum of anthropology, presents exhibits from all around the globe.

Sculpture at Planten un Blomen

Putting Hamburg on the Map

Hamburg, with almost 1.8 million inhabitants, is Germany's second-largest city. This city-state, for it is also a German province, covers 755 sq km (290 sq miles), and is bordered by Lower Saxony and Schleswig-Holstein. This metropolis on the Elbe river is one of Europe's most important ports and trading centres. Due to its favourable location near the mouth of the Elbe river, it is known as the "gateway to the world".

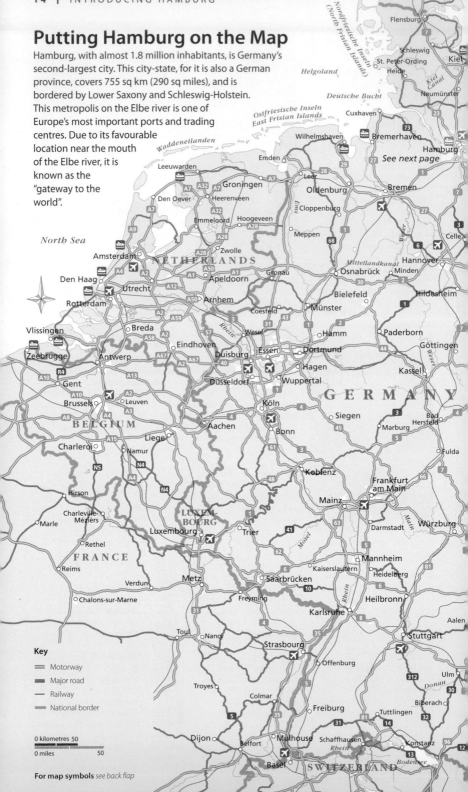

See next page

Key

- ▬ Motorway
- ▬ Major road
- — Railway
- ▬ National border

0 kilometres 50
0 miles 50

For map symbols *see back flap*

Greater Hamburg

The "Free and Hanseatic City" is organized into seven districts (Hamburg-Mitte, Altona, Eimsbüttel, Hamburg-Nord, Wandsbek, Bergedorf and Harburg), which are further divided into a total of 104 city districts. Hamburg is at the heart of an urban conurbation that is home to more than four million inhabitants, and continuing to grow. The gigantic HafenCity construction project adds to Hamburg's dynamism.

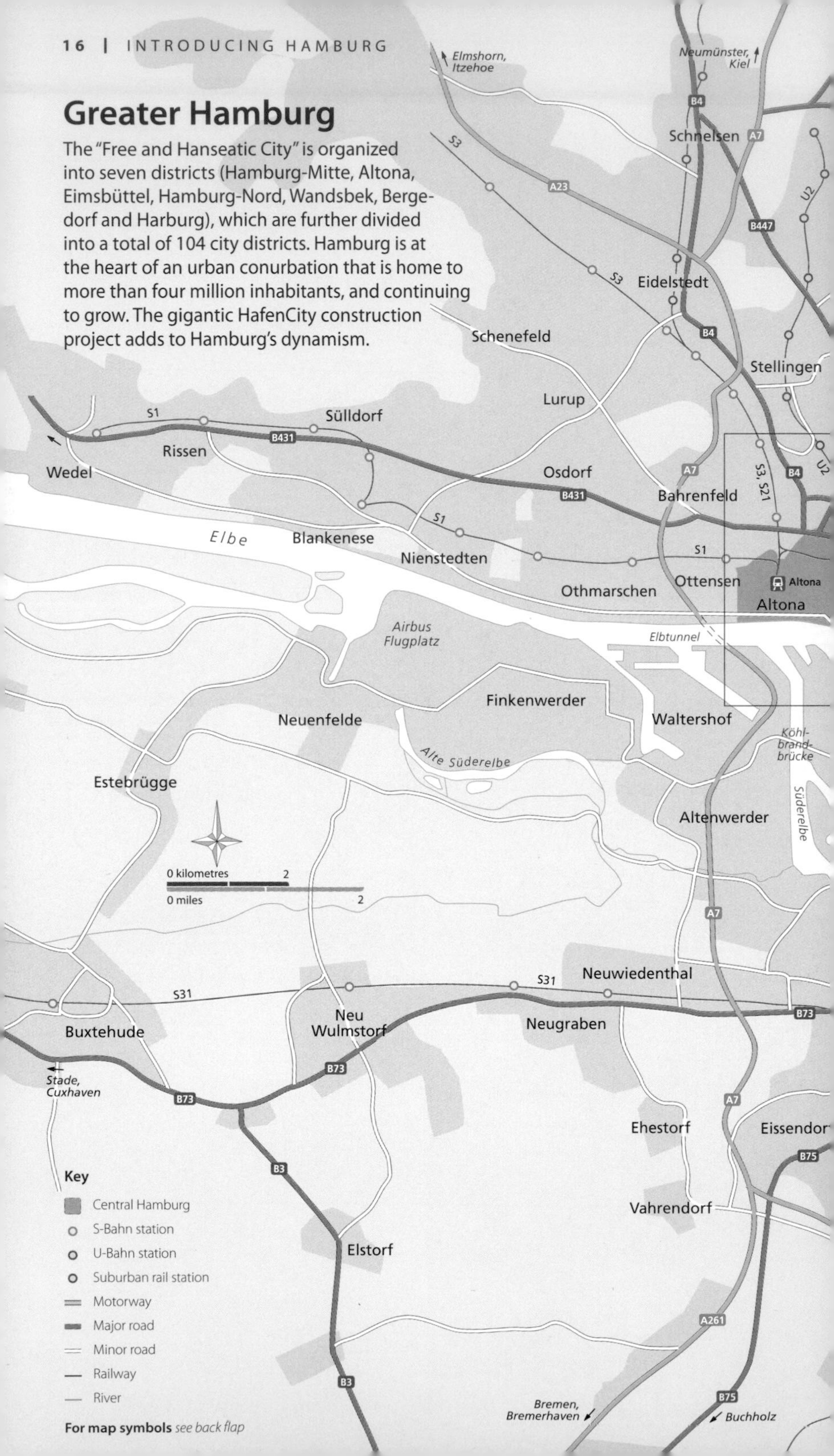

Elmshorn, Itzehoe

Neumünster, Kiel

B4

Schnelsen   A7

S3

A23

U2

B447

S3   Eidelstedt

B4

Schenefeld

Stellingen

Lurup

S1

Sülldorf   A7   S3, S21   B4   U2

B431   Osdorf

Rissen   B431   Bahrenfeld

Wedel   S1

Elbe   Blankenese   S1   Ottensen   S1   Altona

Nienstedten   Othmarschen   Altona

Airbus Flugplatz   Elbtunnel

Finkenwerder

Köhlbrandbrücke

Neuenfelde   Waltershof

Alte Süderelbe   Süderelbe

Estebrügge

Altenwerder

0 kilometres   2

0 miles   2

A7

Neuwiedenthal

S31   S31

Neu Wulmstorf   Neugraben

S31   B73

Buxtehude   B73

Stade, Cuxhaven

B73   A7

B3   Ehestorf   Eissendor

B75

Vahrendorf

Elstorf

Key

- ▢ Central Hamburg
- ○ S-Bahn station
- ○ U-Bahn station
- ○ Suburban rail station
- ▬ Motorway
- ▬ Major road
- ═ Minor road
- ─ Railway
- ─ River

A261

B3

Bremen, Bremerhaven   B75   Buchholz

For map symbols *see back flap*

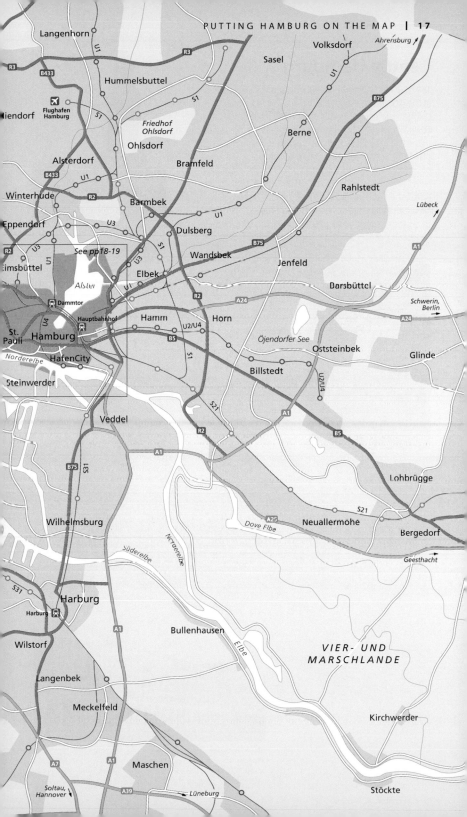

Central Hamburg

The majority of Hamburg's top attractions are located in the city centre, which has been divided into six colour-coded areas. The Old Town (Altstadt) and New Town (Neustadt) are separated by the Alsterfleet. West of the New Town lies the well-known entertainment district of St Pauli, and beyond that Altona, which was an independent town until 1937. South of the Old and New Towns lies the Port and Speicherstadt area. To the north, the area Around the Two Alsters – Binnenalster (Inner Alster) and Außenalster (Outer Alster) – is home to choice residential neighbourhoods, along with the more colourful areas of St Georg and Grindel.

St Michaelis
Lovingly referred to as "Michel" by Hamburgers, this Baroque church has become a symbol of the city *(see pp74 – 5)*.

Rathaus (Town Hall)
Both the city and the city-state are run from the Rathaus. It is one of Germany's grandest government buildings *(see pp60 – 61)*.

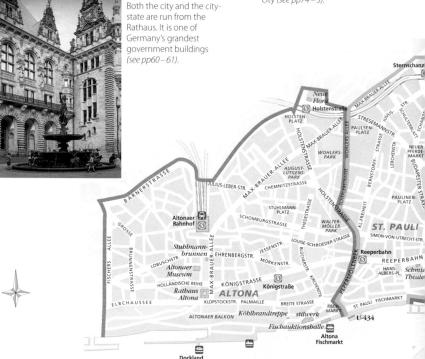

Key

 Star sight

For map symbols *see back flap*

Alster Arcades
Shopping in style right on the water – with the Alster Arcades and 2653 bridges, this area has earned its nickname "The Venice of the North" *(see p58)*.

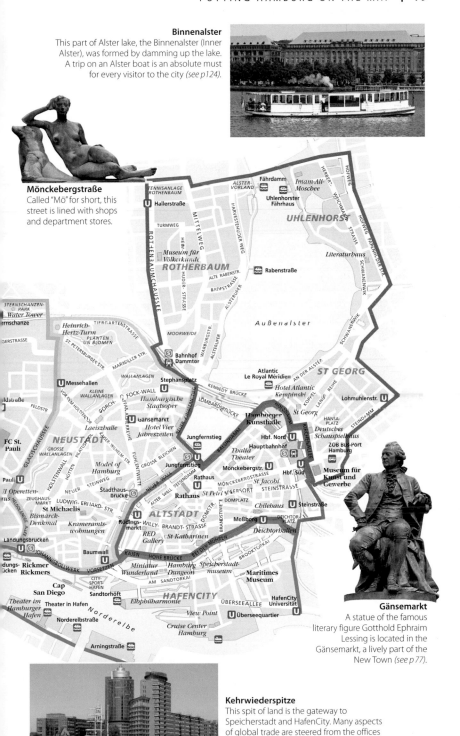

Binnenalster
This part of Alster lake, the Binnenalster (Inner Alster), was formed by damming up the lake. A trip on an Alster boat is an absolute must for every visitor to the city *(see p124)*.

Mönckebergstraße
Called "Mö" for short, this street is lined with shops and department stores.

Gänsemarkt
A statue of the famous literary figure Gotthold Ephraim Lessing is located in the Gänsemarkt, a lively part of the New Town *(see p77)*.

Kehrwiederspitze
This spit of land is the gateway to Speicherstadt and HafenCity. Many aspects of global trade are steered from the offices located in these two chic complexes *(see p84)*.

THE HISTORY OF HAMBURG

Hamburg's origins date back to the 9th century, when Hammaburg castle was built. Since then, it has evolved to become one of Europe's most important trading centres. The city's prosperity is based largely in its vibrant port and its political independence as a "Free and Hanseatic City". In the 21st century, with the building of HafenCity, Hamburg has begun to expand on the other side of the Elbe river.

Early History

Traces of the earliest settlements in the Hamburg area date back to the Middle Stone Age. Discoveries of tools and weapons north of Hamburg testify to the fact that nomadic hunters camped here as early as 8,000 BC. The first permanent settlements can be traced back to the 4th century AD, at which time Saxon tribes settled in the area of today's Old Town.

The Hammaburg

In the beginning of the 9th century, the Saxons were driven out of the area by the Franks under the command of Charlemagne and with the help of their Slavic allies, the Obodrite tribe. After 810, Louis the Pious, who was a son of Charlemagne, built Hammaburg castle, creating the nucleus for modern-day Hamburg. The square fortress, located south of today's church of St Petri, was very imposing with its 130-m (430-ft) high walls. Fifty troops were stationed in the fortress. Merchants, fishermen and innkeepers set up shop in front of its gates, and an early marketplace was founded. Hammaburg castle was not only a defensive stronghold, it was also intended to serve as the bishop's residence.

Hamburg as a Missionary Centre

King Louis the Pious founded the Bishopric of Hamburg in 831, and appointed Ansgar, a Benedictine monk, to be bishop. The terms of the Treaty of Verdun called for the Frankish kingdom to be divided between Louis' two sons. Shortly thereafter, Danish Vikings attacked German settlements on the Elbe river and razed the Hammaburg to the ground. King Louis the German, son of Louis the Pious, combined the diocese of Bremen and Hamburg for Ansgar, as there was little left of Hamburg. During the 10th century, the powerful Archbishop of Hamburg-Bremen, Adaldag, had a new fortress built. The settlement at Hamburg grew rapidly and was awarded market rights, laying the foundation for Hamburg's later prominence as an important centre of trade.

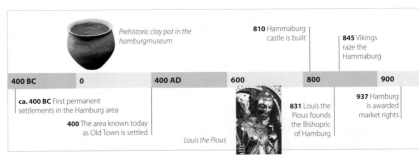

Prehistoric clay pot in the hamburgmuseum

Louis the Pious

400 BC	0	400 AD	600	800	900

810 Hammaburg castle is built

845 Vikings raze the Hammaburg

ca. 400 BC First permanent settlements in the Hamburg area

400 The area known today as Old Town is settled

831 Louis the Pious founds the Bishopric of Hamburg

937 Hamburg is awarded market rights

◄ Doors to the Great Banqueting Hall in the Rathaus *(see pp60 –61)*

Model of the old castle of Hammaburg, which was built by Louis the Pious in the 9th century

From Missionary Centre to Commercial Centre

The emerging market town recovered quickly after being attacked by the Slavic Obodrites in 983. The 11th century was marked by the rivalry between spiritual and earthly powers. As a sign of the might of the church, Archbishop Adalbrand (Alebrand) built a bishop's tower (see p59). To create an earthly counterweight to the bishop's stronghold, Duke Bernhard II, a member of the Billunger dynasty, gave orders for the construction of the Neue Burg (New Castle), which was later known as the Alsterburg. The fate of the church's dominance was sealed in 1066, when the Slavs rebelled against the high tithes they were obliged to pay to the monasteries.

After the Billunger line died out in 1106, the Counts of Schauenburg began to rule Hamburg in 1111. Under their rule, the town boomed. Adolf I expanded the defence works, dammed up the Alster to run a corn mill, and built dikes around several small islands in the Elbe river so that they could be settled. His successor, Adolf II, pursued a policy of consolidation with great success. Under Adolf III, the town of Neustadt (New Town) was founded in the territory surrounding the Neue Berg. It attracted mariners and merchants who settled there, especially along the Nikolaifleet.

The Charter and Its Aftermath

A milestone for future economic development occurred when Emperor Frederick Barbarossa conferred a charter (Freibrief) on the town on 7 May 1189. The document, which recognized the town for the help it had rendered during the third Crusade, awarded Hamburg customs exemption for trade and shipping all the way from the lower Elbe to the North Sea. Citizens were also freed from being conscripted into the army. Instead they were tasked solely with the defense of their own town. They also had the right to fish without paying the usual obligatory taxes.

The original charter granted by Emperor Frederick Barbarossa is not extant; in 1265, a copy, whose contents were most likely forged, was created. Indeed, some historians maintain that the charter was a forgery from the very beginning. Despite this, Hamburgers throw an annual party on May 7 to celebrate their port's birthday (see p85). Rapid economic development followed the bestowal of these trading rights.

St George, the dragon-slayer

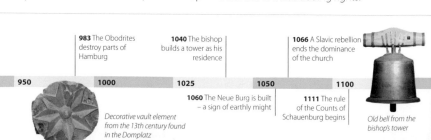

983 The Obodrites destroy parts of Hamburg

1040 The bishop builds a tower as his residence

1066 A Slavic rebellion ends the dominance of the church

950   1000   1025   1050   1100

1060 The Neue Burg is built – a sign of earthly might

1111 The rule of the Counts of Schauenburg begins

Decorative vault element from the 13th century found in the Domplatz

Old bell from the bishop's tower

A 19th-century painting showing the view of Hamburg as it would have looked in 1150

Self-reliance in Difficult Times

After the Danes conquered Hamburg and the surrounding area in 1201, the city was administered by a Danish governor. Under the occupying power, the Old Town and the New Town grew together politically as well as architecturally. By 1216, Hamburg had one town hall and one court of justice with its own laws. The city began to direct its own external affairs and to determine its own economic policy, entering into trade alliances with other cities such as Lübeck, as well as with dominions both near and far.

In 1227, a coalition of German princes drove out the occupying Danes, and the Schauenburg Count Adolf IV began to rule the city. After this period of political turmoil came to an end, trade flourished once again. The first merchant guilds were established, and foreign trading companies set up their own branches in Hamburg.

Lid of the sarcophagus of Adolf IV of Schauenburg

The city developed rapidly in the following centuries as the Alster was dammed up to form a lake, and new fortifications consisting of walls, towers and moats were built to protect the city centre. Towards the mid-13th century, these fortifications encircled the entire area of the present-day Old Town. Today, names such as Millerntor, Alstertor and Lange Mühren bear testimony to the locations of those former fortifications. The citizens of Hamburg demonstrating the self-confidence of true merchants – drew up their own town charter in 1270 and recorded it in their *Ordeelbook*.

The thriving city suffered a terrible setback on 5 August 1284 when a devastating fire roared through it, burning down the houses of the approximately 5,000 inhabitants. Reconstruction, however, started quickly again, and shortly thereafter the city enjoyed a large wave of immigration. There were plenty of jobs to be had, especially in the beer-brewing industry. In fact, at times, there were several hundred Hamburg breweries producing beer, a very important commodity during that time. The city's many and various trading alliances were exceptionally stable, and Hamburg continued to increase in prosperity. The city was also able to acquire a number of properties in the area. At this time, too, many important church buildings were completed and stately homes were built.

1188 New Town is built to the west of Old Town

1189 Emperor Barbarossa awards Hamburg its charter

1227 End of Danish rule

1250 The new fortifications encircle the entire city centre

1284 A huge fire destroys many buildings

1175   **1200**   **1225**   **1250**   **1275**

1201–27 Hamburg falls under Danish rule

1216 Old Town and New Town are amalgamated

1270 Hamburg is awarded a town charter

Hanseatic seal

A miniature decorates the cover of the revised Hamburg Stadtrecht of 1497 (created 1503 –1511)

The Hanseatic League (1321)

In 1321, Hamburg became a member of the Hanseatic League, an alliance of north German cities that had been in existence since the 12th century. Joining the League resulted in an enormous stimulus to the city. Through its membership in this important trade alliance, Hamburg became the leading German trading and warehousing city between the North Sea and the Baltic Sea. Another benefit was that, for several centuries to come, membership in the Hanseatic League secured existing trade routes and promoted the creation of new routes.

Hamburg was dealt a particularly heavy blow in 1350. During an outbreak of the plague, almost half of its entire population – nearly 6,000 inhabitants – perished.

Moorwerder Island (1395)

Towards the end of the 14th century, Hamburg acquired several towns in the surrounding area. Given this significant growth, the port had to be expanded to sustain the economic might of this Hanseatic city. In 1395, Hamburg acquired an island called Moorwerder. This was a strategically important move and an act of great political prescience. For it was here that the Elbe river divided into two branches. One branch, the more southerly one that carried the largest volume of water, flowed toward Harburg. After acquiring Moorwerder, Hamburg regulated the water flow so that Harburg, its rival to the south, was literally cut off from its water supply. Later, the construction of a number of waterworks ensured that the northern Elbe river around Hamburg became the more important branch of the mighty river. Thus was laid the cornerstone for the city's continued growth.

Pirates

The prosperity of the city awakened the greed of privateers, among whose ranks Klaus Störtebeker (see p43) could be found. Hamburg sent its own fleet to attack the band of pirates he led, and Störtebeker was beheaded in 1401 in Hamburg in front of a large crowd.

A Kogge was the most common type of ship in the North Sea and the Baltic Sea during the 15th century

(see p43)

1321 Hamburg joins the Hanseatic League

1350 An outbreak of the plague kills almost 6,000 people

1401 Klaus Störtebeker, the privateer, is executed

1410 The first Hamburg constitution is passed

Maria mit Kind im Strahlenkranz (hamburgmuseum)

1529 Hamburg becomes a Protestant city

1510 Hamburg becomes a Free Imperial City

1558 Börse (stock exchange) founded

Skull of Klaus Störtebeker

1300   1400   1450   1500   1550   1600

A Change of Course

Hamburg's first constitution came into effect in 1410. After the death of the last Schauenberg Count in 1459, the city fell under Danish rule. Even so, it became a Free Imperial City in 1510. In 1558, Hamburg merchants founded the stock market (see p66).

Not until the early 18th century did any significant changes occur. In 1712, to end the power struggles between the town's council and citizens, a new constitution was drawn up, giving both parties equal status. In 1768, the treaty of Gottorp ended the conflict with Denmark.

Klaus Störtebeker (circa 1360–1401), the most famous pirate

Hamburg in the 19th Century

Napoleon's troops occupied Hamburg in 1806. At that time it was a city of some 130,000 inhabitants. The Continental System, an embargo on trade with Great Britain dictated by France, proved to be an utter catastrophe for Hamburg: its economy collapsed almost entirely. Many formerly wealthy merchants had become impoverished by the time the French troops withdrew in 1812.

In 1815, Hamburg joined the German Confederation, and by 1819 it named itself "Freie und Hansestadt" (Free and Hanseatic City). The march to prosperity was halted abruptly by the Great Fire of 1842 (see p67). Afterwards, growth seemed to

accelerate even more. With the arrival of the steamship, trade flourished. In 1847, HAPAG – the Hamburg-American Line – was founded. It quickly grew to become the world's largest shipping company, and ensured Hamburg's trading might throughout the world. After 1850, millions of Europeans emigrated to North America, especially to the United States, on HAPAG ships.

After the German Reich was founded in 1871, Hamburg was at first allowed to store goods in the port area without paying excise duties. In 1888, the city was obliged to join the German Customs Union. After the cholera epidemic of 1892, during which more than 860 people lost their lives, Hamburg again demonstrated its self-confidence with the completion of the Rathaus in 1897 (see pp60–61).

Massive damage was inflicted during the Great Fire of 1842

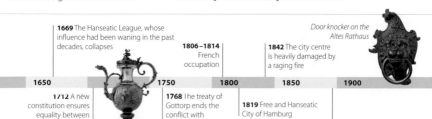

1669 The Hanseatic League, whose influence had been waning in the past decades, collapses

1806–1814 French occupation

1842 The city centre is heavily damaged by a raging fire

Door knocker on the Altes Rathaus

1650   1750   1800   1850   1900

1712 A new constitution ensures equality between citizenry and council

1768 The treaty of Gottorp ends the conflict with Denmark

1819 Free and Hanseatic City of Hamburg

1897 The city hall is completed

Pitcher used by captains of the citizen's militia

The Beatles during one of their legendary shows in the
Star-Club in Hamburg

Hamburg in the 20th Century

In 1910, Hamburg became a city of a million
inhabitants; just two years later, its port had
become the third-largest in the world after
those of London and New York. In 1911, the
first tunnel under the Elbe river was built.
After World War I (1914–18), under the terms
of the Treaty of Versailles, Hamburg was
compelled to surrender a large part of its
trading fleet. However, the merchant spirit
of the city remained intact, and Hamburg
acquired new ships. The city's
prosperity was reflected
architecturally in building
projects such as the imposing
Kontorhausviertel (see p63).

Under the Nazis, who came
to power in 1933, the Greater
Hamburg Act was passed,
which incorporated Altona,
Harburg and Wandsbek into
the city. At this time,
Hamburg's Jewish population
was 19,900. Over the next four years,
roughly half that number emigrated or
were expelled; almost all the remaining
Jews were killed in concentration
camps during World War II (1939–45).

Hamburg was a major target of wartime
Allied bombing, due to its large port and
industrial centre. Huge sections of the city
were destroyed. The heaviest air raid took
place in July 1943, claiming some 50,000
lives. On 3 May 1945, Hamburg surrendered
to British troops. In 1949, it became an
independent German province.

The North Sea Flood of 1962

During the night of 16 to 17 February 1962,
Hamburg was devastated by heavy
flooding from a severe storm. As gale-force
winds caused high volumes of Baltic Sea
water to surge forward, the protective dikes
were breached, causing water to surge into
almost one-sixth of the city. An exemplary
rescue action was mounted by Helmut
Schmidt, then Police Senator (see p42).
In direct contravention of the German
Constitution, he ordered the army to be
deployed to assist during a civil emergency.
His efficient management of the
crisis made him a German household name. Despite the amazing
efforts of several thousand
volunteers, more than 3,000
people perished, and tens of
thousands were made
homeless. Since the
flood, the dike near the
mouth of the Elbe has
been raised twice.
It now stands at 8 m
(26 ft). This effectively
prevented further
flooding, notably
during the 1976 and
1990 storms.

Books about the
North Sea Flood of 1962

1910 Hamburg's
population reaches
1 million

1943 Heavy air raids reduce large
sections of Hamburg to rubble

*The Beatles' key to the backdoor
of the Star-Club*

1952 The constitution comes
into effect

| 1900 | 1915 | 1930 | 1950 | 1960 |

1937 Greater Hamburg Act
is passed; the city grows by
incorporating smaller towns

1949 Hamburg becomes a
German province

1962 A disastrous flood
inundates the city centre
with water

*Albert Ballin
(1857–1918)*

Hamburg Booms

In the 1980s, container ship traffic in the port increased substantially and Hamburg became Europe's leading container port. In addition, the opening up of Eastern Europe gave further impetus to the port's development. Hamburg has, in fact, become one of the most important shipping centres in the Baltic Sea area. Hamburg continually strengthened its position as Germany's leading media centre *(see pp40 – 41)*, and also established itself as the country's musical capital. Each year, the number of tourists visiting this thriving Hanseatic city increases.

The futuristic office building of Dockland, located on the Elbe river near Altona

Hamburg after 2000

Since the end of World War II, the Social Democratic Party (SPD) customarily received the most votes in the city-state, with few exceptions. Therefore, it always appointed the First Mayor, who is the head of government. The most recent First Mayors were Hans-Ulrich Klose (1974 – 81), Klaus von Dohnanyi (1981–88), Henning Voscherau

Poster showing Helmut Schmidt

(1988–97), and Ortwin Runde (1997–2001). But in 2001, during the Bürgerschaft election, which determined who would sit in Hamburg's parliament, the Christian Democratic Union (CDU) won an absolute majority and took up the reigns of power under the leadership of Ole von Beust. After the Bürgerschaft elections in February 2008, the first ever coalition between the CDU and Green party at the state level was formed. In July 2010 von Beust retreated. In the following elections the SPD won an absolute majority, and in March 2011 Olaf Scholz became First Mayor.

Hamburg's pace of development in recent years has been rapid. The Trade Fair has been expanded, the airport enlarged, and downtown areas (such as Domplatz) renovated. Once HafenCity and the Elbphilharmonie are completed in 2016, one of the most ambitious urban building projects in Europe will have been realised. During this period the city was also given the European Green Capital Award, 2011.

The Elbphilharmonie, likely to enhance Hamburg's draw as a cultural destination

1974 The Köhlbrandbrücke is completed

1975 Opening of the Elbe tunnel for the A7 autobahn

1989 The 800th birthday of the port

2000 Building of HafenCity begins

2006 Some of the football World Cup games are held in Hamburg

Udo Lindenberg's star

1970	1980	1990	2000	2010	2020

1987 Town twinning with Dresden

Uwe Seeler's foot in front of the HSV-Arena

2001 The CDU takes power for the first time. Ole von Beust becomes First Mayor

2008 A coalition of the CDU and Green party under Ole von Beust

2011 The SPD wins absolute majority and takes power under Olaf Scholz

The south side of Hamburg Dammtor station, built in 1906 *(see p125)* ▶

HAMBURG AT A GLANCE

More than 100 places of interest are described in the *Area by Area* section of this guide. They range from the lively Landungsbrücken *(see p93)* to stately churches, such as St Michaelis *(see pp74–5)*; from the dignified Speicherstadt *(see pp80–99)* to the ultramodern HafenCity *(see pp90–91)*; from the grand Elbchaussee *(see p118)* to the elegant Jungfernstieg *(see pp124–25)*. To help you make the most of your stay in Hamburg, the following pages provide you with a guide to the very best that Hamburg has to offer. Museums and galleries, architectural masterpieces, and beautiful parks and gardens are all featured, as well as an overview of famous Hamburgers and the important role the city plays as a media centre. Below are the top ten attractions to start you off.

Hamburg's Top Ten Attractions

Rathaus
See pp60–61

Speicherstadt
See pp80–99

Landungsbrücken
See p93

St Pauli Fish Market
See p108

St Michaelis
See pp74–5

Planten un Blomen
See pp78–9

Reeperbahn
See pp102–3

Hamburger Kunsthalle
See pp64–5

Rickmer Rickmers
See pp94–5

Museum für Kunst und Gewerbe
See pp130–31

◀ View from St Nikolai's Church of the Rathaus tower

Hamburg's Best: Museums and Galleries

There are over 80 museums and collections in Hamburg, ranging from the Afghan to the Zoological Museum. Many historically significant works of art can be found here, and some Hamburg museums are among the most renowned in Europe. Collections dedicated to the history of Hamburg are impressive, but enthusiasts of special collections will also find much to enjoy. Unique to the city are the ship museums and those related to seafaring and trade. Once a year in April, the museums stay open until the early hours for the Long Night of the Museums.

hamburgmuseum
A trip in time from Hamburg's beginnings to the present day. Harbours and ships are central themes in this historical museum *(see p73)*.

Evangelist at the hamburgmuseum
This carved figure of an evangelist was created in the 15th century.

Altonaer Museum
Numerous exhibits on the cultural history of Northern Germany, with an emphasis on Altona, are displayed here *(see pp116–17)*.

St Pauli

Altona

Norderelbe

Rickmer Rickmers
This three-masted schooner, built in 1896, has been anchored off the Landungsbrücken since 1897 *(see pp94–5)*.

| 0 kilometres | 1 |
| 0 miles | 1 |

Speicherstadtmuseum
Experience one of Hamburg's greatest traditions in an old warehouse in the middle of Speicherstadt. Tools once used by people living in this part of the city and storage techniques are on show here *(see p85)*.

Museum der Arbeit
The changing world of work since the dawn of the Industrial Age is the main focus of this museum housed in a former rubber factory *(see p135).*

Museum für Völkerkunde
This museum is far more than just a series of exhibits, it is also dedicated to promoting dialogue between peoples and is a lively meeting place *(see p128).*

Around the Alster

New Town

Old Town

Hamburger Kunsthalle
From famous works of the old masters to contemporary art, the Kunsthalle houses the city's most important art collection *(see pp64–5).*

Port and Speicherstadt

Speicherstadt-museum

Deichtorhallen
The staging of bold shows has brought these exhibition halls international recognition. Exhibits showcasing the body of work of important artists are combined with interdisciplinary exhibitions *(see pp62–3).*

Museum für Kunst und Gewerbe
The entire range of applied arts is found here under one roof. This institution is one of the leading museums of its kind in Europe *(see pp130–31).*

Exploring Museums and Galleries

A number of art museums are concentrated along the "museum mile", near the Hauptbahnhof. The themes of museums located in the Speicherstadt range from the history of trade in Hamburg to the city's future development. Some museums cover specialized areas, from trains to wax figures, football (soccer) to fossils, and cinnamon to import duty. The Museumsschiffe (boat museums) are unique.

Portrait of Johannes Brahms in front of the Musikhalle

Medieval wood-carving in the Museum für Kunst und Gewerbe

Fine Art & Arts and Crafts

Among all the museums, the showpiece is definitely the **Hamburger Kunsthalle**. With its collection of important paintings from the Renaissance onwards, it is one of Hamburg's top attractions. Artists such as Rembrandt, Rubens and Manet are represented here. The adjoining Galerie der Gegenwart displays contemporary art. A visit to this museum complex is a trip through several centuries of art history.

The two **Deichtorhallen** (former market halls) are counted among the largest exhibition spaces in Europe. The halls have a special focus on photography, especially art photography and fashion photography.

In the bright yellow buildings of the **Museum für Kunst und Gewerbe**, everything revolves around applied arts. Highlights include a collection of historic and modern keyboard instruments.

Together, these three important cultural sites are the stars of the so-called "museum mile", which runs north and south of the Hauptbahnhof. They are complemented by

smaller collections, including the **Bucerius Kunst Forum** at Rathausmarkt, which mounts four top-quality exhibitions each year.

Two smaller museums are located in Jenischpark. **Jenisch Haus** contains an exhibition of oil paintings and furniture which demonstrates how Hamburg's upper middle class lived. **Ernst Barlach Haus** features the artistic output of this north German artist.

Contemporary History

The history of the city from its beginnings around the Hammaburg to the dynamic metropolis it is today is vividly documented in the **hamburgmuseum** (known as the Museum für Hamburgische Geschichte prior to 2006). It houses the largest collection of city history in Germany. A number of model ships and many other exhibits related to shipping round out the collection. The **Krameramtswohnungen** is a branch of this museum. Here, in this 17th-century apartment building, visitors can tour a period apartment decorated with furniture typical of the time.

Doing double duty as a visitor site and a memorial is **St Nikolai** (Mahnmal St Nikolai) in the Old Town. Significantly damaged during World War II air raids, parts of the church have now been restored, including the tower, which is 147 m (483 ft) high. Exhibits in the adjacent documentation centre provide information about the history of the church.

Cultural history collections from Northern Germany, with an emphasis on fishing and shipping, are found in the **Altonaer Museum**. Photos and documents in the S**peicherstadtmuseum** convey a great deal of knowledge about the history of this unique cluster of warehouses.

The **HafenCity InfoCenter** has been housed in the 100-year-old Kesselhaus (boiler house) of the Speicherstadt, since construction started on this multi-purpose development in 2000. A detailed model introduces and documents the project.

View of the Hanseatic city around 1600, displayed in hamburgmuseum

Cultural History

Ethnological collections from every continent are housed in the **Museum für Völkerkunde**, which is one of the largest of its kind in Europe. The museum hosts a variety of festivals and markets, making it a meeting place for people from around the world throughout the year.

The various changes in the world of work can be traced back to the beginning of the machine age in the **Museum der Arbeit**. Here, visitors learn about work routines in a variety of work places, discovering, for example, what it was like to be employed in a fish factory, or a printing shop.

Much more exotic is the **Afghanisches Museum** (Afghan museum), which presents the rich cultural history of this South Asian country. It exhibits typical Afghani arts and crafts such as colourful carpets and metalwork. In the same building in Speicherstadt, **Spicy's Gewürzmuseum** shows nearly everything that revolves around the precious spices that so delight our taste buds – a festival for the sense of smell.

The Shipping Trade

A number of museums in Hamburg are dedicated to the shipping trade, which played such a vital role in the city becoming a flourishing port. Some of these museums are located on ships.

A glance behind the scenes of the Cold War can be had by visiting the Russian U-boat **U-434**. Prior to 2002, it belonged to the Russian navy and was employed on espionage missions.

Near the Landungsbrücken, more ship museums lie at anchor. Two very different epochs in shipping history come alive aboard the three-masted schooner **Rickmer Rickmers** and the cargo freighter **Cap San Diego**. For lovers of old ships, a visit to the **Museumshafen Övelgönne**

Das Eismeer (The Polar Sea) (1823–24) by Caspar David Friedrich, Kunsthalle

is a must. Here, you can enjoy seeing many old-timers, among them a high-sea cutter and a fire ship.

Model ships, navigation instruments, globes, maps and many more interesting exhibits illustrating the 3,000-year history of seafaring are found in the **Maritimes Museum**. There are some traditional steamers and rigs moored in the Sandtorhafen shipping basin in HafenCity *(see p91)*.

Old radio telephone in the Deutsches Zollmuseum

Special Museums

Hamburg offers a decent number of unusual museums. The **Deutsches Zollmuseum** (German customs museum) provides an overview of customs history. Of interest are the inventive ways people tried to smuggle goods, only to be caught red-handed. In **Panoptikum**, the largest wax figure exhibition in Germany, more than 120 prominent figures from politicians to entertainers are on display. The racing and sports cars displayed in the **Prototyp Museum**, which

The ship museum *U-434*, once a Russian U-boat

opened in 2008, spellbind autosport enthusiasts. The **HSV-Museum** in the Volksparkstadion pays homage to the successes of this tradition-rich football club. In **Miniatur Wunderland**, a first-class model railway attracts aficionados both old and young. The Earth is the topic of the unique **RED Gallery**, with its amazing collection of fossils, gemstones and minerals. The **Johannes-Brahms-Museum** is devoted to the life and works of the famous German composer. In **Dialog im Dunkeln** (Dialogue in the Dark), the blind lead visitors through pitch-black rooms and let them enjoy a world of sounds and scents. **BallinStadt – Auswandererwelt Hamburg** tells the story of the numerous emigrants who sought their fortune in faraway countries.

Museums

Afghanisches Museum *p147*
Altonaer Museum *pp116–17*
BallinStadt – Auswandererwelt Hamburg *p93*
Bucerius Kunst Forum *p58*
Cap San Diego *pp98–9*
Deichtorhallen *pp62–3*
Deutsches Zollmuseum *p88*
Dialog im Dunkeln *p89*
Ernst Barlach Haus *p138*
HafenCity InfoCenter *p147*
Hamburger Kunsthalle *pp64–5*
hamburgmuseum *p73*
HSV-Museum *p134*
Jenisch Haus *p138*
Johannes-Brahms-Museum *p73*
Krameramtswohnungen *p72*
Maritimes Museum *pp86–7*
Miniatur Wunderland *p84*
Museum der Arbeit *p135*
Museum für Kunst und Gewerbe *pp130–31*
Museum für Völkerkunde *p128*
Museumshafen Övelgönne *p135*
Panoptikum *p104*
Prototyp Museum *p89*
RED Gallery *p67*
Rickmer Rickmers *pp94–5*
Speicherstadtmuseum *p85*
Spicy's Gewürzmuseum *p84*
St Nikolai Memorial *p66*
U-434 *p108*

Hamburg's Best: Architecture

Hamburg's architecture varies markedly. Whether the buildings are made of dark red brick, covered with green copper roofs, or are modernistic constructions of steel and glass, the charm of this Hanseatic city is based in part on its traditional as well as its contemporary architecture. The range is broad: stately, solid buildings expressing Hanseatic prosperity vie with architectural expressions of a new light-heartedness. Here and there both these styles are united to create a harmonious whole, as in the Elbphilharmonie, for example. Hamburg's maritime tradition is reflected in many buildings, not just those right on the water.

St Michaelis
Hamburg's skyline is dominated by the towers and steeples of its principal churches. Chief among them is the 132-m (433-ft) tall steeple of St Michaelis, known as "Michel" (see pp74 – 5).

Dockland
Looking a bit like a luxury liner, with its prow jutting out over the water, this futuristic office building was completed in 2005. The five-storey glass-and-steel construction is one of the city's most spectacular (see p149).

St Pauli

Altona

0 kilometres	1
0 miles	1

Norderelbe

Statue at Bucerius Kunst Forum
The façade of the Bucerius Kunst Forum (the former Reichsbank) is adorned with numerous statues representing the traditional trades of Hamburg (see p58).

Landungsbrücken
The central hall of this "floating railway station", built in 1907 – 09 in Jugendstil (German Art Nouveau style), is 200 m (220 yards) long (see p93).

Rathaus
This august building, adorned with sculptures and crests, is the seat of the Bürgerschaft (parliament) and the Senat (government) of the Freie und Hansestadt *(see pp60–61).*

Hauptbahnhof
This Neo-Renaissance building, housing Germany's largest train station, was opened in 1906. It is covered by an enormous roof made of glass and steel *(see p62).*

Around the Alster

Chilehaus
More than five million bricks were used in this world-famous office building designed in the Expressionist style *(see p63).*

New Town

Old Town

Port and Speicherstadt

Elbphilharmonie
This ambitious project, due for completion in 2016, places a futuristic concert hall on top of an old warehouse. The design of the tent-like-roof is reminiscent of waves and mountains *(see pp88–9).*

Verlagshaus Gruner + Jahr
With its nautical appearance, this building resembles a steamship. It houses one of the most important media companies in the city *(see p146).*

Exploring Hamburg's Architecture

Hamburg's cityscape is dominated by buildings dating from the 19th and 20th centuries; only a few older buildings still stand today. This is due to the enormous destruction caused by the Great Fire of 1842, and the hail of bombs that rained on the city during World War II. Another factor is that Hamburg's citizens have always had a preference for tearing down old buildings and replacing them with new ones, making their penchant for rebuilding famous even beyond the city's borders. As a merchant town, Hamburg traditionally looks to the future and the current HafenCity project is one of the most ambitious architectural undertakings in Europe.

The Bucerius Kunst Forum, which mounts four exhibitions a year

"Old" Hamburg

For many centuries, people in Hamburg used bricks to build apartment buildings, warehouses and factories. A few of these architectural links to "old" Hamburg can still be found in the Old and New Towns – for example on Nikolaifleet in the southwest part of the Old Town. Despite the Great Fire of 1842 breaking out immediately next door, a rare cluster of historic buildings still stands today for all to admire. The warehouses to the back of the brick buildings on **Deichstraße** could be conveniently accessed from the adjacent Fleet canal.

In the New Town, the **Krameramtswohnungen** provide a glimpse into the way Hamburg's prosperous citizens lived in the 17th century. The half-timbered buildings of the **Beylingstift** in Peterstraße were reconstructed in perfect detail. On **Palmaille**, a lovely street along the bank of the Elbe river, there remain a few apartment buildings that were built for the well-to-do. Built in the Neo-Classical style, these buildings are a testament in stone to Hanseatic wealth and merchant pride.

The 19th Century

Buildings constructed during the 19th century borrowed in part from the Italians. The **Alster Arcades**, an elegant colonnade in the Venetian style, was built immediately after the Great Fire. The **Börse** (stock exchange) was also built at this time. This late-Classical building was designed by Carl Ludwig Wimmel and Franz Gustav Forsmann. No sign of Hanseatic restraint can be seen in the Neo-Renaissance **Rathaus** (city hall). The Rathausmarkt (city hall square) was intended to be a kind of Hanseatic Piazza San Marco. All later re-designs of the square remained true to this Venetian theme.

In the late 19th century, the three-halled **Fish Auction Hall**, the **Hotel Vier Jahreszeiten** on Binnenalster and **Rathaus Altona** (Altona city hall) were built. The latter was a centrepiece for the city of Altona, which was independent up to 1937. The **Speicherstadt** (warehouse district) was also built at this time. To erect this ensemble of buildings made of red bricks, the most common construction material in Hamburg, workers' settlements were razed, and some 20,000 people were relocated.

Window in the Fish Auction Hall

Old Hamburg merchant houses located on Deichstraße

The City's Five Principal Churches

Hamburg's skyline is dominated chiefly by the towers and spires of its five main churches. Only a few vestiges remain of the original structure of four of the five: **St Michaelis**, **St Jacobi**, **St Katharinen** and **St Petri**. Surprisingly, some of the interior ornamentation of these places of worship withstood the tests of fire and air raids. **St Nikolai** was erected in 1960–62 to replace the Nikolaikirche that was destroyed in World War II. Its tower is preserved as a memorial, the Mahnmal St Nikolai (*see p66*). St Michaeliskirche, a massive Baroque church, was rebuilt three times. In 1750, after lightning destroyed the original 17th-century church, a new one arose in its place. This second Michaeliskirche burned to the ground in 1906, but was rebuilt almost immediately. Today St Michaelis' most recent incarnation has become a symbol of the city.

The 20th Century

Shortly after 1900, the **Landungsbrücken** quays in St Pauli were built. Some of Hamburg's most important cultural institutions were also built at the beginning of the 20th century. Among them is the **Bucerius Kunst Forum**, located in the former Reichsbank building, and the Neo-Baroque Musikhalle (which was re-named **Laeiszhalle** in 2005). These were designed by Martin Haller (see p42), an architect who oversaw construction of the Rathaus.

In the 1920s, architects rediscovered the city's red-brick building tradition. When the Kontorhausviertel was built in the Old Town, a new generation of red-brick buildings arose – one of daring shapes. A prominent example of this building style is the Expressionist **Chilehaus** by Fritz Höger (see p42). The building's pointed shape is reminiscent of a ship's prow. Around the same time, Fritz Schumacher (see p42) built the Museum für Hamburgische Geschichte (called **hamburgmuseum** since 2006) with its imposing roof.

Impressive examples of Industrial architecture from the beginning of the 20th century are **Bahnhof Hamburg Dammtor**, **Hauptbahnhof** and the **Deichtorhallen**. **Heinrich-Hertz-Turm**, which was built by Fritz Trautwein (see p42), stands 279.8 m (918 ft) high –the tallest building in the city.

Transportation routes of note are the **Alter Elbtunnel**, built in 1911, the new tunnel serving the A7 Autobahn, and the **Köhlbrandbrücke**. Notable city centre buildings include **Verlagshaus Gruner + Jahr**, **Kehrwiederspitze** at the entrance to the Speicherstadt, and also the **Passages** located between Rathausmarkt and Gänsemarkt that give a definite flair to the city .

The Elbphilharmonie, HafenCity's star, as it will look on completion

"New" Hamburg

Architects such as Bothe, Richter and Teherani (BRT) and Herzog & de Meuron are responsible for the city's newest architecture. In recent years, futuristic office buildings such as **Dockland**, Berliner Bogen, Deichtor Center, Tanzende Türme as well as ZOB – Bus-Port Hamburg, with its distinctive sickle-shaped roof, have been built. Several buildings of the **HafenCity** complex, due to be completed between 2020 and 2025, are ready. The flagship will be the **Elbphilharmonie** (The Hamburg Philharmonic Hall). Due to open in 2016, this glass roof-top structure will be built on top of Kaispeicher A, a warehouse that was built between 1963 and 1966. The spectacular concert hall will be wave-shaped and visible from a great distance.

Architecture

Alster Arcades p58
Alter Elbtunnel p93
Bahnhof Hamburg Dammtor p125
Beylingstift p73
Börse p66
Bucerius Kunst Forum p58
Chilehaus p63
Deichstraße p67
Deichtorhallen pp62–3
Dockland p149
Elbphilharmonie pp88–9
Fish Auction Hall pp118–19
HafenCity pp90–91
hamburgmuseum p73
Hauptbahnhof p62
Heinrich-Hertz-Turm p77
Hotel Vier Jahreszeiten p125
Kehrwiederspitze p84
Köhlbrandbrücke p135
Krameramtswohnungen p72
Laeiszhalle p73
Landungsbrücken p93
Palmaille p118
Passages p76
Rathaus pp60–61
Rathaus Altona p117
Speicherstadt pp80–99
St Jacobi p62
St Katharinen p63
St Michaelis pp74–5
St Nikolai p66
St Petri pp58–9
Verlagshaus Gruner + Jahr p146

132 m (433 ft) tall, completed in 1878

St Petri

124.5 m (408 ft) tall, renovated in 1963

St Jacobi

116.7 m (383 ft) tall, rebuilt in 1957

St Katharinen

132 m (433 ft) tall, rebuilt with a steel frame in 1906–12

St Michaelis

147.3 m (483 ft) tall, completed in 1874

St Nikolai

Hamburg's Best: Parks and Gardens

When Hamburgers want to enjoy nature they do not have to go far. Several lovely recreation areas are located within the city limits – and these are often just a few U-Bahn or S-Bahn stops away from the centre. Hamburg's recreation areas are perfect for taking long, leisurely walks. And, for those who love playing sports or picnicking, the Alstervorland or the Stadtpark are ideal spots. Several museums can be found in the grounds of Jenischpark. Friedhof Ohlsdorf is well suited to contemplation. In Tierpark Hagenbeck, animals from every continent can be admired.

Volkspark
Despite the presence of the Volksparkstadion (see p134) and the O2 World Hamburg, Volkspark remains a quiet recreation area. Among its attractions is the oldest dahlia garden in Europe. Joggers appreciate the hilly terrain.

```
0 kilometres        1
0 miles      0.5
```

Eierhütte
The egg hut in Jenischpark has egg-shaped windows. The hut was built in 1995 on the place occupied by a block house built in 1790.

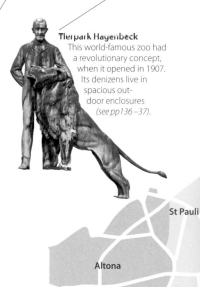

Tierpark Hagenbeck
This world-famous zoo had a revolutionary concept, when it opened in 1907. Its denizens live in spacious out-door enclosures (see pp136–37).

St Pauli

Jenischpark
In this extensive park covering 42 hectares (103 acres) there are two art museums: Jenisch Haus and Ernst Barlach Haus (see p138).

Altona

Norderel

Heine-Park
This area, with its wonderful old trees, is part of a green belt that runs along the Elbe river. The former home of the banker, Salomon, is today used for exhibitions.

Friedhof Ohlsdorf
This cemetery was laid out in the style of an English landscape garden. It still serves as a final resting place, but is also an example of landscaping artistry *(see pp134 – 35)*.

Planten un Blomen
This lovely park forms a green corridor linking St Pauli with the Alster. Its greenhouse and tea ceremony add a touch of the exotic *(see pp78 – 9)*.

Stadtpark
This 150-ha (370-acre) park feels like the city's "living room". Locals come here to enjoy a cold brew in a beer garden, swim, have a barbecue or simply relax *(see p134)*.

Around the Alster

New Town

Old Town

Port and Speicherstadt

Alstervorland
This green space on the western shore of the Außenalster *(see p128)* is a popular recreation area. Cafés offer patios with a view of the water.

Binnenalster
A trip on an Alster boat provides a beautiful view of the many stately buildings that line the Binnenalster *(see pp124)*.

Highlights: The Media in Hamburg

Hamburg is Germany's most important media city. More than 13,000 companies in the industry are headquartered here. Among the prominent firms are some of Europe's most profitable publishing houses, such as Axel-Springer-Verlag (although the editorial departments of *Bild* and *BamS* newspapers moved to Berlin in 2008 and some of the magazines have been sold). Norddeutscher Rundfunk (NDR) is one of the ARD's biggest television stations. It was in Hamburg that the dpa rose to become Germany's most important press agency. Many successful movies have used Hamburg as a backdrop.

Ad agency Jung von Matt
In 1991, Holger Jung and Jean-Remy von Matt founded an ad agency that has become highly successful. Now employing more than 800 people, this creative think tank has come up with many slogans that have entered the German public consciousness.

ZDF-Studio in Hamburg
The seventh floor of the Deichtor Center in HafenCity accomodates the offices, where the journalists of the ZDF's regional studio in Hamburg create their reports.

0 kilometres 1
0 miles 0.5

St Pauli

Altona

Norderelbe

GEO
GEO, one of the leading magazines in Germany, has been published monthly since 1976 by Verlagshaus Gruner + Jahr.

Verlagshaus Gruner + Jahr
The largest magazine and newspaper publisher in Europe publishes about 500 titles in over 30 countries. As early as 1948, even before the German Republic was founded, the first edition of stern appeared.

Tagesschau
German television's longest-running news show is produced in Hamburg by the NDR. More than ten million viewers tune in each evening to watch the day's news, shown here with Susanne Daubner.

NDR
This ARD television station produces several of the popular police-drama series Tatort. Here, Maria Furtwängler is shown in her role as police detective Charlotte Lindholm.

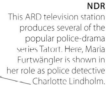

Around the Alster

New Town

Old Town

ZDF-Studio

Port and Speicherstadt

DIE ZEIT
The editors of the weekly newspaper *DIE ZEIT* work from Pressehaus am Speersort, a brick building that forms part of the Kontorhausviertel (warehouse district).

DER SPIEGEL
With a circulation of over 900,000 copies, *DER SPIEGEL* is the most widely read news magazine in Germany. The editorial team works in this building in HafenCity.

stern
Since 1948 stern has been giving its readers an overview of the most important themes of the past seven days. *stern* enjoys the highest circulation of any popular magazine in Germany.

Famous Residents of Hamburg

Among the famous people of Hamburg are the great musicians who have lived and worked here, and the many architects who placed their unmistakable stamp on the city. Forward-looking entrepreneurs have achieved great success here, contributing to the rapid development of the city's economy. Hans Albers, a beloved German actor, expressed the city's soul. Numbered among the many famous personalities intrinsically linked to Hamburg are a former German Chancellor, a boxing world champion, and a legendary pirate who terrorized ships on the Baltic Sea.

German rock star Udo Lindenberg (born 1946)

Composer and pianist
Johannes Brahms (1833–1897)

Musicians

Among the musical directors of Hamburg's five principal churches were Georg Philipp Telemann (1681–1767) and his successor, Carl Philipp Emanuel Bach (1714–1788), son of Johann Sebastian Bach. Born in Hamburg, Johannes Brahms (1833–1897) was among the 19th century's most important composers. Felix Mendelssohn Bartholdy (1809–1847), one of the leading musicians in the European Romantic movement, also rose to prominence in Hamburg.

In the field of popular music, Freddy Quinn (born 1931), singer of seamens' chanties, and rock star Udo Lindenberg (born 1946) – each expressed some of Hamburg's attitude to life in his own way.

Architects

Ernst Georg Sonnin (1713–1794) constructed St Michaelis (see pp74–5). One of the proponents of late Classicism is Franz Gustav Forsmann (1795–1879), who built stately villas, such as Jenisch Haus (see p138). The Rathaus (city hall) (see pp60–61) was built under the direction of Martin Haller (1835–1925), who also built the Laeiszhalle (see p73). With the Davidwache (see p105) and the hamburgmuseum (see p73), Fritz Schumacher (1869–1947) made his mark on the city's architecture. Fritz Höger (1877–1949) designed several office buildings, among them Chilehaus (see p63).

Fritz Trautwein (1911–1993) was a key figure behind the rebuilding of Hamburg after World War II. In addition to apartment buildings, he designed several U-Bahn stations and the Heinrich-Hertz-Turm (see p77). With projects such as Dockland (see p34),

Berliner Bogen and Tanzende Türme (see p102), Hadi Teherani (born 1954) represents the Hamburg of the future. In 1991, Teherani founded the firm of architects BRT. It is based in the Deichtor Center (see p40), which also has been designed by Teherani.

Politicians

The communist Ernst Thälmann (1886–1944) was elected chair of the KDP (German Communist Party) in 1925. After his arrest in 1933, he spent the rest of his life in concentration camps. Theodor Haubach (1896–1945), also killed by the Nazis, was one of the founders of the democratic protest movement Reichsbanner Schwarz-Rot-Gold. Former German Chancellor Helmut Schmidt (born 1918) earned great respect for his handling of the 1962 Hamburg flood. At the time he was the minister of police.

Authors

Barthold Heinrich Brockes (1680–1747) was an important literary figure of the early Enlightenment. The fame of Friedrich Gottlieb Klopstock (1724–1803) stems largely from his principal work Der Messias. Hans Erich Nossack (1901–1977) became famous due to his prose work Der Untergang. Draußen vor der Tür by Wolfgang Borchert (1921–1947) is an important play of the early post-war period. Other famous authors are Mathias Claudius (1740–1815) and Siegfried Lenz (b 1926).

Ernst Barlach Haus, which displays the works of this North German artist

Painters and Sculptors

Meister Bertram (circa 1340 – 1415), a Gothic painter, enriched Northern German painting by bringing in Italian influences. His chief work, the *Grabower Altar*, can be admired in the Kunsthalle (*see pp64 – 5*). Philipp Otto Runge (1777 – 1810) is one of the most important representatives of early Romantic art.

Works by Ernst Barlach (1870 – 1938), a North German Expressionist artist and playwright, are on display in Ernst Barlach Haus (*see p138*). The animal sculptures of Martin Ruwoldt (1891 – 1969) grace Alsterpark, Stadtpark and Planten un Blomen.

The Ohnsorg Theater – synonymous for decades with star Heidi Kabel

Entrepreneurs

Friedrich Christoph Perthes (1772 – 1843) is one of the key figures in the German book and publishing trade. In 1796, he founded the first bookstore in Germany here in Hamburg – the cornerstone of today's book trade.

Under the direction of Albert Ballin (1857 – 1918), HAPAG developed into the world's most important shipping concern. BallinStadt – Auswandererwelt Hamburg (*see p93*), which opened in 2007, is named after Ballin.

Animal merchant and zoo director Carl Hagenbeck (1844 – 1930) set a new standard for the treatment of zoo animals when he opened Tierpark Hagenbeck (*see pp136 – 37*) in 1907.

Hamburg, the headquarters of so many newspapers and magazine publishing houses (*see pp40 – 41*), owes its position to publishers such as Gerd Bucerius (1906 – 1995), Axel Springer (1912 – 1985), Henri Nannen (1913 – 1996) and Rudolf Augstein (1923 – 2002), whose publications dominate the German newspaper and magazine industry.

Albert Darboven (born 1936), owner of a global coffee roasting company, is considered Germany's "coffee king".

Actors

Hans Albers (1891 – 1960) excelled in films such as *Der blaue Engel* (1930), *Große Freiheit Nr.7* (1944), *Auf der Reeperbahn nachts um halb eins* (1954) and *Das Herz von St Pauli* (1957). The actor Gustaf Gründgens (1899 – 1963) directed the Deutsches Scauspielhaus from 1955.

Ida Ehre (1900 – 1989) opened the Hamburger Kammerspiele in 1945, which evolved to become Germany's leading theatre. The very popular actor Heidi Kabel (1914 – 2010) was the unchallenged star of the Ohnsorg Theater (*see p129*).

Raimund Harmstorf (1939 – 1998) specialized in portraying tough guys. His biggest success was in the role of the brutal Captain Wolf Larsen in a four-part series called *Der Seewolf*.

Evelyn Hamann (1942 – 2007) was best-known as the partner of Loriot, a beloved German comedian, in many hugely popular comedy sketches.

Sculpture of Uwe Seeler's foot, HSV-Arena

Sports Greats

Max Schmeling (1905 – 2005) was the Heavyweight World Boxing Champion from 1930 – 32. In 1991, he entered German boxing history as the first German to be named to the International Boxing "Hall of Fame". In 1999 Schmeling was voted Germany's sportsman of the century. Born in Hamburg in 1936, football great Uwe Seeler, affectionately called "our Uwe" by Hamburgers and other Germans, played for Hamburger SV throughout his entire career as well as in four world cups. Between 1954 and 1972, he was a member of the German national team and played in 72 games.

Axel Springer, publisher

Klaus Störtebeker (ca. 1360 – 1401)

All Hamburg came out to watch his execution. "Our Klaus" was, after all, a hero – someone who stole from the rich and gave to the poor. But did he really deserve such a display of public affection? Wasn't he really just a bloodthirsty pirate? Many legends have grown up around him, including one that says he was born in Hamburg, though others say he was born elsewhere. Störtebeker was the leader of the Vitalienbrüder, a group of pirates who seized numerous ships that plied the Baltic Sea. His goal was to capture Hanse ships, but he was chased off into the North Sea. Klaus Störtebeker was finally caught off the coast of Helgoland and, on 20 October 1401, he was beheaded at Grasbrook, near Hamburg.

The skull of Klaus Störtebeker

HAMBURG THROUGH THE YEAR

Hamburg is an exciting city to visit at any time of the year. The wealth of things to do includes a wide range of cultural events. In summer, there is a lot of activity on the Alster, where a variety of watersports attract young and old. On the Elbe, there is a definite Mediterranean feeling. Three times a year (in spring, summer and winter) a popular festival lasting several weeks is held at the cathedral's Heiligengeistfeld. Among the most-visited attractions are the Fischmarkt, which is held every Sunday morning, as well as the port's annual birthday party at the beginning of May. When it rains, Hamburg's many great museums beckon. Information about current events is available from tourist information offices *(see p203)*.

Spring

Spring is a particularly good time to travel to Hamburg, because the city turns green extremely early and more events are held outside. As early as May, the season begins in the beach clubs on the shores of the Elbe. The plants in Planten un Blomen park bloom in full glory. This is also a good time to amble along Hamburg's luxury shopping streets, admiring the latest fashions.

Hamburg City Beach Club, perfect for relaxing by the water

March
Frühlingsdom *(end Mar – end Apr)*. The season of fairs begins here on the Heiligengeistfeld. Numerous and varied attractions offer fun and games for young and old.

April
Osterfeuer *(Easter Saturday)*. Easter fires are lit along the banks of the Elbe (Övelgönne to Blankenese) in the evening. The best views are from aboard a boat on the river.
Lange Nacht der Museen *(one Sat in Apr)*. As many as fifty museums are open for

exhibitions and guided tours until 2am.
Hamburg Marathon *(one Sun in Apr or May)*. More than 20,000 amateur runners supported by numerous spectators compete alongside professionals on the challenging 42-km (26-mile) course which leads them across the entire city.

May
The Port's Birthday Bash *(around 7 May)*. A three-day weekend event held at the port between Fish Auction Hall and Kehrwiederspitze. There's action on land, water and in the air. A high point is the Schlepperballet (tug boat ballet; *see p85*).
Internationale Musikfest Hamburg *(one week in May)*. Concert orchestras, bands and soloists from the world of classical and jazz convene in Hamburg.
Hamburger Surffestival *(five days in mid-May)*. Surfers and skateboarders meet in the city to party and to spread the subculture through film, fashion and demonstrations.

Japanese Cherry Blossom Festival *(mid-May)*. To celebrate the cherry blossoms, the Japanese community holds a festival on Außenalster. Around 10:30pm a large fireworks provides a lovely end.
Elbjazz Festival *(a weekend end May)*. Jazz in all varieties around HafenCity.
Dschungelnächte (Jungle Nights) *(three Sats after the end of May)*. In Tierpark Hagenbeck, Bengal fire, Caribbean rhythms and many more exciting shows captivate visitors until midnight.

People enjoying themselves in Tierpark Hagenbeck

Crowds at the Port's Birthday Bash, celebrated every May

Average Daily Hours of Sunshine

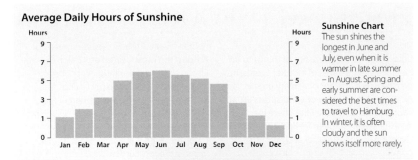

Sunshine Chart
The sun shines the longest in June and July, even when it is warmer in late summer – in August. Spring and early summer are considered the best times to travel to Hamburg. In winter, it is often cloudy and the sun shows itself more rarely.

Summer

Summer is *the* outdoor season in Hamburg, when artists and visitors alike are drawn outside to jazz concerts, theatre performances and sporting events. Many of these events take place on or near the water. Films are screened under the starry skies around the city. The many neighbourhood festivals are on a smaller scale, but they offer lots of entertainment and delicious food.

Planten un Blomen looking lush and attractive in summer

June

Altonale *(first half of Jun)*. The largest district festivals, this one draws many visitors with live music, circus acts, theatre, flea markets and much more. At the closing Spaßparade (fun parade), masks, costumes and artistry create a fun-filled atmosphere.

Summer on the Magellan-Terrassen *(Suns early Jun – end Aug)*. Performances, lectures, shows and tango-workshops are staged on this open space in HafenCity.

July

International German Open Tennis Tournament *(Jul)*. Many tennis greats from around the world compete in this 1892 established tournament at Rothenbaum.

Fleetinsel Festival *(Duckstein Festival; ten days in Jul)*. Art, culture and culinary delights on Fleetinsel. There is music (from Latin to jazz) on a floating stage, street theatre and outdoor booths.

Schleswig-Holstein Music Festival *(mid-Jul – end Aug)*.

Classical concerts are held in several North German cities. Some of the festival's events are held in Hamburg.

Sommerdom *(end Jul – end Aug)*. The second four-week fair is held at the Heiligen geistfeld. Fun for the whole family.

Summer Movies in Sternschanzenpark *(early Jul – early Sep)*. Open-air screenings in a lovely park located in the heart of the famous Schanzenviertel.

August

Romantik-Nächte *(three Saturdays in Aug)*. Romantic music and classical tones can be heard on every path as visitors stroll around Tierpark Hagenbeck. The musicians are students of Hochschule für Musik und Theater Hamburg.

Hamburg Cruise Days *(a weekend in Aug; every two years)*. Maritime event with parades of boats and ships.

International Summer Festival *(two weeks in Aug)*. Dance and theatre festival.

Enter the Dragon *(one weekend in Aug / Sep)*. A two-

day Dragon Boat festival on the Binnenalster with rowing teams from around the world. The boats start in front of Alsterpavillon.

Alstervergnügen *(Thu – Sun end Aug/early Sep)*. A fair held on Binnenalster with music, shows, vendors, children's events and a food mile. On the first three days, there is a spectacular fireworks display.

The Sylt fried-fish stand, part of the Alstervergnügen festivities

Average Monthly Rainfall

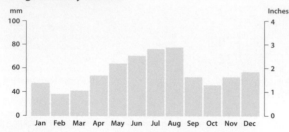

Rainfall Chart
In Hamburg, rainfall is distributed unevenly throughout the year. This is typical for a city located near a coast. The wettest time of year is summer, the driest time is late winter. Whatever the season, visitors should always be prepared for rain.

Exhibition in the crypt of St Michaelis

Autumn

In September, many events still take place outdoors in Hamburg. However, it is becoming a bit too chilly for sports events to be held outside. Still, autumn has its own special mood, especially in the parks, such as in Planten un Blomen. It is also lovely along the Elbe river at this time of year. A stiff breeze often blows off the harbour, but boat trips of the port area are still available. Autumn is also the season for theatre and literature festivals and events dedicated to boats and boating.

Early autumn on the Elbe's shore

September
Stadtpark Revival *(first weekend in Sep)*. Pure nostalgia at the Stadtpark for this Oldtimer Grand Prix, with its 1.7-km (1.05-mile) long racetrack that attracts motor sports lovers.
Hamburger Theaternacht *(one Sat early Sep)*. At the start of the new season, theatres invite the public to a long night with a full programme.
Harbour Front Literaturfestival *(ten days mid-Sep)*. Authors of all kinds of genres present their books at numerous venues, including the Landungsbrücken, Speicherstadt and HafenCity.
Reeperbahn Festival *(last weekend in Sep)*. National and international bands perform in clubs on the Reeperbahn, and at open-air venues. One of the best music festivals in Hamburg.
Filmfest Hamburg *(end Sep / early Oct)*. This film festival shows selected films in several cinemas. Classics of the silver screen supplement the premieres being screened.
Hamburger Theater Festival *(end Sep – end Oct)*. Performances by companies from Germany, Austria and

Switzerland are staged in various theatres.

October
Hanseboot *(end Oct / early Nov)*. International boat show at the trade fair grounds. Over the course of a week, the latest boats and the newest trends in watersports are presented to boating enthusiasts.

Water-Light-Concert in Planten un Blomen *(see pp 78 – 9)*

November
Hamburger Krimifestival *(one week early Nov)*. Crime writers present their latest murder mysteries. Among the "sites of crime" are the Literaturhaus *(see p129)*, several theatres and numerous bookstores.
Winterdom *(early Nov – early Dec)*. This is the third and last of the yearly fairs held at Heiligengeistfeld. Even in late autumn, the view over the city from the giant Ferris wheel is spectacular. A special attraction at the Winterdom are the jugglers dressed in traditional medieval costumes.

Average Monthly Temperature

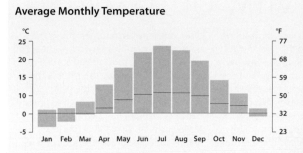

Temperature Chart
The chart shows the average minimum and maximum temperatures for each month. Hamburg is hottest in summer when the thermometer climbs above 30 °C (86 °F). In winter, it can be bitterly cold, with temperatures falling below freezing.

Winter

A festive atmosphere prevails at the Christmas markets in the centre of town and the adjoining districts. The cold in January and February, which can sometimes be bitter, does not spoil the good mood of Hamburg's citizens. In fact, they embrace the weather and, when the Alster lakes freeze over, have great fun ice skating. In the winter months, bookstores and cultural institutions, such as the Literaturhaus, hold many readings.

December

Weihnachtsmärkte (Christmas markets) *(end Nov–24 Dec).*
The whole city gets into the festive mood as Christmas markets spring up here and there around the city. Especially popular and crowded are the markets at Rathausplatz, Gerhart-Hauptmann-Platz, around St Petri church and at the Gänsemarkt. In addition to these larger markets located in Old Town and New Town, the smaller markets held for example in St Pauli, Eimsbüttel or Ottensen also are very fascinating. Each market has its own Christmas tree. Stalls vend various culinary delights.
New Year's Eve *(31 Dec)*. As one year ends and the next begins, Hamburgers are noticeably relaxed. There are large crowds

on the waterfront, especially at the Landungsbrücken, where a concert of ships' sirens greets the new year, the heavens above the harbour light up colourfully with spectacular fireworks, thousands of champagne corks pop and complete strangers wish each other a happy New Year. The cheerful celebrations continue long after midnight until the early morning hours.

January

Ice Fun on the Alster *(when the ice is thick enough)*. When it is bitterly cold outside, and the ice covering the Alster is deemed by the city to be thick enough to be safe, innumerous walkers and ice skaters throng here. It is easy enough to warm up at one of the many mulled wine stands which are set up on the river banks and on the frozen Alster. Sometimes, though, Hamburgers wait expectantly and eagerly for enough of a freeze to create thick ice to skate over, only to be disappointed when it does not happen.

February

Reisen Hamburg *(early Feb)*. At this international tourism fair, about 900 exhibitors from around the world showcase their products. Visitors, however, are not only attracted by the informative displays, but also by the opportunity to book their next holiday.

The Hamburger Dom takes place three times a year

Iced-over ship's prow in Hamburg's wintery harbour

Maskenzauber an der Alster
(weekend before Shrove Tuesday).
Carnival the Hanseatic way, with style, elegance and "noblesse" held in front of the Venetian-style backdrop of the Alster Arcades. The highlight of the festival is the historic masquerade ball which is held in varying venues. Classes are offered to visitors who wish to learn how to dance historical dances.
LILaBe *(after Ash Wednesday)*.
The largest North German carnival is held at the Fachhochschule Bergedorf. Ten thousand revellers make this two-day festival a giant party.

Holidays

New Year's Day (1 Jan)
Good Friday (varies)
Easter Monday (varies)
Workers' Day (1 May)
Ascension Day (varies)
Whit Monday (varies)
German Unity Day (3 Oct)
Christmas (25 / 26 Dec)

A RIVER VIEW OF HAMBURG

A trip to Hamburg's harbour is an absolute must for every visi- tor to the city. "If you haven't been to the harbour, you haven't been to Hamburg", the locals say. The best way to get to know this area is to take a round trip on one of the boats that depart from all along the Landungsbrücken. The small boats can manoeuvre through even narrow canals as well as the Speicherstadt canals (also known as the Fleete). Large ships offer tours of the container port. Their captains are as witty and knowledgable as they are chatty; they are chock full of maritime lore, which they happily recount. You learn a great deal about the port and its ships, and you

often can see even large freighters from up close. Ferry routes service practically all corners of the harbour. If you are willing to travel a bit further, you can explore the entire water's edge, from the Landungsbrücken up-river to the newly built HafenCity *(see pp90–91)*, then further up-river to Museumshafen Övelgönne *(see p135)* and on to Teufelsbrück. The south shore has its appeal, too. Departing from the Blohm + Voss shipyard, a ferry travels to the Seemannshöft pilot station, on to Finkenwerder and then to the Airbus factory. Flights over the city provide an especially spectacular view of the harbour area.

- Loudspeaker system that greets all ships

Elbe

- Teufelsbrück
- Airbus Factory

Seemannshöft •

Finkenwerder •

Round trip of the Port
No trip to Hamburg is complete without taking one of the harbour or container port round trips on offer.

HADAG ferry No. 62
This harbour ferry *(see p135)* offers an interesting trip along the Elbe river from Landungsbrücken to Finkenwerder. It also goes to the Museum Övelgönne.

Loudspeaker system
All ships entering and leaving Hamburg's busy port are greeted and bid farewell via a loudspeaker system that also plays the national anthems for each ship's home country.

Kreuzfahrtterminal (Hamburg Cruise Center)
The largest and best-known cruise ships in the world dock at the Hamburg Cruise Centers – the liner Clubschiff *AIDAvita* docks here, too.

Musical-Express
HADAG ferry number 73 takes patrons to the theatre in the harbour.

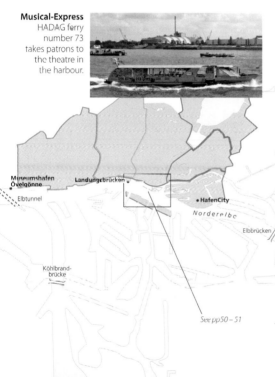

DIRECTORY

Harbour Round Trips

Barkassen-Centrale
Tel 319 91 61 70.
w barkassen-centrale.de

Barkassen Meyer
Tel 317 73 70.
w barkassen-meyer.de

Bergedorfer Schifffahrtslinie
Tel 73 67 56 90.
w barkassenfahrt.de

Elbe Erlebnistörns
Tel 219 46 27.
w elbe-erlebnistoerns.de

Hamburg City Tour
Tel 32 31 85 90.
w hamburg-city-tour.eu

Touristik Kontor
Tel 334 42 20.
w touristik-kontor.de

Harbour Ferries

HADAG Seetouristik und Fährdienst AG
Tel 311 70 70.
w hadag.de

Max Jens GmbH
Tel 36 66 81.
w mj-hafenrundfahrt.de

Air Tours

Air Hamburg
Tel 70 70 88 90.
w air-hamburg.de

CANAIR Luftfahrt-unternehmen
Tel 35 51 52 62.
w canair.de

Hanseatic Helicopter Service
Tel 54 80 29 97.
w hanseatic-helicopter.de

See pp 50 – 51

0 kilometres 4

0 miles 4

Köhlbrandbrücke
The pylons of this steel-and-cable bridge, designed by Egon Jux, rise 135 m (443 ft) above high tide. Since 1974, this bridge has spanned the 325-m (105-ft) wide Köhlbrand in Hamburg's harbour.

From the Alter Elbtunnel to HafenCity

This section of the Elbe river flows through the heart of Hamburg. There is no other place where the city shows itself to be so confident, so worldly and so dynamic, and nowhere else is it changing so radically. Change is ongoing, with the HafenCity project being an enormous architectural challenge. Most of Hamburg's attractions are found on the north shore of the Elbe.

Alter Elbtunnel
Pedestrians and cyclists reach the south shore of the Elbe river via this tunnel, built in 1911. From the south shore, you can enjoy a fabulous view of the city *(see p93)*.

Landungsbrücken
No visitor to the city should miss the chance to take a walk on the gently moving floating quays and watch the many ships as they glide slowly by *(see p93)*.

BEI DEN ST. PAULI
LANDUNGSBRÜCKEN

Landungsbrücken

Access to the Alter Elbtunnel: Elevators transport cars 23.5 m (77 ft) down into the tunnel's depths *(see p93)*.

Alter Elbtunnel

| 0 metres | 200 |
| 0 yards | 200 |

The Hafen-Hochbahn (elevated port railway) was opened in 1912. A fascinating view of the port can be enjoyed between the stops at Rödingsmarkt and Landungsbrücken *(see p92)*.

Rickmer Rickmers
Since 1987, this three-masted schooner, built in Bremerhaven in 1896, has been anchored at the Landungsbrücken as a ship museum *(see pp94–5)*.

Blohm + Voss
At the Blohm + Voss GmbH shipyard, ships are still being built and repaired. The shipyard was founded in 1877. Since then, many famous ships have been launched from its docks.

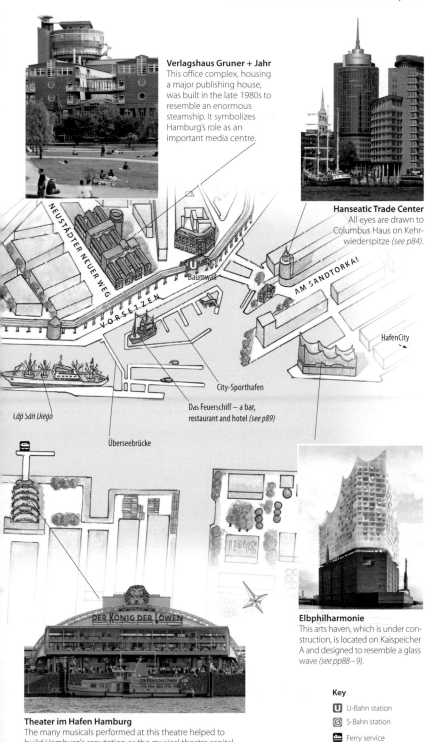

Verlagshaus Gruner + Jahr
This office complex, housing a major publishing house, was built in the late 1980s to resemble an enormous steamship. It symbolizes Hamburg's role as an important media centre.

Hanseatic Trade Center
All eyes are drawn to Columbus Haus on Kehrwiederspitze *(see p84)*.

HafenCity

City-Sporthafen

Das Feuerschiff – a bar, restaurant and hotel *(see p89)*

Lap San Diego

Überseebrücke

Elbphilharmonie
This arts haven, which is under construction, is located on Kaispeicher A and designed to resemble a glass wave *(see pp88 – 9)*.

Theater im Hafen Hamburg
The many musicals performed at this theatre helped to build Hamburg's reputation as the musical theatre capital of Germany *(see p92 and pp208–11)*.

Key

🅄 U-Bahn station
🆂 S-Bahn station
🛳 Ferry service
🛳 Boat boarding point

The Landungsbrücken tower with Columbus Haus behind it on Kehrwiederspitze ▶

HAMBURG
AREA BY AREA

Old Town   **54 – 67**

New Town   **68 – 79**

Port and Speicherstadt   **80 – 99**

St Pauli   **100 – 111**

Altona   **112 – 119**

Around the Alster   **120 – 131**

Further Afield   **132 – 141**

Three Guided Walks   **142 – 149**

Beyond Hamburg   **150 – 169**

OLD TOWN

Even from afar you can easily recognize the Old Town by the towers and spires of its four main churches. Here, archaeologists still find remnants from Hamburg's past, but unfortunately the visitor won't see many buildings older than 150 years. Large sections of the Old Town were destroyed in the Great Fire of 1842. Today there are only a few old houses in the Deichstraße still standing to bear testimony to the beauty that old Hamburg once possessed.

A new architectural era, and a new epoch in the city's history, was heralded by the Kontorhäuser (office buildings) built around Burchardplatz in the 1920s. One of the most beautiful squares in Hamburg is the Rathausmarkt and its imposing Rathaus (city hall), in whose construction all Hanseatic re serve was abandoned. Especially impressive is the view of the square from the Alster Arcades. With its gleaming white, rounded colonnade, Hamburg expresses its Venetian side.

Sights at a Glance

Churches
- ❹ St Petri
- ❼ St Jacobi
- ⓬ St Katharinen
- ⓭ St Nikolai Memorial

Museums and Galleries
- ❷ Bucerius Kunst Forum
- ⓿ Hamburger Kunsthalle pp64–5
- ❿ Deichtorhallen
- ⓰ RED Gallery

Historic Buildings and Monuments
- ❶ Rathaus pp60–61
- ❺ Domplatz

Streets and Squares
- ❽ Alster Arcades
- ⓱ Deichstraße

Theatres
- ❻ Thalia Theater

Other Attractions
- ❾ Hauptbahnhof
- ⓫ Chilehaus
- ⓮ Börse
- ⓯ Alsterfleet

☐ Restaurants
see p188
1. Alt Hamburger Aalspeicher
2. Café Paris
3. Daniel Wischer
4. Deichgraf
5. Fillet of Soul
6. Golden Cut
7. Mama
8. Le Plat du Jour
9. Saliba Alsterarkaden
10. Ti Breizh
11. Tschebull
12. Weltbühne

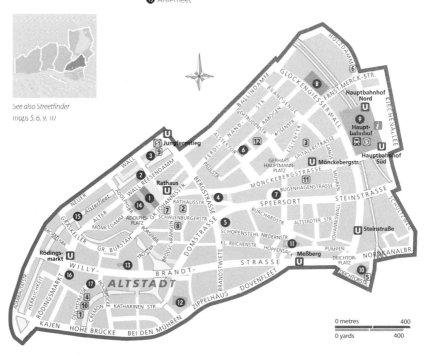

See also Streetfinder maps 5, 6, 9, 10

0 metres 400
0 yards 400

◀ Hamburg's Rathaus (city hall), topped by its striking 112-m (370-ft) tall tower *(see pp60–61)*   **For map symbols** *see back flap*

Street-by-Street: Rathaus and Alster Arcades

Built in the Neo-Renaissance style, Hamburg's Rathaus (city hall) is one of its landmark buildings. Both its façade and interior are adorned with lavish ornamentation and opulent decoration. After walking across the extensive Rathausmarkt, you reach the Alster Arcades. Tucked inside the white colonnade are many exclusive shops that entice visitors in for some serious shopping. Take a break and wander into one of the many bistros and cafés here, which offer an excellent view of the Alster.

❷ ★ Bucerius Kunst Forum
Since autumn 2002, the former Reichsbank building has been home to the Bucerius Art Forum. Every year four stellar exhibitions are mounted in this imposing Neo-Classical building.

★ Hygieia Fountain
After the city had recovered from a cholera epidemic in 1892, this lovely fountain with three basins was built in the interior courtyard of the Rathaus. On top, Hygieia, the Greek goddess of health, watches over the waters.

Key

— Suggested route

0 metres	100
0 yards	100

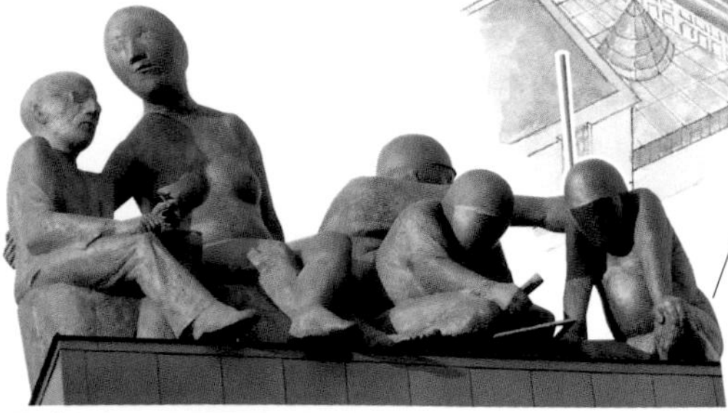

SCHLEC BRÜCK

ALSTERFLEET

ALTER WALL

ADOLPHSPLATZ

JOHANNISSTRASSE

Sculpture
Designed by sculptor Waldemar Otto, this group of figures was installed on the portal of the Börse in 2005.

Lion statue
Large stone lions sit outside the Rathaus.

❸ ★ Alster Arcades
After the Great Fire of 1842 that reduced most of the Old Town to rubble and ash, architect Alexis de Chateauneuf designed this colonnade with a Venetian flair.

Locator Map
See Street Finder maps 5–6 & 9–10

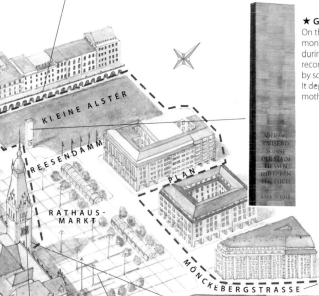

★ Gedenkstein
On the back of this monument to those slain during World War I is the reconstruction of a relief by sculptor Ernst Barlach. It depicts a grieving mother with her child.

The Mönckebergstraße
is one of the most popular shopping streets in the city. Extending from the Rathausmarkt to the Hauptbahnhof, it counts among the most visited shopping streets in Germany.

The Rathausmarkt is used year-round for a wide variety of events – from summer concerts to the Weihnachtsmarkt (Christmas market) in winter.

❶ ★ Rathaus
Built in 1886–97 in the Neo-Renaissance style, the Rathaus dazzles visitors with its huge dimensions and its 112-m (367-ft) high tower.

Portal
The entrance portal of the Rathaus is adorned with sculptures, paintings and Hamburg's coat of arms. It attests to the pride of the city state.

Façade of the Bucerius Kunst Forum in the former Reichsbank building

❶ Rathaus

See pp60–61.

❷ Bucerius Kunst Forum

Rathausmarkt 2. **Map** 10 D3. **Tel** 360 99 60. Ⓤ Jungfernstieg, Rathaus. Ⓢ Jungfernstieg. ⬜ 3, 4, 5, 6, 31, 34, 35, 36, 37. **Open** 11am–7pm daily (Thu to 9pm). **Closed** 24 Dec.

Ⓦ buceriuskunstforum.de

The Bucerius Kunst Forum (Bucerius Art Forum), established in 2002, is housed in the former Reichsbank building near the Rathaus. The Neo-Classical building, which dates from 1914–17, has a richly embellished façade. Depicted on the gables are workers in various professions and trades – from Senator to water carrier – that are typical for this Hanseatic city.

Inside the building are 700 sq m (735 sq ft) of gallery space for the Forum's exhibitions. With its work supported by the ZEIT foundation, the institution mounts exhibitions covering themes from classical times to the present day.

One of the mandates of the Bucerius Kunst Forum is to build bridges between old art and contemporary art, as well as between European and foreign cultures. For this reason the themes covered in each exhibition are broad. The programme consists of four top exhibitions a year, put together by renowned guest curators, supplemented by lectures and readings.

❸ Alster Arcades

Map 10 D3. Ⓤ Jungfernstieg, Rathaus. Ⓢ Jungfernstieg. ⬜ 3, 4, 5, 6, 31, 34, 35, 36, 37.

Alongside the Kleine Alster run the Alster Arcades (Alsterarkaden), among Hamburg's most exclusive addresses for high-quality shopping and elegant dining. Boutiques and fashion stores selling designer goods invite visitors to linger for a while, as do the wine bars and bistros. The latter contribute to the Mediterranean flair – especially in summer.

The Alster Arcades were constructed after the Great Fire of 1842, in which the majority of the buildings between Binnenalster and Rathausmarkt burned down. Architect Alexis de Chateauneuf designed the colonnade in Venetian style and also created the buildings behind them. Many other architects and designers took

inspiration from this complex. The numerous street cafés offer a lovely view of the water.

At the south end of the Alster Arcades is the Schleusenbrücke, a bridge with a weir that helps regulate the amount of water flowing into the Binnenalster.

❹ St Petri

Kreuslerstraße 6. **Map** 10 E3. **Tel** 325 74 00. Ⓤ Jungfernstieg, Rathaus. Ⓢ Jungfernstieg. ⬜ 4, 5, 6, 31, 34, 35, 36, 37. **Open** 10am–6:30pm Mon–Fri (Wed to 7pm), 10am–5pm Sat, 9am–8pm Sun. Ⓦ sankt-petri.de

Named after the Apostle Peter, this house of worship is the oldest of Hamburg's five parish churches. It is thought to have been built in the 11th century and was first mentioned in 1195. Around 1310, the church began to expand into a triple-naved Gothic hall church. Once the second south nave was added around 1420, construction of the church was finally complete.

In 1842 the church fell victim to the Great Fire. Very little was left of the façade. However, the most important treasures stored inside were saved, such as the well-known bronze door knocker (1342) in the form of a lion's head on the west entrance.

The church was rebuilt on the old foundations in the Neo-Gothic style, and was modelled on the original. It was consecrated in 1849. St Petri

The Gedenkstein, a sober monument to the victims of war

Domplatz with cuboids indicating the layout of the Mariendom

church survived World War II with relatively little damage. Some of its works of art, among them a Gothic panel (circa 1460) and a wooden statue (circa 1480), depict Bishop Ansgar of Hamburg and Bremen (801–865) who was canonized by Pope Nicolas I. Gracing the façade are sculptures of the Evangelists, among others.

The church spire, which rises 133-m (436-ft) high, was completed in 1878. Visitors can climb 544 steps to the 123-m (402-ft) level, where there is a viewing platform. The view of the inner city from here is fabulous, and the climb is worthwhile.

❺ Domplatz

Map 10 E3–4. Ⓤ Jungfernstieg, Rathaus. Ⓢ Jungfernstieg. 🚌 4, 5, 6, 31, 34, 35, 36, 37. Showroom: Kreuslerstraße 4. **Tel** 325 74 00. **Open** 10am–1pm & 3–5pm Mon–Fri, 10am–1pm Sat.

The Domplatz is considered to be the birthplace of Hamburg. Here, the remains of a building complex were uncovered, which were first thought to be the legendary Hammaburg castle (see p21). The castle was built in 817 by the Franks, and destroyed by the Vikings in 845. Research, however, revealed that the finds were parts of the Mariendom (St Mary's Cathedral), and not the remains of the Hammaburg, from which the city derives its name.

After the excavation, which had been carried out under the direction of the Helms-Museum für Archäologie (Hamburg's archeological museum), was

completed, greenery was planted on the Domplatz. The layout of the Mariendom is indicated by 30 white plexiglass cuboids, which can be used as benches. At night, when the cuboids are illuminated, the atmosphere on the Domplatz is particularly enchanting.

At the northern edge of the Domplatz, a stone ring some 19 m (62 feet) in diameter was discovered during excavations carried out in 1962, at a depth of around 3 m (10 ft). These foundations are understood to belong to the Bishop's Castle (Bischofsburg). Dating from the 11th century, it is one of the oldest stone fortresses north of the Elbe. Some excavation finds are on display in the lower level of St Petri's parish house.

❻ Thalia Theater

Alstertor 1. **Map** 10 E3. **Tel** 32 81 40. Ⓤ Mönckebergstraße, Jungfernstieg. Ⓢ Jungfernstieg. 🚌 4, 5, 6, 31, 34, 35, 36, 37. 🎭 only groups & per appointment. Box office: **Tel** 32 81 44 44. **Open** 10am–7pm Mon–Sat, 4–6pm Sun, hols. 🌐 **thalia-theater.de**

Named after the Muse of comedy, Thalia Theater is a time-honoured Hamburg institution. It was founded in 1843 by Charles Maurice Schwartzenberger (1805–1896). Since then, the city's oldest theatre company has moved house several times.

Door knocker, St Petri church

In 1912, a playhouse was opened in the theatre's current location. That building was destroyed in 1945, but was later rebuilt in 1960, at which time a full programme of plays were staged once again.

Even though today's theatre is not as splendid as others, such as the Deutsches Schauspielhaus (see p129), Thalia Theater definitely numbers among Germany's most famous stages. In 1989, 2003 and 2007 it was voted "Theatre of the Year". Its repertoire includes about 30 productions that change daily. The range of drama covered is broad – from Sophocles to William Shakespeare, Friedrich Schiller and Franz Kafka to contemporary playwrights like Elfriede Jelinek. The tradition-rich Thalia Theater is also well known for its decisive direction: famous directors such as Peter Zadek and Jürgen Flimm have had great successes here.

The Thalia Theater is one of the venues of the Hamburger Theater Festival (see p46), which is held in autumn.

The muse of comedy on the façade of Thalia Theater

❶ Rathaus

The Rathaus (city hall) certainly does not reflect that well-known Hamburg characteristic – understatement. Nothing was held back in the construction of this Neo-Renaissance palatial building, erected in 1886 – 97. Its dimensions are huge (111 m by 70 m / 365 ft by 230 ft), and its tower is impressive 112 m (365 ft) high. Its façade is richly adorned with sculptures. Among the sculptures are 20 German emperors facing out towards the Rathausmarkt. The seat of the Hamburg City Council and Senate is built atop 4,000 wooden stakes and contains 647 rooms.

★ Parliament Chamber
The seat of parliament is both one of the largest rooms in the Rathaus and also the starkest.

Entrance to the Great Banquet Hall
The interior of this hall was only completed at the beginning of the 20th century.

Main entrance

★ Lord Mayor's Chamber
All eyes are drawn to the oil painting by Hugo Vogel in this richly decorated room. It depicts Senators clothed in their official garb during the dedication of the Rathaus in 1897.

★ Great Banquet Hall
This hall is dominated by three enormous chandeliers. The painting in the background is an impression of Hamburg's port at the beginning of the 20th century.

Hygieia Fountain in the courtyard
The bronze figures on the edge of this fountain depict the great significance water holds for many very different professions such as shipping.

Hamburger Wappen am Rathaus

★ Ratsstube
Once a week, the Hamburg Senate goes into session in this chamber. The Lord Mayor takes the place of honour under the canopy, while the Senators and City Council take their seats around the horseshoe-shaped table.

KEY

① **Four copper figures** represent the virtues of a good citizen.

② **The clock face** of the tower clock is 5 m (16 ft) long.

③ **The right wing** of the Rathaus is used exclusively by Hamburg's Senate.

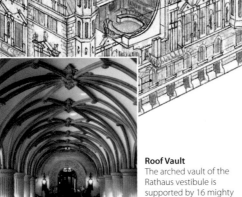

Roof Vault
The arched vault of the Rathaus vestibule is supported by 16 mighty sandstone columns.

❼ St Jacobi

Jakobikirchhof 22. **Map** 10 E3. **Tel** 303 73 70. Ⓤ Mönckebergstraße. Ⓢ Hauptbahnhof. ▥ 4, 5, 6, 31, 34, 35, 36, 37. **Open** Apr–Sep: 10am–5pm Mon–Sat; Oct–Mar: 11am–5pm Mon–Sat. 📷 call ahead. Ⓦ **jacobus.de**

The Gothic church of St Jacobi, one of the parish churches of Hamburg, was erected in the second half of the 14th century. In the 15th century, the triple-nave hall church was expanded when a second aisle was built on the south side. Of the church's three altars, the St Lucas Altar (circa 1500) is the most valuable. It was originally located in Mariendom (St Mary's Cathedral) in Hamburg. Portraits of the benefactors were depicted on an inside panel, as was usual in the Middle Ages. In the left aisle of the church is a statue of the patron saint, St Jacob, which was carved in the 17th century. Paintings on the ceiling illustrate virtues of good citizens.

A real treasure is the church's organ, built in 1689–93 by Arp Schnitger. Located on the west balcony, this celebrated organ is the largest extant Baroque organ in northern and central Europe. Even Johann Sebastian Bach played on this instrument. It has been restored, and can be heard every Sunday during services and in special organ concerts.

St Petri Altar (1508), located in the first of St Jacobi's south naves

❽ Hamburger Kunsthalle

See pp64–5.

❾ Hauptbahnhof

Kirchenallee. **Map** 10 F2–3. Ⓤ Hauptbahnhof. Ⓢ Hauptbahnhof. ▥ 4, 5, 6, 31, 34, 35, 36, 37, 112.

Hamburg's Hauptbahnhof, the main train station located on the eastern edge of the Old Town, is northern Germany's most important railway hub. Trains depart from 14 tracks for numerous destinations. Some 450,000 passengers and visitors frequent this station daily, making it one of the busiest in Germany. Several S-Bahn and U-Bahn lines also converge here. Their tracks are located under or beside the station, making it the hub of Hamburg's internal transport system, Hamburger Verkehrsverbund (HVV for short).

Built in the Neo-Renaissance style, the station opened on 6 December 1906. The main hall is 37 m (122 ft) high and covered with a steel and glass roof. The hall itself is 206 m (675 ft) long and 135 m (443 ft) wide – the largest station forecourt in the country. It was here in 1991 that Wandelhalle opened; this was Germany's first shopping centre to

be located in a train station. Along with 70 speciality stores and a wide range of food choices, the Deutsche Bahn (German railway) has its Reisezentrum (travel information centre) here.

❿ Deichtorhallen

Deichtorstraße 1–2. **Map** 10 F4. **Tel** 32 10 30. Ⓤ Steinstraße, Meßberg. Ⓢ Hauptbahnhof. ▥ 34. **Open** 11am–6pm Tue–Sun (first Thu each month 11am–9pm). 📷 📷 Ⓦ **deichtorhallen.de**

These two monumental halls were erected 1911–14 on the grounds of the former Berliner Bahnhof (train station). Measuring 3,800 and 1,800 sq m (50,000 sq ft and 19,000 sq ft) respectively, their steel construction is an example of Jugendstil industrial architecture. At first they were used as market halls, after 1984 they stayed empty for some time.

The Deichtorhallen has been used for art exhibitions since 1989. Over time, it has evolved into one of Europe's largest exhibition centres. The Internationales Haus der Fotografie (International House of Photography) in the south hall focuses on the evolution of photography since its beginnings. In the north hall, exhibitions featuring the works of contemporary painters and sculptors, both famous and not so famous, are mounted. Discussions with artists round out the programme.

A view of Hamburg's Hauptbahnhof

From the grounds of the Deichtorhallen, the **HighFlyer Hamburg** rises up 150 m (490 ft) into the sky over Hamburg. The view of the city from this ultramodern stationary balloon is breathtaking. The spectacular balloon has a diameter of 23 m (75 ft). The faint of heart will be reassured by the steel cable that permanently anchors the balloon to the ground.

HighFlyer Hamburg
Tel 30 08 69 69.
Open 10am–10pm.
w highflyer-hamburg.de

⓫ Chilehaus

Burchardplatz / Pumpenstraße.
Map 10 F4. **U** Steinstraße, Meßberg.
S Hauptbahnhof. 4, 5, 6, 31, 34, 35, 36, 37. **Open** 9am–4pm daily.

The ten-storey Chilehaus (1922–24) is a striking example of the red-brick architecture of the 1920s. Due to its thin, unconventional form, this best-known of all Hamburg office buildings has been nicknamed "Ozeanriese" (ocean giant). With its angular form and a design that emphasizes the vertical, the building is reminiscent of the prow of a ship, especially when viewed from the prow side in

A symbol of Expressionist architecture: the Chilehaus

the east. In order to create this building, designed by architect Fritz Höger, nearly five million bricks were used.

The name Chilehaus was chosen because the man who commissioned the building, Henry Brarens Sloman, was a Hamburg merchant and shipping magnate who had made his fortune in the saltpetre trade in Chile.

Kontorhausviertel

The Kontorhausviertel (warehouse district), with its many impressive office buildings, is located around Burchardplatz between Brandstwiete and Klosterwall, and Steinstraße and Meßberg. Typical architectural elements of these buildings, designed in the Expressionistic style of the 1920s, include using reinforced concrete and red-brick façades, accentuating the vertical by using pillars, installing wide windows and creating imposing entrances. Some of the offices have Paternosters (open-style lifts) that are in use to this day. The most remarkable of all these office buildings is Chilehaus. Other interesting examples are the Sprinkenhof, which is the largest office complex, Montanhof, with its many bay windows, and the Meßberghof, with its elegant spiral staircase that winds its way up eleven storeys.

Façade of the Sprinkenhof, built in 1927–43

⓬ St Katharinen

Katharinenkirchhof 1. **Map** 10 D4.
Tel 30 37 47 30. **U** Meßberg,
Rödingsmarkt. **S** Jungfernstieg.
3, 4, 6. **Open** 10am–5pm Mon–Fri,
11am 5pm Sat & Sun.
w katharinen-hamburg.de

Given its proximity to the water, St Katharinen church is also known as the "Mariners' Church". One of the five parish churches in Hamburg, it was first mentioned in 1256. The only remnant of the original building is the base of the tower. In 1656 7 the top of the tower of this church was capped by a Baroque-inspired steeple with arches – a significant feature of Hamburg's skyline.

After incurring heavy damage during 1943–44, the exterior of the church was rebuilt in its old form. The in former times richly decorated interior is now fairly simple. Among the very few old artworks is a beautiful wooden carving of St Catherine from the 15th century as well as some late Renaissance tomb-stones dating from the 16th and 17th centuries. After extensive restoration, the church re-opened in autumn 2012.

❽ Hamburger Kunsthalle

The Hamburger Kunsthalle is the most interesting art gallery in northern Germany. It has a tradition dating back to 1817, when the Kunstverein (friends of the fine arts) was established. The museum opened to the public in 1869. The collection provides a chronological review of European art movements, with an emphasis on 19th-century German Romantics, with works by Caspar David Friedrich and Philipp Otto Runge. A four-storey, cubelike extension, the Galerie der Gegenwart (contemporary gallery), was built in 1996 to a design by the architect O M Ungers. The building is reached by an underground link from the basement of the main gallery.

★ **Morning** (1808)
This painting by Philipp Otto Runge was intended to be part of a series called *Times of the Day*, but the artist died before completing it.

Hannah and Simeon in the Temple (c. 1627)
Thanks to his mastery of a sense of drama, Rembrandt succeeded in conveying the psychological make-up of his elderly subjects, who have recognized the Saviour in an unspoken message conveyed to the temple by Mary and Joseph.

High Altar of St Petri Church (1379)
This painted panel, displaying a wealth of detail, was created by Master Bertram of Minden, the first German artist to be identified by his name. He worked in Hamburg for most of his life.

Cupola Room

Rotunda

Café George Economou

Main entrance

Ground floor

Hubertus Wald Foru

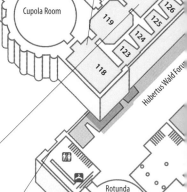

★ **The Polar Sea** (1823–24)
Caspar David Friedrich's dramatic seascape, with a sinking ship behind the rising ice-floes, is rife with symbolism.

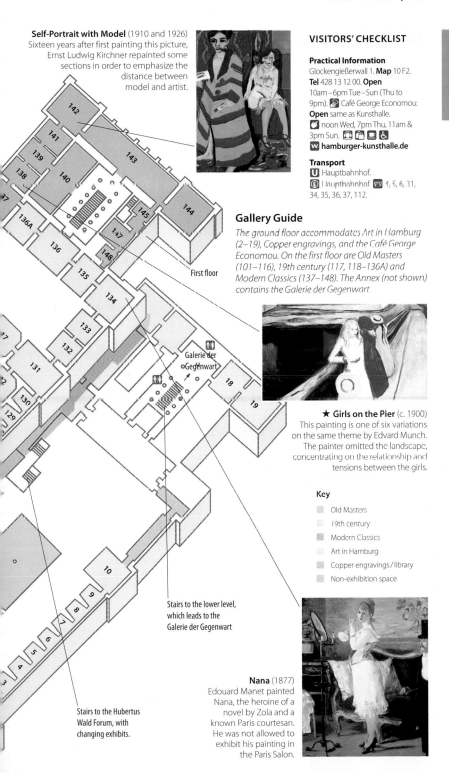

Self-Portrait with Model (1910 and 1926)
Sixteen years after first painting this picture, Ernst Ludwig Kirchner repainted some sections in order to emphasize the distance between model and artist.

VISITORS' CHECKLIST

Practical Information
Glockengießerwall 1. Map 10 F2.
Tel 428 13 12 00. **Open**
10am–6pm Tue–Sun (Thu to 9pm). Café George Economou:
Open same as Kunsthalle.
noon Wed, 7pm Thu, 11am & 3pm Sun.
w hamburger-kunsthalle.de

Transport
Hauptbahnhof.
Hauptbahnhof. 4, 5, 6, 31, 34, 35, 36, 37, 112.

Gallery Guide

The ground floor accommodates Art in Hamburg (2–19), Copper engravings, and the Café George Economou. On the first floor are Old Masters (101–116), 19th century (117, 118–136A) and Modern Classics (137–148). The Annex (not shown) contains the Galerie der Gegenwart

First floor

Galerie der Gegenwart

★ **Girls on the Pier** (c. 1900)
This painting is one of six variations on the same theme by Edvard Munch. The painter omitted the landscape, concentrating on the relationship and tensions between the girls.

Key

- Old Masters
- 19th century
- Modern Classics
- Art in Hamburg
- Copper engravings/library
- Non-exhibition space

Stairs to the lower level, which leads to the Galerie der Gegenwart

Stairs to the Hubertus Wald Forum, with changing exhibits.

Nana (1877)
Edouard Manet painted Nana, the heroine of a novel by Zola and a known Paris courtesan. He was not allowed to exhibit his painting in the Paris Salon.

⑬ St Nikolai Memorial

Willy-Brandt-Straße 60. **Map** 10 D4.
Tel 37 11 25. Ⓤ Rödingsmarkt. Ⓢ
Stadthausbrücke. 🚌 3, 31, 35, 37.
Open May–Sep: 10am–8pm daily;
Oct–Apr: 10am–5pm daily. 🎧 ✓
2pm on Sat and by appointment. 📷
Ⓦ **mahnmal-st-nikolai.de**

The ruins of the church, called
Mahnmal St Nikolai, serve both
as an attraction and a memorial.
The earliest mention of an
ecclesiastical building at this
location was in 1195. By the
middle of the 14th century, the
church had been enlarged into
a triple-naved hall church;
thereafter it remained relatively
unchanged for about 500 years.
In 1842 it was destroyed during
the Great Fire. Afterwards, this
house of worship was rebuilt in
the Neo-Gothic style from
1846–74. The church's tower,
which at 147 m (482 ft) was one
of the highest in Germany, was
completed in 1874.

During the air raids of 1943,
St Nikolai church suffered heavy
damage. Due to generous
benefactors and public funds, it
would have been possible to
restore the nearly destroyed
tower and the remains of the
walls. However, the decision
was made not to attempt a
complete restoration; instead, in
1960–62, a new St Nikolai
church was erected to the
northwest of the Außenalster
(Harvestehuder Weg No. 114).
The ruins of the original church

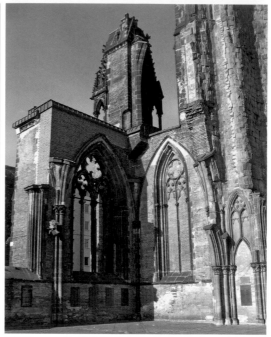

St Nikolai – a memorial to the victims of war and violence

have become a memorial to the
tragic consequences of war and
serve as a sober plea for world
peace. In 2013, the crypt was
converted into a museum with
a permanent exhibition on the
destruction of Hamburg
entitled "Gomorrah 1943".

A glass elevator, added to the
tower in 2005, has become a
popular tourist attraction,
whisking visitors up to a
viewing platform 76 m (250 ft)
high. From here there are wonderful view of the surrounding
area, as well as historical
photographs of the cityscape,
allowing comparison of the
skyline before and after 1943.

The church's carillon is played
at noon on Thursdays and at
5pm on Saturdays Apr–Oct.

⑭ Börse

Adolphsplatz 1. **Map** 10 D3.
Tel 36 13 83 60. Ⓤ Rathaus.
Ⓢ Stadthausbrücke. 🚌 3, 4, 5, 6, 31,
34, 35, 36, 37. ✓ by appointment.

The Hamburg Börse (stock
exchange) was established in
1558 and is considered the
oldest institution of its kind
in central and northern Europe.
As the trade in goods from
the colonies increased, the
stock exchange was moved in
1841 from its original location
on the Trostbrücke to the
current location on
Adolphsplatz. Designed by Carl
Ludwig Wimmel and Franz
Gustav Forsmann in the late-
Classical style, this building
survived the Great Fire that
ravaged the city the following
year. The stock exchange is
connected to the Rathaus,
which was built in 1886–87.
Together, these two buildings
create an impressive ensemble.

The Börse is run by the
Hamburg Chamber of
Commerce, which also has
its headquarters here. Floor
trading of stocks and securities
ended in 2003. Only a board
hanging on the wall with stock
prices testifies to this past
activity. Today, traders work in
three halls, linked by arcades,
using telephones and
computers. The Grain Exchange
is the only active commodity
exchange that still remains.

The 51-bell, four-octave carillon, added to
the spire of St Nikolai in 1993

⓯ Alsterfleet

Map 9 B5 – C3. **U** Rödingsmarkt. **S** Stadthausbrücke. 🚌 31, 35, 37.

The Alsterfleet is a canal linking the Binnenalster with the river Elbe. It runs south of the Kleine Alster basin between the Schleusenbrücke and the Schaartorschleuse, where it meets the Elbe river at Baumwall. As early as the 12th century, the water level of Alster lake was regulated when the Alsterfleet was created by straightening out a previously meandering waterway. Today, the Schaartorschleuse, a lock which was built in the Alsterfleet in 1967, serves as a protection against high tides. It ensures a constant level of water, which is about 3 m (10 ft) below sea-level. In 2003, the city constructed a pathway allowing pedestrians to walk along the Alsterfleet all the way to the Elbe river.

⓰ RED Gallery

Rödingsmarkt 19. **Map** 9 C4. **Tel** 36 90 03 19. **U** Rödingsmarkt. **S** Stadthausbrücke. 🚌 3, 6, 31, 35, 37. **Open** 10am – 6pm Mon – Fri, 10am – 2pm Sat.. 📷 🏢 **W** redgallery.de

On the premises once occupied by the Museum SteinZeiten, the RED Gallery was opened in October 2009. The gallery's name – RED stands for "Rare Earth Decor" – is an indication of its unique

Old Hamburg merchant houses on Deichstraße

concept: In fashionable settings, geological objects such as fossils, minerals and gemstones are presented as "geogenic art". The collection is truly peerless, and the pieces of modern art created from treasures dating back millions of years can also be bought. Some exhibits, like minerals with fascinating shapes rising some metres high, have been retained unchanged. Others have been given artistic form, and have been turned into articles of daily use. Among the latter is a piece of petrified wood that functions as a decorative table top. It has been created from a trunk of a tree which is about 220 million years old. The petrified trunk has been carved into slabs and polished.

⓱ Deichstraße

Map 9 C4 – 5 **U** Rödingsmarkt. **S** Stadthausbrücke. 🚌 3, 4, 6, 31, 35, 37.

This old merchant street on Nikolaifleet will be associated forever with a sad chapter in the city's history. For it was here that a fire broke out in 1842, a fire that turned into a huge conflagration lasting several days. Starting on 5 May, in the warehouse of the house at No. 42, it rapidly spread to the surrounding streets and, finally, engulfed the entire inner city. On Deichstraße, too, several houses fell victim to the raging flames. However, the majority of these buildings have since been restored to their original state.

During a stroll along Deichstraße, you pass by the oldest extant merchants' houses in Hamburg. Painted roof beams still decorate the interior of No. 25. Bardowicker Speicher at No. 27, which was built in 1780, is one of the oldest warehouses in the city. In spite of the ravages of the fire, the house at No. 37 survived relatively unscathed; it is the last merchant house in Hamburg that has remained in its original state.

Restaurants have opened up in several of these old houses, a few are decorated in traditional Hamburg style. Also worth seeing are the narrow channels that run between the houses and lead to the water.

Wasserträger Hummel

This Hamburg symbol is known far beyond the borders of the Hanseatic city. A real person stands behind the character nicknamed "Wasserträger Hummel" (Hummel, the water carrier): Johann Wilhelm Bentz (1787 – 1854). At the time, water carriers supplied clean drinking water to those who did not live near the Alster. As Johann went about his labours, children playing on the streets taunted the stick-thin water carrier with cries of "hummel, hummel!" ("bee, bee"). Because he was carrying a heavy load, Johann could not chase away his little tormentors. He could only reply, gruffly, "Mors, Mors" (which in Low German means "bottom", or in this case, "little asses"). The slogan of Hamburg's football fans "Hummel, Hummel! – Mors, Mors!" derives from this exchange.

Wasserträger Hummel

NEW TOWN

A t first glance the name of this part of Hamburg is a bit confusing. After all, this area dates back to the 17th century. An important moment in the development of the New Town occurred when the church of St Michaelis was designated a principal church, considerably enhancing the area's stature. In the 19th century, the old fortifications on the north and west edges of the city were turned into parks and gardens (Alter Botanischer Garten, Große and Kleine Wallanlagen, Elbpark). Locals and visitors alike come here to relax after shopping in the passages between Gänsemarkt and Alsterfleet. Unlike the Old Town, the New Town, which still seems idyllic, has remained a popular place in which to live. Großneumarkt is the area's main square; ringed with restaurants, its weekly market is one of the most colourful in the city.

Sights at a Glance

Churches
1. St Michaelis pp74–5

Museums and Galleries
6. hamburgmuseum
7. Johannes-Brahms-Museum

Historic Buildings and Monuments
2. Krameramtswohnungen
5. Bismarck-Denkmal

Streets and Squares
3. Großneumarkt
10. Colonnaden
11. Passages
13. Gänsemarkt

Theatres
10. Laeiszhalle
12. Hamburgische Staatsoper

Other Attractions
4. Model of Hamburg
9. Fleetinsel
14. Planten un Blomen pp78–9
15. Heinrich Hertz Turm

See also Streetfinder maps 4, 5, 9–10

Restaurants
see pp188-189

1 Die Bank
2 Marblau
3 Marinehof
4 Matsumi
5 [m]eatery
6 La Mirabelle
7 Old Commercial Room
8 Rialto
9 Shalimar
10 Zu den alten Krameramtsstuben am Michel

◀ The headquarters of Gruner + Jahr with the tower of St Michaelis off to the right (see pp74–5)   **For map symbols** see back flap

Street-by-Street: New Town

The visual landmark of New Town is the church of St Michaelis, with its 112-m (367-ft) tall steeple. Located close by are the Krameramtswohnungen. This impressive housing complex was built in the 17th century for widows of small store owners, and it gives an excellent idea of how Hamburg's burghers, the well-off middle class, once lived. After passing by a statue of Zitronenjette, a well-known Hamburg personality, you reach Großneumarkt. This lovely market square was built in the 17th century. With its many restaurants and cafés, it is a favourite with Hamburgers.

Pelikan-Apotheke
This pharmacy has been occupying these rooms since 1651. Its interior is undeniably charming.

NEUER STEINWEG

GROS NEU MAR

City Landmark
The sparkling windows of this skyscraper reflect the tower of St Michaelis church.

LUDWIG - ERHARD - STRAS

❶ ★ St Michaelis
The observation platform of this Hamburg landmark offers spectacular views that reach far beyond New Town.

KRAY

0 metres	50
0 yards	50

Key

— Suggested route

❷ ★ Krameramts-wohnungen
Widows first dwelled in these two-storey half-timbered houses dating from the 17th century. Today, one of the apartments is open to visitors.

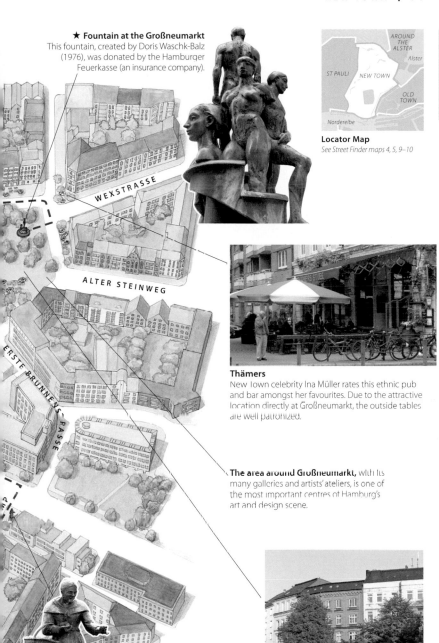

★ Fountain at the Großneumarkt
This fountain, created by Doris Waschk-Balz (1976), was donated by the Hamburger Feuerkasse (an insurance company).

Locator Map
See Street Finder maps 4, 5, 9–10

WEXSTRASSE

ALTER STEINWEG

ERSTE BRUNNENSTRASSE

Thämers
New Town celebrity Ina Müller rates this ethnic pub and bar amongst her favourites. Due to the attractive location directly at Großneumarkt, the outside tables are well patronized.

The area around Großneumarkt, with its many galleries and artists' ateliers, is one of the most important centres of Hamburg's art and design scene.

★ Zitronenjette
"Zitroon! Zitroon!" ("Lemons! Lemons!") This call signalled the approach of Zitronenjette, whose real name was Johanne Henriette Marie Müller. Day and night she would walk the city selling the fruits that she had just purchased from sailors.

ZITRONENJETTE

❸ Großneumarkt
The tree-lined market square in the centre of New Town was built in the 17th century. At the northern and eastern edges a number of buildings dating from this era can still be admired.

❶ St Michaelis

See pp74–5.

❷ Krameramts-wohnungen

Krayenkamp 10. **Map** 9 B4. **Tel** 37 50 19 88. 🚌 36, 37. 🅄 Baumwall, Rödingsmarkt. Ⓢ Stadthausbrücke. **Open** 10am – 10pm daily (Museum: Apr – Oct: 10am – 5pm Tue – Sun; Nov – Mar: 10am – 5pm Sat, Sun). 🎭 (museum only). 🆆 **kramer-witwen-wohnung.de**

The Krameramtswohnungen are an ensemble of houses thought to be the last examples of 17th-century Hamburg courtyard apartment dwellings. In 1676 the guild of small shop owners (Krameramt) that had existed since the 14th century bought this piece of land across from St Michaelis and commissioned two-storey half-timbered houses to be built there. The complex was designed for the widows of small shop owners. After the Krameramt was disbanded in 1863, the houses were acquired by the city and continued to be used as homes for the elderly until 1968.

In 1974, the Krameramtswohnungen were refurbished and some were rented out again. Today you'll find here an art gallery, several shops, a used bookshop, and a restaurant, Zu den alten Krameramts-stuben *(see p189)*, which serves Hamburg special-ities. One of the apartments is exhibited by a branch of the hamburg-

Cosy Krameramtsstuben restaurant, part of the Krameramtswohnungen

museum, complete with furnishings that were typical of the age. This is an excellent way to learn how Hamburg's well-off middle class once lived.

❸ Großneumarkt

Map 9 B3. 🅄 Rödingsmarkt, Gänsemarkt. Ⓢ Stadthausbrücke. 🚌 3, 35, 37.

A popular meeting spot for both Hamburgers and visitors is the Großneumarkt. It was created in the 17th century when the New Town was being built, and was given its name to distinguish it from an older market (called Neumarkt) that was held near the church of St Nikolai. Of the original buildings, there are still a few Neo-Classical houses remaining. The square is especially lively on market days – Wednesdays and Saturday mornings.

There are a number of restaurants around the Großneumarkt. Almost all of them offer an opportunity to sit outside and watch the market bustle, when the weather allows. On such days, a beer garden atmosphere springs up on the square. While some restaurants offer inter-national fare, others draw many guests with hearty tra-ditional food. The fountain is an eye catcher.

Fountain on Großneumarkt

❹ Model of Hamburg

Wexstraße 7. **Map** 9 B3. **Tel** 428 40 21 94. 🅄 Rödingsmarkt, Gänsemarkt. Ⓢ Stadthausbrücke. 🚌 3, 35. **Open** 10am – 5pm Tue – Fri, 1 – 5pm Sat, Sun. 🎭

In the exhibition hall of the city's development and environment department (Behörde für Stadtentwicklung und Umwelt), there is a giant 111 sq m (1,200 sq ft) wooden model of Hamburg's inner city on a scale of 1 : 500. It depicts the area from Övelgönne in the west to Rothenburgsort in the east, and from Harvestehude in the north to HafenCity in the south. There is a model of practically every building within this area. Those that already exist are painted white; planned buildings or those under construction are left in plain wood. Streets, greenspaces, and bodies of water are also replicated. This constantly updated model gives a perfect overview of exactly what is being built in the city – and this almost in "real time".

❺ Bismarck-Denkmal

Map 4 E4. 🅄 Landungsbrücken, St. Pauli. Ⓢ Landungsbrücken. 🚌 36, 37, 112. **Closed** for safety reasons.

One of the largest monuments in Germany, the statue of Otto von Bismarck (1815 –1898) is 34.3 m (113 ft) tall. Standing on a mighty pedestal, the granite figure is 14.8 m (49 ft) high. It depicts the first Chancellor of the German Empire leaning on a sword that itself is 8 m (26 ft) long. Reliefs illustrating scenes from German history embellish the pedestal of the monument. Architect Emil Schaudt and sculptor Hugo Lederer created this impressive memorial between 1903 and 1906. The granite blocks were quarried in the Black Forest (Schwarzwald). Due to its prominent location, this 625-tonne statue can be seen from far away, and especially from the water.

The Johannes-Brahms-Museum in the Peterstraße

❻ hamburg-museum

Holstenwall 24. **Map** 4 E3. **Tel** 428 13
21 00. **U** St. Pauli. 36, 37, 112.
Open 10am–5pm Tue–Sat, 10am
–6pm Sun.
w hamburgmuseum.de

In 2006, the Museum für
Hamburgische Geschichte
(Museum of Hamburg History)
was renamed the hamburg-
museum. It possesses the
largest collection of city history
in Germany. As visitors progress
through the exhibits, they take
a trip back in time through the
history of Hamburg – from the
construction of Hammaburg
castle in the 9th century to
the city's development in
modern times.

Central themes covered in
the hamburgmuseum are the
port and shipping as well as
industry and trade. Among the
many highlights are the ships'
models (among them a
reproduction of a 14th-century
Hanseatic boat) and
a model railway.

This red-brick
building was
designed by the
architect Fritz
Schumacher in 1922.
With its lovely
staircase and
imposing roofline,
the hamburgmuseum is
one of Hamburg's most
beautiful cultural
institutions. The large interior
courtyard was covered over
with a glass roof in 1989. It is

Propeller in front of the
hamburgmuseum

here, in this light-flooded
expansive space, that larger
exhibits are on display and
special events are held.

❼ Johannes-Brahms-Museum

Peterstraße 39. **Map** 9 A3. **Tel** 48 83 27,
41 91 30 86. **U** St. Pauli, Baumwall.
36, 37, 112. **Open** 10am–5pm
Tue–Sun. Telemann-Museum: **Open**
10am–5pm Tue, Thu–Sun.
w brahms-hamburg.de

Photographs, letters, sheets of
music, concert programmes, a
piano and other mementos
documenting the life and work
of Johannes Brahms (1833–1897)
are presented in this small
museum. The Baroque building,
which dates from the 18th century, stands not far from the
house in which the composer
came into the world, it, unfortunately, was destroyed in 1943.
The museum contains an interesting small reference library of
about 600 volumes
and all Brahms'
compositions on
CD. The building also
houses a museum on
Baroque composer
Georg Philipp
Telemann (1681–
1787).
Located beside the
museum is the
Beylingstift, founded in
1751. This picturesque
set of half-timbered buildings
grouped around a courtyard has
been painstakingly recreated.

❽ Laeiszhalle

Johannes-Brahms-Platz. **Map** 9 B2. **Tel**
357 66 60. **U** Gänsemarkt, Mes-
sehallen. 3, 5, 34, 35, 36, 112.
w elbphilharmonie.de/laeiszhalle

At the heart of Hamburg
concert life is the Laeiszhalle
(pronounced "Leisshalle"),
the city's former music hall.
Constructed in 1904–08 in
magnificent Neo-Baroque style,
this concert hall is a wonderful
place to enjoy an evening of
classical music. Top orchestras,
ensembles and soloists can be
heard here. The hall is the home
of the NDR Symphony
Orchestra, the Hamburg
Symphony and the Hamburg
Philharmonic, among others.
Concerts featuring international
players are held here, too.

There are two concert halls
in the Laeiszhalle: the large hall,
with 2019 seats, and the small
hall, with 639 seats. On the
basement level is the
Klingendes Museum (musical
museum), where visitors can
try their hand at playing one of
100 instruments.

Renaming the museum in
2005 from the Musikhalle to the
Laeiszhalle acknowledges the
great contribution that was
made by a foundation set up
by the Laeisz family. This
foundation financed the
building. The square on which
the Laeiszhalle stands was
named after famous German
composer Johannes Brahms in
1997 on the 100th anniversary
of his death.

The hamburgmuseum, where visitors can
take a trip through time

❶ St Michaelis

The newest of Hamburg's main churches serves as the city's landmark. Hamburg's skyline would not be the same without the presence of the 132-m (433-ft) high tower, affectionately called "Michel" by Hamburgers. This place of worship has undergone many transformations. The first church, built in 1649–61, was destroyed in 1750 by a strike of lightning; the second (built 1750–62) burned down to the ground in 1906. With the help of numerous donors, the second church was completely rebuilt in 1907–12. The long-standing tradition of the church horn-blowers has endured and can be heard weekdays at 10am and 9pm, and Sundays at noon.

Main Entrance
Above the entrance, Satan writhes at the feet of the Archangel Michael who is shown defeating the Devil with a cross-shaped lance, an allegory for the might of God.

KEY

① **The viewing platform** is located at 82 m (270 ft). It can be reached by 452 steps or by a lift, which was installed in 1911. On request, the platform is also open late evenings (**www.nachtmichel.de**).

② **The clock face** of the tower clock is 8 m (26 ft) in circumference. It is Germany's largest.

③ **Six bells** are hidden away in the belfry. The heaviest of them weighs 7.5 tons.

④ **The church balconies** are curved and give a sense of movement to the interior of the church.

Side entrance

★ Altar
St Michaelis' Neo-Baroque-style altar is an imposing 20 m (65 ft) high. Its centrepiece is a glass mosaic, created in 1911, that shows the risen Saviour with hands raised in blessing.

Organ Detail
On the balcony above the main entrance looms a Steinmeyer organ that was dedicated in 1962. With its 6,665 pipes, it is the largest of the three organs in St Michaelis.

★ Font
Three angels made of white marble support the font's basin, which is still in use today. The font was made in 1763, in Livorno, and donated to the church by Hamburg merchants who lived there. Along with the reliquary, the font withstood the Great Fire of 1906 unscathed.

★ Pulpit
This elegant pulpit, made of marble, was created after the devastating 1906 fire in the form of a large chalice.

★ Reliquary
Ernst Georg Sonnin, who built the second St Michaelis church, donated this reliquary (1763).

Warehouse façade on Fleetinsel

❶ Passages

Map 9 C1–3, 10 D2. **U** Gänsemarkt, Jungfernstieg. **S** Jungfernstieg. 🚌 3, 4, 5, 34, 35, 36.

The covered arcades and passages between Rathausmarkt and Gänsemarkt in the city centre are a shopping paradise in any weather. The variety of shops, which are mainly small, encompass a wide range of wares – from stylish items for the home to the latest fashions, from arts-and-crafts to jewellery, from delicatessens to books. Cafés and restaurants, found in every passage, are perfect places to stop and enjoy a break from shopping.

Designed as an exclusive private passage for the owners of luxury apartments, the first passage, the Colonnaden, was built in the 19th century. It is lined with Neo-Renaissance façades, lending an Italian flair. One after the other, new passages were created, among them the Gänsemarkt-Passage, the Galleria and the Bleichenhof. One of the most spectacular passages was built in 1980 – the glass-roofed Hanse-Viertel. The city now has an extensive network of covered shopping streets and they have become extremely popular meeting places.

❾ Fleetinsel

Map 9 B5–C4. **U** Rödingsmarkt. **S** Stadthausbrücke. 🚌 31, 35, 37.

More a tongue of land than an island, Fleetinsel is crossed by Admiralitätsstraße and lies between Herrengrabenfleet to the west and Alsterfleet to the east. Many of the old warehouses and office buildings once located here were destroyed in World War II, and the area was deserted for decades. In the 1970s, a few industrial buildings and office buildings were constructed. Then, finally, buildings started to become more varied. Today, historic and ultramodern buildings are found side by side here. Along with original merchants' offices and contemporary office buildings, there are also several galleries, shops, and cafés as well as the luxurious Steigenberger Hotel.

Each year, in July, Fleetinsel changes character entirely when the Fleetinsel festival (Duckstein Festival) devoted to art, culture and the culinary arts is held here. Over the course of ten days the area turns into a bustling piazza pulsating with energy. Enthusiastic crowds enjoy music, street theatre, artists and comedy. The festival has become a "must-attend" event for Hamburgers *(see p45)*.

The Weihnachtsmarkt (Christmas market) on Fleetinsel is also very popular. The Fleetinsel can be accessed via a number of bridges.

❿ Colonnaden

Map 9 C1–10 D2. **U** Gänsemarkt, Stephansplatz, Jungfernstieg. **S** Jungfernstieg. 🚌 4, 5, 34, 36, 112.

The pedestrianized area which includes Gustav-Mahler-Platz is one of the most popular shopping streets in Hamburg. The Colonnaden are lined by jeweller's shops, fashion boutiques, delicatessens and many other specialist shops with a broad choice of products that please every taste. In spite of the large range of shops and boutiques, the Colonnaden offer a more tranquil atmosphere than, for example, the Mönckebergstraße in Old Town. The name Colonnaden stems from the arcade on the eastern side of the street which is reminiscent of Italian structures. On both sides of the Colonnaden a number of late 19th century houses with Neo-Renaissance façades remain. On a shopping expedition, the Colonnaden are an ideal addition to areas like the Jungfernstieg or Neuer Wall. The various restaurants and cafés offering alfresco dining provide shoppers with an opportunity to rest their feet.

A popular passage in the Hanse-Viertel

The Hamburgische Staatsoper, one of the world's leading stages

⑫ Hamburgische Staatsoper

Große Theaterstraße 25. **Map** 9 C2.
Tel 35 68 68. Ⓤ Gänsemarkt,
Stephansplatz. Ⓢ Dammtor. 🚌 4, 5,
34, 36, 112. Box office: **Open**
10am–6:30pm Mon–Sat.
Ⓦ **hamburgische-staatsoper.de**

When it was founded in 1678,
the Staatsoper (State opera
house) was the first opera
house in Germany that was
open to the public. Previously,
only the nobility had been able
to enjoy this musical art form.
Here was something very new:
whoever could pay would be
admitted. The location of this
opera house changed often;
the opera house on
Dammtorstraße opened
in 1955 with a
performance of Mozart's
Magic Flute. Since then,
not only have the
"classics" been
performed but also
more contemporary
operas. Today the
programme ranges
from Handel to Henze.
For many inter-
national stars, such
as Plácido Domingo,
engagements in
Hamburg proved to be
milestones of their careers.
The opera house has also been
considered a stronghold of
German ballet ever since John
Neumeier, a renowned Ame-
rican dancer and choreographer,
started a new company here in
1973 along with a ballet centre
and integrated ballet school.
Most of the operas and ballets are
accompanied by the Hamburg
Philharmonic State Orchestra.

Pillar on
Gorch-Fock-Wall

⑬ Gänsemarkt

Map 9 C2. Ⓤ Gänsemarkt,
Stephansplatz. Ⓢ Jungfernstieg.
🚌 4, 5, 34, 36, 112.

The Gänsemarkt is located in the
northern part of the New Town,
and is one of the liveliest squares
in this district. Contrary to its
name ("geese market"), geese
have never been traded on this
almost triangular square. Lined
by stores, cafés and restaurants,
it is an ideal starting point for a
shopping trip. The Jungfernstieg
and several passages (*see p76*)
converge here.
In 1678, when the Stadt-
theater (municipal theatre) was
built, the square became a
focal point of the city's
cultural life. After the
Stadttheater had been
demolished, the
Hamburger National-
theater was built (1765).
Financial problems led to
it closing only after a few
repertory seasons in
1769. A statue created
by Fritz Schaper (1881)
commemorates Gotthold
Ephraim Lessing, an
important literary figure
of the Enlightenment
who held the post of
dramaturge at the
Nationaltheater.
The Gänsemarkt boasts
interesting architecture from
historic red-brick buildings to
modern office buildings. The
Deutschlandhaus ist a fine
example of red-brick architecture.
Completed in 1929, it served to
house the Ufa-Palast, a cinema
equipped with 2600 seats. At
this time, the Ufa-Palast was the
largest cinema in Europe.

⑭ Planten un Blomen

See pp78–9.

⑮ Heinrich-Hertz-Turm

Lagerstraße 2. **Map** 7 A3.
Ⓤ Sternschanze, Schlump.
Ⓢ Sternschanze. 🚌 35.

Rising up 279.80 m (918 ft),
this tower, named after the
Hamburg-born physicist
Heinrich Hertz (1857–1894), is
the city's tallest building. With
a nod to the city's landmark
church tower, the "Michel"
(*see p74–5*) the television
tower, completed in 1968, is
also referred to as "Tele-Michel".
At 128 m (420 ft), the
observation deck would be the
perfect spot from which to
enjoy a panoramic view of the
city and area, as would the
revolving restaurant, 4 m (13 ft)
higher up. Unfortunately, since
2001 both the observation deck
and the restaurant have been
closed indefinitely for repairs.

The Heinrich-Hertz-Turm – Hamburg's
tallest building

⑭ Planten un Blomen

Located within the former walls of the city, this park, whose Low German dialect name means "plants and flowers", does its name justice. Flower beds delight the eye with their many-coloured blossoms. Idyllic streams and lakes as well as lovingly created theme gardens invite visitors to linger. Those with cultural interests will also find plenty to do here. The multitude of events held in summer include concerts in the music pavilion and water-light-concerts on the lake. This green girdle on the edge of the New Town continues south into the Wallanlagen and south-east into the Alter otanischer Garten.

Rose Garden
More than 300 kinds of roses bloom in this garden. The open-sided pavilion tells visitors all about roses and their care.

Waterfalls
Built in 1935, these waterfalls are among the oldest attractions in the park.

ST. PETERSBURGER STRASSE

★ Water-Light-Concerts
Held on the lake from May to August at 10pm daily (9pm from September to mid-October), these concerts with colourful fountains and music are a popular attraction.

On the Hamburgbaum, a wooden sculpture carved in 1980, you can discern various figures as well as the Hamburg coat-of-arms.

KEY

① Rose Garden
② Music Pavilion
③ Medicinal Garden
④ The Television Tower is Hamburg's tallest building (see p77).
⑤ Waterfalls
⑥ Park Lake with water-light-concerts
⑦ Playground
⑧ Pony riding
⑨ Greenhouses
⑩ Wallanlagen
⑪ Japanese Landscape Garden
⑫ Congress Centrum Hamburg
⑬ Japanese Garden with Teahouse

★ Japanese Garden with Teahouse
Rocks, waterfalls, plants and ponds are combined into a harmonious ensemble in this tranquil Japanese garden. In the teahouse, the tea ceremony is celebrated.

Japanese Landscape Garden
Yoshikuni Araki designed this garden, which opened in 1988. There seems to be a world of time here to reflect on the elements of nature that have been arranged so artistically.

Greenhouses
Since 1963, plants from many climate zones have thrived in these greenhouses that cover 2,800 sq m (30,000 sq ft).

```
0 metres        100
0 yards         100
```

★ Wallanlagen
Surrounded by greenery, everything you need for outdoor fun is to be found here: there is roller-skating and a mini-golf course. Afternoons from May to August, children can work in a pottery studio.

This monument to Emperor Wilhelm I was unveiled in 1902 on Rathausmarkt and moved to the Wallanlagen in 1930.

The Landungsbrücken with a view of the Theater im Hafen Hamburg

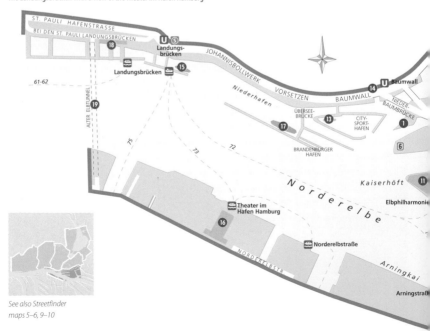

See also Streetfinder
maps 5–6, 9–10

PORT AND SPEICHERSTADT

The true heart of Hamburg is its port. One of the world's busiest in terms of cargo turnover, it is a universe unto itself, a place where modern technology and heavy industry work together effectively. With the construction of HafenCity, a new area of the city being built on under-used port lands, Hamburg is thrusting into the Elbe river itself. The Elbphilharmonie, a concert hall with a daring contemporary design above a warehouse, is due for completion in 2016 and indicative of the direction Hamburg is headed. Speicherstadt, an ensemble of red-brick buildings constructed on oak piles, has also seen much change. The area was established at the end of the 19th century, when Hamburg joined the German customs union. It was a place for traders to store their wares duty-free. But since modern container shipping needs less and less warehouse space, media companies, advertising agencies, and several museums have now found a home in the Speicherstadt among the carpet and spice warehouses.

Sights at a Glance

Museums and Galleries
2 Miniatur Wunderland
3 Spicy's Gewürzmuseum
5 Speicherstadtmuseum
6 *Maritime Museum pp86–7*
8 Deutsches Zollmuseum
12 Prototyp Museum
13 Das Feuerschiff
15 *Rickmer Rickmers pp94–5*
17 *Cap San Diego pp98–9*
20 BallinStadt – Auswandererwelt Hamburg

Historic Buildings
18 Landungsbrücken
19 Alter Elbtunnel

Theatres
11 Elbphilharmonie
16 Theater im Hafen Hamburg

Other Attractions
1 Kehrwiederspitze
4 Hamburg Dungeon
7 *HafenCity pp90–91*
9 Hamburg Cruise Center
10 View Point
14 Hafen Hochbahn

Restaurants
see pp189–190
1 CARLS
2 La Baracca
3 MEERWEIN
4 Oberhafen Kantine
5 Schönes Leben
6 Stricker's KehrWiederSpitze
7 VLET
8 Wandrahm

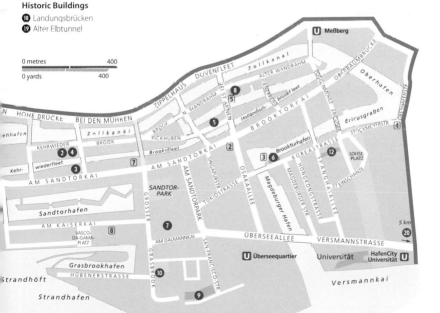

Street-by-Street: Speicherstadt

The world's largest warehouse district is located on Brookinsel. Construction began in 1885 as the city prepared for the opening of the freeport of Hamburg in 1888. Dark red brick Neo-Gothic warehouses front the canals which flow here. Inside, precious commodities such as coffee, tea, tobacco, spices and oriental carpets waited to be released from customs. Since the 1980s, Speicherstadt has been undergoing a transformation into an elegant office building and business district.

❹ In Hamburg Dungeon dark, dramatic events from the city's past come alive.

❷ Miniatur Wunderland has the world's largest model railway.

NIEDER-BAUM-BRÜCKEN

KEHRWIEDER-SPITZE

BINNEN-HAFEN

KEHRWIEDER

KEHRWIEDER

KE

KEHRWIEDERFLEET

KEHRWIEDERSTEG

BROOKSFLEET

AM SANDTORKAI

SANDTORHAFEN

Canal Barge Tour
A trip on a barge through the canals is a treat on sunny days and also during evenings, when the warehouses are illuminated.

Key

— Suggested route

0 metres	400
0 yards	400

❸ ★ Spicy's Gewürzmuseum
Over 700 exhibits introduce visitors to the world of spices, showing how they are cultivated, processed and packaged. You can also rub many spices between your fingers, smell them, and even taste them.

A Typical Warehouse
Warehouses are five to eight storeys tall and equipped with winches. Most are built in the red-brick Neo-Gothic style found in many North German Hanseatic cities.

❼ HafenCity InfoCenter
A model of HafenCity, Hamburg's newest district, is the heart of this information centre, located in a former boiler house.

❽ Deutsches Zollmuseum
This customs museum in Kornhausbrücke, a former customs building, has wonderful exhibits documenting the history of customs over the centuries.

Locator Map
See Street Finder maps 5–6 & 9–10

The Bridges denote the borders of the port's duty-free zone from which the Speicherstadt has been excluded since 2003.

★ Kornhausbrücke
Flanking the entrance to this bridge, named after corn warehouses, are statues of maritime explorers Christopher Columbus and Vasco da Gama by Carl Boerner and Herman Hosaeus (1903).

Dialog im Dunkeln
Blind and seeing-impaired staff guide visitors through pitch-black rooms where recreations of daily occurences, such as street noise, turn into a completely new experience.

❺ ★ Speicherstadtmuseum
Work equipment and sample wares as well as historic photographs are on display in this museum, which recounts the story of Speicherstadt.

Wandrahmsfleet
This canal was named after the Dutch cloth-makers who stretched out their fabric on frames here for it to dry.

❶ Kehrwieder-spitze

Map 9 B5. **U** Baumwall. 🚌 3, 4, 6.

One of the most photographed subjects in the Hanseatic city is this spit of land jutting out from Kehrwieder Island. This is due, above all, to the striking buildings located here, between the Elbe river and the canals, that, when seen together, create a futuristic-looking ensemble. The tower of Columbus Haus is 100 m (328 ft) high, for example.

As the gateway to Speicherstadt and HafenCity, Kehrwiederspitze is an important landmark: everyone who decides to visit the historic warehouses or learn about Europe's biggest construction project will come past here.

❷ Miniatur Wunderland

Kehrwieder 4, Block D. **Map** 9 C5. **Tel** 300 68 00. **U** Baumwall. 🚌 3, 4, 6. **Open** 9:30am – 6pm Mon – Fri (Tue to 9pm, Fri to 7pm), 8am – 9pm Sat, 8:30am – 8pm Sun. 🅿 📷
W miniatur-wunderland.de

The eyes of railway fans, both large and small, light up with delight in this extraordinary miniature world. For this is the home of the world's largest computer-controlled model railway, which covers a surface of 1300 sq m (14,500 sq ft). Around 930 trains pull nearly 14,500 wagons along 13 km (8 miles) of tracks through models of real landscapes. Some 3,700 houses, 8,900 cars,

The impressive modern architecture on Kehrwiederspitze

215,000 tiny people and 230,000 trees are integrated into the model. Push buttons allow visitors to step into the miniature action and make windmills spin or cause spectators to break out into cheers as a goal is scored in the HSV-Arena.

More than ten million people have already visited this model railway, which is constantly being expanded and improved upon. Numerous countries are modelled including Austria, Switzerland (both with their gorgeous alpine landscapes), Hamburg's coast, Scandinavia and the USA (including natural attractions such as the Grand Canyon and glitzy cities such as Las Vegas). Italy is under construction, and more regions are being planned – among them England, France and Africa. The behind-the-scenes tour is highly recommended. Since only a limited number of visitors can be accommodated at any given time, lines can be long. Book your ticket on the Internet in advance.

❸ Spicy's Gewürzmuseum

Am Sandtorkai 34, Block L. **Map** 9 C5. **Tel** 36 79 89. **U** Baumwall. 🚌 3, 4, 6. **Open** 10am – 5pm Tue – Sun (Jul – Oct: also 10am – 5pm Mon). 📷
W spicys.de

Fennel and curry powder, cloves, cardamom and saffron, vanilla and cinnamon – in this unusual spice museum, the scent of more than 50 spices perfumes the air. A notice telling visitors to "follow their noses" sends them to the second floor of this warehouse, where the museum has been located since 1993. The museum informs visitors about how to use, properly store, and assess the quality of spices. Photos, maps and displays show where our spices come from and the processes used before they wind up in our food, from cultivation onward.
Spicy's is also a hands-on museum in which you are encouraged to touch, smell and even sample the spices on display. Along with the pungent spices themselves, there are a lot of exhibits of tools and other equipment used around the world to gather, process and transport spices.

Miniatur Wunderland – a playground for railway fans

❹ Hamburg Dungeon

Kehrwieder 2, Block D. **Map** 9 C5. **Tel** 36 00 55 20. Ⓤ Baumwall. ⬛ 3, 4, 6. **Open** 10am–6pm daily (Jul & Aug: to 7pm). ⬛ 🗗 ⬛ Ⓦ the-dungeons. com/hamburg.de

Torture, fear and gloom await visitors to this dark cellar. Down in these catacombs the gruesome history of over 2,000 years of Hamburg is featured, although the city is not even 1,200 years old. Even so, this trip through time offers visitors a great many horrors, taking them through the bloodiest periods and documenting the grisliest scenes in the city's history. These include the Inquisition, the cholera epidemic, the execution (by beheading) of the pirate Störtebeker, raging infernos and a terrible flood – all of which are experienced up-close during the 90-minute interactive tour.

Special effects, eerie background sounds, and clever lighting increase the ghastly atmosphere. A visit here is not recommended for children under ten years of age, but older children and adults will have fun – as long as their nerves hold up, of course.

❺ Speicherstadt-museum

Am Sandtorkai 36. **Map** 10 D5. **Tel** 32 11 91. Ⓤ Meßberg. ⬛ 3, 4, 6. **Open** Apr–Oct: 10am–5pm Mon–Fri, 10am–6pm Sat, Sun; Nov–Mar: 10am–5pm Tue–Sun. ⬛ 🗗 11am Sun (Apr–Oct: also 3pm Sat). ⬛ 🗗 Ⓦ speicherstadtmuseum.de

Experience an old as well as typical part of Hamburg. A building that is over 100 years old gives the authentic setting for this exciting experience. In this privately operated branch of the Museum der Arbeit (Labour Museum; *see p135*), the history of Speicherstadt (Dockland) is documented very lively. Typical work tools and trade goods – among them sampling implements and coffee sacks, tea chests and

The Brooksbrücke in Speicherstadt, which opened in 1888

balls of rubber – provide a glimpse into the world of those who worked in this warehouse district which once was the largest around the world. These warehouse employees appraised the goods, sorted them and were responsible for their proper storage.

This is definitely not your usual museum collection where you can look but not feel. Here, you can also touch the exhibits and sometimes even taste them.

The exhibit is accompanied by historic photographs on the history of Speicherstadt and gives an interesting insight into long forgotten occupations that were once carried out here. Coffee, cocoa and tea tastings are held at the museum on a regular basis, as well as readings by writers of crime fiction.

The Port's Birthday

Hamburgers consider 7 May 1189 to be the birthday of their port. It was supposedly on this day that Emperor Friedrich Barbarossa awarded customs-exempt status to ships that sailed the Elbe river all the way from the city to the North Sea, guaranteeing the city's merchants the trading privileges they had long sought. Even when the relevant document later turned out to be a fake, Hamburgers persist in believing in its veracity. Every year, on 7 May, thousands flock to the port to celebrate its birthday. The first gigantic party was held in 1989 in honour of the port's 800th anniversary. The highpoints of the three-day festivities are the parade of tall ships, the dragon boat races and the tugboat ballet. All along the harbour promenade between Kehrwiederspitze and the Fish Auction Hall you can listen to music and see dance, shows and much more.

Hamburg Port's Birthday Bash – the largest port festival in the world

❻ Maritime Museum

The International Maritime Museum is the largest seafaring museum in the world. When it was opened in 2008, Prof Peter Tamm's huge private maritime collection found a home fittingly situated at the waterfront in HafenCity. The museum's more than 100,000 exhibits occupy ten storeys or "Decks", as the exhibition spaces are called. Model ships in various scales, navigation instruments, nautical charts, and numerous other items are proof to the important role seafaring plays in the fields of economy, science, history, politics, arts and culture.

Kaispeicher B
The museum in HafenCity.

ROV Cherokee
This remotely operated underwater robot collects data and samples from a depth of up to 1,000 metres.

U-Bahn station
Meßberg

Lighthouse
The original lighthouse (»Roter Sand«, 1883 – 85) at the mouth of the Weser river was in operation until 1986.

★ Queen Mary 2
This model of the famous British liner is seven metres long. It took 1200 hours to assemble the around 780,000 LEGO bricks the model ship is made of.

Sandtorkai ferry

Cruise ships
Visitors are bound to get itchy feet at the sight of these model ships – the luxury liners seem to sail into the blue horizon.

VISITORS' CHECKLIST

Practical Information
Kaispeicher B, Koreastraße 1.
Map 6 D4. **Tel** 30 09 23 00.
Open Tue–Sun 10am–6pm.
Sun 2pm, additional tours by appointment
(**Tel** 428 13 10).
w internationales-maritimes-museum.de

Transport
Meßberg 3, 4, 6

★ **High-Tech- Globe**
Geological processes and climate scenarios are projected onto the outer membrane.

KEY

⓪ **Deck 0** Foyer and Museum Shop

① **Deck 1** Explorers of the World (Navigation)

② **Deck 2** Ships under Sail

③ **Deck 3** Shipbuilding

④ **Deck 4** Service on Board

⑤ **Deck 5** Navies of the World

⑥ **Deck 6** Trade and Travel

⑦ **Deck 7** Ocean Expeditions

⑧ **Deck 8** Art Gallery and Treasure Chamber

⑨ **Deck 9** The Big World of Little Ships

⑩ **Deck 10** Events and special exhibitions

Entrance

★ **Wapen von Hamburg III**
This convoy ship (1722) protected the citizens of Hamburg against pirate attacks. On a scale of 1:5, the museum's largest model ship represents one historic gem of Hanseatic admiralty.

Astrolabe
Together with other navigation instruments, this goniometer – a copy of a 17th-century original – made orientation on the high seas possible.

❼ HafenCity

See pp90–91.

❽ Deutsches Zollmuseum

Alter Wandrahm 16. **Map** 10 E4–5.
Tel 30 08 76 11. Ⓤ Meßberg. 🚌 3, 4, 6. **Open** Tue–Sun 10am–5pm. 📷♿
📷 Ⓦ zoll.de

Is it possible for a subject as dull as customs and excise to be exciting? The Deutsches Zollmuseum (German customs museum) proves it can be: On two floors, the history of customs is traced back into the ancient past in a very lively way. After all, smugglers have shown a great deal of ingenuity in trying to get around customs regulations.Evidence of their creativity is seen in the various objects displayed, which have been used for smuggling: cocaine has been hidden in golf clubs or artificial legs, cigarettes in hats and marijuana woven into wooden baskets.

Other sections of the museum are dedicated to product piracy and customs officers' uniforms. The various customs responsibilities, from the prevention of drug smuggling to environment and consumer protection, are also represented.

Hamburg Cruise Center, where the world's largest cruise ships dock

❾ Hamburg Cruise Center

Großer Grasbrook 19.
Map 5 C5. 🚌 3, 4, 6.
Ⓦ **hamburgcruisecenter.eu**

When luxury liners such as the *Queen Mary II* or the *Freedom of the Seas* pay Hamburg the honour of a visit, they are welcomed by their national anthem booming out of the loudspeakers at Willkommhöft *(see p139)*, and then by crowds of spectators at Hamburg Cruise Center, the city's main cruise ship terminal (Kreuzfahrtterminal). In 2012, a total of 164 ocean giants carrying 400,000 passengers steered for the terminal, which had been enlarged in 2006 with a second hall nearby so that the terminal could accommodate two large cruise ships at the same time. Most cruise ships dock at HafenCity, although there is another cruise terminal in Altona *(see p149)*, which deals with ships when the HafenCity terminal is at capacity.

The Cruise Shop located next to the terminal sells travel essentials and souvenirs. The café is frequented by cruise ship passengers and city tourists alike.

❿ View Point

Map 5 C5. 🚌 3, 4, 6.

There is a fantastic view of the port from View Point observation platform. When it opened in 2004, it quickly proved to be a magnet for visitors. Up to 25 people at a time are allowed on the observation platform to survey HafenCity. There is often a crowd, since this is also the best vantage point for watching the luxury cruise liners dock at the nearby Hamburg Cruise Center.

When designing View Point, the architects borrowed elements from periscope design. As the HafenCity development grows, the View Point, is constantly moved along its set of rails.

⓫ Elbphilharmonie

Dalmannkai. **Map** 5 B5. Ⓤ Baumwall. 🚌 3, 4, 6.

Once it is completed in 2016, the Elbphilharmonie (Elbe Philharmonic Orchestra) will be one of the architectural highlights of HafenCity. Here, classical music, 21st-century music and other serious music will have a striking new performance space. The Elbphilharmonie has been conceived of as an 110-m (360-ft) high cultural "lighthouse" which will attract many from the surrounding areas. Under a glass tent-like construction that resembles a wavy seascape, two concert halls are being

View Point, which offers amazing port views

built with approximately 2,150 and 550 seats a piece, as well as a high-end hotel and luxury apartments.

The Elbphilharmonie is being built atop Kaispeicher A (the warehouse on quay A), a 37-m (120-ft) tall structure dating from 1963–66. The original façade will remain intact. As conceived by the Swiss architectural firm Herzog & de Meuron, the port's trading past and its new cultural identity will be united in the building's design.

Visitors will travel up an elevator from the parking levels in the warehouse to the roof. Here, a meeting place for all Hamburg is planned: an admission-free plaza with an arching multi-planed roof, from where the public will have great views over the port. The plaza will lead into the foyer of the Elbphilharmonie.

A pavilion on the Magellan-Terrassen *(see p91)* houses a model of the large concert hall on a scale of 1:10.

⑫ Prototyp Museum

Shanghaiallee 7. **Map** 6 D4. **Tel** 39 99 69 70. Ⓤ Meßberg. 🚌 3, 4, 6. **Open** Tue–Sun 10am–6pm. 🚗📷📁💻
Ⓦ prototyp-hamburg.de

This museum, which opened in 2008, is dedicated to the fascination of automobiles. The exhibits are displayed on three floors. The emphasis lies on German racing and sports cars dating from the 1940s to the 1960s.

Motorsport aficionados are enthralled by the museum's inventive mode of presentation: The venue exudes the ambience of a meeting place for automobile enthusiasts rather than the atmosphere of a museum; in addition to the 50 or so cars that are on display from Borgward to Volkswagen and Mercedes to Porsche – interactive displays draw visitors into the world of car racing. The driving simulator in a Porsche 356 Speedster is

The coast guard cutter Oldenburg alongside the Deutsches Zollmuseum

fascinating. A soundbox, in which the genuine road noise of historic racing cars can be heard, displays embedded into the floor and a library which contains photographs of racing drivers, are among the further attractions at the Prototyp Museum.

⑬ Das Feuerschiff

City-Sporthafen. **Map** 9 B5. **Tel** 36 25 53. Ⓤ Baumwall. Ⓢ Landungsbrücken. Restaurant: **Open** 11am–10pm daily. Turmbar: **Open** 11am–1am daily. Ⓦ das-feuerschiff.de

Das Feuerschiff offers a unique kind of maritime ambience. In the middle of the port, this

former lightship (floating lighthouse) welcomes guests who come to enjoy food and drinks in the restaurant and bar (the Turmbar). Another gathering spot is the pub in the machine room, where jazz is played on "Blue Mondays" after 8:30pm and on Sundays after 11am. Cabarets and readings are also staged here.

Built in 1952, this lightship was a navigation aid along the English Channel before being replaced by a larger vessel in 1989. It was sold and rebuilt and has been anchored in front of City Sporthafen since 1993. Guests can also spend the night in one of several cabins which have been kept in their original state.

Dialogue in the Dark

"An exhibition to discover the unseen" – this is the motto of Dialog im Dunkeln (Dialogue in the Dark) – a world of ex-periences located in the Speicherstadt at Alter Wandrahm 4. The idea behind this project, which was established in 2000, sounds simple enough: blind staff members lead visitors in small groups through the pitch-black rooms of an exhibit in which there is literally nothing to see. The tour does,

A new level of sensory experience can be reached here

however, open up a world of scents, sounds and textures – the world of the blind and seeing impaired – as visitors smell, listen and touch. The guides ensure that no one loses their way. During "Dinner in the Dark", visitors' taste buds and table manners are keenly tested. The exhibition is only open for tours (9am–5pm Tue–Fri, 10am–8pm Sat, 10am–6pm Sun), which must be arranged ahead of time by calling 0700 44 33 20 00. Be sure to book an English-speaking guide.

❼ HafenCity

Maritime flair shapes this new city district being built on 155 hectares (380 acres). A "city within a city", it will include apartments for 12,000 people, 40,000 workplaces, cultural institutions and leisure facilities. HafenCity will expand the Hamburg inner city by approximately 40 per cent. Nowhere else does the Hanseatic city show its dynamism more than here. Construction began in 2001, and completion is planned for 2020 – 2025. The rapid progress being made can be seen in HafenCity InfoCenter in the Kesselhaus.

★ Sandtorhafen
Sandtorhafen is the oldest harbour basin in Hamburg. Along Sandtorkai (Sandtor quay) pontoons, traditional Hamburg ships are docked.

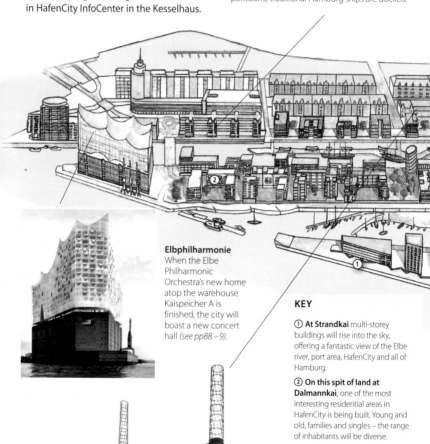

Elbphilharmonie
When the Elbe Philharmonic Orchestra's new home atop the warehouse Kaispeicher A is finished, the city will boast a new concert hall *(see pp88 – 9)*.

★ Kesselhaus
The HafenCity InfoCenter is located in a red brick building built in 1886–87. A detailed scale model of HafenCity gives visitors a good overview of this ambitious development.

KEY

① **At Strandkai** multi-storey buildings will rise into the sky, offering a fantastic view of the Elbe river, port area, HafenCity and all of Hamburg.

② **On this spit of land at Dalmannkai**, one of the most interesting residential areas in HafenCity is being built. Young and old, families and singles – the range of inhabitants will be diverse.

③ **To the east of Magdeburger Hafen** are many historic buildings. Here, along with squares and boulevards, a new HafenCity university will be established.

④ **The Science Center** will bring an aquarium and a science theatre to the Überseequartier, stimulating attractions for both young and old.

★ Kaispeicher B
The oldest preserved warehouse in HafenCity has been home to the Maritime Museum *(see pp86–7)* since 2008. The exhibition showcases more than 100,000 objects related to shipping. The exhibits are presented on ten levels.

0 metres 100
0 yards 100

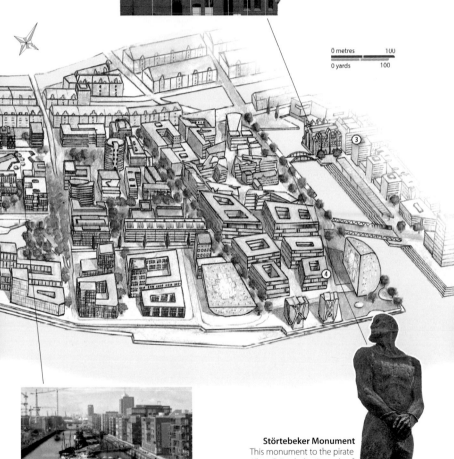

Störtebeker Monument
This monument to the pirate Klaus Störtebeker is made of roughly two tons of bronze and was unveiled in Magdeburger Hafen in 1982. Since 2006, this sculpture by Hansjorg Wagner stood in Großer Grasbrook. After the completion of Maritimes Museum it was relocated back to its former site across from Kaispeicher B.

Traditional boats at Sandtorkai
About 20 old steamers, fishing boats and yachts have been moored just outside the Magellan-Terrassen..

The elevated Hafen-Hochbahn port railway, which provides an impressive view of the port

⑭ Hafen-Hochbahn

Map 4 E – F5, 5 A4 – B3.
Ⓤ Rödingsmarkt, Baumwall,
Landungsbrücken.

In 1912, after six years of construction, the city's first underground line opened. This meant that Hamburg became the second city in Germany, after Berlin, to have an underground railway. More lines followed. One of the most interesting stretches in the entire Hamburg public transport system is the Hafen-Hochbahn (elevated port railway). This is the section of the U3 U-Bahn line that runs between Rödingsmarkt and Landungsbrücken stations.

A ride on this stretch of the railway offers passengers a wonderful view over Hamburg's bustling port. Starting from Rödingsmarkt station, the train crosses slowly over the bridges along Binnenhafen. Between Baumwall and Landungsbrücken stations, the view opens up to show the harbour. The trip in the opposite direction is just as scenic. Just bear in mind that the sightseeing tour will end after three stations, when the U-Bahn train will go underground once again.

⑮ Rickmer Rickmers

See pp94 – 5.

⑯ Theater im Hafen Hamburg

Norderelbstraße 6. **Tel** 42 10 00.
Ⓤ Landungsbrücken.
Ⓢ Landungsbrücken. 🚢
Ⓦ **loewenkoenig.de**

Without a doubt, Hamburg is the musical theatre capital of Germany. One of the most popular stages is a theatre built in an old shipyard in 1995, the Theater im Hafen Hamburg *(see also p211)*. This tent-like building, located on the south side of the port, covers over 5,000 sq m (54,000 sq ft). When the theatre was built, the architects made sure that none of the 1,406 seats on the parquet floor was more than

25 m (80 ft) from the stage. The balcony holds a further 624 seats. Through the glass-fronted façade of the foyer, theatre-goers enjoy a marvellous view of Hamburg's skyline – especially impressive at night when everything is lit up. Bars and the Skyline Restaurant offer a first-class experience. A boat that departs from Landungs-brücken shuttles people to and from the theatre across the Elbe. The shuttle-boat fare is included in the price of your theatre ticket.

The Lion King has been playing at the Theater im Hafen Hamburg since 2001. This Disney spectacle, with its compelling music, opulent lighting design and inventive costumes, draws young and old alike into its magical world.

The Theater im Hafen Hamburg, located in an old shipyard

⑰ Cap San Diego

See pp98–9.

⑱ Landungs-brücken

Between Fischmarkt and Niederhafen.
Map 4D–E5. 🚇 Landungsbrücken.
🚊 Landungsbrücken. 🚌 112.

The Landungsbrücken with floating pontoons – a symbol of the city

Hamburg would not be Hamburg without the Landungsbrücken (landing bridges). Every traveller comes here at least one time to stroll along the swaying pontoons, breathe in the sea air and allow the smells of the port to linger in their nostrils. The Landungsbrücken consists of ten floating pontoons, measuring 700 m (2,300 ft) altogether. The long passenger hall, which forms part of the complex, was built in 1907–09. The tower at the east side of the hall displays the water level and the time, with a ship's bell ringing every half hour.

The first Landungsbrücken were built in 1839 as a place for steamships to dock before heading overseas. During World War II, the complex was heavily damaged, so in 1953–55 new pontoons were built.

Numerous restaurants, bars and food stalls are found along the Landungsbrücken, perfect for a break. This is the place where round trips of the harbour, offered by various tour companies, begin and end. The passenger ferries also depart from here *(see pp240–41)*. Displays show the development of the Port of Hamburg, and accordion players, souvenir stands and boat companies touting their tours add to the colourful hustle and bustle here. To cap it all off, a visit to the museum ship *Rickmer Rickmers (see pp94–5)*, moored at Fiete-Schmidt-Anleger, is an absolute must for visitors.

Statue on the harbour promenade

⑲ Alter Elbtunnel

An den Landungsbrücken. **Map** 4 D4.
🚇 Landungsbrücken. 🚊 Landungsbrücken. **Open** for pedestrians and cyclists: 24 hrs daily; for vehicles: 5:30–8pm Mon–Fri. 🅿 for vehicles.

The Alter Elbtunnel (the old tunnel under the Elbe), which links the districts of St Pauli and Steinwerder, is also part of the Landungsbrücken complex. When it opened in 1911, the 4.26-km (2.65-mile) long tunnel was a sensation. Since the opening of the new A7 motorway tunnel in 1975, the old one has become a nostalgic place. The tunnel was built as a way for workers living on the north side of the Elbe to get to the shipyards on the south side, where they were employed.

Elevators transport visitors 23.5 m (77 ft) down into the tunnel's depths. Drivers also must take their cars on the elevators, since there are no access ramps. Then, after walking or driving underneath the Elbe, they go topside again by elevator.

The two tunnels are 6 m (20 ft) in diameter and are decorated with light-blue ceramic tiles. Glazed terracotta reliefs depict subjects associated with the Elbe.

The tunnel is undergoing extensive restoration but remains open.

⑳ BallinStadt – Auswandererwelt Hamburg

Veddeler Bogen 2. **Tel** 31 97 91 60.
🚊 Veddel. 🚌 34. 🔓 **Open** Apr–Oct: 10am–6pm daily; Nov–Mar: 10am–4:30pm daily. 🅿
🌐 **ballinstadt.de**

BallinStadt opened its doors in 2007. The exhibit is dedicated to the fate of more than five million people who emigrated from their homes in Hamburg to North America between 1850 and 1934. Along with the themes of departure, the sea journey and arrival in New York, the exhibition also documents the reasons why people emigrated and the initial experiences of the emigrants in their new homeland. The complex is located on the grounds of a historic emigrant city built by Albert Ballin, the former General Director of the HAPAG shipping company.

A glimpse into the Alter Elbtunnel under the Elbe river

⑮ Rickmer Rickmers

This three-masted sailing ship *Rickmer Rickmers* is 97 m (318 ft) long, and was built at the Rickmers shipyard in Bremerhaven in 1896. On its first journey it was sent to Hong Kong, where it was loaded with rice and bamboo for the return trip. Later, the freighter was used in the saltpetre trade with Chile. In 1912, the Portuguese Navy commandeered the ship and used it as a school ship until 1962, quartering cadets where freight was once stored. The "Windjammers for Hamburg" association acquired the ship in 1983 and completely restored it. Since 1987, this vessel has been moored as a museum ship at Landungsbrücken.

Washroom
As was the case on most ships, there was not much space here for personal ablutions – even the captain had to make do with the basics.

Deck
In order to protect the wooden deck, the rule on board is "No stiletto heels allowed".

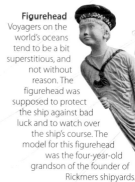

Figurehead
Voyagers on the world's oceans tend to be a bit superstitious, and not without reason. The figurehead was supposed to protect the ship against bad luck and to watch over the ship's course. The model for this figurehead was the four-year-old grandson of the founder of Rickmers shipyards.

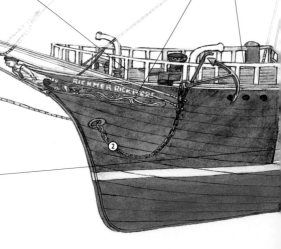

★ Cinema
In the cinema, museum visitors can watch films about the history of maritime travel, including some famous ships such as the *Gorch Fock*.

KEY

① **The keelson** (inside keel) runs the length of the ship and strengthens the keel.

② **The heavy anchor chain** increases the effectiveness of the anchor.

③ **The museum** has a permanent exhibition that includes nautical instruments and historic pictures.

④ **The restaurant** on board serves light meals daily from 11am.

VISITOR'S CHECKLIST

Practical Information
St Pauli Landungsbrücken
(Brücke 1). **Map** 4 E5.
Tel 319 59 59. **Open**
10am–6pm daily. 🎨 🚫
W rickmer-rickmers.de

Transport
Ⓤ Baumwall.
Ⓢ Landungsbrücken.

Doctor's Office
Rickmer Rickmers was often at sea for months on end, so a ship's doctor was on board, who was responsible for the crew's health. Great store was set on the quality of the medical equipment and the medicines carried on board.

★ **Map Room**
The ship's captain needed precise navigation instruments and nautical charts to find his way on the high seas. A selection of navigational aids are on display in the map room.

The life-saver, a key part of a ship's safety equipment, serves here as decoration.

★ **Officer's Mess**
This elegantly decorated officer's mess was a place for the ship's officers to dine and relax.

⑰ Cap San Diego

The world's largest museum ship, the *Cap San Diego* was built in Hamburg and launched in 1961. Her seaworthiness is demonstrated when she makes excursions to Cuxhaven and Kiel or takes part in great parades. During the rest of the year, this general cargo vessel, which once sailed between Europe and the east coast of South America, lies anchored at its dock at the Überseebrücke. You can get a good idea of what it was like to live on board from the museum's displays, or by having a meal in the restaurant. Rooms can be rented for parties, concerts, exhibitions and overnight stays. Not only young guests are regularly invited to "Klabauternacht" (goblin night). During these spooky evenings, maritime history comes alive.

★ Permanent Exhibits
The exhibition "A Suitcase Packed With Hope" documents the fate of emigrants who left Europe from Hamburg's port.

★ Shaft Tunnel
The shaft tunnel is a very narrow room that houses the shaft drive. Visitors can walk through the 40-m (130-ft) long tunnel, which links the machine room with the ship's propeller.

KEY

① **On-board cranes** meant that the *Cap San Diego* was not dependent on the infrastructure of the ports where it docked.

② **The *Cap San Diego*** has five cargo hatches. Two rooms below deck are used for cold storage.

Medical Instruments
The *Cap San Diego* had its own sick bay so that those who fell ill on the high seas could be properly treated.

◀ The tanker Loch Rannoch in dry dock

★ Radio Room
The radio room in the Cap San Diego is in its original condition. Thanks to the help of former marine radio operators, the equipment – such as the receiver or the USW – is kept in top condition.

The Bridge
The bridge is the most important place on a ship. The radar equipment and the steering column, with its compass and automatic pilot, are found here, as is the speaking-tube linking the bridge with the captain's cabin and the machine room.

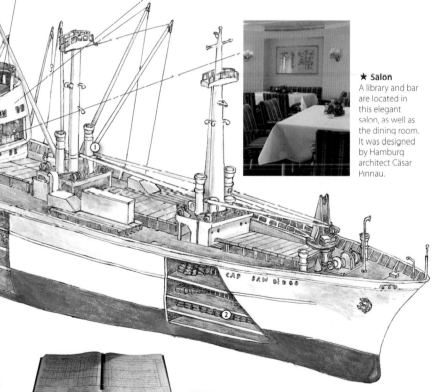

★ Salon
A library and bar are located in this elegant salon, as well as the dining room. It was designed by Hamburg architect Cäsar Pinnau.

Ship's Log
The ship's log, which documented the ship's journeys, is stored in the chart room along with the maritime charts.

ST PAULI

Once an unloved suburb, today St Pauli probably is Hamburg's best-known district. In the 18th century, booths for an annual fair were set up on Spielbudenplatz. Soon after, workers in the "world's oldest profession" moved in, and seamen recovered from their long journeys in the arms of attractive women, leaving a portion of their wages behind on the bedside table. Even today, the erotic industry dominates the neighbourhood. And yet, the red light is beginning to fade – St Pauli is undergoing a transformation. The Reeperbahn (the red-light district) of the future is, due to redevelopment, becoming more mainstream and less the exclusive province of a subculture. The first step was the rebuilding of Spielbudenplatz. Popular attractions such as the Schmidt Theater will be preserved by the developers of the "new" St Pauli, and the local football club, FC St. Pauli, will certainly survive.

Sights at a Glance

Museums and Galleries
① Panoptikum
⑤ St Pauli Museum
⑥ U-434

Streets and Parks
⑧ Hafenstraße
⑩ Schanzenviertel
⑪ Sternschanzenpark
and Water Tower

Theatres
② Schmidt Theater
and Schmidts Tivoli
③ TUI Operettenhaus

Other Attractions
④ Davidwache
⑦ St Pauli Fish Market
⑨ FC St. Pauli pp110–11

See also Streetfinder
maps 3–4

☐ **Restaurants**
see p190

1 Bullerei
2 Fischerhaus
3 Hamborger Veermaster
4 Luxor
5 Man Wah
6 Nil
7 Schauermann

◀ A Caribbean feeling at the beach of the Elbe river on warm, sunny days   **For map symbols** see back flap

Street-by-Street: The Reeperbahn

This district of Hamburg is one of the most famous in Germany, thanks to the Reeperbahn (red-light district), the fish market, the actor Hans Albers and FC St Pauli football club. Here, the alternative culture scene has space to unfold. Bizarre stores, noisy pubs, curious museums and ribald theatres all contribute to St Pauli's appeal. Many events are held on the renovated Spielbudenplatz, among them concerts, theatrical performances and markets. You can learn more about the district's raucous culture and interesting history at the St Pauli Museum *(see p105)*.

❶ ★ Panoptikum
In this wax museum, more than 120 well-known figures are on display: politicians, actors, pop stars, scientists, and athletes.

❸ ★ TUI Operettenhaus
This venue is one of the largest musical theatres in Hamburg. Shows like *Cats* and *Mamma Mia* have attracted millions of visitors for years.

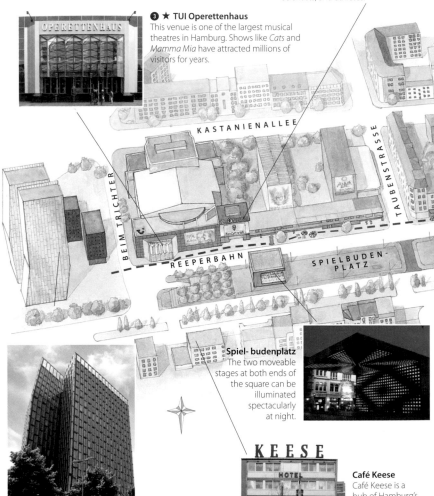

KASTANIENALLEE

BEIM TRICHTER

TAUBENSTRASSE

REEPERBAHN

SPIELBUDEN- PLATZ

Spiel- budenplatz
The two moveable stages at both ends of the square can be illuminated spectacularly at night.

Tanzende Türme
The two towers – striking architectural landmarks designed by Hadi Teherani – are reminiscent of a dancing couple.

0 metres   50
0 yards   50

Café Keese
Café Keese is a hub of Hamburg's nightlife and music scene. The Hotel Café Keese resides above this popular gathering place.

❷ ★ Schmidt Theater
With vaudeville, comedy and live music, the Schmidt Theater is synonymous with St Pauli's colourful culture.

❼ Schmidts Tivoli
This intimate musical theatre has long gained recognition for hosting fancy shows.

Locator map
See Street Finder maps 3–4

KEY

— Suggested route

Statue of Hans Albers
Hans Albers was a beloved Hamburg actor and singer. His bronze likeness was created in 1986 by Jörg Immendorff.

Herzblut St Pauli is one of the most ethnic bars/restaurants in the Reeperbahn. Maritime, St Pauli and football paraphernalia adorn its interiors.

St Pauli Theater
The performances of classical and modern plays staged in this theatre wittingly take their cue from New York City Broadway shows (see pp208–209).

❹ Davidwache
The most famous police station in Germany was built in 1913–14 and now stands under heritage protection.

❶ Panoptikum

Spielbudenplatz 3. **Map** 4 D4. **Tel** 31 03 17. Ⓤ St. Pauli. Ⓢ Reeperbahn. 🚌 36, 37, 112. **Open** 11am–9pm Mon–Fri, 11am–noon Sat, 10am–9pm Sun. 🚻 📷 ♿ **W panoptikum.de**

Hamburg's Panoptikum is the oldest and largest wax figure museum in Germany. Over 120 personalities from the worlds of politics, culture, science, showbusiness and sport are on display, each dressed in the appropriate garb. Anyone who is anyone can be seen here, from Napoleon to Madonna, Lady Di to Albert Einstein, Cleopatra to Elvis Presley, or from Michael Schumacher to Romy Schneider playing the role of Sisi. Of course unique Hamburgers such as Uwe Seeler and Hans Albers are not forgotten either. Two new figures are added each year. Among the more recent additions is fashion designer Karl Lagerfeld. An audio tour provides detailed information about each figure.

Even when the face of St Pauli is constantly changing, the Panoptikum is an institution that remains the same. It was opened in 1879 by Friedrich Hermann Faerber and since then has stayed in the hands of the family. Now, a fourth generation of the family runs this wax museum.

The raucous and highly original Schmidt Theater

Wax mask in the Panoptikum

success of this stage is the owner and actor Corny Littmann (alias Herr Schmidt) along with Ernie Reinhard (alias Lilo Wanders). The "Schmidt" became well-known throughout the country due to monthly television broadcasts of the Schmidt Show, which started in the early 1990s. The theatre gained a reputation as a crucible for talent, and it proved to be a springboard for the careers of artists such as Rosenstolz and Helge Schneider.

At the beginning of 2004, the theatre had to close because the building was in such disrepair it had to be torn down. In summer 2005 (on 8 August, naturally), the theatre reopened and celebrated with a colourful gala. Some of the funds for the new building were raised by finding seat sponsors, and many prominent Hamburgers purchased seats. Now there are 400 seats serving a very mixed audience in the restored theatre.

Schmidts Tivoli opened next door in 1991. It is known for its musicals, which are created in-house from the first spark of an idea to the premiere. A long-running hit was the 1950s revue *Fifty-Fifty*; the St Pauli musical *Heiße Ecke* is legendary with more than one million spectators.

❷ Schmidt Theater and Schmidts Tivoli

Spielbudenplatz 24–25 and 27–28. **Map** 4 D4. **Tel** 31 77 88 99. Ⓤ St. Pauli. Ⓢ Reeperbahn. 🚌 36, 37, 112. 🅿 📷 **W tivoli.de**

Raucous entertainment, comedy and musical theatre are the calling cards of the Schmidt Theater *(see also p211)*. Its mission to be different showed on its very first performance starting at 8/8/1988 at 8:08pm. The cornerstone of the terrific

The Reeperbahn – once thought to be "the world's most sinful mile"

❸ TUI Operetten-haus

Spielbudenplatz 1. **Map** 4 D4. **Tel** 31 11 70. Ⓤ St. Pauli. Ⓢ Reeperbahn. 🚌 36, 37, 112. 🖵 *See also p210.* 🔲 **tuioperettenhaus.de**

A theatre stood where this operetta house now stands up until World War II. In 1912, the hit song well-known to most Germans *Auf der Reeperbahn nachts um halb eins* (On the Reeperbahn at Twelve-thirty at Night) was first performed on the original stage. Music has always been an important feature of this location and today the TUI Operettenhaus is one of Hamburg's most important stages for large scale musical productions.

Starting in 1986, one of the world's most successful musicals – *Cats* – was staged here for a total of 15 years. Following in the footsteps of this huge success was a German version of *Mamma Mia*. This musical brought the top hits of the Swedish group ABBA to the big stage, and was an enormous box office success right from its premiere in November 2002. This production was the first non-English version of the musical, although the songs themselves were sung in their original language, English.

In September 2007, *Mamma Mia* was performed for the last time and was replaced by a musical by Austrian pop star Udo Jürgens called *Ich war noch niemals in New York* (I Have Never Been to New York). It premiered in December 2007 and included over twenty of the European superstar's infectious and very popular songs. *Sister Act* followed on in 2010, entertaining audiences with the tumultuous story of a lounge singer on the run from gangsters who goes into hiding as a nun.

A stage version of the boxing film *Rocky* has been running at TUI Operettenhaus since November 2012. This exciting German production was exported to Broadway in 2014.

The TUI Operettenhaus, with its eye-catching façade

❹ Davidwache

Ecke Spielbudenplatz / Davidstraße. **Map** 4 D4. Ⓤ St. Pauli. Ⓢ Reeperbahn. 🚌 36, 37, 112.

The Davidwache is home to Hamburg's police station No. 15. The building was constructed in 1913–14 by Fritz Schumacher in the style of a middle-class Hamburg home. About 120 police officers are stationed here, working in four shifts. They patrol a district that is only 0.85 sq km (0.33 sq miles) in size; it is the smallest police beat in the city. Given its location in the heart of the red-light district, it is also the "hottest" beat.

Davidwache became well known mainly through numerous film and TV productions such as the movie *Polizeirevier Davidwache* (Davidwache

The Davidwache police station, in the heart of the red-light district

police station), which opened in 1964. The Davidwache served as model for the popular TV series *Großstadtrevier* (metropolitan police district), although it was filmed in other buildings. Protected as a heritage building, the red brick Davidwache was expanded in 2005 when a modern annex was added.

❺ St Pauli Museum

Davidstraße 17. **Map** 4 D4. **Tel** 439 20 80. Ⓤ St. Pauli. Ⓢ Reeperbahn. 🚌 36, 37, 112. **Open** 11am–7pm Tue, Wed, 11am–10pm Thu–Sat, 11am–6pm Sun 🖼 🖼 🔲 **kiezmuseum.de**

This museum provides insight into the colourful history of the district of St Pauli from the Middle Ages right up until today. The indepth exhibits concentrate on how the entertainment quarter around the Reeperbahn has developed, making it the perfect introduction to the neighbourhood and a good place to visit before exploring the nearby streets.

Costumes of Hamburg born actor and singer Hans Albers are on display, as well as posters announcing concerts by the Beatles in the legendary Star Club. There's also jewellery that belonged to Domenica, a local prostitute and activist, and a St Pauli icon.

❻ U-434

St. Pauli Fischmarkt 10. **Map** 2 F4
Tel 32 00 49 34.
🅤 Landungsbrücken. 🆂
Reeperbahn, Königstraße. 🚌 112.
Open 9am–8pm Mon–Sat, 11am–
7pm Sun. 🚻 📷 🅦 u-434.de

This submarine was built in 1976 at a shipyard in the Russian city of Gorki (today Nishnij Nowgorod), and served as a spy submarine in the Russian North Sea flotilla until 2002. The U-434 was also used for secret operations in US territories like the Atlantic seaboard. Today, the submarine functions as a museum.

During a visit to the U-boat, which is 90 m (295 ft) long and barely 9 m (30 ft) wide, visitors learn all about life on board. The crew consisted of 84 people (16 officers and 52 men), and there were provisions to last them up to 80 days. Also on board were about 32,000 litres (7,000 gallons) of fresh water.

The largest space in the U-434 is the torpedo room with its six torpedo tubes. Up to 24 torpedos could be carried on board. Some sections of the U-boat are off limits – for example the command centre – but can be visited as part of a guided tour. Tours last approximately 45 minutes.

❼ St Pauli Fish Market

Between Hafenstraße and Große Elbstraße. **Map** 3 B5. 🅤
Landungsbrücken. 🆂 Reeperbahn, Königstraße. 🚌 112.
Open Apr–Oct: 5 – 9:30am Sun; Nov–Mar: 7 – 9:30pm Sun.

A stroll through the St Pauli Fish Market (Fischmarkt) is an absolute must for every visitor to the city. Probably no other weekly market in Germany attracts such a crowd. The mix is unique: night owls and early-risers, bargain-hunters and shoppers looking for a unique experience, business people and punks flock to the fish market starting in the wee hours of the morning. And it's worth getting up early. The best bet is to skip breakfast and indulge in the delicacies offered here at every turn. More than just fish is for sale. Along with trout, eel, flounder and other fish, market-criers, screaming at the top of their voices, hawk many other kinds of wares. These include potted plants, fruit, small animals, jewellery, bric-à-brac, souvenirs and much more. And when "cheese Tommi", "eel Dieter", or "banana Fred" praise their wares, large crowds gather around their stands to listen. Haggling is part of the fun, and many of the sellers, who are known as "rappos", have a rapier-quick

Statue of a fisherman

Graffiti art on a building located in Hafenstraße

repartee – this is also part of the charm of the St Pauli fish market.

But all those who can't or won't get up at such an early hour might still find a bargain when they do arrive. As the market draws to a close, the unsold wares are often hawked at cut-rate prices. At 9:30am, a gong is struck, and the vibrant market is over.

The market's party centre is the Fish Auction Hall (Fischauktionshalle; see pp118–19). No fish have been auctioned off here for a long time. Instead, the hall is now a place where people meet for an early drink. With free admission and live music, people enjoy jazz and rock well into the afternoon.

❽ Hafenstraße

Map 4 D – E4. 🅤 Landungsbrücken.
🆂 Landungsbrücken. 🚌 112.

For many years, a dispute centred around the Hafenstraße kept the city in a state of high alert. A mayor resigned, protests and demonstrations were watched anxiously throughout Germany, and the situation was even described as being akin to a civil war. It all began, when empty houses on the Hafenstraße (Nos. 116–126) – as well as some buildings in the Bernhard-Nocht-Straße nearby (Nos. 16 – 24) – were slated to be torn down to make way for a modern building on the harbour's edge. Alternative

Lively crowds at the Sunday morning St Pauli Fish Market

◀ Brew kettles on the former grounds of the Bavaria-Brauerei in St Pauli types occupied the houses, and there were repeated violent encounters between the squatters, their sympathizers and the police. It was only during the mid 1990s that the conflict was defused, after the houses were sold to a cooperative. Hamburgers are reminded of those turbulent times by graffiti and protest paroles in front of the houses.

House No. 89 – which, however, is located a bit further down the Hafenstraße directly on the Elbe river – is home to the Beachclub Strand Pauli (end Apr–end Sep: noon–11pm Mon–Thu, noon–midnight Fri, Sat, 10am–11pm Sun).

9 FC St. Pauli

See pp110–11.

10 Schanzenviertel

Map 3 C1–4 E1. Ⓤ Sternschanze, Feldstraße. Ⓢ Sternschanze. 🚌 3, 15.

Lying north of the Heiligengeistfeld, the district of Schanzenviertel is known simply as "Schanze" among locals. This lively neighbourhood is known for its alternative scene, its multicultural atmosphere, quaint shops and many bars and cafés. The Schanzenstraße forms its central axis with the neighbourhood stretching out from either side, but the Schulterblatt is at the very heart of the district and where things really happen. It is lined with numerous restaurants, from Spanish bars offering tapas to vegetarian eateries, from pubs

to Portuguese restaurants and Greek tavernas. Schulterblatt is the street to come to if you are looking for rare vinyl or CDs, for second-hand clothes or organic products. Numerous little vintage shops can be found in the area and browsing their eclectic inventories is a pleasure.

The Schanzenviertel hit the headlines in 1989, when the theatre Flora, at Schulterblatt 71, was taken over by squatters who were protesting plans to transform the playhouse into a musical theatre. After a long battle and plenty of controversy, the building finally opened as a cultural and community centre called the Rote Flora.

Many residents of the Schanzenviertel appreciate the district's unique atmosphere which sets it apart from other more commercially oriented quarters of the city; it is the polar opposite of the area surrounding the Reeperbahn.

The water tower in Sternschanzenpark has housed a hotel since 2007

11 Sternschanzenpark and Water Tower

Ⓤ Sternschanze, Schlump. Ⓢ Sternschanze 🚌 4.

The Schanzenviertel is named after the Sternschanzenpark, a popular spot for recreation all year round. People from the neighbourhood flock to the 12-hectare park to go for a walk or a run, to play *boules*, or to go sledding in winter. There is also a varied programme of cultural events held in the park including the immensely popular Summer Movies *(see p45)*.

Built in 1909, a water tower, rises up 57.5 m (189 ft) from the top of the hill in the southern part of the Schanzenpark. It is the area's main landmark and can be seen from miles around. After it was decommissioned in 1961, the city considered various ways to use the water tower, which had fallen into a state of disrepair. However, for one reason or another, none of the proposals could be carried out.

It was only in 2003, some 13 years after being sold to an investor, that a decision about the fate of this industrial monument was finally made. By allowing the Mövenpick Hotel Hamburg *(see p177)* to be built inside the tower (which is under heritage protection), it at last became possible to ensure the tower's future. Since 2007 the tower has been in use once again – after a 45-year break.

Climbing wall Kilimanschanzo at Florapark in Schanzenviertel

❾ FC St. Pauli

An essential element of St Pauli is its football (soccer) club, which was founded in 1910. While it cannot boast the world-renowned players or championship titles of the more successful (and wealthier) clubs like rival HSV *(see p 134),* FC St. Pauli is loved by local residents. The fans do not seem to mind which of the three professional German leagues the team plays in. A great time is guaranteed at every home game on the Heiligengeistfeld. Up to 29,000 spectators fill the seats of the Millerntor stadium, which is undergoing renovation through 2014. The football season runs from August to May.

Pirate Flag
FC St. Pauli's flag with skull and crossbones harks back to Hamburg's history of piracy embodied by Klaus Störtebeker; the team itself is considered to be a "league raider".

FC St. Pauli returned to the first German league for the 2010 season. Fans were key to this success; at home games, the stadium becomes a cauldron seething with emotion.

Since its founding in 1910, FC St. Pauli's home field has been the Heiligengeistfeld. During its eventful history it has been the subject of many newspaper headlines.

Offices
Distances within the club are short: The new office building is also located at the stadium.

The emblem on the club's premises testifies to the self-confidence and creativity of the team and its fans.

This club symbol, carved from stone, is located at the south entrance of the stadium at Millerntor.

The League's Pirates
The pirate flag was first hoisted in the stadium in the mid-1980s and has become a symbol of the rebellious and combative nature of the club and its fans.

Former Clubhouse
This FC St. Pauli clubhouse, where cups and pictures documenting club history were displayed, was torn down in 2007. In the course of refurbishing the stadium grounds, a new clubhouse was built; it is integrated into the grandstand.

Retter (Saviour) T-shirt
FC St. Pauli is strapped for cash and only survives thanks to a range of large-scale "Retter" (saviour) campaigns.

The Hamburg city gate is at the heart of the club's logo.

The Stadium

Millerntor-Stadion (Millerntor Stadium) was called Wilhelm-Koch-Stadion from 1970 – 98. By 2014, if all goes according to plan, it will have been completely rebuilt. It has been the site of many memorable football games. Fans still rave about the game on 6 February 2002 when the club, which was ranked at the bottom of the Bundesliga listings, bested FC Bayern München 2 to 1. Since the famous Munich club had won the World Cup a few days earlier, FC St. Pauli fans celebrated their "World Cup champion beaters" in a big way. In 2007, FC St. Pauli was promoted from the amateur league to the second Bundesliga, in 2010 it once again joined the first Bundesliga for one season. But, no matter what the league, the club can rely on the support of its fans. Depending on the score, the fans chant or the team is spurred on to even greater effort with cries of "St. Pauli! St. Pauli!"

The Heart of St Pauli
The club enjoys many different kinds of support. Along with Relentless, Captain Morgan and Do You Football, Astra beer is another major sponsor of FC St. Pauli.

ALTONA

Prior to 1937, Altona was an independent city belonging to Schleswig-Holstein. With the formation of Greater Hamburg, the city became part of its larger neighbour, a neighbour of which it had always been critical. Even today, Altona's residents think of themselves as Altonaers and not as Hamburgers. But even for many Hamburgers, Altona was too close. Their rivalry stretches back into the distant past. A sore point was always the question of who had jurisdiction

over the lucrative fish market, Altona, or Hamburg and St Pauli? Altona is an excellent starting point for a stroll along Hamburg's port lands. The best view of this area is from the Altonaer Balkon. Most of the area's other attractions are also located south of the railway station (Altonaer Bahnhof), around the Platz der Republik. Both the lovely street of Elbchaussee and the Elbuferweg, an attractive path along the Elbe, start in Altona.

Sights at a Glance

Museum
- ③ Altonaer Museum

Historic Buildings
- ⑤ Rathaus Altona
- ⑩ Fish Auction Hall

Streets and Squares
- ① Platz der Republik
- ⑦ Elbchaussee
- ⑧ Palmaille

Other Attractions
- ② Stuhlmannbrunnen
- ④ Monument by Sol LeWitt
- ⑥ Altonaer Balkon
- ⑨ Köhlbrandtreppe
- ⑪ stilwerk
- ⑫ Neue Flora

Restaurants
see pp190-191
1. Altamira
2. Au Quai
3. Bolero
4. Breitengrad
5. Eisenstein
6. Fischereihafen Restaurant
7. Haifischbar
8. Henssler & Henssler
9. IndoChine
10. Lutter & Wegner
11. Rive
12. Das Seepferdchen
13. Shikara
14. La Vela
15. Zum Schellfischposten

See also Streetfinder maps 1–2

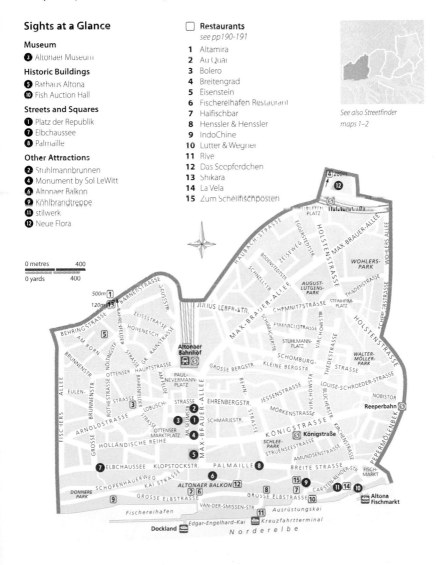

Street-by-Street: Altona

One of the major highlights of a walk through Altona, a district of Hamburg, is the white Rathaus (city hall), which is located in a former railway station. Across from the Rathaus is the Platz der Republik, an oasis of tranquillity richly adorned with sculptures. Benches on the Altonaer Balkon beckon you to stop and rest. From here, there is a wonderful view of the port and the Elbe with the Cruise Center, which opened in 2010. With a bit of luck you can watch an ocean giant steering the terminal. Also worth seeing is the Palmaille, a boulevard laid out in the 17th century.

❽ ★ Palmaille
The tree-lined boulevard dates from the 17th century. It ends in the Elbchaussee.

❺ ★ Rathaus Altona
In front of the grand Rathaus (city hall) of Altona, this equestrian statue of Emperor Wilhelm I recalls the time of Prussian rule (1867–71) and the ensuing integration into the German Empire .

PALMAILL

MAX-BRAUER-ALLEE

KÖNIGSTR.

MAX-BRAUER-ALLEE

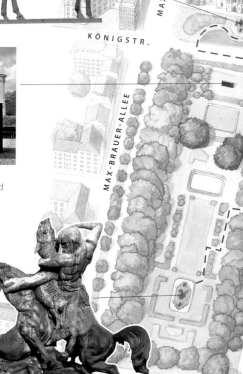

❹ ★ Denkmal von Sol LeWitt
This black cube in front of the Rathaus is entitled Black Form – Dedicated to the Missing Jews (1987). It is a memorial to the Altona Jews who were murdered by the Nazis.

❷ Stuhlmannbrunnen
Two giant centaurs fighting over a fish are the focus of this fountain, which was erected in 1900. They symbolize the age-old rivalry between the two fishing ports of Altona and Hamburg.

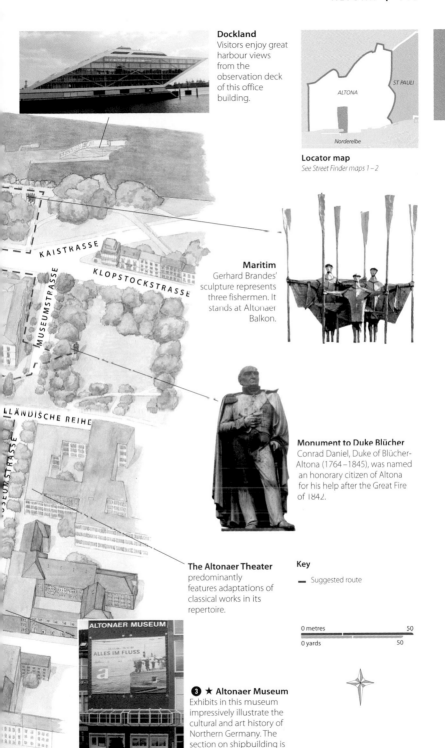

Dockland
Visitors enjoy great harbour views from the observation deck of this office building.

Locator map
See Street Finder maps 1–2

ST PAULI

ALTONA

Norderelbe

KAISTRASSE

KLOPSTOCKSTRASSE

MUSEUMSTRASSE

LLÄNDISCHE REIHE

SEUMSTRASSE

Maritim
Gerhard Brandes' sculpture represents three fishermen. It stands at Altonaer Balkon.

Monument to Duke Blücher
Conrad Daniel, Duke of Blücher-Altona (1764–1845), was named an honorary citizen of Altona for his help after the Great Fire of 1842.

The Altonaer Theater
predominantly features adaptations of classical works in its repertoire.

Key

— Suggested route

ALTONAER MUSEUM

ALLES IM FLUSS

0 metres   50
0 yards   50

❸ ★ **Altonaer Museum**
Exhibits in this museum impressively illustrate the cultural and art history of Northern Germany. The section on shipbuilding is especially worth seeing.

The green expanse of the Platz der Republik

❶ Platz der Republik

Map 1 C3–4. Ⓢ Altona, Königstraße. 🚌 1, 2, 15, 20, 25, 36, 37, 112.

This green park-like square between the Rathaus (city hall) and the railway station is 250 m (820 ft) long. Built in 1895, it was intended by the city fathers to be an oasis of tranquillity in the middle of a bustling district. Around the square are several imposing buildings in the Historical style. These include the railway station and the Rathaus (city hall) as well as the Altonaer Museum and the Königliche Eisenbahndirektion (royal railway administration), among others. Here, city administration, culture and economy are grouped together.

This square with its monuments – Stuhlmannbrunnen at the north end and the Monument by Sol LeWitt at the south end – is popular with Altona's residents as a place for walks. Visitors to the Altonaer Museum also enjoy the green expanse.

❷ Stuhlmannbrunnen

Platz der Republik. **Map** 1 C3. Ⓢ Altona, Königstraße. 🚌 1, 2, 15, 20, 25, 36, 37, 112.

Berlin sculptor Paul Türpe chose a highly dramatic scene for this fountain, created in 1900. It presents two mighty centaurs – creatures from Greek mythology with the upper bodies of humans and the lower bodies of horses – in the throes of fighting over the prize, an enormous fish. The fountain's main water jet shoots up high out of the fish's mouth. Surrounding the combatants are other bronze mythological figures – Triton, the son of the ocean god Poseidon, and a Nereid, a sea nymph – as well as four lizards spouting extra jets of water; they are seemingly upset by the fact that a fish has been caught.

This striking fountain tableau symbolizes the long-standing rivalry between the fishing ports of former neighbours Altona and Hamburg that dates back to the 16th century. At the time, Altona was

considered to be the centre of the German fishing industry. However, the more Hamburg rose in prominence, the more bitterly it fought Altona over fishing rights.

The fountain, which is 7.5 m (25 ft) high, was named after its benefactor, Günther Ludwig Stuhlmann, a wealthy citizen of Altona.

In the 1970s, extensive restoration work was carried out since parts of the bronze figures had begun to show signs of severe corrosion. Repairs were financed primarily through donations given by Altona residents.

In the year 2000, a hundred years after its creation, the Stuhlmannbrunnen once again regained its former lustre and was re-dedicated on the Platz der Republik.

Sign for the Altonaer Museum of Northern German cultural history

❸ Altonaer Museum

Museumstraße 23. 1 C3. **Map** 1 C3. **Tel** 42 81 35 35 82. Ⓢ Altona, Königstraße. 🚌 1, 2, 15, 20, 25, 36, 37, 112. **Open** 10am–5pm Tue–Sun. 📷 📸 call ahead. 🖥 📷 ♿ 🌐 **altonaermuseum.de**

The daily life and history of Northern Germany are the primary themes explored in the Altonaer Museum's collection. The typical ways in which country people lived is shown in reconstructed living quarters and mills.

In 2008, the ship-building exhibition was expanded; it documents the maritime side with ships' figureheads, nautical instruments and model ships. There is also a gallery with

Stuhlmannbrunnen: two mighty centaurs battling over a giant fish

The blinding white Rathaus Altona (city hall), built in 1896 – 98

landscape paintings and arts and crafts (including porcelain, glassware and pottery). Folk costumes and other garb trace the history of peasant and middle-class fashions through the 18th and 19th centuries.

❹ Monument by Sol LeWitt

Platz der Republik. **Map** 1 C4. Ⓢ Altona, Königstraße. 🚌 1, 2, 15, 20, 25, 36, 37, 112.

At the south end of the Platz der Republik is a cuboid stone monument to Altona's decimated Jewish community. Titled *Black Form – Dedicated to the Missing Jews*, it is a memorial to the deportation and murder of Altona's Jews during the Nazi period, and also to their unborn children.

Altona's Jewish community originated in the 16th century. In 1691, the Jewish communities of Hamburg, Altona and Wandsbek joined together to form a "triple community"; the seat of the Chief Rabbi was located in Altona. The community thrived and grew steadily, especially during the 19th century, due to immigration by Jews from Eastern Europe.

The deportation of Altona's Jewish citizens began in 1941; barely two years later, there were no Jews left in the city. The synagogues were destroyed in 1943 during bombing-raids.

Sol LeWitt (1928 – 2007), an American artist and a proponent of minimalist art, finished this sculpture in 1989. Concrete blocks were cemented together to form a cuboid structure covering an area of 5.5 m (18 ft) by 2 m (6.5 ft) and rising up 2 m (6.5 ft) high. Once formed, the monument was finished in dark black. In keeping with the artist's minimalist style, the memorial has no inscription.

❺ Rathaus Altona

Platz der Republik 1. **Map** 1 C4. **Tel** 428 11 01. Ⓢ Altona, Königstraße. 🚌 1, 2, 15, 20, 25, 36, 37, 112.

Altona's architectural showpiece is its Rathaus (city hall). It was built in 1896 – 98 on the grounds of the first Altona railway station, which was in use from 1844 – 1895, after which a new station opened. The Rathaus, which has four wings, was designed by Joseph Brix and Emil Brandt in the Neo-Renaissance style. The relief of a ship sailing into stormy waters, which decorates the gable above the entrance, was carved by sculptors Karl Garbers and Ernst Barlach. It is entitled *Ein Genius geleitet das Stadtschiff* (a genius steers the city ship).

The Rathaus was severely damaged during World War II and there was not much left of the interior.

Lizard, Stuhl-mannbrunnen

In front of the city hall is an equestrian statue of Emperor Wilhelm I, which was created in 1898 by Gustav Eberlein. Grouped around his feet are smaller monuments to Prussian heroes.

❻ Altonaer Balkon

Map 2 D4. Ⓢ Altona, Königstraße. 🚌 1, 2, 15, 20, 25, 36, 37, 112.

Stretching to the south of the Rathaus and running parallel to the Elbe river is this park, the Altona "Balcony". Tourists and locals alike come here to enjoy one of the very best views of the city. From here, there is a fantastic view of the Elbe river, the Köhlbrandbrücke (*see p135*) that crosses it, and of the port area, whose true extent can only truly be appreciated from this vantage point. On New Year's Eve, residents of Altona and the nearby district of Ottensen flock to the Altonaer Balkon to enjoy the fireworks.

The park is home to the bronze sculpture *Maritim* (1965) by Gerhard Brandes, which depicts three fishermen holding aloft their six oars.

There is plenty of activity in the park, especially in good weather. Then, the benches are full, people play boules and visitors enjoy the view on the docks and the passing ships through binoculars.

The Elbuferweg, a path running along the shore, begins here. You can walk or cycle along it towards Blankenese and Övelgönne, with its historical ships, or stroll along the path to the centre of town.

View from the Altonaer Balkon – one of the best in the city

A villa entrance on the Palmaille

❼ Elbchaussee

Map 1 A4 – C4. 🚌 36.

The Elbchaussee is definitely the most famous street in the city after the infamous red-light Reeperbahn. Its fame is due in part to its wonderful location high above the Elbe, and partly to the large number of elegant villas that were built here.

The Elbchaussee is about 9 km (6 miles) long, runs parallel to the Elbe and links Altona with Blankenese. Among wealthy Hanseatics this street is considered to be the best address in the city. A small difference plays a big role here, however: houses with an uneven number face the Elbe and are considered to be on the "right" side of the street.

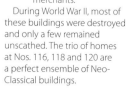
Decoration on the Palmaille

Visitors do not have to worry about such distinctions, but may encounter another problem. Today, there is a lot of traffic on the Elbchaussee. But as long as you stay on the Elbe side, you'll enjoy walking past impressive villas, surrounded by beautifully manicured gardens. Many of the villas were built in the 18th and 19th centuries, when Blankenese was located outside the gates of Hamburg and rich merchants wanted to live at a dignified distance from their city offices. Some of these dwellings were used only on weekends or exclusively as summer homes.

The atmosphere along the Elbchaussee was an inspiration for many artists. In 1902, during a stay in Hotel Louis C. Jacob (see p183), Max Liebermann painted *Die Terrasse im Restaurant Jacob in Nienstedten*, which today hangs in the Hamburger Kunsthalle (see pp64 – 5).

❽ Palmaille

Map 2 D4. 🇸 Königstraße. 🚌 36, 37.

This magnificent boulevard runs east parallel to the Elbe river above the Altonaer Balkon. The street's name is derived from *palla a maglio*, a ball game imported from Italy that is a cross between croquet and golf. Duke Otto V of Holstein-Schaumburg had three lanes built here in 1638 – 39 for playing this game. After suffering extensive damage in a fire in 1713, the area was planted with four rows of linden trees at the beginning of the 18th century.

Starting in 1786, the regional architect for Holstein, Christian Frederik Hansen, built several Neo-Classical homes here for the well-to-do. Those living here at the time included noblemen, magistrates and wealthy merchants.

During World War II, most of these buildings were destroyed and only a few remained unscathed. The trio of homes at Nos. 116, 118 and 120 are a perfect ensemble of Neo-Classical buildings.

❾ Köhlbrandtreppe

Between Carsten-Rehder-Straße and Breite Straße. **Map** 2 E4. 🇸 Königstraße. 🚌 36, 37.

The massive Neo-Gothic Köhlbrandtreppe, built in 1887, looks especially monumental when seen from the edge of the Elbe. This stairway enabled workers to move easily from their homes in the densely populated upper part of town down to their shifts on the port. The construction of the staircase was financed by Prussians; Altona once belonged to Prussia. Still today, a small figure of Roland guards the coats-of-arms of Prussia and Altona that are carved above the small fountain. Ornamental ovals depict Neptune and Mercury as symbols of seafaring and trade. From the staircase, there is a view of the shipyard Blohm + Voss on the opposite shore.

❿ Fish Auction Hall

Map 2 E4. **Tel** 570 10 52 00. 🇸 Königstraße, Reeperbahn. 🚌 36, 37, 112. 🌐 **fischauktionshalle.de**

It can be very quiet here on weekdays, but when the "Fischmarkt" (fish market) opens in St Pauli on Sunday mornings, hordes of people flock to Altona's Fish Auction Hall (Fischauktionshalle). Live music (mainly jazz, rock and oldies) entertains the crowds, and

A splendid villa with well-tended gardens on the Elbchaussee

breakfast is available between 6am and noon. On the gallery, you can choose between the captain's brunch or a classic Altona fish market buffet. Downstairs, there are food stalls selling Fischbrötchen (fish in a bun), crabs or Matjeshering (salted herring). Beer, champagne, coffee and tea are also available.

The triple-naved hall was built in 1896. Two years later, Hamburg – ever the competitor – built its own Fish Auction Hall in St Pauli. In 1933, the two fish markets were combined, but Altona's auction hall had a big advantage: it had a direct link to the railway, which meant that more fish were sold here.

The Hamburg Fish Auction Hall was torn down in 1971. Altona's hall has been completely reconstructed after sustaining severe bomb damage in World War II. It is now an event centre. The solid construction of the building ensures its survival in case of flooding during storm tides. Yet, with its domes and gables, it is very appealing.

Entrance to the Fish Auction Hall in Altona

⑪ stilwerk

Große Elbstraße 68. **Map** 2 E4. **Tel** 30 62 11 00. Ⓢ Königstraße, Reeperbahn. Haus. **Open** 10am–7pm Mon–Fri, 10am–6pm Sat, 1–6pm Sun. 🖥️
🌐 stilwerk.de/hamburg

It's all about style in stilwerk. The centre for interior design has branches in Berlin, Düsseldorf, and Vienna. The Hamburg subsidiary spreads over 11,000 sq m (118,000 sq ft) of space. The vendors sell upmarket household and garden furniture, beds, home accessories, consumer electronics, carpets, lamps, fabrics, and gift items. But stilwerk is not just another shopping mall; the architecture of this building is interesting in itself. Stilwerk is located in a red-brick building (1910), which once housed a malt

factory. The building's history transfers visitors back into Hamburg's Hanseatic past. Within the centre, more than 35 shops over seven floors are grouped around a covered interior courtyard. Glass elevators transport visitors between floors. A popular way of experiencing the centre, is to go to the top floor by elevator, and then walk downstairs, getting an

Fountain below the Köhlbrandtreppe

overview of the select choice of commodities presented on the individual floors, and a thorough impression of the building's interior design.

Exhibitions form an integral part of stilwerk's concept. In the lobby, displays present the latest trends from internationally renowned designers.

⑫ Neue Flora

Stresemannstraße 159a. **Map** 2 E1. **Tel** 43 16 50. Ⓞ Holstenstraße. 🚌 3. See also Entertainment p213.
🌐 neueflora.de

Since it opened with *Phantom of the Opera*, the Neue Flora theatre (built in 1989–90) has become famous throughout Germany. From *Titanic* to *Dance of the Vampires* to *Dirty Dancing*, big musicals continue to be staged here. In November 2008, Phil Collins' musical Tarzan premiered at the Neue Flora and in 2013 *Phantom of the Opera* returned to the theatre.

The theatre has almost 2,000 seats arranged in amphitheatre style. There is a live music club here, too, as well as facilities for banquets and conferences.

AROUND THE ALSTER

Two lakes, the smaller southern Binnenalster (Inner Alster) and the larger northern Außenalster (Outer Alster), form a delightful part of the cityscape. They were created by the damming of the Alster river; they were separated when the Wallanlagen fortifications were built in the 17th century.

Crossing the lakes today are two major bridges: the Lombardsbrücke and the Kennedybrücke. The district around the Alster is considered to be a prestigious address. The Jungfernstieg is one of Europe's best-known promenades, and world-famous stars and celebrities stay in the Atlantic Kempinski and Vier Jahreszeiten hotels. Both Pöseldorf, an elegant residential district second only to Blankenese, and Grindel, with its university and student quarter, are located on the Außenalster. Cultural attractions are well represented here by several museums and the Deutsches Schauspielhaus.

Sights at a Glance

Museums and Galleries
0 Museum für Völkerkunde
12 Museum für Kunst
   und Gewerbe pp130–31

Historic Buildings
4 Hotel Vier Jahreszeiten
5 Bahnhof Hamburg
   Dammtor
9 Hotel Atlantic Kempinski

Districts and Streets
3 Jungfernstieg
6 Pöseldorf
10 St Georg

Other Attractions
1 Binnenalster
2 Alsterpavillon
7 Außenalster
11 Deutsches Schauspielhaus
13 Ohnsorg-Theater
14 Literaturhaus
15 Imam Ali Mosque

☐ **Restaurants**
   see pp191–192

1 ALEX im Alsterpavillon
2 Brasserie Flum
3 Brodersen
4 Cox
5 Haerlin
6 Jahreszeiten Grill
7 Kajüte
8 Küchenwerkstatt
9 Max & Consorten
10 Piazza Romana
11 Raven
12 Ristorante Galatea
13 Ristorante Portonovo
14 Suzy Wong
15 Turnhalle St Georg

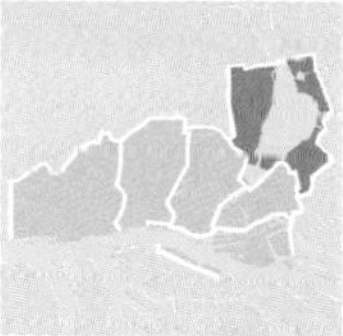

See also Streetfinder
maps 5–6, 7–8, 9–10

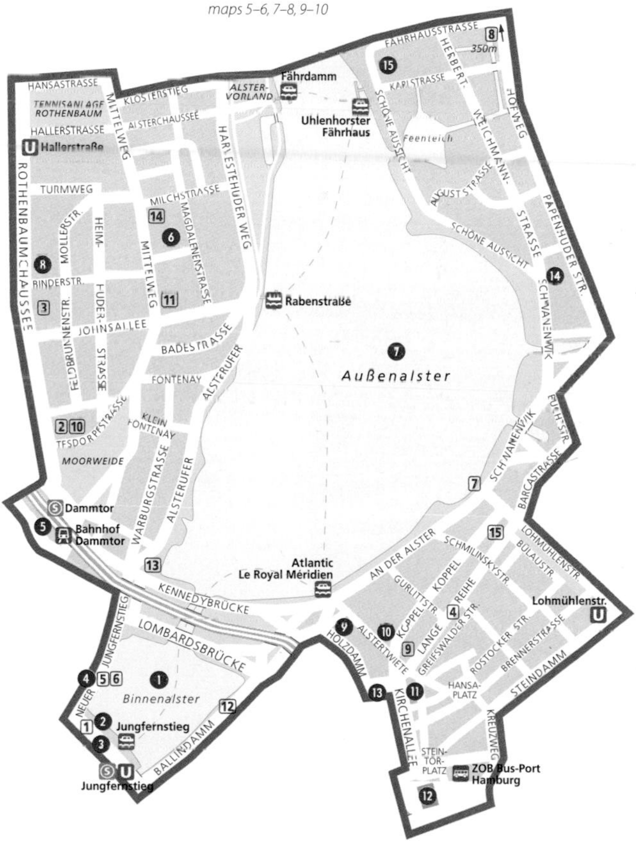

0 metres 300
0 yards 300

Street-by-Street: Around the Alster

Some districts that border the Alster, including
Rotherbaum and Harvestehude, are counted among
the most prestigious addresses in Hamburg. Visitors
will also feel welcome here, since the Binnenalster
is lined with acclaimed hotels, and the Jungfernstieg
is one of Europe's most attractive shopping streets.
Cafés, such as the Alsterpavillon, are a delightful place
to stop and relax and enjoy a view of the water. It is a
matter of debate among Hamburgers as to which
spot along the shore of the Alster offers the best view
of the almost 40-m (131-ft) high Alster fountain.

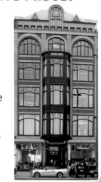

★ Heine-Haus
Ricardo Bahre
designed this
beautiful Jugendstil
building in 1903. It is
named for the
residence of Salomon
Heine that once
stood here.

❷ ★ Alsterpavillon
The terrace of this
popular café offers an
unforgettable view of
the Binnenalster.

❸ ★ Jungfernstieg
The Jungfernstieg is an ideal place for
shopping, strolling and relaxing.

JUNGFERNSTIEG

**BINNEN-
ALSTER**

Swans live on the
Außenalster (Outer
Alster) from spring to
autumn. An officially
appointed "Father of
Swans" takes care of
them and ensures
their wellbeing.

| 0 metres | | 50 |
| 0 yards | | 50 |

Nivea Haus
An oasis of wellness in the city centre; visitors to the Nivea Haus are pampered with relaxing massages (*see pp200–201*).

Alsterkunst
(Art along the Alster). Numerous statues adorn the embankment of the Alster.

Locator Map
See Street Finder maps 5–6 & 9–10

Amsinck-Palais
This palace was built in 1831 by Franz Gustav Forsmann and was sold to the merchant Gustav Amsinck in 1899. It is well-known for its guilded railings.

NEUER JUNGFERNSTIEG

❹ Hotel Vier Jahreszeiten
For over 100 years, the Hotel Vier Jahreszeiten (Hotel Four Seasons) has been welcoming international guests to the Binnenalster. When it first opened in 1897, there were only 11 rooms, but under the direction of its first owner Friedrich Haerlin, it developed into a luxury hotel.

❶ Binnenalster
The Binnenalster covers some 18 hectares (44 acres). One of the best ways to view its wonderful fountain and the imposing buildings lining its shores is by excursion boat

Alsterdampfer
Numerous tour boats cruise the Alster. A trip on board provides a perfect vantage point for viewing the stately buildings along the Alster, with many points for disembarking.

Key

— Suggested route

The terrace at the Alsterpavillon – Hamburg's best-known café

❶ Binnenalster

Map 10 D – E2. Ⓤ Jungfernstieg.
Ⓢ Jungfernstieg. 🚌 4, 5, 34, 36.

Hamburg's inner city owes much of its charm to the Binnenalster (Inner Alster). When the city was reconstructed after the Great Fire (1842), the lake shore was reconfigured to make it accessible from all sides. The lake covers 18 ha (44 acres) and is separated from the larger Außenalster (Outer Alster) by the Kennedybrücke and the Lombardsbrücke.

In the middle of the lake, shooting water nearly 60 m (197 ft) into the air, is the Alster fountain. It operates between 9am and midnight from spring to autumn. Alster excursion boats dock at the southwest side of the lake. An impressive backdrop is provided by stately buildings (such as the Hotel Vier Jahreszeiten), office buildings, including HAPAG-Lloyd's headquarters, and the shopping oases Alsterhaus and Nivea Haus.

Windsbraut on the Binnenalster

❷ Alsterpavillon

Jungfernstieg 54. **Map** 10 D2.
Tel 350 18 70. Ⓤ Jungfernstieg.
Ⓢ Jungfernstieg. 🚌 4, 5, 34, 36.
🕐 8am – 1pm Mon – Thu, 8am – 3am Fri – Sat, 9am – 1am Sun.

From this café, directly on the Binnenalster, you can enjoy one of the loveliest views in Hamburg. The wide steps offer a perfect place to relax, and are also used for events.

The Alsterpavillon (Alster Pavilion) survived the extensive rebuilding which took place at the start of the 21st century and changed the southern shore of the lake.

Hamburg's best-known café has enjoyed a long history. The first pavilion to be located here was built in 1799. Patrons of the fifth pavilion (built in 1914), came to enjoy swing music at tea dances in the Roaring Twenties. During the National Socialist period, this dance café was frowned upon; it was given the nickname "Jew aquarium" and was set on fire in 1943.

The current Alster-pavillon – a half-circle with a flat roof – was built in 1953, but has failed to regain the glamour of former days. Many different operators have tried to make a go of it here using various concepts. During

The 40-m (131-ft) high fountain in the Binnenalster

the summer months, the terraces of the Alex im Alsterpavillon café are very popular, and the all-you-can-eat buffet (served 8am – noon Mon – Sat) and the Sunday brunch (9am – 2:30pm Sun) also attract the hordes.

❸ Jungfernstieg

Map 9 C2, 10 D2 – 3.
Ⓤ Jungfernstieg. Ⓢ Jungfernstieg.
🚌 4, 5, 34, 36.

The Jungfernstieg is one of Hamburg's oldest streets. It acquired its name in the 17th century after it had become the most popular promenade for well-to-do Hamburgers – especially among young women ("Jungfern").

In this sense, it hasn't changed to this day, although its look is different. The first change was in 1838, when Jungfernstieg became the first street in Germany to be asphalted. Then after the Great Fire of 1842, the south side was completely rebuilt. In 2004 – 2006 the pavements were widened and, with the exception of the Alster-pavillon, all the buildings along the water's edge were demolished. With the addition of new grandstand-like steps along the edge of the shore, Hamburg can now claim to have one of Europe's most attractive promenades.

A good part of this is due to the presence of Alsterhaus (see p198), a department store with a long tradition. Flagship stores of major fashion houses are also located here, alongside exclusive jewellery and interior design shops.

Together with two other streets, Große Bleichen and Neuer Wall which lead off to the southwest, Jungfernstieg is today a luxury shopping mile made even more attractive by the white arches of the Alster Arcades *(see p58)*.

Neuer Jungfernstieg is a street running along the west side of the Binnenalster. Its appeal lies less in shopping opportunities than in the impressive buildings which line it.

Hotel porter

❹ Hotel Vier Jahreszeiten

Neuer Jungfernstieg 9–14. **Map** 7 C5. **Tel** 349 40. 🚇 Jungfernstieg, Gänsemarkt, Stephansplatz. Ⓢ Jungfernstieg. 🚌 4, 5, 34, 36. 🌐 hvj.de

Ever since the Swabian Friedrich Haerlin acquired houses along the Binnenalster's western shore and opened up a luxury hotel in 1897, the Vier Jahreszeiten (Four Seasons) has welcomed guests from around the world. A who's-who of the German Empire and the Roaring Twenties frequented this grand hotel. Under the direction of Haerlin's son, Fritz, who took over the hotel in 1932, and his descendants, the hotel has remained a favourite with the rich and famous. Film stars such

as Sophia Loren, opera singers such as Plácido Domingo, business czars including Aristotle Onassis, and rock musicians such as the Rolling Stones have stayed in this magnificent white building. The hotel has been part of the luxury hotel group Fairmont Hotels & Resorts since 2007. Hanseatic understatement has always been a hotel trademark; you won't find glitter and opulent furniture here. But the ambience is splendid – not least due to the Gobelins (tapestries) and oak in the salon off the entrance.

❺ Bahnhof Hamburg Dammtor

Theodor-Heuss-Platz. **Stadtplan** 7 B4. **Karte** H/J5. 🚇 Stephansplatz. Ⓢ Dammtor. 🚌 4, 5, 34, 112.

Without a doubt, this glass-and-steel Art Nouveau building is Hamburg's most beautiful train station. At the time it was built, in 1903, state guests were greeted here; it was therefore also known as the "Kaiserbahnhof" (the Emperor's train station). Due to its proximity to the Messezentrum (trade fair) and Kongresszentrum (conference centre), Dammtor is now also called the "Messebahnhof"

(trade fair station). Each day, about 200 long-distance trains (including ICE and IC trains), 80 local trains and 500 S-Bahns serving three lines stop here.

The station's hall is 23 m (75 ft) high, 112 m (367 ft) long and 35 m (115 ft) wide. Around 100 years after it was first built, the hall and train platforms were extensively renovated. Its appeal comes from its ceiling, which resembles a vaulted roof.

❻ Pöseldorf

Stadtplan 7 C1–2, 8 D1–2. **Karte** J1–K2. 🚇 Hallerstraße. 🚌 34.

Between the Außenalster and Mittelweg and between Harvestehuder Weg and Badestraße lies Pöseldorf, the Alster's finest area. Its character is best expressed by the antique dealers, galleries and exclusive fashion boutiques here. German fashion designer Jil Sander opened her first store here in the Milchstraße in 1967. The most fashionable villas outside of Blankenese are located in Pöseldorf. Among the large companies headquartered in this area is the publisher Milchstraße am Mittelweg. Despite the elite ambience, a lively bar scene has sprung up here. The Hochschule für Musik und Theater (Music and Theatre School) is also here, on Harvestehuder Weg No. 12.

The railway station Hamburg Dammtor – an Art Nouveau building dating from 1903

The Hotel Atlantic Kempinski, located directly on the Alster

❼ Außenalster

Map 8 D1 – F4 🚌 6, 25, 34, 37

This lake, measuring some 3 km (1.8 miles) in length, was formed by damming up the river Alster. It is a perfect place to sail or paddle a boat. A large number of restaurants line its shore; these are often hopelessly crowded during good weather. Excursion boats ply the Alster on a zig-zag course, and passengers can embark and disembark at the dock of their choice. Along the lake's western shore stretches an expansive green space, the Alstervorland, which is used for leisure activities. Joggers in particular love the 7.6-km (4.7-mile) loop through the park.

Sculpture, Hotel Atlantic Kempinski

❽ Museum für Völkerkunde

Rothenbaumchaussee 64. Map 7 B2. Tel 428 87 90. Ⓤ Hallerstraße. 🚌 34. Open 10am – 6pm Tue – Sun (Thu to 9pm). 🚇 🗎 📷 ♿ Ⓦ voelkerkundemuseum.com

A cross-section of the world's cultures is on display in this anthropological museum, which was founded in 1879. Since 1912, it has been housed in its current stately building. About 350,000 items and almost as many documentary photographs are on display here. The exhibits have been gathered from areas as disparate as Africa, Oceania, the Americas and the Far East. Unique in Germany is the archive dedicated to exploring the modern-day belief in witchcraft.

Each autumn, a "Peoples' Market" is held in the museum's rooms, with exhibitors from around the world showing and selling their works.

❾ Hotel Atlantic Kempinski

An der Alster 72 – 79. Map 8 D4. Tel 288 80. Ⓤ Hauptbahnhof. Ⓢ Hauptbahnhof. 🚌 4, 5, 6, 31, 34, 35, 36, 37. Ⓦ atlantic.de

Hamburgers fondly call this hotel, which was built in 1909, "the white palace on the Alster". In its 245 spacious rooms and suites, travellers from around the world are provided with every comfort to make their stay in Hamburg perfect. The guest book contains names of such luminaries as Herbert von Karajan, Charles de Gaulle and Michael Jackson. Politicians meet in the Atlantic Kempinski to exchange opinions at the highest level.

The hotel's façade, as well as its multifaceted interior, has often served as a location for films and television shows. In 2004 the Hotel Atlantic Kempinski created a splash by being the first to open a private cinema in a German hotel. Up to eight people can watch films in this deluxe cinema.

The Außenalster – popular for sailing, rowing and canoeing

◀ Southwest view of the Binnenalster, with the towers of the Rathaus and St Nikolai Memorial in the distance

⑩ St Georg

Map 8 D4–F5. **Ⓤ** Hauptbahnhof, Lohmühlenstraße. **Ⓢ** Hauptbahnhof. **🚌** 4, 5, 6, 31, 34, 35, 36, 37.

From the splendid buildings along the Alster to student digs, from pricey restaurants to local eateries, from boutiques to corner shops – this district can hardly be beaten in terms of diversity. The street Lange Reihe exudes multicultural flair. Snack bars and shops selling arts and crafts can be found here. German actor Hans Albers was born on this street (No. 71). "Koppel 66" (No. 75) is home to ateliers for jewellery-making, book design and writing instrument design, as well as a vegetarian café.

⑪ Deutsches Schauspielhaus

Kirchenallee 39. **Map** 8 F5. **Tel** 24 87 13. **Ⓤ** Hauptbahnhof. **Ⓢ** Hauptbahnhof. **🚌** 4, 5, 6, 31, 34, 35, 36, 37. Kasse: **Open** 10am–7pm Mon–Sat. **🖥** **W** schauspielhaus.de

Germany's largest traditional theatre was built at the end of the 19th century in the Neo-Classical style. In 1900, it opened with a performance of Goethe's *Iphigenie auf Tauris* (*Iphigenia in Taurus*). It became world-renowned under the direction of Gustaf Gründgens (1955–63), when plays such as Goethe's *Faust* were staged. The Peter Zadek era (1985–89) ruffled feathers due to its provocative, socially engaged productions. The stage has kept up this experimental tradition. It was voted "Theatre of the Year" in 1996, 1997, 2000 and 2005.

The building's façade is decorated with busts of the most famous German literati, among them Goethe, Schiller, Lessing and Kleist. The theatre accommodates 1,200 people and features two balconies, loges, gilded ornamentation and classic red seats.

⑫ Museum für Kunst und Gewerbe

See pp130–31.

Entrance to the turquoise-coloured Imam Ali Mosque

⑬ Ohnsorg-Theater

Heidi-Kabel-Platz 1. **Map** 10 F2. **Tel** 350 80 30. **Ⓤ** Hauptbahnhof. **Ⓢ** Hauptbahnhof. **🚌** 4, 5, 6, 31, 34, 35, 36, 37. Box office: **Open** 10am–7pm Mon–Sat, 2–6pm Sun. **🖥** **W** ohnsorg.de

The theatre is an integral part of Hamburg. It has become famous throughout Germany due to televised broadcasts featuring Heidi Kabel & Co. Based in new premises since 2011, the stage still premieres several comedies in a repertory season. Sometimes the programme includes more serious drama such as Bertolt Brecht's *Mudder Courage*.

Germany's largest traditional theatre, Deutsches Schauspielhaus

⑭ Literaturhaus

Schwanenwik 38. **Map** 8 F2. **Tel** 22 70 20 11. **🚌** 6, 37. **🖥** **W** literaturhaus-hamburg.de

Hamburg has a lively literary scene and many well-known authors live here. An important centre for the German literary world is located in a former merchant's villa built in 1868 and under heritage protection since 1989.

The Literaturhaus does not just see itself as a platform for readings by authors like at the Hamburg Krimifestival (see p46), but also as a forum for public discussion. You can browse to your heart's content in the well-stocked bookstore of this literary meeting place.

The café is considered to be one of the most beautiful cafés in Hamburg, in part due to its lovely plaster work and ceiling paintings. Guests can take their time reading the national and international newspapers here over a cup of tea or coffee.

⑮ Imam Ali Mosque

Schöne Aussicht 36. **Map** 8 E1. **Tel** 22 94 86 10. **🚌** 6, 25. **Open** 9am–8pm daily. **🅿** **W** izhamburg.com

Muslims from around the world meet in the Imam Ali Mosque (Imam-Ali-Moschee), which is also the seat of the Hamburg Islamic Centre. Two minarets flank the mosque's turquoise-coloured exterior, which is crowned by a dome. Displayed in the prayer room is the largest hand-knotted round carpet in the world. Twenty-two carpet-makers laboured for three years to create this amazing 200-sq m (2,200-sq ft) carpet, which weighs one ton; the rug alone makes a visit to the Iman Ali Mosque worthwhile.

⑫ Museum für Kunst und Gewerbe

The MKG, one of Europe's leading applied arts museums, is housed in a Neo-Renaissance building dating from 1876. Its collection, which ranges from the ancient world to the present day, is displayed on four floors. The European, Near Eastern and Far Eastern collections show extraordinary diversity. Among the highlights are the Japanese art collection with its teahouse and woodblock prints, the collection of historical musical instruments, the photography collection with 100,000 images and the Art Nouveau (Jugendstil) collection with its Parisian room. Some collections are closed for restoration.

Poster Art
French Art Nouveau posters form the cornerstone of this collection of 20th-century posters, along with many international works.

Second floor

First floor

★ Historical Keyboard Instruments
Some 400 European and 30 non-European instruments, each one a stunning example of artistry, are displayed in this collection.

★ Middle Ages
The European collection (Byzantium to Historicism) includes a large number of excellent works from the Middle Ages.

Entrance to the museum
🏛 🖼 👫 ♿ ℹ

In Hubertus Wald Kinderreich
children can try their hands at being designers, architects or artists.

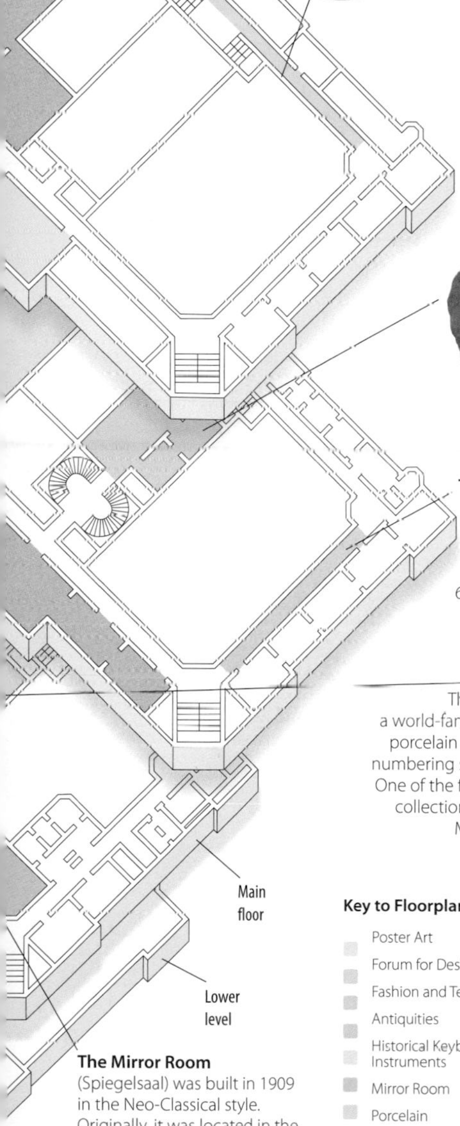

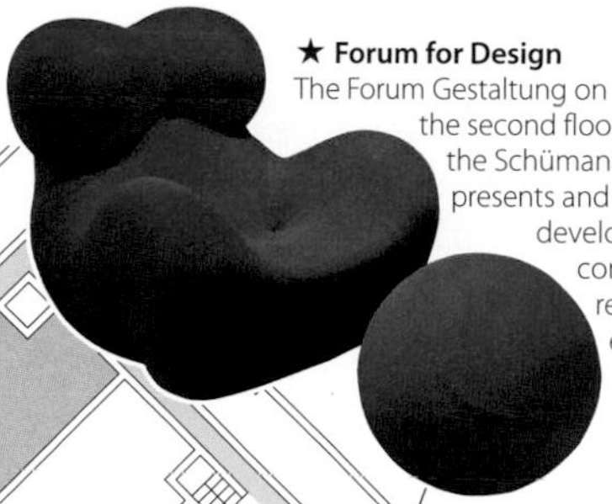

★ **Forum for Design**
The Forum Gestaltung on the second floor of the Schümann Wing presents and reflects developments in contemporary and recent design. The exhibitions are changed every one or two years.

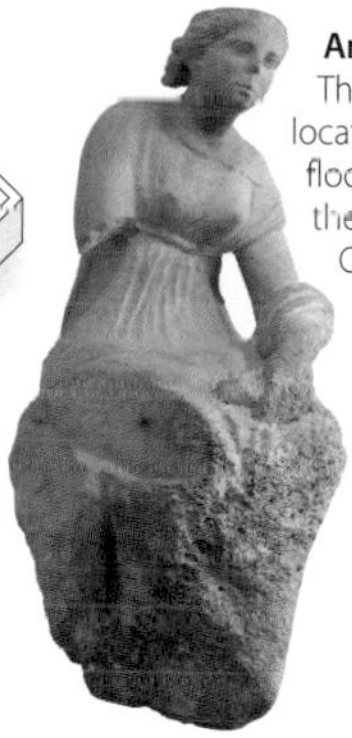

Antiquities
The Antiquities collection is located on the museum's first floor. It includes works from the ancient Orient, Egypt and Classical antiquity, represented by items such as burial urns, reliefs from Attic tombs, pottery, bronzes and sculptures.

The Fashion and Textiles collection is extensive, with up to 60,000 exhibits.

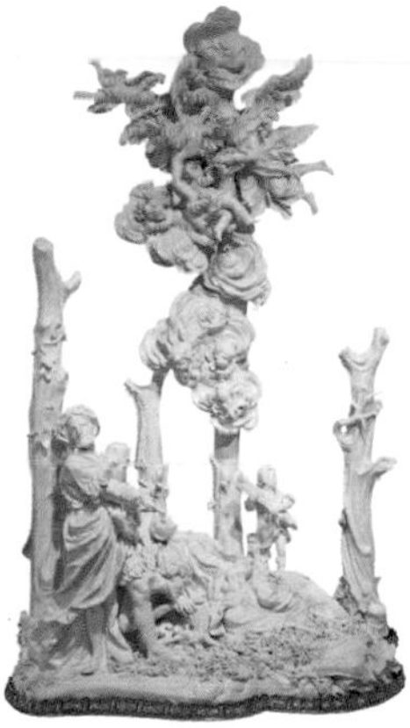

★ **Porcelain**
The MKG possesses a world-famous collection of porcelain and faience ware, numbering some 1,500 items. One of the focal points of the collection is the acclaimed Meissen porcelain.

Main floor

Lower level

The Mirror Room
(Spiegelsaal) was built in 1909 in the Neo-Classical style. Originally, it was located in the Budge Palace and was rebuilt in the MKG.

Key to Floorplan

☐ Poster Art
☐ Forum for Design
☐ Fashion and Textiles
☐ Antiquities
☐ Historical Keyboard Instruments
☐ Mirror Room
☐ Porcelain
☐ Middle Ages
☐ Special Exhibitions

Gallery guide

On the ground floor are objects from the Middle Ages, Renaissance, Baroque and 19th century. Among other things, the first floor is devoted to Antiquities, Art Nouveau, Modernism, East Asia and Islamic art. The second floor displays poster art, photography and – in the Forum for Design – modern design. On the lower level are the library and the DesignLabor (Design lab).

FURTHER AFIELD

A long with the many attractions found in its centre, the nearby districts and outlying areas of this Hanseatic city also have much to offer. Sights include modern architecture, interesting museums and, above all, extensive parks, which provide Hamburgers with a place to retreat from the stresses of daily life. These varied destinations outside the city gates make for ideal excursions, whether your interest lies in greeting or bidding farewell to ships in Willkommhöft,

admiring the gorgeous floral displays in Altes Land or watching the birds and seals on the North Sea and in the tidal mud flats of the Wattenmeer (Wadden Sea). Trips inland offer an agreeable change of pace from the bustling city centre. Most excursions can be made using public transport, but there is one special experience that is exclusive to automobile drivers: a drive over the Köhlbrandbrücke with its magnificent view of Hamburg's skyline.

Sights at a Glance

Museums and Galleries
- ⑤ Museum der Arbeit
- ⑦ Museumshafen Övelgönne

Parks and Green Spaces
- ② Tierpark Hagenbeck pp136–37
- ③ Stadtpark
- ④ Friedhof Ohlsdorf
- ⑧ Jenischpark

Modern Architecture
- ① HSV-Arena and HSV-Museum
- ⑥ Köhlbrandbrücke

Other Attractions
- ⑨ Altes Land
- ⑩ Blankenese
- ⑪ Willkomm-Höft
- ⑫ Hamburg Wadden Sea National Park pp140–41
- ⑬ Neuwerk

Key
- ▨ Hamburg city centre
- ✈ International airport
- Ⓡ Railway station
- ▬ Motorway
- ▬ Major road
- ═ Minor road
- — Railway

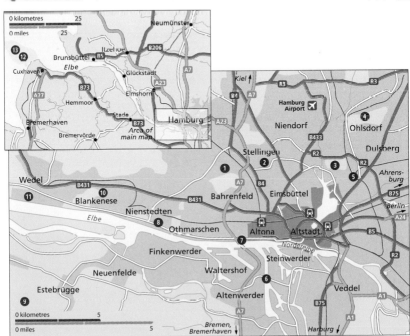

For map symbols see back flap

◀ The Museum der Arbeit, in a former boiler house, demonstrating change in an industrialized world (see p135)

The HSV-Arena, the home stadium of the Hamburg football club

❶ HSV-Arena and HSV-Museum

Sylvesterallee 7. **Tel** 41 55 15 50.
🚇 Stellingen. 🚌 22. 🕐 noon, 2pm, 4pm Mon – Fri, 10:30am, noon, 2pm, 4pm Sat, Sun (except on game days).
Museum: **Open** 10am – 6pm daily. 🚹
🚹 🚾 **imtech-arena.de hsv-museum.de**

The home stadium of HSV, the Hamburg football (soccer) club, has had many names. Originally it was called Volksparkstadion, since 2001 AOL Arena, since 2007 HSH Nordbank Arena, and since 2010 its official name is Imtech Arena. The stadium was the site of five games during the FIFA World Cup in 2006, including a quarter-final game. 2010 it hosted the UEFA Europa League Final.Not only is it one of Europe's most modern football stadiums, but it also has an interesting construction history.

Unlike the other FIFA World Cup stadiums, the arena wasn't built from scratch, but on the grounds of the Volksparkstadion, which was torn down in several stages starting in June 1998. The playing field was "rotated" and new stands were built. In August 2000, the last roof membrane was attached. All 57,000 seats (including a 10,000 person standing room section and 3,400 business-seats) are covered.

A 90-minute tour gives visitors a look inside the world of professional football. The HSV often plays to a full stadium, so book early for tickets to home games. From time to time the stadium also holds open-air concerts, featuring rock and pop stars, such as the Rolling Stones or Bruce Springsteen.

In 2004, the HSV-Museum opened here. Visitors can learn everything there is to know about the HSV, which was founded in 1887. Along with trophies, there are original shirts belonging to legendary HSV players.

❷ Tierpark Hagenbeck

See pp136 – 37.

❸ Stadtpark

Winterhude. 🚇 Saarlandstraße, Borgweg, Sierichstraße, Hudtwalckerstraße. 🚇 Alte Wöhr. 🚌 6, 20, 23, 25, 26.

With its large number of leisure activities, this is one of Hamburg's most beloved and largest parks. The city acquired the grounds of this former hunting preserve in 1902, and created the Stadtpark on an area of 150 ha (371 acres). There are sun-bathing meadows, a lake with boats for hire, an outdoor public pool, an open-air stage, a festival meadow, a beer garden, barbecues, restaurants, trails and football fields.

An architectural highlight within the park is the water tower (1912 – 15), which has been home to the **Planetarium** since 1930. The massive dome measures 21 m (69 ft) in diameter. Thanks to state-of-the-art computer software and simulation technology, this planetarium presents stunning 3-D shows. On the reclining seats, visitors can relax as they turn their attention from Earth to the stars. Special shows also take viewers deep inside the universe, focus on the Big Bang and the Earth's creation, or investigate cosmic collisions, making the science of astronomy a true adventure.

🏛 **Planetarium**
Hindenburgstraße 1b. **Tel** 42 88 65 20.
Open 10am – 5pm Mon, Tue, 10am – 9pm Wed, Thu, 10am – 9:30pm, Fri, noon – 9:30pm Sat, 10am – 8pm Sun. 🚹 🚹 🚹
🚾 **planetarium-hamburg.de**

❹ Friedhof Ohlsdorf

Fuhlsbüttler Straße 756. **Tel** 59 38 80.
🚇 Ohlsdorf. 🚇 Ohlsdorf. 🚌 39.
Open Apr – Oct: 8am – 9pm; Nov – Mar: 8am – 6pm.
🚾 **friedhof-hamburg.de/ohlsdorf**

Friedhof Ohlsdorf is one of the largest cemeteries in the world. With its impressive garden design and countless artfully sculpted grave stones, it is a place of international importance. Since it opened in 1877, some 1.4 million burials have taken place in the cemetery.

Many well-known people have been laid to rest in Friedhof Ohlsdorf, such as actors Hans Albers and Gustaf Gründgens, zoo founder Carl

The Stadtpark's planetarium, with its impressive dome

The Köhlbrandbrücke spanning the Elbe

Hagenbeck, shipbuilder Hermann Blohm and shipping magnate Albert Ballin. A stroll through this burial ground takes you back in time through Hamburg's history.

❺ Museum der Arbeit

Wiesendamm 3. **Tel** 428 13 30.
🅄 Barmbek. Ⓢ Barmbek. **Open** 1pm – 9am Mon, 10am – 5pm Tue – Sat, 10am – 6pm Sun. 🎨 🛗 🏛 🎦 🖵
🆆 **museum-der-arbeit.de**

Industrial history is featured in this excellent museum of work, which opened in 1997 in a former rubber factory. The central themes of the museum are the changes to the way people have lived and worked since the mid-19th-century. Whether printing plant, office, harbour or fish factory – you can learn about traditional Hamburg professions here. Great store is laid on lively presentation: visitors can set machines in motion and create things in various workshops.

A large collection on the history of tobacco, the Tabakhistorische Sammlung Reemtsma, displays everything to do with smoking. The exhibition covers four centuries of tobacco history, with displays that include tobacco pouches, pipes, advertising posters and cigarette packaging from around the world.

The Museum der Arbeit has two branches: the Speicherstadtmuseum (see p85), and the Hafenmuseum Hamburg (harbour museum), located at Australiastr., Kopfbau Schuppen 50A.

❻ Köhlbrandbrücke

5 km (3 miles) southwest of the city centre

Serving both as a landmark and a major traffic route, the 3.6-km (2.25-mile) long Köhlbrandbrücke was opened in 1974 after four years of construction. The bridge arches gracefully over the Köhlbrand channel, linking two parts of the Elbe – the Norderelbe and the Süderelbe. The four-lane highway on-ramps, supported by 75 pillars, lead to the cable-stayed bridge, with its two 135-m (443-ft)-high pylons.

The Köhlbrandbrücke is for use by motor vehicles exclusively; bicyclists and pedestrians are not allowed to cross it. Even at high tide, large ships can easily pass under this bridge, with its clearance of 53 m (174 ft).

❼ Museumshafen Övelgönne

Övelgönne, Anleger Neumühlen.
Map 1 A5. **Tel** 41 91 27 61.
🚌 36, 112. 🚢 62. **Open** daily.
🚢 by appointment.
🆆 **museumshafen-oevelgoenne.de**

Ferries sailing for Landungsbrücken or Finkenwerder stop at the Neumühlen ferry docks, where the Museumshafen Övelgönne (Övelgönne museum harbour) is located. Founded in 1977 by the "Vereinigung zur Erhaltung historischer Wasserfahrzeuge", an association dedicated to preserving historic ships and boats, the museum harbour survives without state subsidies; its work is supported only by membership fees and donations.

It is a magical draw for old-ship enthusiasts, with many to be admired from the dock here. There are German and Dutch flat-bottomed boats, the former lightship *Elfriede 3* (built in 1888), the lighter *Elfriede* (1904), the tugboats *Tiger* (1910) and *Claus D.* (1913), and even an icebreaker, the *Stettin* (1933). All these "old-timers" are still seaworthy. Some still make excursions – mainly on weekends – so it is best to view the boats during the week. When the owner or crew is present, you can often go on board for a peek below deck.

Hadag Ferry No. 62

If you want to see the Elbe shore from the water, the best way is to ride the HADAG ferry No. 62 (see also pp240–41). The ferry departs every 15 minutes from the Landungsbrücken (at pier 3) and, after a 28-minute journey, arrives at Finkenwerder on the south shore of the Elbe. There are several places where you can break up your journey and re-embark later: the ferry docks of Altona (below the Altonaer Balkon, see p117), Dockland (near the futuristic-looking office building of the same name, see p115), or Neumühlen (where the Museumshafen Övelgönne is located). Finally, the ferry crosses over to the opposite Elbe shore and lands at Finkenwerder. With luck, you will be able to see the Airbus planes that are built there taking off or landing. (www.hadag.de)

HADAG Ferry No. 62 – an ideal form of transport for visitors

❷ Tierpark Hagenbeck

Opened by Carl Hagenbeck in 1907, the world's first cageless menagerie revolutionized the way animals were kept in zoos. Today, it is owned by the sixth generation of Hagenbecks. Some 1,850 animals representing 210 species live in free outdoor enclosures spread across 25 ha (62 acres) of land. Especially notable is the zoo's elephant breeding programme. In 2007, the Tropical Aquarium was built; it contains more than 14,000 exotic animals from 300 species. The on-site Lindner Park-Hotel *(see p178)*, the world's first zoo-themed hotel, opened in 2009.

Japanese Island
Bronze statues, fountains and three ginkgo trees beautify this island. Flamingos live on the water here, too.

0 metres   100
0 yards   100

Key

① Nepalese Temple
② Tropical Aquarium
③ Elephant House
④ Elephants' Outdoor Enclosure
⑤ Orangutan House
⑥ Thailand Pavilion
⑦ Siberian Tigers
⑧ Leopards
⑨ Pink Pelicans
⑩ Japanese Island
⑪ Bird House
⑫ Hagenbeck's Old Training School
⑬ Humboldt Penguins
⑭ Polar Bears
⑮ Himalaya Tahr Cliffs
⑯ Lion Ravine
⑰ African Panorama
⑱ Pavilion
⑲ Kamtschatka Bears
⑳ Historic Jugendstil Entrance

GAZELLENKAMP

TIERPARKALLEE

HAGENBECKALLEE

Flamingo Lodge, open during the summer

Himalayan Tahr Cliffs
Himalayan tahrs, which are related to wild goats, live on an artificial cliff that has been under heritage protection since 1997.

Statue of Hagen-beck with a lion

African Panorama
Mainly Chilean and Cuban flamingos live on the large pond here. The lion ravine is an outdoor enclosure without any bars, surrounded by a wide moat.

Siberian Tigers

These tigers, who have produced several sets of offspring, are an example of the great success of the zoo's breeding programmes. In the wild, they are threatened with extinction.

VISITORS' CHECKLIST

Practical Information

Lokstedter Grenzstraße 2. **Tel** 530 03 30. **Open** Mar–Oct: 9am–6pm daily (July, Aug: to 7pm); Nov–Feb: 9am–4:30pm daily (box office closes one hour before). Tropen-Aquarium: **Open** 9am–6pm daily. **W hagenbeck.de**

Transport

U Hagenbecks Tierpark. 22, 39.

Year-round restaurant at the playground

⑧ ⑦ ⑨ ⑥ ⑤ ④ ③ ② ① ⑱ ⑲ ⑳

LOKSTEDTER GRENZSTRASSE

★ **Orangutan House**

Visitors love watching these large simians play and climb here. The house is covered by a glass dome that can be partly opened.

★ **Kamtschatka Bears**

Four of these brown bears have lived at the zoo since 2007. When they stand upright, they can loom as tall as 3.20 m (10.5 ft).

Location of the Lindner Park-Hotel Hagenbeck

Pink Pelicans

On land, these birds appear to be clumsy and slow. But when they take wing, they are elegant fliers. Since they are used to a warm climate, they winter in heated quarters.

Main entrance

★ **Tropical Aquarium**

Experience sharks here as well as land animals from the tropics and sub-tropics.

❽ Jenischpark

Othmarschen. ⑤ Klein Flottbek.
🚌 15, 21, 36, 39.

North of the Elbchaussee, in the
Othmarschen quarter of Altona,
is the Jenischpark, which
stretches over 42 ha (104 acres)
of land. It is considered to be
one of the most outstanding
examples of an English landscape garden in Northern
Germany. This beautiful park,
with its giant old maples, oaks
and chestnut trees, was
designed in 1797 for the
merchant Johann Caspar
Voght. Afterwards, it became
the property of the merchant
and, later, Senator, Martin
Johann von Jenisch.

Jenisch commissioned architect Karl Friedrich Schinkel to
draw up plans for a Neo-
Classical villa to be built on
the highest spot in the park.
Completed in 1831 – 34, it is
today known as Jenisch Haus.
As a branch museum of the
Altonaer Museum, it displays
artworks and applied arts. The
various periods are displayed in
an interesting fashion: the Neo-
Classical rooms on the ground
floor are decorated with
furniture and paintings made
during the time the house was
created. The rooms on the first
floor are decorated with
Baroque, Rococo and
Biedermeier furnishings. The
second floor is reserved for an
exhibit on painting, drawing,
garden design and architecture.

Nearby is Ernst Barlach Haus,
which opened in 1962 as the
first private museum in the
Hanseatic city, thanks to the
financial support of the tobacco
company's Hermann
F. Reemtsma Foundation. The
museum displays a collection of
lithographs, bronzes and
ceramics by the North German
artist Ernst Barlach (1870–1938).

🏛 **Jenisch Haus**
Baron-Voght-Straße 50. **Tel** 82 87 90.
Open 11am–6pm Tue–Sun. 🖼 🖥
♿ limited. 🆆 **jenischhaus.org**

🏛 **Ernst Barlach Haus**
Baron-Voght-Straße 50a. **Tel** 82 60 85.
Open 11am–6pm Tue–Sun. 🖼 📷
🆆 **barlach-haus.de**

Ernst Barlach Haus in Jenischpark

❾ Altes Land

Südwestl. von Hamburg. **Tel** (04142)
81 38 38. ⑤ Neugraben, then bus.
📧 🆆 **tourismusverband-stade.de**
or **tourismus-altesland.de**

The Altes Land (old country) is
the largest continuous fruit-
growing district in central
Europe, with over 4,000 ha (3,500
acres) of orchards. This fertile
marshland is located on the
south side of the Elbe, just
outside the gates of Hamburg,
and stretches between Stade and
Buxtehude. About three quarters
of the Altes Land is planted with
apple trees; especially high yields
are given by the Gravenstein,
Jonagold, Holstein Cox and Elstar
varieties. Cherry and pear trees
are also cultivated.

The area was settled as early as
the 12th and 13th centuries by
the Dutch, who made it arable
and erected dikes to protect the
cultivated areas. The Altes Land is
a popular destination, especially
in spring, when the entire region
is a sea of blossoms. But also in
summer this is an ideal area for
enjoying long hikes and cycling
trips. During the autumn harvest,
the area bustles with activity.
The Museum Altes Land in Jork
shows how the Altes Land

Jenisch Haus, standing at the highest point
in the park

developed. On summer
weekends, HADAG boats *(see
p240)* bring sightseers here from
the Landungsbrücken. The Lühe-
Schulau ferries sail year-round
between Willkomm-Höft and
Lüheanleger, a gateway to the
Altes Land.

🏛 **Museum Altes Land**
Jork, Westerjork 49. **Tel** (04162) 57 15.
Open Apr – Oct: 11am – 5pm
Tue – Sun; Nov – Mar: 1 – 4pm Wed,
Sat, Sun. 🖼

❿ Blankenese

⑤ Blankenese. 🚌 1, 22, 36, 48, 49.

Hamburg's most elegant
suburb started off as a small
fishing village and was once
considered a great distance
from the gates of the city. For a
long time, it was an important
stop for ferries. Well into the
18th century, residents of
Blankenese lived mainly from
seafaring and fishing. Then,
wealthy Hamburg merchants
discovered this idyllic village
and built imposing country
houses here. Not much has
changed in this respect:
Blankenese is still an affluent
area to this day.

A walk through the Trep-
penviertel (stair district) is
especially interesting. This district
is a chaotic mix of stairways and
alleyways located between
Strandweg along the Elbe shore
and Am Kiekeberg, a road that
runs along the cliffside. Your
efforts at climbing the stairs are
rewarded by a superb view over
the Elbe river and the opposite
shore. Carefully tended parks
such as Goßlers Park, Hessepark
and Baurs Park are also lovely
places for a stroll.

⓫ Willkomm-Höft

Wedel, Parnaßstraße 29, Schulauer
Fährhaus. **Tel** (04103) 920 00. Ⓢ
Wedel. 🚌 189. **Open** 8am to sunset
daily (at the latest 8pm). Museum:
Open Mar–Oct: 10am–6:30pm daily;
Nov–Feb: 10am–6pm Sat, Sun. 🎨
🔲 🖥 9:30am–10pm.
W **schulauer-faehrhaus.de**

Every ship that sails into the
port of Hamburg or leaves the
Hanseatic city via the Elbe river
has to pass by Willkomm Höft
(Welcome Point), a battery of
loudspeakers belonging to the
city of Wedel in Holstein. The
system began operation in
1952. It is located on the shore
of the Elbe on the grounds of
the Schulauer Fährhaus, a popular sightseeing destination
with a café and restaurant.

Loudspeakers greet or bid
farewell to every passing ship
that registers over 1000 gross
tons. They're greeted in the
ship's national language,
followed by a rendition of their
national anthem. More than
150 anthems are stored on the
hard drive of the computer-
controlled system.

The Ships Reporting
Service provides visitors to
the Schulauer Fährhaus with
information on the routes and
cargo of the ships which have
just been welcomed or given
a farewell.

The best views of the passing
ships can be enjoyed from the
huge terrace of the restaurant
and café located in the
Schulauer Fährhaus. From April
to October the bar on the
beach is also a nice place to sit

and watch. The Sunday
brunch at the
restaurant (from
9:30am) is very popular.

In the basement of
the Schulauer Fährhaus,
a model ship museum
displayed more than
200 different model
ships in bottles until it
closed down in 2012.
The museum's exhibits
have all been sold.

The sea shell
museum, which had
also been affiliated with
the Schulauer Fähraus,
also closed its doors for
good recently. It used
to display over 1000
sea and snail shells
from oceans across
the globe.

A house in the elegant Blankenese district

⓬ Nationalpark Hamburgisches Wattenmeer

See pp140–41.

⓭ Neuwerk

110 km (68 miles) northwest of
Hamburg 🚢 from Cuxhaven
W **neuwerk-insel.de**

This small North Sea island is
part of the Free and Hanseatic
City of Hamburg. At low tide it
can be reached from Cuxhaven
by walking over the mud flats;
you can also get there on
horseback or in a horse-drawn
carriage with **Wattwagenfahren
Werner Stelling**. Just be sure to
keep an eye on the tides! At
high tide, it is accessible by

boat. The island's landmark is its
substantial lighthouse. It dates
back to the early 14th century,
when it was a fortified tower
protecting the mouth of the
Elbe from North Sea pirates.

A walk around the island on
the main dike takes about an
hour. A section of Neuwerk is a
designated bird refuge. If you
would like to stay overnight on
the island and wait for the next
low tide, there are a variety of
guest rooms available.

🚢 **Reederei Cassen Eils**
Cuxhaven, Bei der Alten Liebe 12
Tel 0180 522 86 61
W **cassen-eils.de/neuwerk**

Wattwagenfahrten Werner Stelling
Tel (04721) 297 26.
Cuxhaven, Swiensweg 1.
W **wattwagen-cux.de**

Willkomm-Höft with its battery of loudspeakers to greet huge vessels from around the world

⑫ Hamburg Wadden Sea National Park

In 1990, this park (the Nationalpark Hamburgisches Wattenmeer) was created to protect the Wadden Sea west of the mouth of the Elbe. The area, which covers 137 sq km (53 sq miles), encompasses several islands and vast tidal mud flats; 97 per cent of it is under water. Many animals call this park home: seabirds find ideal breeding grounds, and countless migratory birds pause here on their journey. Harbour seals and grey seals feel right at home, too. Favourite activities in this area are walking on the tide flats, bird-watching and viewing seals from the banks. The national park was declared a World Heritage Site by UNESCO in 2011. There is one bathing beach and several boat docks.

★ Wagon Ride
Riding in a horse-drawn wagon on the islands in the national park is both an ideal method of transport and a wonderful experience. Riding is possible when the tide goes out and the mud flats start to dry.

NIGEHÖRN

SCHARÖRNLOCH

NORDERTILL

WITTSANDLOCH

HAMBURG
WADDEN SEA
NATIONAL PARK

Oystercatchers
One of the common birds on the North Sea Coast is the oystercatcher. Adults have long, bright-red beaks.

Salt Marshes
The Wadden Sea is a unique environment. In the marshes between the mainland and the sea, the soil's salt content is high, and salt-tolerant plants have rooted here. These salt marshes are an important breeding ground for many types of birds.

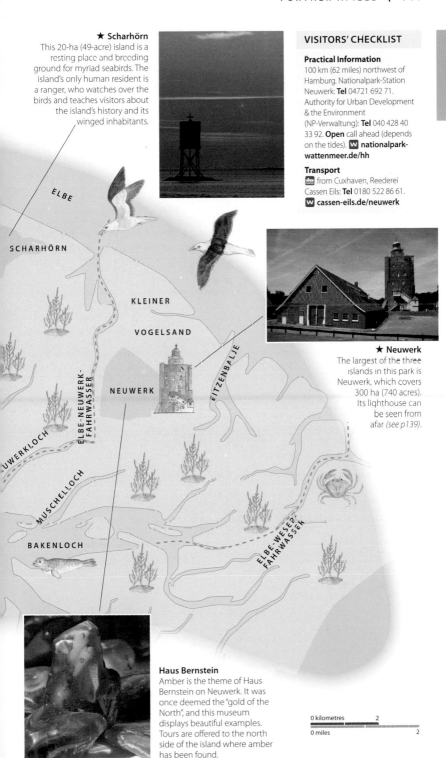

★ Scharhörn
This 20-ha (49-acre) island is a resting place and breeding ground for myriad seabirds. The island's only human resident is a ranger, who watches over the birds and teaches visitors about the island's history and its winged inhabitants.

VISITORS' CHECKLIST

Practical Information
100 km (62 miles) northwest of Hamburg. Nationalpark-Station Neuwerk: **Tel** 04721 692 71. Authority for Urban Development & the Environment (NP-Verwaltung): **Tel** 040 428 40 33 92. **Open** call ahead (depends on the tides). **W** nationalpark-wattenmeer.de/hh

Transport
from Cuxhaven, Reederei Cassen Eils: **Tel** 0180 522 86 61. **W** cassen-eils.de/neuwerk

★ Neuwerk
The largest of the three islands in this park is Neuwerk, which covers 300 ha (740 acres). Its lighthouse can be seen from afar (see p139).

ELBE

SCHARHÖRN

KLEINER

VOGELSAND

ELBE-NEUWERK-FAHRWASSER

NEUWERK

FITZENBALJE

UWERKLOCH

MUSCHELLOCH

BAKENLOCH

ELBE-WESER-FAHRWASSER

Haus Bernstein
Amber is the theme of Haus Bernstein on Neuwerk. It was once deemed the "gold of the North", and this museum displays beautiful examples. Tours are offered to the north side of the island where amber has been found.

0 kilometres   2
0 miles   2

THREE GUIDED WALKS

Hamburg is an excellent city for walking, since most of its attractions lie close to one another. Several city passages and shopping streets, as well as the harbour promenade, are reserved for pedestrians. Hamburg's many parks and green spaces offer a welcome respite from the bustle of the city centre, and many stretches along the Elbe shore are pedestrianized. The walks suggested in this chapter take you on routes of discovery through very different parts of the city.

The first walking route runs through the Old Town, which is criss-crossed by many canals, taking you from the Hamburg Rathaus through the Kontorhausviertel to Deichstraße. The distinctive buildings that are found here chronicle the various eras of the city's history – from its origins right up until the 21st century.

The second walk takes you east along the harbour promenade, starting at the Landungsbrücken and on past the Speicherstadt to HafenCity. The contrast – contemporary architecture is fascinating. In HafenCity, you can see clearly how dynamically the Hanseatic city is evolving.

The third walking route takes you from the Landungsbrücken on the Elbe's shore west to Altona. Many spots along the way offer an intriguing view over the portlands. All the walk routes start and end within easy reach of public transport. For each walk, suggestions are made for perfect places to take a break.

CHOOSING A WALK

The Three Walks
The map shows the location and routes of the three guided walks in relation to the main sightseeing areas in Hamburg.

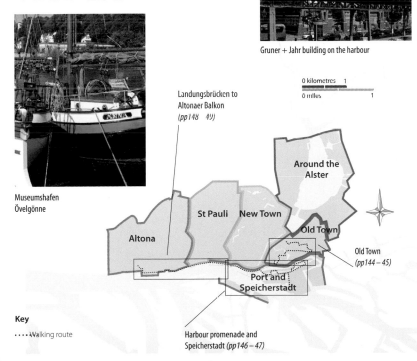

Gruner + Jahr building on the harbour

Museumshafen
Övelgönne

Landungsbrücken to
Altonaer Balkon
(pp148–49)

0 kilometres 1

0 miles 1

Around the
Alster

St Pauli New Town

Old Town

Altona

Old Town
(pp144–45)

Port and
Speicherstadt

Key

···· Walking route

Harbour promenade and
Speicherstadt *(pp146–47)*

◀ Small fountain on the Neo-Gothic Köhlbrandtreppe *(see p149)* from 1887

A Two-Hour Walk in the Old Town

Although many of its buildings were razed in the Great Fire of 1842 or destroyed in World War II, a walk through the Old Town allows you to trace the history of Hamburg back to its beginnings. A more recent chapter in the city's history is evidenced by the Kontorhausviertel, out of which Hamburg grew to become an economic centre from the 1920s onward. The Old Town gets its ambience from many of the city's most striking ecclesiastical buildings, as well as several publishing houses, and the remaining canals and modern commercial streets which are partly pedestrianized.

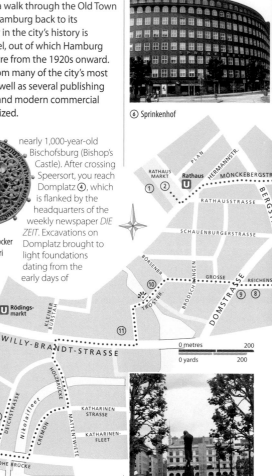
⑥ Sprinkenhof

Rathaus to Kontorhausviertel

Dating from 1897, the Hamburg Rathaus (city hall) ①, with its 112-m (367-ft) high tower, impresses not only with its sheer size but also its opulently decorated façade, which includes several statues of emperors. At first glance, this splendour might not seem typical of the utilitarian architecture more usually found in Hamburg. However, due to its important role as the seat of parliament and Senate, Hamburg's citizens loosened their purse-strings. Rathausmarkt ② is an imposing square; its builders took inspiration from St Mark's Square in Venice.

Leave the Rathausmarkt via Mönckebergstraße, Hamburg's main shopping street, which leads east. After about 200 m (660 ft), turn right into Kreuslerstraße, where the entrance to the church of St Petri ③ is located. In the basement of the parish house, there is a showroom displaying foundations of the

③ Door knocker on St Petri

nearly 1,000-year-old Bischofsburg (Bishop's Castle). After crossing Speersort, you reach Domplatz ④, which is flanked by the headquarters of the weekly newspaper *DIE ZEIT*. Excavations on Domplatz brought to light foundations dating from the early days of

Hamburg's history. Follow Speersort east, where it turns . into the Steinstraße. Soon you will reach a courtyard, Jacobi-kirchhof, which surrounds the church of St Jacobi ⑤.

Across from the church, leading off from Steinstraße, is Mohlen-hofstraße. Walk south along it and you will come to Burchardplatz. This square is at the heart of the Kontorhausviertel, an architect-urally impressive office building quarter from the 1920s. The largest of these office buildings, with their red-brick façades, is Sprinkenhof ⑥ on the east side

④ The headquarters of *DIE ZEIT*

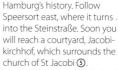
② Rathausmarkt with the Alster Arcades in the background

of Burchardplatz. Terracotta orna-ments decorated with symbols of trade and industry embellish its façade. A bit more conspic-uous due to its angular shape is Chilehaus ⑦, opposite Sprinken-hof. It was built in 1922–24 by Fritz Höger and is considered to be a groundbreaking example of red-brick Expressionism.

Kontorhausviertel to Rödingsmarkt

Walk east around the "prow" side of Chilehaus and follow Pumpen street west. As it continues, the street changes its name several times. Just before it meets Domstraße – at this point it is called Große Reichenstraße – you will see Afrikahaus ⑧ at No. 27 on the left side of the street. This building was commissioned by the shipping company Woermann and built in 1899. It marries utilitarianism

⑧ Entrance to Afrikahaus

with a showy façade. Among the striking African-themed decorations is the figure of a warrior at the entrance, as well as two cast-iron elephants and a palm mosaic in the inner courtyard.

The contrast between old and new architecture can be seen most clearly when you turn left into Domstraße and pass by Zürichhaus ⑨. This building, erected in 1989–92, continues the Hamburg office-building tradition but, with its red brick, steel and glass exterior, also represents a style that began in the early 1990s, and is typical for newer office building design.

Cross Domstraße and return to Große Reichenstraße. After a short walk, turn left onto the bridge, the Trostbrücke ⑩. The first bridge to be built here was mentioned in 1266. It linked the town of the bishopric around Hammaburg castle with the new merchant town. Statues of the founders – Bishop Ansgar of Hamburg and Bremen as well as Duke Adolf III of Schauenburg – flank the bridge. Follow the short street Neue Burg, then turn right into Willy-Brandt-Straße. Here, the ruins of St Nikolai church ⑪, destroyed in World War II, have been

preserved as a memorial – the Mahnmal St. Nikolai.

After continuing for about 150 m (492 ft), turn left onto the Holzbrücke, a bridge, and cross over Nikolaifleet. Then turn right into Cremon, a street lined with several old warehouses. At the end of this street, keep to the right and cross over the Nikolaifleet again and turn right into Deichstraße ⑫, which provides a very good idea of how old Hamburg once looked. Plaques on the exteriors of the buildings provide information about the rich history of some of the houses here.

Deichstraße leads into Willy-Brandt-Straße, which takes you west towards Rödingsmarkt street. From here, you can return back to your starting-point on U-Bahn line No. 3.

⑩ View from the Trostbrücke

Statue on Mönckebergstraße

Key

• • • Walking route

⧗ Viewpoint

Ⓤ U-Bahn station

⑪ St Nikolai Memorial

Tips for Walkers

Starting point: Rathaus.
Length: 3 km (2 miles).
Duration: 2 hours.
Getting there: U-Bahn line 3.
St Petri: Open 10am–6:30pm Mon–Fri (to 7pm Wed), 10am–5pm Sat, 9am–9pm Sun *(see p58)*.
St Jacobi: Open Apr–Sep: 10am–5pm Mon–Sat; Oct–Mar: 11am–5pm Mon–Sat *(see p62)*.
St. Nikolai: Open 10am–6pm daily *(see p66)*.
Stopping-off points: There are a large number of restaurants in the Old Town. Some of the most popular ones are located in the Deichstraße, including the Kartoffelkeller (No. 21), Zum Brandanfang (No. 25), and an eel restaurant, Alt Hamburger Aalspeicher (No. 43, *see p188*).

A Three-Hour Harbour and Speicherstadt Walk

Each visitor to this Hanseatic city comes to the Landungsbrücken at least once. It is not only the unique atmosphere and the wonderful water views that draw people here, but also the many museum ships. Speicherstadt, a giant warehouse complex, embodies more than 100 years of port and trading history. Carpets, coffee, tea, and cocoa and other trading goods are still stored behind the red-brick exteriors. Recently, however, Speicherstadt has been undergoing a huge change due to the reduced demand for storage space. Museums, and even a theatre, have moved into former warehouses. South of Speicherstadt a whole new city district – HafenCity – is being built.

① Accordion player at the Landungsbrücken

Landungsbrücken to Kehrwiederspitze

Starting at the Landungs-brücken ①, walk east along the broad promenade at the water's edge. As you stroll by the accordion players singing chanties, and captains touting round-trip excursions on their boats, you experience the typical harbour flair. The 97-m (318-ft) long, three-master *Rickmer Rickmers* ②, built in

1896, has been anchored here as a museum ship since 1987.

A tide-marker on the shore shows how high the Elbe reached during the devastating flood of 1962. A bit further east, you can visit the 160-m (525-ft) long freighter *Cap San Diego* ③, which was brought back to Hamburg's port in 1986. A little further still and you reach a lightship ④, anchored since 1993 in Hamburg's City-Sporthafen. On the other side

of the street is the headquarters of publisher Gruner + Jahr ⑤, with its four main sections facing the Elbe, looking like a gigantic steamship. Behind Baumwall U-Bahn station you will see Slomanhaus ⑥ on the left.

Tips for Walkers

Starting point: S- and U-Bahn station Landungsbrücken.
Length: 5 km (3 miles).
Duration: 3 hours.
Getting there: S-Bahn 1, 3, U-Bahn 3.
Rickmer Rickmers: Open 10am – 6pm daily (see pp94 – 5).
Cap San Diego: Open 10am – 6pm daily (see pp98 – 9).
Hamburg Dungeon: Open 10am – 6pm daily (Jul – Aug: 10am – 7pm) (see p85).
Miniatur Wunderland: Open 9:30am – 6pm Mon – Fri (to 9pm Tue, to 7pm Fri), 8am – 9pm Sat, 8:30am – 8pm Sun (see p84).
Stopping-off points: Cafés at the Landungsbrücken, one in the coffee roasting house and a bistro in HafenCity InfoCenter.

① The Landungsbrücken, seen from the floating quays

⑱ View Point, offering the best view of the port

whose treasures can be viewed, there is a place to buy Persian goods. On the opposite side of the street is the most northerly row of buildings in HafenCity (see pp90–91). Walk back a short way along Sandtorkai, turn right, and cross over the canal, Kehrwiederfleet, via Kehrwiedersteg. Keep right and you will reach Theater Kehrwieder ⑨,

where musical entertainment, variety theatre, and plays are part of the regular programme. A few steps further along is a coffee roasting house, where coffee from around the world, from Costa Rica to Ethiopia to Indonesia, is wrapped up in sacks. Attached to the roasting house is a museum featuring everything to do with coffee. This warehouse also is home to Miniatur Wunderland ⑩ and Hamburg Dungeon ⑪; long lines often form in front of these two attractions. At the end of the building, turn left and cross the canal Brooksfleet on the bridge Auf dem Sande. On the corner of Am Sandtorkai is an old boiler house which houses the Hafen-City InfoCenter ⑫; the entrance is in the back. Here you'll find a scale model of the city and all sorts of information about the HafenCity project.

Walk a short distance west. On the first floor of Am Sandtorkai 32 is the Afghanisches Museum (Afghan museum) ⑬ and on the second floor Spicy's Gewürzmuseum ⑭ – the spice

museum. Now walk east along Sandtorkai. After about 0.5 km (0.3 miles) keep to the left, walk over the Neuerwegsbrücke, and then turn right. Here you pass by the Speicherstadtmuseum ⑮, located at St. Annenufer. Behind this museum, first turn left into the street Bei St. Annen and then right into Alter Wandrahm. The Deutsches Zollmuseum (German customs museum) ⑯ is at No. 16. At No. 4 you can experience "Dialog im Dunkeln" ("Dialogue in the Dark") ⑰.

Speicherstadt to HafenCity
Continue walking south along Poggenmühle street, then turn right into Brooktorkai and keep going along this street – past more warehouses – until you come to Große Grasbrook. Turn left here and walk to View Point ⑱. Along the way, you will get an impression of the tremendous upheaval this section of Hamburg is undergoing. From the View Point observation platform there is a fantastic view over the HafenCity construction site, the Kreuzfahrtterminal (Cruise Center) ⑲, the Speicherstadt and the Elbe.

Return by first taking MetroBus No. 3, 4 or 6 from the Marco-Polo-Terrassen stop to the Rathaus and then U-Bahn line 3 back to the Landungsbrücken, or walk to Überseequartier station and take U4 to Jungfernstieg to get on either the S1 or S3 line.

This office building, constructed in 1908–09, is the headquarters of Reederei Sloman, a shipping company. Now turn right and cross over a bridge, the Niederbaumbrücke. You are nearing Kehrwiederspitze ⑦ at the entrance to Speicherstadt.

Speicherstadt
Once you have passed Kehrwiederspitze, keep walking south. Turn left into the street called Am Sandtorkai, which is at first lined with buildings that belong to the Hanseatic Trade Center complex. Awaiting you behind Kehrwiedersteg, in Persienhaus ⑧ on Sandtorkai, is something exotic: along with a carpet warehouse,

Key
• • • Walking route

🔆 Viewpoint

U U-Bahn station

S S-Bahn station

⑫ The frequently updated scale model in HafenCity InfoCenter

A Two-Hour Walk to Altonaer Balkon

This walking route ambles west along the Elbe river. It starts at the Landungsbrücken and continues on to the Fischmarkt (fish market) – a magnet for night owls and tourists – then on to Altona and the Altonaer Balkon. Along the way are many vantage points offering some of Hamburg's most beautiful and panoramic views. You also will discover the latest changes to the area, as construction along the Elbe shore is proceeding apace. Here – and at HafenCity further east – you will see at first hand the impressive architectural growth of the city.

④ Fish Auction Hall (Fischauktionshalle)

⑤ Stadtlagerhaus – a warehouse topped by a modern glass cube

entrance, continue along the Hafenstraße to the St Pauli Fischmarkt ③. On Sunday mornings the crowds are huge, but at other times of the week you can enjoy the view of the water in peace and quiet. Here, Pepermölenbek street leads off to the north; it once marked the boundary between Altona and Hamburg. On the left side of Große Elbstraße is the Fish Auction Hall (Fischauktionshalle) ④ built in 1896. The U-boat

U-434 moored in front of it is now a museum.

Recently, Große Elbstraße has been undergoing massive reconstruction. In accordance with the city fathers' wishes, city planners are designing a promenade with a nautical flair here. To this end, old industrial buildings and warehouses are being turned into exclusive apartment buildings, shopping centres and company headquarters. Warehouses are

Landungsbrücken to Köhlbrandtreppe

Starting from the S-Bahn and U-Bahn station Landungsbrücken, walk west past the striking domed passenger halls serving the Landungsbrücken ① and past the entrance to the Alter Elbtunnel ② (old Elbe tunnel), a walking and cycling tunnel to the south shore of the river. Once you have passed the tunnel

Key

••• Walking route

☆ Viewpoint

Ⓤ U-Bahn station

Ⓢ S-Bahn station

The once embattled Hafenstraße in St Pauli, declaring "No man is illegal"

being expanded and modernized, or completely rebuilt in the process. The rebuilding of the quays of this former lumber port began with Stadtlagerhaus (No. 27) ⑤, an old storehouse. A multi-storey glass cube was set on top of this building between 1998 and 2001. It is one of the architectural pearls along the Elbe shore, receiving design praise.

The seven-storey stilwerk ⑥ suits the newly conceived Große Elbstraße. Opened in 1996, this shopping centre is known for stocking home furnishings and home decor in a red-brick building dating from 1910.

In stilwerk's lobby there are occasional exhibitions presenting the latest home-decorating trends.

After walking a bit further along, it is worth looking to your right to admire the Neo-Gothic stairway – the Köhlbrand-treppe ⑦ with its small fountains, constructed in 1887. Here, too, is the famous Haifischbar ⑧ (*see p193*), a bar steeped in tradition, whose decorations still include ships-in-bottles, dusty ships' models and old photographs of Hamburg entertainment greats such as Hans Albers, Heidi Kabel and Freddy Quinn. In recent years, the pub has faced increasing competition from modern bars and restaurants.

③ **Figure on a fountain at Fischmarkt**

Center in HafenCity. West of here is Dockland ⑩, an office building in the shape of a parallelogram with its bow jutting out over the water. From the observation deck of this building visitors enjoy great harbour view. The cruise terminal and Dockland are important links in the "pearl necklace", as the city planners like to call the row of modern buildings that are continually being constructed along the Elbe shore.

Turn right into Elbberg street which leads up to the Altonaer Balkon ⑪ (Altona balcony) located above the Große Elbstraße and parallel to the Elbe river. This terrace offers the loveliest view in Hamburg of much

⑧ Relaxing at the Haifischbar

To return to the beginning of the walk and your starting point on the Elbe shore, take the S-Bahn (lines 1, 3, 11 or 31) from Bahnhof Altona (Altona station). To get to the station, turn north, cross over Klopstockstraße, walk past the Rathaus Altona (city hall), the Platz der Republik and continue straight ahead to the station.

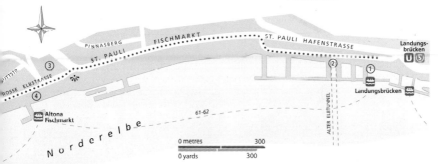

Altona Fischmarkt · PINNASBERG · FISCHMARKT · ST. PAULI · ST. PAULI HAFENSTRASSE · Landungsbrücken · GROSSE ELBSTRASSE · WITTSTR · ALTER ELBTUNNEL · 61-62 · Norderelbe

0 metres 300
0 yards 300

Köhlbrandtreppe to Altonaer Balkon

Continuing along the shore of the Elbe river to the west, you reach the cruise terminal (Kreuzfahrtterminal) Altona ⑨, that opened in 2011. Occasionally, luxury liners call at this terminal. This new terminal supports the Hamburg Cruise

of the portlands and the Köhlbrandbrücke. The Elbuferweg, a path along the Elbe, starts here on this green space with its wonderful panoramic view. You can walk or cycle along the water all the way to Museumshafen Övelgönne and further west to Blankenese, without being disturbed by cars.

Tips for Walkers

Starting point: S-Bahn and U-Bahn station Landungsbrücken.
Length: 3 km (1 mile).
Duration: 2 hours.
Getting there: S-Bahn 1 or 3, U-Bahn 3.
Stopping-off points: There are a lot of restaurants along the route, some with terraces directly on the Elbe shore. Among the best-known restaurants are Lutter & Wegner (Große Elbstraße 49, *see p191*), Au Quai (Große Elbstraße 145b – d, *see p191*) and the Riverkasematten (Fischmarkt 28 – 32). Hearty Hanseatic fare is served in the restaurant Haifischbar (Große Elbstraße 128, *see p190*).

⑩ Dockland office building, shaped like a ship's prow

Pavilion on the beach promenade in Borkum (*see p160*) ▶

BEYOND HAMBURG

Sylt   156–157

North Frisian Islands   158

Helgoland   159

East Frisian Islands   160–161

Kiel Canal   161

Bremen   162–167

Museumsdorf
   Cloppenburg   168–169

BEYOND HAMBURG

For those wanting to venture beyond the city, there are plenty of enticing getaways. The Free and Hanseatic City of Hamburg is bordered by Lower Saxony and Schleswig-Holstein; both provinces offer a host of attractions for day trips or excursions lasting several days. Among the most fascinating destinations are the North and East Frisian Islands. The city-state of Bremen also has much to offer.

Nature-lovers and water-sports fans are drawn to the North Sea coast. Unique flora and fauna can be found in the two parks that line it – the Wadden Sea National Park of Lower Saxony and the Wadden Sea National Park of Schleswig-Holstein. Both are parts of the region Wadden Sea that was declared a World Heritage Site by UNESCO in 2009. The Frisian Islands are known for their beaches and sand dunes. Watersports fans love it here, and on sunny days wicker beach chairs stretch as far as the eye can see. Some of the islands are car-free, allowing visitors to enjoy nature at its best on foot, by bicycle, or in a horse-drawn carriage.

One of the special attractions of this land within the-sea is walking on the Watt, as the tidal flats of the Wadden Sea are known locally. Walks are best undertaken with a guide, who will explain the unique and fascinating Wadden Sea environment.

Those who yearn for a more action-filled getaway can journey to the Island of Sylt, which is known for its parties and visiting celebrities. In the evenings you can plunge into the nightlife scene, while days can be spent relaxing or embarking on some upscale shopping.

The architecture of the Old Town of Bremen with its Weser Renaissance buildings, is fascinating. Its Rathaus and Roland statue were declared a World Heritage Site in 2004.

Alternatively, you can visit Museumsdorf Cloppenburg and learn about the hard lives of farmers. Or to keep with a nautical theme, visit the Kiel Canal. Every year some 40,000 large ships sail by on it, almost close enough to touch. The canal links the North Sea with the Baltic Sea.

The East Frisian Islands with their sand dunes under an endless sky *(see p160 – 61)*

◀ Lighthouse and thatched house on Sylt *(see pp 156 – 57)*

Exploring Beyond Hamburg

With so many attractions in the surrounding area, Hamburg is a perfect jumping-off point for excursions to places such as the North Sea islands or Bremen. The bucolic charms of the North and East Frisian Islands are a pleasing contrast to urban Hamburg. Along with tidal flats, beaches and water sports, the islands also offer a wide range of spas and wellness resorts – just the right thing for a relaxing getaway. Bremen's city centre is of interest for its lovely Renaissance buildings; the port of Bremerhaven on the Weser river has a completely different character to the port of Hamburg. Museumsdorf Cloppenburg, a museum village, documents the hard existence of farmers in earlier times.

The Bremer Town Musicians – a symbol of this Hanseatic city

Sunset above the Wadden Sea (Wattenmeer)

Sights at a Glance

❶ Sylt
❷ North Frisian Islands
  Amrum
  Föhr
  Halligen
  Nordstrand
  Pellworm
❸ Helgoland
❹ East Frisian Islands
  Baltrum
  Borkum
  Juist
  Langeoog
  Norderney
  Spiekeroog
  Wangerooge
❺ Kiel Canal
❻ Bremen
❼ Museumsdorf Cloppenburg

For additional map symbols see back flap

The northern beach on the East Frisian Island of Borkum

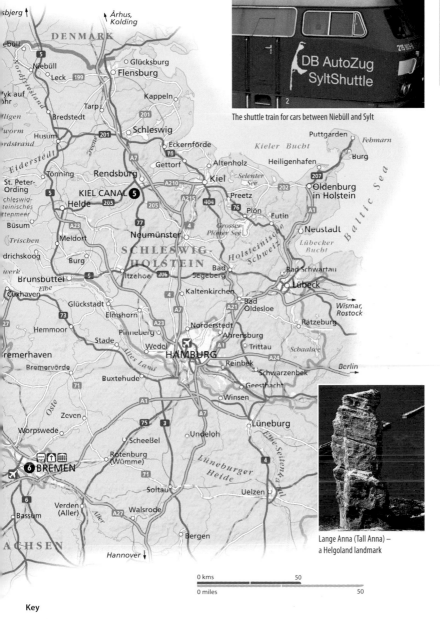

The shuttle train for cars between Niebüll and Sylt

Lange Anna (Tall Anna) –
a Helgoland landmark

0 kms   50

0 miles   50

Key

━━ Motorway

━ Major road

═ ═ Secondary road

┄ Railway

⋯ Ferry route

━ State border

━━ National border

🔻 National park

Getting Around

The easiest way to explore the area beyond Hamburg is by car. Motorway A1 leads from Hamburg to Bremen. To reach the East Frisian Islands you continue through Bremen or Oldenburg. The North Frisian Islands are reached by motorway A23, followed by the well-built country highways. Ferries depart for the individual islands from the coast. Motorway A7 leads from Hamburg to Kiel. There is also regular train service. Many North Sea islands are car free.

① Sylt

Sylt is the largest of the North Frisian Islands *(see p158)*, covering an area of 99 sq km (38 sq miles). Since 1927, it has been linked with the mainland by the Hindenburgdamm, a causeway reserved solely for train traffic. The fine sand beaches of Sylt are renowned, and on lovely summer days more than 12,000 wicker beach chairs are set up for visitors. The island's main town, Westerland, offers a wide range of activities year-round. There's dining and shopping, spas and nightlife, beach saunas and art previews, beach parties and New Year's Eve galas. Westerland's motto is "see and be seen", but the island's other towns also have their charms. Sylt is a paradise for watersport lovers.

★ Dune Landscape
Long stretches of dunes are typical of the Sylt landscape. Some of these "hills of sand" are overgrown with plants, including protected species.

★ Red Cliffs
These 30-m (100-ft) high cliffs (Rotes Kliff) between Wenningstedt and Kampen owe their red colour to oxidized iron particles. The cliffs are an island landmark and a navigation aid for sailors.

★ Westerland
A lively town encircled by beautiful nature, Westerland is the heart and soul of Sylt. Those who holiday here combine nights of parties with relaxation in the Syltness-Center.

Sandy Beaches
Beach chairs as far as the eye can see are a typical feature.

Leuchtturm Westerellenbogen
ELLENBOGEN
Leuchtturm Osterellenbo
MÖVENBERG
SANDBERG
LIST-LAND
List
Mellhörn
Westerheide
Süderheidetal
Klappholttal
Vogelkoje
Blidsel-bucht
ROTES KLIFF
Kampen (Sylt)
Wenningstedt (Sylt)
Braderup
Munkmarsch
SYLTER WELLE
Regional-flughafen Westerland/Sylt
WESTERLAND
Keitum (Sylt)
Tinnum (Sylt)
Archsum
MORSUMK
MUNKH
Morsum
Osterende
RANTUM-BECKEN
Vogelkoje
Rantum (Sylt)
Vogelkoje
Puan Klent
Hörnum (Sylt)
Lister Landtief
Lister Ley
Pandertief
Helgoland

The Wadden Sea (Wattenmeer) – UNESCO World Heritage Site since 2009 – is ruled by the rhythm of the tides. Walks along the flats at low tide are popular.

NP Schleswig-Holsteinisches Wattenmeer

Wester Ley

Rømø/ Havneby

Højero

MARGRETHE-KOOG

DENMARK

RICKELS-BÜLLER KOOG

HINDENBURGDAMM

Autotransport Sylt–Niebüll (50 Min.)

GERMANY

FRIEDRICH-WILHELM-LÜBKE-KOOG

Niebüll

Wester Ley

Oster Ley

Hörsbüllsteert

ALTER KOOG

NP Schleswig-Holsteinisches Wattenmeer

0 kilometres | 5
0 miles | 3

Holiday Paradise
Sylt attracts many visitors with more than 1,700 hours of sunlight a year, pleasant temperatures, a healthy North Sea island climate, attractive coastal villages and easy access via car shuttle train.

Key

▬	National border
····	National park border
▬	Road
—	Railway
🚉	Railway station
⛴	Ferry service
✈	Domestic airport
🏖	Beach
🗼	Lighthouse
⛺	Camping
⛳	Golf course
🌲	Scenic area
🏛	Archeological site, ruins
❊	Viewpoint

For map symbols *see back flap*

❷ North Frisian Islands

This group of islands (the Nordfriesische Inseln) lies off the western shores of Schleswig-Holstein. Between the larger islands of Föhr, Amrum, Pellworm and Nordstrand lie the smaller Halligen islands. Storm tides have repeatedly left their mark here; in 1634, a storm tide forever separated the islands of Pellworm and Nordstrand. Among the most popular seaside resorts are Westerland and Kampen, on the largest island of Sylt (see pp156 – 57), and Wyk on Föhr. Although the islands are surrounded by the Wadden Sea National Park of Schleswig-Holstein, they do not belong to this nature reserve.

Sand dunes in a nature reserve in the north of Sylt, the largest of the North Frisian Islands (see pp156 – 57)

Föhr

160 km (100 miles) northwest of Hamburg. 🏔 8600. 🚢 from Dagebüll. 🌐 foehr.de

The largest town on this 82-sq km (32-sq mile) island is the seaside resort of Wyk, located in the southeast. It is known for its year-round health and wellness facilities. One of Föhr's special attractions is AQUAFÖHR (www.aquafoehr.de), the popular waterwaves pool. For something different, a visit to the Bronze Age burial mounds in the southwest is rewarding.

Nowhere on the island is more than a 15-minute walk from a beach. Every year on 21 February "Biikebrennen" time is celebrated. This time-honoured ritual is also observed on other North Sea islands, when island residents light bonfires to chase away the long, dark winter.

One of many seals that can be seen on the Wadden Sea sandbanks

Amrum

150 km (95 miles) northwest of Hamburg. 🏔 2300. 🚢 from Dagebüll. 🌐 amrum.de

Amrum's biggest dunes reach 32 m (105 ft) in height. In the centre of the island, drifting dunes meet wooded areas and heath. In the harbour of Wittdün, the main town, ferries and fishing boats vie for space. Among the interesting sites to visit are Viking graves. Ornithologists treasure the rich birdlife. In the 19th century, before tourism became the main source of income, this 20-sq km (8-sq mile) island lived from whaling.

Pellworm

140 km (87 miles) northwest of Hamburg. 🏔 1200. 🚢 from Strucklahnungshörn to Nordstrand. 🌐 pellworm.de

A large part of Pellworm (36 sq km/14 sq miles) lies under sea level. It is protected from the sea by a dike measuring 8 m (26 ft) high and 28 km (17 miles) long. There are no sand beaches, but it is possible to swim. The island's landmark is the 12th-century church of St Salvator in the west, whose organ, dating from 1711, is still used to give concerts.

Nordstrand

120 km (75 miles) northwest of Hamburg. 🏔 2000. 🌐 nordstrand.de

In contrast to the other North Frisian Islands, Nordstrand (50 sq km/19 sq miles) can be reached by car over a causeway linking the island to the mainland. Many tourists come here between May and July to enjoy the North Frisian Lammtagen (lamb days), when they can learn all about herding sheep. An entertaining time for all is guaranteed, thanks to the exhibits, music and markets. The rose garden at Osterdeich is worth a visit.

Halligen

🏔 300. 🌐 halligen.de

These ten marsh islands around Pellworm cover a total area of 23 sq km (9 sq miles); some were once parts of larger islands that were divided by storm tides. Several of the Halligen islands are not protected by dikes, so are constantly eroded as storm tides wash over them. Buildings on the inhabited islands are erected on artificial mounds of earth to protect them from the tides. Walking tours of the tidal flats, salt marsh explorations and bird-watching expeditions are popular activities. It is lovely here in late summer, when lavender transforms the islands into a blanket of violet blossoms.

❸ Helgoland

In 1890, Germany received Helgoland from Britain in exchange for Zanzibar. Lying well out in open seas, 70 km (44 miles) from the mainland, the island always held great strategic importance. After 1945, Britain used Helgoland as a bombing target before returning it to Germany in 1952. The main island covers about 1 sq km (0.39 sq mile). The nearby dune, a popular spot for swimming and sunbathing, is a stretch of land measuring 0.7 sq km (0.27 sq miles).

VISITORS' CHECKLIST

Practical Information
70 km (44 miles) from mainland.
🚇 1400. ℹ Lung Wai 28 (04725 20 67 99). 🆆 **helgoland.de**

Transport
✈ Bremerhaven, Cuxhaven, Büsum. 🚢 Hamburg, Bremerhaven, Cuxhaven, Wilhelmshaven.

① **Harbour**
On the flat part of the island is Unterland, a small post-war town with a harbour. Fishermen store their nets in the characteristic colourful little houses known as Hummerbuden (lobster huts)

③ **Lange Anna**
Tall Anna, 48 m (157ft) high, is a red sandstone cliff. A small nature reserve can be found in Lummenfelsen.

③ Lange Anna

0 metres 400
0 yards 400

Oberland ②

① Hafen

② **Oberland**
In the upper part of the island stands the St Nikolai church, dating from 1959. Nearby, and worth a visit, are 16th-century tombs.

Key
— Suggested route

Tips for Walkers

Starting point: Harbour.
Length: 1.7 km (1.1 miles).
Stopping-off points: Restaurants all over the island.
Tips: Go bird-watching at the Lummenfelsen.

❹ East Frisian Islands

The islands of Borkum, Juist, Norderney, Baltrum, Langeoog, Spiekeroog and Wangerooge form a chain extending from west to east along the coast of Lower Saxony. The western shores of these East Frisian Islands (Ostfriesische Inseln) are slowly being eroded by constant winds, but protective structures save them from heavy damage. These islands, together with the Watt tidal mud-flats, belong to the Wadden Sea National Park of Lower Saxony. All the East Frisian Islands are car-free, except for Borkum and Norderney.

The Große Kaap (1872) on Borkum, a historic navigation aid

Borkum

220 km (137 miles) west of Hamburg.
🏔 5200. 🚢 from Emden.
ⓦ borkum.de

The most westerly of the East Frisian Islands, and the largest in the group, Borkum covers 31 sq km (12 sq miles). It is a North Sea therapeutic spa, offering a wide range of spa facilities. Interesting buildings include the old and new lighthouses – the Alter Leuchtturm (1576) and the Neuer Leuchtturm (1879). Family fun is guaranteed at the wellness and adventure pool complex, Gezeitenland (www. gezeitenland.de). It offers treats such as a sauna with a North Sea view. Every year, in December, a Blues festival is held on the island.

Juist

210 km (137 miles) west of Hamburg.
🏔 1800. 🚢 from Norddeich.
ⓦ juist.de

The charming island of Juist, with its lovely 17-km (11-mile) sandy beach, is appropriately named "magic land" by its tourist board. The 16.4-sq km (6.3-sq mile) island has several bird sanctuaries and the largest freshwater lake on the East Friesians, the Hammersee. In 2008, the Seebrücke Juist (Juist pier) opened. You can stroll along it as far as the harbour entrance. Each year, at the end of May, the Juister Musikfestival (Juist Music Festival) is held, featuring bands from across Europe.

Norderney

190 km (118 miles) west of Hamburg.
🏔 6000. 🚢 from Norddeich.
ⓦ norderney.de

Sandy beaches stretching 14 km (9 miles) offer pure relaxation on this 26-sq km (10-sq mile) island, which also has an extensive hiking-trail network. Other popular attractions are the Kurtheater (spa theatre), dating from 1894, and the observatory.

In 1797, Norderney became the first North Sea therapeutic spa in Germany. The Bademuseum (bath museum) features the history of the island's spa culture.

Baltrum

190 km (118 miles) west of Hamburg.
🏔 500. 🚢 from Neßmersiel.
ⓦ baltrum.de

Wellness spas and fabulous bathing fun in SindBad make Baltrum a popular destination for all those seeking relaxation. The island is only 6.5 sq km (2.5 sq miles) in size, so small that everything can be reached easily on foot.

Langeoog

170 km (106 miles) west of Hamburg.
🏔 2000. 🚢 from Bensersiel.
ⓦ langeoog.de

Dunes and sandy beaches are the hallmarks of this 20-sq-km (7.7-sq-mile) island. The spa and wellness centre offer many kinds of therapies. You can also visit the maritime distress

A car ferry plying the Kiel Canal at Brunsbüttel

observation station, the Schifffahrtsmuseum (seafaring museum), the Heimatmuseum (local history museum) and the water tower. Lale Andersen ("Lili Marleen") is buried in the cemetery, Dünenfriedhof.

Spiekeroog

160 km (99 miles) west of Hamburg.
🚇 800. 🚢 from Neuharlingersiel.
W spiekeroog.de

Unusual for a North Sea island are the relatively large tree populations to which Spiekeroog owes its nickname, "the green island". The first forests were planted in the mid-19th century. Spiekeroog is 18 sq km (7 sq miles) in size. Its church (1696) is the oldest house of worship on the East Frisian Islands. The Spiekerooger Muschelmuseum (Spiekeroog shell museum) has a collection of over 3,000 shells. A lovely thing to do is to take a trip on the Museumspferdebahn, a horse-drawn railway, which operates from April to September. Sporty people can participate in the game of Bosseln, a popular ball-game played throughout the East Frisian Islands.

Wangerooge

150 km (93 miles) west of Hamburg.
🚇 1000. 🚢 from Harlesiel.
W wangerooge.de

The most easterly of the East Frisian Islands is tiny Wangerooge, measuring only 5 sq km (2 sq miles). Since 1884, it has been accredited as having seawater therapeutic baths. A lighthouse, the Alter Leuchtturm (1856), houses the Inselmuseum, a museum of local history. The Nationalpark-Haus, open year-round, displays exhibits related to the Watt tidal mud-flats.

❺ Nord-Ostsee-Kanal

Herring Gull

Known in Germany as the Nord-Ostsee-Kanal but internationally as the Kiel Canal, this man-made waterway is the most travelled in the world. Each year, as many as 35,000 ships traverse this canal between the mouth of the Elbe and the Kiel fjords as a short-cut, saving themselves roughly 320 km (200 miles) that it would otherwise take to go around Denmark. The canal links the North Sea at Brunsbüttel with the Baltic Sea at Kiel. It is 98 km (61 miles) long and 11 m (36 ft) deep with a maximum width of 162 m (531 ft) at the water line and 90 m (295 ft) at the bottom. After eight years of construction, the canal (originally named Kaiser-Wilhelm-Kanal) opened on 21 June 1895. It was re-named Nord-Ostsee-Kanal in 1948.

Eight roads and four railway lines cross over the canal on ten bridges. Ferries ply the waters between the north and south shores. There are locks at both ends of the canal to control the differences in water levels caused by the tides.

The Kiel Canal – important in international freight shipping

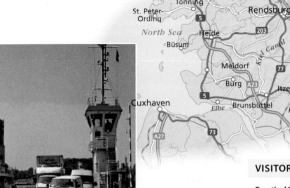

One of 14 ferries that transport cars across the Kiel Canal

0 kilometres 25
0 miles 25

VISITORS' CHECKLIST

Practical Information
ℹ️ Tourist-Information, Schiffbrücken Galerie, Rendsburg.
Tel (04331) 211 20. **W** tinok.de

❻ Bremen

Bremen, together with its deep-water port Bremerhaven, constitutes a separate city-state. The townscape is dominated by what the citizens call "the parlour", the area around the statue of Roland, the magnificent cathedral and the town hall. In 787 Bremen became a diocesan town, in 965 it was granted market rights and in 1358 it joined the Hanseatic League. The harbour of Bremen was developed in 1827, and during the 19th century the city's wealth was based on the tobacco, coffee and cotton trades. Today, Bremerhaven is Europe's biggest port-of-loading for the fishing and automobile industries.

Statue of the Bremen Town Musicians by Gerhard Marcks

Gabled houses and the statue of Roland on the Marktplatz

Exploring Bremen

Most of Bremen's sights are located in the Old Town, on the east bank of the Weser river. The area is surrounded by a green belt – the Wallanlagen, the site of the city's former fortifications. The Überseemuseum (ethnography museum) is close to the Hauptbahnhof (central train station). A 10-minute tram ride takes you from here to the Marktplatz, and in 15 minutes you reach Schwachhausen, where the Focke-Museum is based.

🏛 Marktplatz

On the main square of medieval Bremen are the town hall, cathedral and the Schütting (guildhall); gabled houses are on the west side.

In front of the town hall stands the largest statue of Roland in Germany, measuring 10 m (32 ft). Together with the town hall, it was named a UNESCO World Heritage Site in 2004. Roland was a peer in Charlemagne's court. Over time, he has come to symbolize market rights and freedom in Germany.

Roland's gaze is directed towards the cathedral, the residence of the bishop, who often sought to restrict the city's autonomy. The sword of justice symbolizes the judiciary's independence; the inscription cites the emperor's edict, conferring town rights on Bremen.

Also here is a monument dedicated to the **Bremen Town Musicians** (1953) – a donkey, dog, cat and cockerel, characters from a Grimms fairy tale.

🏛 Rathaus

See pp 164–65.

🏛 Schütting

Marktplatz.

Opposite the town hall stands a mansion used by the Merchants' Guild for their conventions. It was built in 1537–39 by the Antwerp architect, Johann der Buschener, in the Dutch Mannerist style. Its eastern gable is by local builder, Carsten Husmann (1565).

🏛 Pfarrkirche Unser Lieben Frauen

Unser-Lieben-Frauen-Kirchhof 27.
Open 11am–4pm Mon–Sat, noon–1pm Sun.

Work on this three-aisled early Gothic hall-church started in 1229. The Romanesque tower of a previous church on the site was integrated as the building's northern spire. At the end of the 14th century, the choir was extended, and a southern aisle was added. The church's colonnade dates from the 19th century. Striking 14th-century frescos adorn the crypt.

The late Renaissance façade of Bremen's Rathaus (town hall)

⬆ St-Petri-Dom

Sandstraße 10–12. **Open** 10am–5pm Mon–Fri, 10am–2pm Sat, 2–5pm Sun. Tower: **Open** Apr–Oct: 10am–4:30pm Mon–Fri, 10am–1:30pm Sat, 2–4:30pm Sun (Jun–Sep: until 5:30pm Mon–Fri, Sun). 🔁 Bleikeller: **Open** Apr–Oct: 10am–4:45pm Mon–Sat, noon–4:45pm Sun (Jun–Sep: until 5:45pm Mon–Fri, Sun). 🔁 Museum: **Open** 10am–4:45pm Mon–Fri, 10am–1:30pm Sat, 2–4:45pm Sun. 🗎 🕮
ⓦ stpetridom.de

This magnificent cathedral, with its vast twin-towered façade, dates from the 11th century. Enlarged in the 16th century and extensively rebuilt at the end of the 19th, the church contains numerous architectural styles, from Romanesque to late Gothic. It was closed from 1532 to 1638, during the Reformation.

The Mannerist Schütting (guildhall), a meeting place for merchants

Inside you can view the old chancel (1518), which now functions as the organ parapet, fragments of Gothic stalls and the beautifully carved pulpit (1638). There are also multi-coloured memorials, including one to Provost Segebade Clüver (1547). The eastern crypt has cubiform capitals, while in the western crypt visitors can

VISITORS' CHECKLIST

Practical Information
100 km (62 miles) SW of Hamburg.
🚆 550 000. 🚹 Obernstr. 1.
Tel 0421 308 00 10. Harbour cruises: (1.5 hrs) Martinianleger, (0421 33 89 89). May–Sep: 10:15 & 11:45am, 1:30pm, 3:15pm & 4:45pm daily; Mar, Apr & Oct: 11:45am, 1:30pm & 3:15pm daily; Nov, Dec & Feb: 1:30pm & 3:15pm Sat, Sun. 🔁 🖼 Sat, Sun.
🎭 Bremer Sambakarneval (Mar/Apr); Osterwiese (Apr); Bremer Freimarkt (late Oct/early Nov).
ⓦ bremen-tourismus.de

Transport
🚉 ✈ 5 km (3 miles) SW of Bremen.

admire the sculpture of Christ the Omnipotent (1050) and the baptismal font with its 38 bas-reliefs, supported by four lions with riders. In the **Bleikeller** (lead cellar), six preserved mummies are on show. The **Museum** records the history of the cathedral and archbishopric, and stores treasures retrieved from the tombs of Bremen's archbishops. Opened in 1998, the cathedral's garden is a peaceful retreat.

Bas-reliefs on the western choir stalls in the St-Petri-Dom

Bremen Town Centre

① Marktplatz
② Rathaus
③ Schütting
④ Pfarrkirche Unser Lieben Frauen
⑤ St-Petri-Dom
⑥ Böttcherstraße
⑦ Schnoorviertel
⑧ Kunsthalle
⑨ Überseemuseum

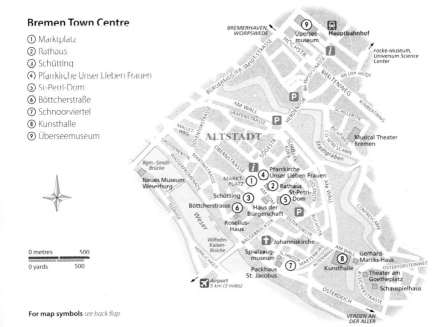

0 metres 500
0 yards 500

For map symbols see back flap

Bremer Rathaus

Bremen's town hall was built in 1405–10. The late Gothic red-brick building is decorated with medieval statuary, including lifesize sandstone sculptures of the Emperor Charlemagne and the seven Electors. The façade, having been completely reworked by the architect Lüder von Bentheim in 1608–12, is considered to be an outstanding example of Weser Renaissance architecture. The frieze above the arcade represents an allegory of human history. The town hall and the statue of Roland were named as World Heritage Sites by UNESCO in 2004.

Façade
The original Gothic building was clad with an outstanding Weser Renaissance façade designed by Lüder von Bentheim in 1608–12.

★ **Upper Hall**
This magnificent banqueting hall occupies the entire second floor. The city's most splendid receptions and concerts are held here.

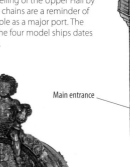

Model Ships
The model sailing ships suspended from the ceiling of the Upper Hall by heavy iron chains are a reminder of Bremen's role as a major port. The oldest of the four model ships dates from 1545.

Main entrance

★ **Ratskeller**
The Gothic Ratskeller stores hundreds of wine barrels adorned with figures such as Bacchus.

★ **Ornamental Gable**
The architect Lüder von Bentheim embellished the town hall façade by adding a Flemish-style stepped gable that is five storeys high.

The Judgment of Solomon
The mural (1532) of Solomon's court in the Upper Hall is a reference to the room's former dual function as a council-chamber and courtroom.

Arcades
Above every arcade there are figures representing the history of Bremen and the virtues of the state.

Art Nouveau Room
The lower room of the two-storey Gülden-kammer owes its 1905 Art Nouveau (Jugendstil) makeover to the artist Heinrich Vogeler. The gilded leather wallpaper dates from the early 17th century.

KEY

① **The roof** is covered with copper tiles.

② **The middle projection** with the striking pediment was added in the 17th century.

🔲 Böttcherstraße

Paula-Modersohn-Becker-Museum, Museum im Roselius-Haus: Böttcherstraße 6–10. **Tel** (0421) 338 82 22. **Open** 11am–6pm Tue–Sun. 🔊 📷 **W** pmbm.de

From 1924–31, this street was transformed into an Expressionist-style lane by Ludwig Roselius, a wealthy coffee merchant. Later the Nazis preserved the Böttcherstraße as an example of degenerate art. On the entrance gate is Bernhard Hoetger's bas-relief, *Der Lichtbringer* (1920), which represents the Archangel Michael fighting a dragon.

Today the lane is lined by museums and shops. The Paula-Modersohn-Becker-Museum displays paintings and graphic art by the artist as well as Bernhard Hoetgers' oeuvre. In the 16th century Roselius-Haus you can admire the original period interiors as well as low German art from the 14th to the 19th centuries.

🔲 Schnoorviertel

Spielzeugmuseum im Schnoor Schnoor 24: Schnoor 24. **Tel** (0421) 32 03 82. **Open** 11am–6:30pm Mon–Fri, 11am–6pm Sat. 🔊

The Schnoor is part of Bremen's oldest district. One of the city's poorest and most densely populated areas before World War II, it miraculously escaped wartime destruction. It has been restored gradually since 1958 and now teems with restaurants,

Der Lichtbringer bas-relief at Böttcherstraße

cafés and galleries. In the centre of the district is the Gothic **Johanniskirche** (14th century). The red-brick church once belonged to the Franciscans. In accordance with the order's rules it has no tower, although this is compensated for by a decorative gable with blind arcades on the western façade. The **Spielzeugmuseum** (toy museum) is also worth a visit.

🏛 Kunsthalle Bremen

Am Wall 207. **Tel** (0421) 32 90 80. **Open** 10am–9pm Tue, 10am–5pm Wed–Sun. 🔊 **W** kunsthalle-bremen.de

The gallery showcases masterpieces from the 14th century to contemporary art. The Old Masters wing features works by Dürer, Altdorfer, Rubens and Rembrandt. The French artists' section is striking, as are German 19th and 20th century artists such as Beckmann and Kirchner. A renovation has exapnded the gallery space.

🏛 Überseemuseum

Bahnhofsplatz 13. **Tel** (0421) 16 03 81 01. **Open** 9am–6pm Tue–Fri, 10am–6pm Sat & Sun. 🔊 📷 🖊 **W** uebersee-museum.de

Opened in 1896, this museum was originally devoted to German colonialism. Today, it is still a museum of overseas countries, transporting visitors to faraway lands and explaining their cultural history, ecology and current situation. While largely dedicated to the culture of non-European nations, there is also an exhibition entitled "Bremen – Hanseatic City by the River". The spacious halls are filled with palm trees, models of South Pacific houses and boats, temples and a Japanese garden. Innumerable plants and stuffed animals are placed next to ethnological exhibits.

🏛 Focke-Museum

Schwachhauser Heerstraße 240. **Tel** (0421) 699 60 00. **Open** 10am– 9pm Tue, 10am–5pm Wed–Sun. 🔊 🎨 ♿ 🖥 📷 **W** focke-museum.de

This excellent museum presents Bremen's art and culture from the Middle Ages to the present day. Exhibits from patrician houses and original sculptures from the façade of the town hall testify to the wealth of this Hanseatic city. Other sections are devoted to the archeology of the region and to whaling.

The nearby **Rhododendron-Park**, part of the Bürgerpark, offers a pleasant respite from the museums. Covering 46 ha (114 acres), it includes 2,000 varieties of rhododendron and azalea, which turn the park into a sea of blossoms from late April to June.

🏛 Universum Science Center

Wiener Straße 1a. **Tel** (0421) 334 60. **Open** 9am–6pm Mon–Fri 10am–6pm Sat & Sun 🔊 📷 🖊 **W** universum-bremen.de

In this centre, the wonders of the world are spectacularly presented. The fantastic journey across the "continents" (Humankind, Earth and Cosmos) features experimental areas and large-scale projections. It is fun for adults and children alike.

Camille Pissarro's *Girl Lying on a Grassy Slope* at the Kunsthalle Bremen

Paula Modersohn-Becker (1876–1907)

A pupil of Fritz Mackensen and the wife of Otto Modersohn, Paula Modersohn-Becker was the most significant artistic figure in Worpswede.

She learned about the Impressionist use of colour during visits to Paris, and her own unique style was a precursor to Expressionism. She became famous for naturalistic paintings of poor, starving, and even dying country folk, as well as self portraits and still lifes. Her watercolours and prints were also acclaimed. She died in childbirth at the age of 31. Her tombstone, by the sculptor Bernhard Hoetger, is in the cemetery at Worpswede.

Girl playing a flute in birch woods (1905)

Exhibits in the Große Kunstschau in Worpswede near Bremen

Environs

50 km (31 miles) to the north lies **Bremerhaven**, with the Deutsches Schifffahrtsmuseum. This superb marine museum, designed by Hans Scharoun, displays originals and models of a wide range of ships, dating from the beginnings of seafaring to the present day. One of the highlights is the Hansekogge (1380), an oak wood merchant ship retrieved from the Weser river in 1962. In the open-air section of the museum are the last great German sailing boat Seute Deern, the polar ship Grönland and Wilhelm Bauer, a U-boat from World War II.

The Klimahaus Bremerhaven 8° Ost, the city's most recent attraction, opened in 2009. The exhibition revolves around climate and climate change. Visitors embark on a journey following the 8th degree of longitude, crossing different climate zones.

From 1884 to World War II, the small village

of **Worpswede**, 28 km (17 miles) northeast of Bremen near the Teufelsmoor, was a famous artists' colony. Apart from poets such as Rainer Maria Rilke, and architects including Bernhard Hoetger, the village's fame rested principally on the painters Fritz Mackensen, Otto Modersohn, Hans am Ende, Fritz Overbeck and Heinrich Vogeler. The greatest artist here was Paula Modersohn-Becker. Work by the founding members is on display in the Große Kunstschau and the Worpsweder Kunsthalle.

Verden an der Aller, the quaint bishop's residence and once a free town of the Reich, is known to sports enthusiasts thanks to its horse-breeding centres and the Deutsches Pferdemuseum (horse museum). In the city centre, the early 13th-century Andreaskirche contains the brass tomb of

Bischof Yso, and the Johanniskirche (12th–15th century) features Gothic murals and ceiling frescos. Above the town rises the Dom (1290–1490) with a copper saddle roof. The tower, cloister and the eastern section of the three-aisled hall-church are Romanesque. North of the cathedral, the Domherrenhaus (1708) houses the Historisches Museum, with exhibits on cultural history and ethnology.

🏛 Deutsches Schifffahrtsmuseum
Bremerhaven, Hans-Scharoun-Platz 1. **Tel** (0471) 48 20 70. **Open** Mar–Oct: 10am–6pm daily; Nov–Feb: 10am–6pm Tue–Sun. 🔗 **W** dsm.museum

🏛 Klimahaus Bremerhaven 8° Ost
Am Längengrad 8. **Tel** (0471) 902 03 00. **Open** Apr–Aug: 9am–7pm Mon–Fri, 10am–7pm Sat, Sun; Sep–Mar: 10am–6pm daily. 🔗 📷 **W** klimahaus-bremerhaven.de

🏛 Große Kunstschau Worpswede
Lindenallee 5. **Tel** (04792) 13 02. **Open** mid-Mar–Oct: 10am–6pm daily; Nov–mid-Mar:10am–6pm Tue–Sun. 🔗 📷 **W** grosse-kunstschau.de

🏛 Worpsweder Kunsthalle
Bergstraße 17. **Tel** (04792) 12 77. **Open** 10am–6pm daily. 🔗 📷 **W** worpsweder-kunsthalle.de

🏛 Deutsches Pferdemuseum
Verden, Holzmarkt 9. **Tel** (04231) 80 71 40. **Open** 10am–5pm Tue–Sun. 🔗 📷 **W** dpm-verden.de

🏛 Historisches Museum – Domherrenhaus
Verden, Untere Str. 13. **Tel** (04231) 21 69. **Open** 10am–1pm, 3–5pm Tue–Sun. 🔗 **W** domherrenhaus.de

The Dom in Verden an der Aller, with its unusually high-pitched roof

❼ Museumsdorf Cloppenburg

Over 50 structures built in Lower Saxony between the 16th and 19th centuries can be viewed in this 20-ha (49-acre) open-air museum. Moved from their original locations and reassembled here, these buildings document the development and variety of rural architecture, Lower Saxon artisanry and the way rural people lived. The region's main building styles are the half-timbered, thatch-roofed, Lower German Hallenhaus and the East Frisian Gulfhaus, a type of farmhouse in which people and animals lived together under one roof. Special themed exhibitions expand and complement the collections.

Dutch Mill
Just the timber cap of the windmill needs to be turned in this type of windmill (1764) from Bokel in Cappeln.

★ **Haake Farmstead**
The Haake farmstead from Cappeln (1793) is supported by four rows of posts and is therefore known as a Vierständerhaus (four-posted house).

Storage building
This type of multi-purpose building (before 1792, from Norddöllen) served as carriage house and workshop. The attic was used for storage.

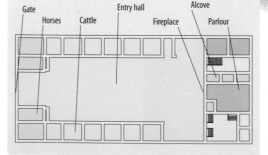

Plan of a Farmstead

The entry hall is also the heart of the farmstead. It is a covered courtyard with farmhouse gate and stable doors. The living quarters surround the parlour.

Gate
Horses Cattle
Entry hall
Fireplace
Alcove
Parlour

KEY

① **Zaunscheune, a type of stable, from Varenesch**

② **Brewing outbuilding from Visbek**

★ Fireplace
Close to the wall of the living quarters was an open fireplace that warmed the entire house. The fire also was used for food preparation.

VISITORS' CHECKLIST

Practical Information
150 km (93 miles) southwest of Hamburg. **Tel** (04471) 948 40.
Open Mar–Oct: 9am–6pm; Nov–Feb: 9am–4:30pm.
(04471) 94 84 23.
museumsdorf.de

Alcoves
Alcoves off the living room served as tiny bedchambers. They were locked during the day.

★ Parlour
In winter, this room served as the family living room. On Sundays and holidays, it was the dining and sitting room. It contained the best furniture.

Entry hall
This type of farmstead is known as a Hallenhaus. The entry was the farmstead's principal room and inner courtyard. From here, there was access to the stables, attic and living quarters.

Pig stable
This 18th-century small pig stable from Klein Mimmelage features a thatched roof with deep eaves, which protected the feeding troughs lined up along the wall from the elements.

TRAVELLERS' NEEDS

Where to Stay 172–181

Where to Eat and Drink 182–197

Shopping in Hamburg 198–201

Entertainment in Hamburg 202–215

Children's Hamburg 216–217

WHERE TO STAY

Whether you are on holiday, a business trip or a short jaunt – the Hanseatic city of Hamburg is a great place to stay. With its around 300 hotels, there is something to suit every taste and budget. The accommodations range from the luxurious to the inexpensive, from impeccably appointed five-star hotels to avant-garde designer hotels, from low-cost chains to classic pensions providing excellent value for money. Some hotels have their own spas where guests can relax and be thoroughly pampered after a busy day. If you're looking for something out of the ordinary, you won't be disappointed either: what could be more fitting in this maritime city than spending a night on a ship? The list of hotels provided on pages 176–181 helps you choose a place to stay. The list is organized by area and price category, and includes every type of hotel.

Entrance to the luxurious Hotel Atlantic Kempinski *(see p176)*

Finding a Hotel

Most of Hamburg's attractions are located in the city centre area and can be reached easily on foot or with the excellent public transit system. If your visit is primarily intended to see the sights, then it is best to select a hotel close to the centre of town. Business travellers might prefer a hotel near the airport or the trade fair, depending on their needs.

Several of the finest hotels in Hamburg are found in the elegant city districts located around the Binnenalster and the Außenalster. But even in the district of Blankenese, which is just a few kilometres west of Hamburg, there are a number of exclusive hotels in tranquil settings that are ready to welcome guests. If you are looking for a place to relax, then this might well be the right area for you.

In the Old Town and in St Pauli, there are a great many places to stay for budget-conscious visitors who are not bothered by noise. The entertainment district of St Pauli, in particular, never seems to quiet down completely.

Irrespective of the price category, a hotel room with a view of Hamburg's harbour is always a good choice.

Hotel Categories and Amenities

Hamburg has a wide range of hotels in all price categories. Five-star hotels offer every comfort a traveller could expect. Hotel rooms in these luxury accommodations are spacious and decorated with top-quality furniture. They are usually bright and come equipped with the latest technology, such as sound-proof windows, ingenious bathrooms with upscale fixtures and amenities, as well as the most up-to-date communications gadgets. Along with exquisite and elegant restaurants, luxury hotels usually also offer fitness centres, and wellness areas with saunas, massage and often swimming pools.

An interesting alternative for guests who take a special delight in extravagance are the so-called boutique hotels, which are also known as designer hotels. In recent years, several boldly designed hotels have opened in Hamburg. They captivate with their unique design and colour-schemes as well as their sophisticated use of light. As soon as you enter a boutique hotel, you almost enter another world. Some of these unusual hotels have been constructed in buildings that were originally designed with other purposes in mind. They include a former post office, an old coal storage warehouse and a former high-class brothel. Fortunately, design does not always have to come at a price. The cost of staying in some boutique hotels is certainly in the mid price-range. This is also true for hotels that are located in historic buildings, such as in

Hotel Vier Jahreszeiten *(see p176)* – a fantastic location on the Binnenalster

◄ Terrace of the café and restaurant Alex in Alsterpavillon *(see p191)*

Lobby of the Maritim Hotel Reichshof *(see p177)*

magnificent Art Nouveau (Jugendstil) villas. Even these hotels with their magical ambience do not have to be expensive.

At the other end of the price spectrum are the simple, sparse rooms that usually are furnished with a television and telephone but the bathroom might be down the hall. This kind of accommodation is popular with tourists who spend their time sightseeing and taking in the town, returning just to sleep.

Hotel Chains

When you stay in a chain hotel such as **Best Western, Dorint, Mercure** or **Ramada** you can usually count on a high degree of comfort and cleanliness. Guests here know what to expect if they've stayed in any other of the chain's branches; even between countries amenities are similar. The majority of these hotels cater to the needs of business travellers, and offer conference rooms with the necessary equipment. Chain hotels often have attractive weekend deals to fill up their rooms; it can pay to look into these offers. Also check to see if the hotel has a bonus programme if you travel to Hamburg with an airline or in a rental car. Many chain hotels have agreements with airlines and car rental companies, and you might be eligible for a reward such as a discount or bonus air miles.

Hamburg kleine Hotels (Small Hamburg Hotels) is not a

hotel chain in the usual sense, but rather a loose association of hotels. It consists of nine hotels located around the Alster. Each is distinguished by its intimate atmosphere, and each can be counted among the city's most attractive hotels. This small hotel group considers itself an alternative to international hotel chains.

Ship Hotels

You can also stay overnight in the very place where Hamburg is at its most quintessential – in the harbour. The passenger cabins of the museum ship **Cap San Diego** *(see pp98–9)*, which has been anchored in the harbour since 1986, were renovated in the style of the 1950s; they still exude the charms of the glory days of sea travel. A former lightship, **Das Feuerschiff** *(see p89)*, is also enjoying a second career in

Pure modern style at the boutique hotel East *(see p177)*

tourism just a few ships away. Here guests are gently rocked to sleep in the former captain's cabin and the cabins where the crew slept. The space in these "floating hotels" is a bit snug, but it is also very cosy.

How to Book

As in other countries, you can book your Hanseatic accommodation at your convenience directly by telephone, by fax or online. A good way of learning about the features of a hotel – and what it will cost – is to visit the website of the hotel you are considering. In the hotel listings on pages 176–181, contact information (including websites and phone numbers) has been provided for every hotel that appears. You can also book rooms in practically every hotel in Hamburg through the Hamburg tourist office, **Hamburg Tourismus GmbH**.

It is a very good idea to book ahead, especially in summer, when important trade fairs are being held, and during the Port's Birthday at the beginning of May *(see p85)*. At such times it may be difficult to find a room at short notice.

Of course, many hotels may also offer last-minute discounts for rooms that have not been reserved. A number of hotels catering to business travellers offer special discounts at weekends, making staying in these hotels from Friday to Sunday cheaper than on weekdays.

Hotel Rates and Discounts

Several hotels offer interesting discounts, often combined with the purchase of tickets for musicals or other events. These discounts also often include the much sought-after – and therefore quickly sold-out – tickets for boat tours during the Port's Birthday Bash. All-round packages that include transportation, shuttle from the airport to the hotel, an overnight stay and one or two events are increasingly popular.

The bright colours of the bar in Le Royal Méridien *(see p176)*

Hidden Extras

At some hotels, the cost of the room does not include breakfast. There is often an additional cost for parking. Charges may be incurred for using fitness centres and spa facilities.

Telephone calls made from your hotel or hotel room can be very expensive. You may well pay a steep price for drinks and snacks from the mini-bar. Tipping is usually expected only in the largest and most expensive hotels.

Disabled Travellers

Many of the larger hotels offer rooms with wheelchair access and services tailored to disabled visitors' needs. Often this is not the case in smaller hotels, pensions, and bed-and-breakfasts, which may not even have a lift. Before you book, if you or a travelling companion has special needs, contact the hotel and discuss your requirements, such as lifts or doors that are wide enough for wheelchairs.

The **Senatskoordinator für die Gleichstellung behinderter Menschen der Freien und Hansestadt Hamburg** produces a brochure with information for the disabled. You can also find out more information through **Behinderten-Ratgeber**, who run a comprehensive website for people with special needs.

Travelling with Children

In many hotels, young children can stay in their parents' room for free or for a small extra charge. Children's cots are usually available and can be placed in your room as needed. Some hotels offer special family packages such as two connecting rooms or one large room with a separate sleeping area. Of course, self-catering flats offer more room for the entire family.

The package tour operator Happy Hamburg Reisen, which belongs to **Hamburg Tourismus GmbH**, offers special deals for families who travel to Hamburg by train. The package includes train travel and accommodation at a reasonable price.

Another family-friendly and budget-conscious option is the **A&O Hostel Hamburg**. Just 400 m (0.25 miles) from the Hauptbahnhof, this hostel offers single, double and multi-bed rooms (all with bath), and an option for groups and school classes, as well as for families.

Private Homes and Self-catering Flats

A good yet relatively inexpensive alternative to hotel rooms are rooms in private homes; they often include breakfast. Aside from the price, their attraction for cost-conscious travellers is the chance to stay with local families who usually provide valuable tips and information on sightseeing.

The agency **bed & breakfast** specialises in renting simply furnished rooms in private homes. Some of their package deals are unusual, such as the one offering a two-night stay, breakfast, and a one-hour introductory sailing course.

The agency tailors its offers to your needs and also helps you plan your stay in Hamburg. The online community **airbnb** offers a wide range of rooms and flats in central Hamburg. **Bedroomforyou** rents elegantly decorated rooms in the homes of well-off middle-class Hamburgers.

Ideal for families or for longer stays are self-catering flats. Completely furnished, and well-located near transit routes, they provide accommodation for up to six people. They can be booked through agencies such as **Hamburger Ferienwohnungen**. Private rooms (some with private baths), suites and self-catering flats also are available for rent in several Hamburg districts by **Zimmer Frei Hamburg**.

Budget Accommodation

An inexpensive way of spending time in Hamburg is to stay at one of the city's many youth hostels (Jugendherberge). To be eligible, you must be a member of the **IYHA** (International Youth Hostel Association). You can purchase a membership in person at any affiliated hostel or through a **YHA** website.

The **Jugendherberge auf dem Stintfang** is a very popular hostel located just above the Landungsbrücken. All the two- to six-bed rooms have a shower and toilet. There is a fantastic view of the harbour through the huge lobby windows.

Breakfast room in the Hotel Schwanenwik *(see p179)*

Other popular youth hostels are the Jugendherberge Horner Rennbahn near the Horn racetrack and the **Hamburger Jugendpark Langenhorn** (no youth hostel pass needed) in the north. More budget options are recommended in the hotel listings on page 181.

Camping

For a city, Hamburg and its environs offer an astonishing number of camping sites. Directly on the shores of the Elbe at Blankenese – in the extreme west of Hamburg – stretches the campground **Elbe Camp**.

Approximately 25 km (16 miles) southeast of the city centre (about 30 minutes by car) is the well-equipped campground on the **Elbe Campingplatz Stover Strand**, which has a flat sandy beach and a marina with 100 berths

Novum Hotel am Holstenwall *(see p180)*, which houses Bar 509

for sailboats and motorboats. Almost just as far to the northeast of the city centre (about 35 minutes by car) is the idyllic campground **Campingplatz ABC am Großensee**. Here visitors can enjoy the charms of this landscape with its many lakes formed by glaciers during the Ice Age.

Recommended Hotels

The hotels in this guide are included based on two main criteria – quality and value for money, irrespective of the price bracket. In each area of the city a highly recommended hotel has been highlighted as the DK Choice. It may be set in a historic landmark building or have excellent facilities and service.

DIRECTORY

Hotel Chains

Best Western
Tel 0800 212 58 88.
W bestwestern.de

Dorint
Tel 0180 226 25 24.
W dorint.com

Mercure
Tel (069) 95 30 75 92.
W mercure.com

Ramada
Tel (05691) 87 87.
W ramada.de

Hamburg kleine Hotels
Tel 410 48 92.
W hamburg-kleinehotels.de

Ship Hotels

Cap San Diego
Überseebrücke.
Tel 36 42 09.
W capsandiego.de

Das Feuerschiff
City-Sporthafen.
Tel 36 25 53.
W das-feuerschiff.de

Reservations

Hamburg Tourismus GmbH
Postfach 102249.
Map 10 E3.
Tel 30 05 17 01.
W hamburg-travel.com

Disabled travellers

Behinderten-Ratgeber
W handicap-info.de

Senatskoordinator für die Gleichstellung behinderter Menschen
Osterbekstr. 96.
Tel 428 63 57 25.

Travelling with Children

A & O Hostel Hamburg
Amsinckstr. 2–10.
Tel 644 21 04-56 00.
Hammer Landstr. 170.
Tel 57 01 06 93-55 00.
W aohostels.com/de/hamburg

Private Homes and Self-catering Flats

Airbnb
W airbnb.co.uk

bed & breakfast
Markusstr. 9. Tel 491 56 66.
W bed-and-breakfast.de

Bedroomforyou
Tornquiststr. 1.
Tel 40 18 61 37.
W bedroomforyou.de

Ferienwohnungen in Hamburg
Tel 643 14 34.
W hamburg ferienwohnungen.de

Zimmer Frei Hamburg
Steilshooper Str. 186.
Tel 27 87 77 77.
W zimmerfrei hamburg.de

Budget Accomodation

IYHA
W hihostels.com

YHA
W yha.org.uk

Hamburger Jugendpark Langenhorn
Jugendparkweg 60.
Tel 531 30 50.
W hamburger-jugendpark.de

Jugendherberge auf dem Stintfang
Alfred-Wegener-Weg 5.
Tel 570 15 90.
W hamburg-stintfang.jugendherberge.de

Camping

Campingplatz ABC am Großensee
Trittauer Str. 11.
22946 Großensee.
Tel (04154) 606 42.
W campingplatz-abc.de

Campingplatz Stover Strand
Stover Strand 10.
21423 Drage.
Tel (04177) 430.
W camping-stover-strand.de

Elbe Camp
Falkensteiner Ufer 101.
Tel 81 29 49.
W elbecamp.de

Where to Stay

Luxury

Old Town

Park Hyatt Hamburg €€€
Bugenhagenstraße 8, 20095
Tel *33 32 12 34* **Map** 10 F3
W hamburg.park.hyatt.de
Maritime flair and contemporary
furnishings are combined
beautifully in this hotel located in
a former office building. The
wellness area, Club Olympus Spa
& Fitness, offers everything mere
mortals need to help turn
themselves into gods. The
mixology courses in the Apples
Bar are great fun.

**Steigenberger Hotel
Hamburg** €€€
Heiligengeistbrücke 4, 20459
Tel *36 80 60* **Map** 9 C3
W steigenberger.com/hamburg
This red-brick building on
Alsterfleet looks like a giant ship.
Behind its massive façade a world
of luxury and elegance unfolds.
In addition to the Shiseido Day
Spa – an oasis of calmness –
amenities include a ticket book-
ing service, free newspapers and
a hairdresser. In the Davidoff
Cigar Lounge, you'll find over
30 brands of cigars and cigarillos
on offer.

Around the Alster

Boulevard Hotel €€€
Hofweg 73, 22085
Tel *227 02 20* **Map** 8 E1
W boulevardhotel.de
This splendid Jugendstil villa
dating from 1886 has been
transformed into a luxury hotel
with romantic charm. Pale tones,
luxuriant carpets, stuccoed
ceilings and high-quality finishes
give the rooms a pleasing
atmosphere. For couples, the
rooms beneath the eaves make
for a romantic stay. The lobby
features antique furniture,
Classical sculptures and gilt-
framed paintings.

The George Hotel €€€
Barcastraße 3, 20087
Tel *280 03 00* **Map** 8 F4
W thegeorge-hotel.de
This classy hotel pays homage
to British style. The lobby area
and bedrooms are decorated
in warm colours, with bold,
patterned wallpaper. The Italian
restaurant DaCaio and the
Moroccan-themed day spa
add to the hotel's cool, understated elegance.

Grand Elysée €€€
Rothenbaumchaussee 10, 20148
Tel *41 41 22 00* **Map** 7 B3
W grand-elysee.com
Offering exclusive suites and first-
class cuisine, Grand Elysée ranks
among the city's top hotels. The
reception hall, with its bars, shops
and restaurants, is aptly named
the Boulevard – it's large enough
for a stroll. The wellness and spa
area is a world unto itself.

Hotel Atlantic Kempinski €€€
An der Alster 72 – 79, 20099
Tel *288 80* **Map** 8 D4
W kempinski.com/de/hamburg/
hotel-atlantic
Join the high life and live like a
celebrity at "the white palace on
the Alster" *(see p128)*. Since 1909,
this grand hotel has been the
first choice of celebrities visiting
Hamburg. It has also served as a
set for numerous films.

Hotel Vier Jahreszeiten €€€
Neuer Jungfernstieg 9 –14, 20354
Tel *349 40* **Map** 7 C5
W hvj.de
This venerable institution on the
banks of the Binnenalster *(see p125)*
conjures up turn-of-the-century
nostalgia with wood-panelled
hallways, Art Deco accents and
vintage lifts. The hotel lobby and
rooms are very modern. All nine
restaurants are temples to fine
food, with extensive menus.

Le Royal Méridien €€€
An der Alster 52 – 56, 20099
Tel *210 00* **Map** 8 E4
W leroyalmeridienhamburg.com
This hotel successfully marries
modern luxury and timeless

The legendary white palace,
Hotel Atlantik Kempinski

elegance. Rooms offer views of
the Alster and all have modern
amenities including power
showers and plasma TVs. Le Ciel
restaurant on the ninth floor
serves heavenly dishes.

Further Afield

DK Choice

Louis C. Jacob €€€
Elbchaussee 401 – 403, 22609
Tel *82 25 50*
W hotel-jacob.de
Pampering guests to the
utmost is a matter of honour in
this privately run luxury hotel in
Nienstedten on the Elbe. Its
antique and art collection will
delight art lovers. The view from
the terrace of the Elbe lined
with old Linden trees was a
source of inspiration for the
Impressionist Max Liebermann.

Zollenspieker Fährhaus €€€
Zollenspieker Hauptdeich 141, 21037
Tel *(040) 793 13 30*
W zollenspieker-faehrhaus.de
This hotel offers discreet, understated comfort. The modern
hotel rooms are slick and stylish,
while rooms in the refurbished
13th-century house are tucked
under the wooden beams of the
sloping roof. The lounge offers
views of the Elbe.

Boutique

Old Town

Henri Hotel €€
Bugenhagenstraße 21, 20095
Tel *554 35 70* **Map** 5 D3
W henri-hotel.com
The studios and suites are
decked out in spiffy mid-century
modern furniture, including
Henri club chairs and triangular
tables.

Hotel City House €€
Pulverteich 25, 20099
Tel *280 08 10* **Map** 6 F2
W cityhouse.de/en
This hotel in a villa dating from
around 1890 is an architectural

gem. The rooms have high, stuccoed ceilings, and there is also a library with sofas, wing chairs and an open fireplace.

Hotel Village   €€
Steindamm 4, 20099
Tel *480 64 90*   **Map** 6 E2
w hotel-village.de
The plushness of this hotel hints at its past as a high-end brothel. The rooms are extravagantly decorated with silk wall coverings and patterned carpets, and many rooms have canopy beds or four-posters. Coffee is free at all hours.

Junges Hotel   €€
Kurt-Schumacher-Allee 14, 20097
Tel *41 92 30*   **Map** 6 F2
w jungeshotel.de/en
Bright colours dominate at this contemporary hotel. Family rooms feature bunk beds that pop out of the wall and Studio 405 has its own terrace. There's a Finnish sauna in the wellness centre.

Maritim Hotel Reichshof   €€
Kirchenallee 34 – 36, 20099
Tel *24 83 30*   **Map** 6 E2
w maritim.de
This classic hotel was opened in 1910. Its restaurant ClassiC is decorated in the style of a luxury cruise-liner. The pool area includes a steam bath and sauna. Piano music is played in the bar, which offers a great choice of single malt whiskys

New Town

The Madison Hamburg   €€
Schaarsteinweg 4, 20459
Tel *37 66 60*   **Map** 9 B4
w madisonhotel.de/en
Stylish, yet functional, this hotel offers spacious, colour coordinated rooms and suites with large windows. There's a pool and gym at the Meridian Spa.

DK Choice

SIDE   €€€
Drehbahn 49, 20354
Tel *30 99 90*   **Map** 9 C2
w side-hamburg.de
Clean lines and futuristic design are the signature features of this 12-storey luxury hotel. Behind its stone-and-glass façade, minimalism prevails. Rooms are well designed, some with panoramic views over Hamburg. The ceiling of the long, thin lobby rises up to 28 m (91 ft) dwarfing hotel guests, while computer-controlled light installations adorn the walls.

Room with a view of the Elbe, Louis C. Jacob

Port and Speicherstadt

Gresham Carat Hotel   €€
Sieldeich 5 – 6, 20539
Tel *78 96 60*
w carat-hotel-hamburg.de
If you want to experience the building of HafenCity up close, this stylish hotel is the ideal place to stay. The bedrooms are decorated in warm earthy colours and the all-day restaurant, Limerick, serves German and international cuisine, the Shannon Bar offers Irish food.

The Rilano Hotel Hamburg   €€
Hein Saß Weg 10, 21129
Tel *300 84 90*
w rilano-hotel-hamburg.de
The Rilano is located near the Airbus plant in the district of Finkenwerder. The hotel's own ferry dock allows convenient transfer into the city centre. All the bedrooms are elegant and modern, with spectacular views of the Elbe.

St Pauli

Arcotel Onyx Hamburg   €€
Reeperbahn 1a, 20359
Tel *209 40 90*   **Map** 4 D3
w arcotelhotels.com/en/onyx_ hotel_hamburg
The Arcotel Onyx rises up on the eastern end of the Reeperbahn. Its glossy monolithic façade is punctuated by round blue windows. The hotel combines contemporary design with plush furniture. Its lounge-style Wiener Café is very appealing. There's a fitness area and two saunas.

Mövenpick Hotel Hamburg   €€
Sternschanze 6, 20357
Tel *334 41 10*
w moevenpick-hotels.com
Located in the Sternschanzenpark, this unique hotel is built into a

historic water tower, 57.5 m (189 ft) tall. The suites on the 16th floor offer 360 degree views. The restaurant serves Swiss cuisine; the bar is housed in the red-brick cellar.

East   €€€
Simon-von-Utrecht-Straße 31, 20359
Tel *30 99 30*   **Map** 4 E2
w east-hamburg.de
Near the Reeperbahn, this boutique hotel of the first order was once an old iron foundry and was transformed by star architect Jordan Mozer. This luxurious temple to good living is very trendy, and the rooms, lofts and suites are spacious. The concierge assists guests with ticket bookings and arranges a shuttle service.

Empire Riverside Hotel   €€€
Bernhard-Nocht-Straße 31, 20359
Tel *31 11 90*   **Map** 4 D4
w empire-riverside.de
On the grounds of a former brewery rises this modern hotel. Clean lines characterize the rooms, which are located between the fourth and the 20th floors; each has a panorama window covering an entire wall. Wonderful views from the 20th floor at Skybar 20up.

Altona

Boston Hamburg   €€€
Missundestraße 2, 22769
Tel *589 66 67 00*   **Map** 2 E1
w boston-hamburg.de
This is a modern and tastefully decorated designer hotel directly beside the Neue Flora – the ideal location for a weekend of musicals. The rooms have beautifully designed bathrooms, many with tropical rain showerheads. There is a bar and communal lounge area with an open fireplace.

For more information on types of hotel *see pages 172–3*

Gastwerk Hotel Hamburg €€€
Beim Alten Gaswerk 3, 22761
Tel *89 06 20* **Map** 1 A1
🅦 gastwerk.com/hotels-hamburg/
A successful mix of traditional
comfort and modern design. This
industrial feel, loft-style hotel is
housed in a red-brick coal
warehouse of a former gasworks
built in the 1890s.

Around the Alster

Aussen Alster €€
Schmilinskystraße 11, 20099
Tel *284 07 85 70* **Map** 8 E4
🅦 aussenalsterhotel.de
Hidden behind a white façade is
a hotel that has contemporary
designed bedrooms and
communal areas. The restaurant's
creative Italian cuisine can be
enjoyed on the lovely garden
terrace. It is a very short walk
from the Aussen Alster to the
Außenalster, where a sailboat
owned by the hotel awaits the
hotel's guests.

Hotel Amsterdam €€
im Dammtorpalais
Moorweidenstraße 34, 20146
Tel *441 11 10* **Map** 7 B3
🅦 hotelamsterdam.de
Patrons of this hotel, which is
located in a historic gabled
building, will enjoy a tranquil
stay. The rooms are individually
decorated and themed – some
romantic vintage; some restrained
contemporary. Many of the rooms
have high, stuccoed ceilings and
multi-paned windows.

Hotel Smolka €€
Isestraße 98, 20149
Tel *48 09 80*
🅦 hotel-smolka.de
The Smolka is located in the
district of Harvestehude – a
choice residential area, with
many green spaces. Each guest
room is furnished uniquely, and
the hotel lobby, restaurant and
bar are very elegant. In the
library, the fireplace creates a
cosy ambience. One of the
biggest weekly markets in
Hamburg, the Isemarkt, is held
right around the corner.

Hotel Vorbach €€
Johnsallee 63 – 67, 20146
Tel *44 18 20* **Map** 7 B3
🅦 hotel-vorbach.de
This unusual hotel in the
Harvestehude district stretches
over an assemblage of three Belle
Époque buildings. High ceilings,
plaster ornamentation and Art
Deco elements give the spacious
rooms a unique charm. Hotel
Vorbach is fully equipped and
well suited for longer stays.

Hotel Wagner €€
im Dammtorpalais
Moorweidenstraße 34, 20146
Tel *450 13 10* **Map** 7 B3
🅦 hotel-wagner-hamburg.de
Several very different hotels
are located in this Jugendstil
palace, which is under heritage
protection. Rooms in the Hotel
Wagner are decorated in
contemporary style and
equipped with modern features,
including showers with colour
changing technology. The
breakfast room has the ambience
of a coffee house.

DK Choice

Hotel Wedina €€
Gurlittstraße 23, 20099
Tel *280 89 00* **Map** 8 E4
🅦 hotelwedina.de
This hotel has a colour theme
setting its mood. The "red"
has rooms inspired by the
1980s, the "yellow" has a
Mediterranean ambience, the
"blue" features rooms dedicated
to authors and the "green", with
its Zen garden, is just the thing
for lovers of the avant garde.
The owners have amassed a
collection of books signed by
their guests. All in all, a unique
place to stay.

Nippon €€
Hofweg 75, 22085
Tel *227 11 40* **Map** 8 E1
🅦 nipponhotel.de
Clean lines, bold shapes, muted
colours and a few well-chosen
pieces of furniture, along with
paper screens, sliding doors,
futons and tatami mats – this
hotel has taken on the Japanese
aesthetic right down to the last
detail. It's an ideal place to relax
body and mind, and daily
newspapers are free.

Further Afield

Lindner Park-Hotel €€
Hagenbeck
Hagenbeckstraße 150, 22527
Tel *800 80 81 00*
🅦 lindner.de
This is the world's first zoo-
themed hotel, appropriately
located at Hamburg's own
historic zoo, Tierpark Hagenbeck
(see pp136 –7). The rooms are
decorated in either African
or Asian style, and murals and
photos of animals are found
throughout the building –
including polar bears in the spa
and orangutans in the lift.

Steigenberger Hotel €€
Treudelberg
Lemsahler Landstraße 45, 22397
Tel *60 82 20*
🅦 treudelberg.com
This hotel offers a very special
atmosphere, every convenience
imaginable and great service.
Here in the Alster Valley on the
northern edge of the city, tourists
find utter relaxation. The Hotel
Treudelberg has its own 27-hole
golf course and the day spa
pampers visitors with numerous
treatments. Sunday brunch
in the Szenario restaurant is
very popular.

Strandhotel Blankenese €€€
Strandweg 13, 22587
Tel *86 13 44*
🅦 strandhotel-blankenese.de
This historic Jugendstil hotel
is a beautiful white-washed
building with delicate plaster-
work and Juliet balconies. It is
located in the Treppenviertel in
the elegant district of Blankenese.
Each room has its own character
and style, but all are furnished
with contemporary pieces.
Guests can enjoy a view of the
Elbe as they dine in the elegant
and formal restaurant.

Reception desk at the Young Hotel, YoHo

Character

Old Town

Galerie Hotel Petersen €€
Lange Reihe 50, 20099
Tel *24 98 26* **Map** 6 E2
ⓦ ghsp.eu
Whether in period Biedermeier, Art Deco or contemporary style, the five hotel rooms in this classic town house built in 1790 have been lovingly decorated with choice furnishings and art. Individualists, above all, will delight in the creative atmosphere of this charming hotel.

Hotel Continental €€
Kirchenallee 37, 20099
Tel *18 88 11 50* **Map** 6 E2
ⓦ hotel-continental.de
Hanseatic flair with up-to-date comfort – the Hotel Continental, an upmarket hotel, has a friendly atmosphere that is certain to make its guests feel right at home. All the rooms are very comfortable. The breakfast buffet has an excellent selection.

Hotel Graf Moltke Novum €€
Steindamm 1, 20099
Tel *24 42 41 10* **Map** 6 E2
ⓦ hotel-hamburg-graf-moltke.de
This hotel is ideally situated for exploring the city centre. The generously sized rooms in this five-storey building are decorated in standard contemporary style with neutral shades predominating.

Hotel Senator €€
Lange Reihe 18 – 20, 20099
Tel *24 19 30* **Map** 6 F2
ⓦ hotel-senator-hamburg.de
The rooms in this hotel are furnished with standard fittings and fixtures. Signature features are the winter garden and wellness rooms, which feature a mini spa in the bathroom.

Europäischer Hof €€€
Kirchenallee 45, 20099
Tel *24 82 48* **Map** 6 E2
ⓦ europaeischer-hof.de
Along with generously sized rooms, there is a varied programme of fitness and activities, including gym facilities and a large swimming pool as well as beauty treatments. The EURO-Therme spa has an indoor pool, sauna, whirlpool, squash courts and a 7-storey, 150-m (492-ft) long water slide! Your room pass also serves as a three-day public transit (HVV) pass. The three restaurants offer guests a choice of meals each night.

New Town

Baseler Hof €€
Esplanade 11, 290354
Tel *35 90 60* **Map** 10 D1
ⓦ baselerhof.de
Only a few of the large hotels in Hamburg are still privately run – Baseler Hof is one of them. Included in the room price is a three-day public transit (HVV) pass. The Kaffee- and Weinhaus Kleinhuis serves excellent food and more than 50 different wines by the glass.

Port and Speicherstadt

Hotel am Elbufer €€
Focksweg 40a, 21129
Tel *742 19 10*
ⓦ hotel-am-elbufer.de
Many regular guests at this small hotel appreciate its friendly atmosphere. For those whose rooms look out on the Elbe, giant ocean liners seem close enough to touch. The city centre is a short ferry ride away.

Stella Maris €€
Reimarusstraße 12, 20459
Tel *319 20 23* **Map** 9 A4
ⓦ hotel-stellamaris.de
Nautical and modern – a hotel just like Hamburg. The rooms (sailor's, officer's and captain's class) are decorated in light colours. At cooler times of the year, the *Kaminzimmer* (fireplace room) is especially cosy.

St Pauli

Fritz Hotel €€
Schanzenstraße 101 – 103, 20357
Tel *82 22 28 30*
ⓦ fritzhotel.com
Offbeat and imaginative, the Fritz Hotel blends in well with the Schanzenviertel. The rooms are minimalist and stylish.

DK Choice

Hafen Hamburg €€
Seewartenstraße 9, 20459
Tel *31 11 30* **Map** 4 E4
ⓦ hotel-hafen-hamburg.de
This privately run, traditional hotel above the Landungsbrücken is perhaps the most Hanseatic and the most nautical of all Hamburg hotels. Model ships and nautical clocks hang on the walls. The view of the port from the Tower Bar on the twelfth floor could not be better. Choose between seaman's, cabin, lieutenant's and captain's class room.

Bathroom in African-themed guest room, Lindner Park-Hotel Hagenbeck

YoHo €€
Moorkamp 5, 20357
Tel *284 19 10* **Map** 6 E2
ⓦ yoho-hamburg.de
YoHo is short for "Young Hotel", and the ambience in this white Jugendstil villa is refreshingly young, with guests under the age of 26 receiving a discount. Breakfast at friendly communal tables is an ideal place to strike up a conversation.

Around the Alster

Hotel Fresena
im Dammtorpalais €€
Moorweidenstraße 34, 20146
Tel *410 48 92* **Map** 7 B3
ⓦ hotel-wagner-hamburg.de
Located on the third floor in the architecturally appealing Dammtorpalais. Staff can book tickets for cultural events and arrange bike rental. Guests gain free entry to the Museum für Völkerkunde *(see p128)*.

Hotel-Pension Fink €€
Rothenbaumchaussee 73, 20148
Tel *44 05 71* **Map** 7 B2
ⓦ hotel-fink.de
Excellent hospitality prevails at this lovingly restored Jugendstil villa, which is under heritage protection. Rooms are eclectically furnished, with patterned bedspreads and curtains. The hotel is located in the elegant district of Rothenbaum.

Hotel Schwanenwik €€
Schwanenwik 29, 22089
Tel *220 09 18* **Map** 8 F3
ⓦ hotel-schwanenwik.de
This white villa in the Uhlenhorst district is a peaceful place to stay, with views of the Alster or the park-like garden. The Literaturhaus is only a few steps away and the Alster's banks make for a fine walk.

For more information on types of hotel *see pages 172–3*

Further Afield

Hotel Reiterhof Ohlenhoff €€
Ohlenhoff 18, 22848 Norderstedt
Tel *528 73 20*
Ⓦ hotel-reiterhof-ohlenhoff.de
Not far from the gates of
Hamburg and perfect for those
who would like some North
German countryside after a day
in the centre, this hotel is
idyllically located next to horse
stables. The city is still within easy
reach, and the airport is
20 minutes away.

Landhaus Flottbek €€
Baron-Voght-Straße 179, 22607
Tel *822 74 10*
Ⓦ landhaus-flottbek.de
This 18th-century farmhouse has
been lovingly restored, and combines nostalgic country charm
with modern comforts. The restaurant features Holstein cuisine.

Nige Hus €€
Insel Neuwerk, 27499
Tel *(047 21) 295 61*
Ⓦ inselneuwerk.de
Relax by the sea. This hotel on
Neuwerk island *(see p139)* is an
ideal base for tours of the tidal
mudflats or walks to the
lighthouse. The rooms are
spacious. Guests can borrow a
wicker chair for the beach or a
bicycle to explore the island.

Business

Old Town

Best Western Plus €€
Hotel St. Raphael
Adenauerallee 41, 20097
Tel *24 82 00* **Map** 6 F2
Ⓦ straphael-hamburg.
bestwestern.de
This chain hotel is much loved by
business travellers. Every room
is up-to-date and standardized,
so frequent travellers know what
to expect. Le Jardin, the hotel
restaurant, prepares culinary
delights. In the wellness area,
guests relax above the rooftops
of the city.

Centrum Hotel Königshof €€
Pulverteich 18, 20099
Tel *284 07 40* **Map** 6 E2
Ⓦ novum-hotels.de
This hotel concentrates on the
modern and functional., the
lobby area is bright and modern
and this is reflected throughout
the hotel. Rooms have simple,
clean decor, in white with
splashes of bright green. All are
equipped with desks and
business facilities.

Elegant decor and fine views at Radisson Blu, Hamburg's tallest hotel

Hotel Eleazar Novum €€
Bremer Reihe 12–14, 20099
Tel *878 87 70* **Map** 6 E2
Ⓦ hotel-hamburg-eleazar.de
The rooms are equipped with
sound insulating windows, and
are decorated tastefully. Free
newspapers are available in the
lobby. There is a wellness area
with sauna.

InterCityHotel Hamburg €€
Hauptbahnhof
Glockengießerwall 14/15, 20095
Tel *24 87 00* **Map** 6 D2
Ⓦ en.intercityhotel.com/hamburg
Typical for the InterCity chain,
this hotel is centrally located.
Rooms are decorated in warm
colours. There are five conference
rooms and a business centre. The
restaurant specializes in regional
cuisine. Free use of public transit
(HVV) and free newspapers for
hotel guests.

Quality Hotel Ambassador €€
Heidenkampsweg 34, 20097
Tel *238 82 30*
Ⓦ ambassador-hamburg.de
This hotel caters only for business
travellers. Light furnishings and
first-class technical equipment
characterize the rooms. The
wellness area features a pool
and sauna.

Sofitel Hamburg Alter Wall €€
Alter Wall 40, 20457
Tel *36 95 00* **Map** 9 C3
Ⓦ accorhotels.de
The Sofitel Hamburg Alter Wall
has a choice location right in the
heart of the city on the edge of
the Alsterfleet. From its business
services to its beauty salon, the
five-star hotel caters to both
business travellers and tourists.
The modern multi-storey
building boasts contemporary,
luxury decor, with clean lines and
tasteful hues.

New Town

Mercure Hotel Hamburg Mitte €€
Schröderstiftstraße 3, 20146
Tel *45 06 90* **Map** 7 A3
Ⓦ mercure.com
Located opposite the trade fair
grounds and the Hamburger
Fernsehturm, this hotel offers
rooms with desks and printers
and a conference room for up
to 170 people. The Bar Lemon
serves cocktails, the Olive Tree
restaurant: Mediterranean food.

Novum Hotel am Holstenwall €€
Holstenwall 19, 20355
Tel *31 80 80* **Map** 9 A3
Ⓦ novum-hotels.de
Comfortable rooms are tucked
away behind the 19th-century
exterior of this hotel, located
near the trade fair grounds.
Secretarial service.

Renaissance Hotel Hamburg €€
Große Bleichen, 20354
Tel *34 91 80* **Map** 9 C3
Ⓦ marriott.com
This hotel in a red-brick building
offers state-of-the-art conference
facilities and a traditional
restaurant. The nearby Passages
is handy for shopping.

DK Choice

Radisson Blu Hotel €€€
Marseiller Straße 2, 20355
Tel *350 20* **Map** 5 B1
Ⓦ radissonblu.de/hotel-
hamburg
This 27-floor hotel is Hamburg's
tallest. The rooms provide all
the amenities you might expect
in a four-star hotel, with
"Natural", "Urban" and "New
York Mansion" giving hints
of each room's decor. The
Filini restaurant and bar exude
Italian charm and the food
reflects this.

Port and Speicherstadt

Holiday Inn Hamburg €€
Billwerder Neuer Deich 14, 20539
Tel *0800 181 60 68*
W holidayinn.com
The Holiday Inn is one of the largest and best-equipped hotels in Hamburg. The colours and furnishings in the rooms are perfectly matched, and artworks adorn the lobby. For hotel guests entry to the Golf Lounge *(see p215)* is free. Thrillseekers can book an extra treat: abseiling from the hotel's 18th floor.

Altona

InterCityHotel Hamburg €€
Altona
Paul-Nevermann-Platz 17, 22765
Tel *38 03 40*   **Map** 1 C3
W intercityhotel.com/hamburg_altona
The rooms are tastefully turned out and the conference facilities are state-of-the-art. In summer, al fresco dining on the restaurant's terrace is popular. Included in the room price is a public transit (HVV) pass.

Around the Alster

Barceló Hamburg €€
Ferdinandstraße 15, 20095
Tel *226 36 20*   **Map** 6 D2
W barcelo.com
Innovative, avant-garde design is the hallmark of this hotel. Six conference rooms accommodate up to 200 people. The restaurant serves Mediterranean cuisine.

Crowne Plaza Hamburg-City €€
Alster
Graumannsweg 10, 22087
Tel *0800 181 60 68*   **Map** 8 F3
W ichotelsgroup.com
Rooms come equipped with the latest technology and the business services include PCs, printers, fax machines and photocopiers. Hotel guests can unwind in the wellness area or the King George Bar.

Further Afield

NH Hamburg-Horn €€
Rennbahnstraße 90, 22111
Tel *65 59 70*
W nh-hotels.com
Perfect for horse racing enthusiasts, this hotel is located east of Hamburg at the Galopprennbahn Horn *(see p215)*. The rooms are modern in design and some have views of the racetrack. There is a spa and restaurant serving Spanish cuisine.

Budget

Old Town

Generator Hostel Hamburg €
Steintorplatz 3, 20099
Tel *226 35 84 60*   **Map** 6 E2
W generatorhostels.com
Part of the fun and funky Generator hostel chain, Generator Hamburg in Hauptbahnhof, is close to the train station. All rooms have en-suite bathrooms. The hostel appeals to night owls and late risers, and there's a laundry. Head to the bar for karaoke and pub quizzes.

Hotel-Pension von Blumfeld €
Lange Reihe 54, 20099
Tel *24 58 60*   **Map** 6 E2
W pension-blumfeld.de
Only some of the rooms are en suite, shared bathrooms off the corridors serve the rest. All in all, the Hotel-Pension offers very good value, basic accomodation.

St Pauli

A & O Hamburg Reeperbahn €
Reeperbahn 154, 20359
Tel *317 69 99 46 00*   **Map** 3 C4
W aohostels.com
Why not choose a hostel right on Hamburg's best-known street? Blending in perfectly with the Reeperbahn's lively character, the A&O is the ideal place for night owls and party animals.

Hotel St Annen €
Annenstraße 5, 20359
Tel *317 71 30*   **Map** 4 D3
W hotelstannen.de
This hotel is close to the Reeperbahn and yet very quiet. Each room is different, but the colour-scheme throughout is dominated by warm tones, with high-quality cherry wood

Modern and Industrial feel of the Kitchen Club at Superbude St Pauli

furnishings. The Weinbar is a great place to sample wines, especially those from South Africa. Nice garden terrace.

Superbude St Pauli €
Juliusstraße 1 – 7, 22769
Tel *807 91 58 20*   **Map** 3 C1
W superbude.de
Recycled furniture and bold colours create a unique atmosphere at this hostel, in the heart of the Schanzenviertel. All the rooms are en suite and decorated in an industrial chic design. The kitchen (Kitchen Club) is open day and night, and serves a substantial breakfast buffet. The lobby/lounge sports a 50-m (164-ft) long bar.

Altona

DK Choice

25 Hours Hotel €
Hamburg No. 1
Paul-Dessau-Straße 2, 22761
Tel *85 50 70*   **Map** 1 A1
W 25hours-hotels.com/no1
For those who seek the unconventional, this hostel is the ideal place to stay. Opened as Hamburg's first "Low-Cost-Design Hotel", 25 Hours is a flashpackers extraordinaire. Astute sixties and seventies retro styling means fun and funky rooms that rarely overstep the boundaries of taste. Great roof-top terrace on which to enjoy a drink.

ibis budget Hamburg Altona €
Holstenkamp 3, 22525
Tel *85 37 98 20*
W ibis.com
This is a very good option for budget-conscious travellers. The 180 rooms at this chain hotel are identically furnished and equipped with colour TVs. Generous breakfast buffet. The U-Bahn brings you quickly into the city.

Schanzenstern Altona €
Kleine Rainstraße 24 – 26, 22765
Tel *39 91 91 91*   **Map** 1 C3
W schanze.abcde.biz
Although backpackers stay in the Schanzenstern, this hotel is much more than just a backpackers' hostel. The two apartments on the top floor for example make fine accommodation for families. The breakfast buffet serves organic products. The Schanzenstern branch in St Pauli (Bartelsstraße 12) features an organic restaurant.

For more information on types of hotel *see pages 172 – 3*

WHERE TO EAT AND DRINK

Hamburg's gastronomic scene is diverse and, especially in certain districts such as Pöseldorf or St Georg, constantly changing. Trends come and go, and new establishments are continually opening, sometimes with rather inventive themes. Hamburg is a true gourmet paradise; few other cities in Germany can pride themselves on having so many restaurants with first-class cuisine. However, the city also offers a vast range of reasonably priced restaurants serving very good food. Appropriately, the culinary emphasis in this port city is on fish. Since Hamburg is a cosmopolitan city, you can find specialities from every country in the world here. You can dine on wonderful Portuguese, Greek, Vietnamese or Arab food, as well as a range of other national cuisines. Many of the finest establishments in the city are described in the list of selected restaurants on pages 188–193, which covers a wide variety of price categories. A selection of cafés and snack bars is provided on pages 194–197.

The Fischerhaus *(see p190)* is known for its classic fish dishes

Types of Restaurants

Since many Hamburgers relish good food, it is an excellent sign when a restaurant counts many locals among its patrons. During your stay, you will quickly be able to identify which restaurants cater to tourists and which offer a truly genuine Hanseatic experience. The harbour, of course, gives the city a very special atmosphere. There's nothing quite like dining with a view of the port as you watch the boats or a large ocean-going vessel slowly pass by.

Several upmarket restaurants have opened in the gaps between the newly built office buildings, especially in the stretch along the harbour nicknamed the "pearl necklace" by Hamburgers – between the Fischmarkt and Övelgönne. Most restaurants on the harbour promenade have terraces that sometimes are so close to the water that you are in danger of getting wet. Diners also have a lovely water view from many restaurants around the Alster, especially those with terraces on wooden jetties.

Restaurants located inside former warehouses, such as in the Deichstraße *(see p67)* or in other old buildings including the Krameramtswohnungen *(see p72)* have a very special atmosphere.

One of the city's most active ethnic communities are the Portuguese. In the Portuguese district, which is located around the Ditmar-Koel-Straße to the north of the Landungsbrücken, there are many establishments serving Portuguese cuisine of excellent quality.

One original Hamburg gastronomic idea turned out to be a huge hit – a restaurant chain specializing in steaks called Block House. It was founded in 1968 in the Hanseatic city and now has 14 establishments in Hamburg, as well as subsidiaries throughout Germany and in some other European countries.

Reservations

It is always a good idea to make a reservation for fancy or gourmet restaurants. For the most popular establishments, especially those with a view of the harbour, it is necessary to book several days in advance. For most other restaurants, there is only need to book ahead for Friday and Saturday dining.

Prices and Tips

The range of restaurants covers all price categories. Most establishments post a menu with prices beside the entrance. To avoid surprises, look it over before you go in.

One of the key factors that determines the prices a restaurant charges is its location.

The trendy bar in the lobby of stilwerk *(see p119)*

Die Bank brasserie *(see p189)* in what was once a bank

Prices are usually higher at establishments that are closer to the Elbe, as well as those on elegant boulevards, such as the Jungfernstieg or the Neue Wall. In the most inexpensive restaurants, you can expect to pay about 15 Euros for a three-course meal not including alcoholic beverages. In the top restaurants, or those in a choice location, you can end up paying much more than 50 Euros. Of course, ordering the better wines will usually inflate the size of your bill significantly.

All prices include taxes and service, but it is usual to add about a 10 per cent tip. It's appropriate to tip more for especially good service. While many of the better restaurants accept credit cards, smaller pubs or cafés usually do not.

Vegetarians

Since many restaurants in Hamburg specialize in fish dishes, fish lovers will find a great deal of choice here. Although strict vegetarian restaurants are still rather rare, most dining establishments include dishes without meat or fish on their menus. You can also get good salads just about anywhere.

If you have special dietary requirements, do not hesitate to ask the staff; they will usually make every effort to accommodate your wishes, and may provide a specially prepared meal.

Children

Some Hamburg restaurants – especially those in the higher price brackets – are not geared to the needs of children. However, most of them do have high-chairs on hand and offer children's meals.

While you are out and about with children during the day, the city's fast-food restaurants or snack bars are a convenient choice for a bite to eat (see pp190–201). They do not just offer food that kids like, but some also have a children's section where the little ones can run about and play.

Smoking

Smoking is not permitted in Hamburg's restaurants, cafés or bars. You can only smoke in establishments with separate, well-ventilated rooms.

Disabled Travellers

Many Hamburg restaurants have limited wheelchair access, and in many establishments tables are often placed close together, making it difficult for those in wheelchairs to get around. And, quite often, the toilets are located in the basement, and can only be reached by stairs since there is no elevator. Sometimes the hallway leading to the toilets – even if they are on the ground floor – is very narrow, making it difficult to navigate. To be sure

of a comfortable experience, it is best to check ahead when you make your reservation.

Max & Consorten *(see p191)*, a restaurant on the edge of St Georg

Recommended Restaurants

The restaurants and other eating venues outlined in this guide have been chosen because they offer quality and reasonable value for money. They represent a wide range of price bands, and range from traditional eateries serving *Labskaus (see p187)*, to fine dining temples in the city's luxury hotels or Elbe-side warehouses. Look out for entries that have been highlighted as DK Choice. These restaurants have been chosen for their exceptional features, which may include gourmet food or a wonderfully refurbished building. All DK Choices offer excellent food and a memorable dining experience.

Canal-side dining in style at the Rialto *(see p189)*

The Flavours of Hamburg

The gates of the Elbe metropolis have always stood wide open to welcome the world, and this is reflected in its cuisine. Many ingredients and spices commonly used in Europe today were once unknown or rare, and started their conquest of the Continent from Hamburg's port and warehouses. The cuisine of the Hanseatic city is dominated by a wide variety of fish dishes. Hearty stews and a wide range of vegetables and fruits enrich the gastronomic offerings. The hamburger, famous the world over, actually has nothing at all to do with the city.

Crisp, freshly picked apples from the Altes Land

The daily menu displayed in front of a Hamburg restaurant

Fish Dishes

To get an idea of the many kinds of fish used in Hamburg cuisine, you must stroll through the St Pauli Fish Market *(see p108)* just once. The catch comes in fresh each day from the Elbe river as well as the North Sea and Baltic Sea;

some gourmet restaurants order fish caught in the Mediterranean and Atlantic directly from the Paris market halls. Fish is prepared in every conceivable way in Hamburg. The most popular kinds are eel *(Aal)*, plaice *(Scholle)*, pike *(Hecht)*, herring *(Hering)* and pike-perch *(Zander)*. The fish

may be fried or steamed; baked, smoked or marinated; or made into tasty fish soups and stews.

Potatoes usually accompany traditional North German dishes. They are served either boiled, in their jackets, pan-fried, or as delicious potato salad. Green beans or a green

Franzbrötchen with chocolate

Franzbrötchen with raisins

Franzbrötchen with pumpkin seeds

Croissant

Rye bun

Whole wheat bread

Different kinds of bread, buns and baked goods

Typical North German dishes

Hamburg cuisine is dominated by a mixture of fish dishes and hearty home-style fare. Some dishes are inextricably linked with the city of Hamburg, such as *Labskaus*, Finkenwerder Scholle (a plaice dish) and *Matjes* (salt herring) dishes. *Hamburger Aalsuppe* (Hamburg eel soup) once had everything in it except eel. If the soup does contain eel, then this is a concession to tourists. This soup gets its sweet-sour taste from dried fruit (mainly apples). An odd-sounding yet beloved dish is *Birnen, Bohnen und Speck* (pears, green beans and bacon). The flavour contrast between the smoked bacon, the slightly bitter beans and the sweetness of the pears makes for a delicious combination. If speed is of the essence, then many Hamburgers will choose a *Frikadelle* (kind of hamburger) or a *Fischbrötchen* (fish in a bun) from a *Fischbude*, a booth that sells fish.

Cabbage rolls on cooked carrots

Labskaus is a traditional seaman's dish that gets its characteristic red colouring from red beetroots *(see box on p185)*.

WHERE TO EAT AND DRINK

Prawns, shrimp, crayfish, rollmops, mussels and other fish delicacies

Baked Goods and Desserts

In Hamburg, you can choose from a cornucopia of baked goods. There are many different kinds of bread and pastries such as *Franzbrötchen* (a raised pastry with a sweet filling) and *Hanseat* (pastry fingers with a red-white glaze). *Kopenhagener*, puff-pastry delicacies, are filled with marzipan or jam, *braune Kuchen* are cookies baked until crisp and are a bit like *Lebkuchen* (spice cookies). Mouth-watering desserts include *Rote Grütze*, made of cooked red berries, and *Hamburger Sandkuchen*, a kind of Madeira cake.

salad are also often served with fish dishes. Fish sauces usually have a cream or mustard base. Overall, Hamburg is an ideal city in which to enjoy tasty simple fare as well as creative modern variations.

Soups and Stews

In the countryside surrounding Hamburg there is a lot of farming activity. Livestock graze and crops are cultivated in the fields. There are all sorts of vegetables, potatoes and fruit – important ingredients for hearty soups and stews that Hamburgers love. The fertile Altes Land *(see p138)*, just outside the city gates, is the largest continuous fruit-growing district in Central Europe. Much of the reclaimed arable land is given over to apple orchards. Among the

better-known soups and stews are *Birnen, Bohnen und Speck* (pears, green beans and bacon) and *Grünkohltopf mit Kassler und Kochwurst*, (kale with ham and sausage), and *Labskaus* (seaman's stew).

Dat Backhus outlet located on the Binnenalster

LABSKAUS

This classic Hamburg dish is a traditional seaman's stew that is very popular along the entire North German coast, even though it might look a bit unpromising at first glance. This stew is made of finely chopped salted beef, potatoes, red beetroots and other kinds of vegetables, such as celery and leek, as well as salted herring. A fried egg is placed on top, and dill pickles are served on the side. It is accompanied by flavourful farmer's bread. Nothing tastes better with *Labskaus* than a cool beer.

Finkenwerder Scholle (Finkenwerd plaice) is a common way of preparing plaice. It generally features a bacon-and-onion stuffing.

Matjes (salt herring) with beans is one of the most popular herring dishes. In spring, when "young" herring are available, it is a real delicacy.

Rote Grütze is a mixture of cooked red berries and a bit of red wine. This tasty dessert is often served with vanilla sauce or cream.

What to Drink

Just as in most other regions of Germany, beer is the most popular alcoholic drink in Hamburg, too. The city has a beer-brewing tradition going back centuries. Many Hamburgers are especially proud of the Astra label. The many kinds of schnapps – strong distilled spirits (not all of which are clear) – are typical of Northern Germany, as is tea. Among the alcohol-free refreshments, fritz-kola and Bionade have greatly increased their market shares in the past few years.

Coasters and bottle caps of popular beers

Beer

Beer has a long tradition in the Hanseatic city; in fact, during the Middle Ages Hamburg's reputation stood or fell on the quality of its beer. The Holsten brewery, founded in 1879, is the largest brewery. Located on the Holstenstraße in Altona, it has been part of the Carlsberg-Deutschland Group since 2004. The premium label, Duckstein, is brewed there. The Holsten logo showing a knight on a galloping horse is known around the world. Offerings from other North German breweries are also plentiful in Hamburg; these include Wicküler, Jever, Beck's and Flensburger.

Wicküler beer   Holsten beer   Jever beer

Bright red Astra advertising, an integral part of St Pauli

Astra

Astra is more than "just" a Hamburg beer label. Several different types of beer are sold in the greater Hamburg area under this name: Urtyp, Exclusiv, Pilsener and the slightly stronger Rotlicht. Until 2003, Astra beer (as well as Astra Alsterwasser) was made in the Bavaria-St.-Pauli brewery located between the Reeperbahn and Landungsbrücken. The buildings have since been torn down, and Astra brewery was taken over by Holsten brewery, but this original Hamburg product still remains a Reeperbahn icon.

Rotlicht and Urtyp – two beers from Astra brewery

Alsterwasser

This beverage mix – known in southern Germany as a Radler and in England as a shandy – consists of one-half lemon-flavoured soda and one-half lager. It was once always freshly mixed in restaurants, bars and private homes. Since the German beer tax law was altered in 1993, Alsterwasser and its cousins have been sold in bottles by beverage companies. A tip: if you want to make your own Alsterwasser, first pour in the lemon soda, then the beer, otherwise the beer will not be able to develop a creamy head.

Alsterwasser, a mix of beer and lemon-flavoured soda

Spirits and Liqueurs

There is a wide choice of spirits in shops, restaurants and bars. A schnapps rounds off a meal or provides a bit of welcome warmth on a damp day. Among the classics are herbal liqueurs, such as Wattenläufer, aniseed schnapps such as Küstennebel, or the distilled Aquavit, flavoured with caraway seeds. While sailors once drank straight rum, today, when the weather is miserable in Hamburg, people enjoy a Grog (a shot of rum with hot water).

Wattenläufer   Egg liqueur   Aquavit   Küstennebel

fritz-limo and fritz-kola – non-alcoholic beverages originating in Hamburg

Non-Alcoholic Drinks

It is safe to drink Hamburg tap water – and it has been safe since before the days of Wasserträger Hummel (see p67). But most people order a bottle of mineral water in a restaurant – sparkling or still. Apart from the usual soft drinks found everywhere, there are a few new speciality beverages originating in Hamburg that have become well known throughout Germany and even beyond its borders.

A cola drink by the name of fritz-kola originated in the Hanseatic city and has been on the market since 2003. It has a higher caffeine content than the market leader and was at first only sold in Hamburg bars before moving beyond the city boundaries. Along with fritz-kola, the company created a soft-drink series called fritz-limo.

Bionade is a fermented herbal fruit drink made with natural products. It comes in various flavours – Elderberry, Lychee, Herbs, Ginger & Orange, Quince and Active (with more minerals). In 1997, Bionade began to conquer Hamburg's beverage market – first in fitness-centres, then in trendy bars and finally as a drink for the masses.

Bionade, a herbal, fruit soft drink   Mineral water and "Apfelsaftschorle"   Mineral water

Hot Drinks

Although the American coffee shop, with its bewildering number of flavoured coffee varieties, has become well-established in Hamburg there is still nothing like a good cup of unadulterated coffee – meaning no added flavours. Apart from the commonly available filter coffee, espresso and cappuccino are also popular drinks. There are also some tea salons in Hamburg, where tea preparation is still treated as a real ritual, attracting tea aficionados.

A cup of coffee – espresso or cappuccino

East Frisian black tea

Where to Eat and Drink

Old Town

Daniel Wischer   €
Traditional   **Map** 10 E3
Spitalerstraße 12, 20095
Tel 32 52 58 15   **Closed** Sun
Hamburg's oldest fish fryer opened
in 1924 and is still a good option
for a quick meal. From the beginning, its motto has been "there's
always fish, and fish always sells".
The food ranges from *Matjes*
(salted herring) to pollack. Don't
forget a side of potato salad.

Ti Breizh   €
French   **Map** 9 C4
Deichstraße 39, 20459
Tel 37 51 78 15
This restaurant brings the spirit
of Brittany to the Alster. It serves
delicious *galettes* and crêpes,
filled with either a savoury or
sweet filling – from goat's cheese
and artichoke to scrumptious
cherry flambé.

Café Paris   €€
French   **Map** 10 D3
Rathausstraße 4, 20095
Tel 32 52 77 77
French cuisine served in a lovely
Jugendstil atmosphere at the
foot of the Rathaus. A downtown
mix of stock brokers, shoppers
and visitors to the city dine under
ceiling mosaics on fine dishes
such as *coq au vin*, tripe capped
with puff-pasty, and steak tartar
with capers and mustard.

Fillet of Soul   €€
European   **Map** 10 F4
Deichtorstraße 2, 20095
Tel 70 70 58 00
Art meets gastronomy at this
restaurant in the Deichtorhallen

Mediterranean restaurant Marblau, with
its distinctive azure blue ceiling

(see pp62–3), which considers
itself equal in its own way to the
art displayed in the museum.
Carrot and apple soup with
hazelnut pesto, ocean perch fillet
poached in a Thai curry stock or
beef simmered in stock
(Tafelspitz) with asparagus.

Golden Cut   €€
International   **Map** 10 F2
Holzdamm 61, 20099
Tel 85 10 35 32
Dine and chill out under one roof
in this restaurant and club, a
place to see and be seen. Dine
on breast of duck or fillet of pike-
perch on cabbage cooked with
champagne, then dance the
night away in the lounge.

Mama   €€
Italian   **Map** 10 D3
Schauenburgerstraße 44, 20095
Tel 36 09 99 93
The owners of Mama have created
a modern version of a trattoria.
Their flawless Italian dishes include
pizza, pasta, antipasti and great
desserts. Guests sit either on low
stools with huge cushions, on
traditional wooden benches, or
at a 6-m (20-ft) long table.

Le Plat du Jour   €€
French   **Map** 9 C3
Dornbusch 4, 20095
Tel 32 14 14
French bistro food at its finest.
Choose from the set menu or
eat à la carte. Popular choices
include the hearty home-made
paté, entrées of *scampi provençal*
and roasted rack of lamb with a
rosemary-infused sauce.

Weltbühne   €€
European   **Map** 10 E3
Gerhart-Hauptmann-Platz 70, 20095
Tel 30 39 32 50
For theatre-goers, this café and
bistro in the Thalia Theater is the
ideal place to dine. The traditional
dishes include fillet of halibut
and *Tafelspitz* (beef simmered in
stock) as well as Viennese apple
strudel and *Palatschinken* (pan-
cakes) with apricot jam.

Alt Hamburger   €€€
Aalspeicher
Traditional   **Map** 9 C4
Deichstraße 43, 20459
Tel 36 29 90
Eel is the speciality of this
restaurant in a 16th century
warehouse. Guests first select an
eel and, when the freshly smoked
eel arrives at their table, peel off
the skin with their fingers. They

then clean their hands with
Kornbrannt (corn schnapps).
There's also *Matjeshering* (salted
herring) with pan-fried potatoes.

Deichgraf   €€€
Traditional   **Map** 9 C4
Deichstraße 23, 20459
Tel 36 42 08
If you'd like to dine in a traditional
restaurant that serves authentic
Hanseatic cuisine, head here.
The classic dishes include fillet
of sturgeon on beetroot salad
and mullet in a mussel and
saffron infused stock served on
pearl barley risotto.

Saliba Alsterarkaden   €€€
Syrian   **Map** 10 D3
Neuer Wall 13, 20354
Tel 34 50 21
A touch of the Middle East under
the white arches of the arcade
along Alsterfleet. Hardly anyone
who comes here can resist lamb
cooked with dates and
pomegranates. A strong cup
of coffee rounds off the meal.

Tschebull   €€€
Austrian   **Map** 10 D3
Mönckebergstraße 7, 20095
Tel 32 96 47 96   **Closed** Sun
Authentic Austrian fare such as
Wiener schnitzel and *Kärntner
Käsenudeln* (pasta with cheese)
as well as fish dishes and seafood.
Try *Salzburger Nockerln* (sweet
soufflé) for dessert.

New Town

DK Choice

Marblau   €€
Mediterranean   **Map** 9 B2
Poolstraße 21, 20355
Tel 35 01 65 55
This restaurant serves specialities from the Mediterranean.
Classic Spanish and Italian dishes
are prepared with North African
spices and herbs. The ambience
is perfect: the ceilings are as
azure blue as the summer sky
and evocative photos printed
on canvas adorn the walls.

Price Guide
For a three-course meal per person
including tax, service and half a bottle
of house wine.

€	under €30
€€	€30–€50
€€€	over €50

Marinehof
European   €€   **Map** 9 B4
Admiralitätstraße 77, 20459
Tel *374 25 79*   **Closed** *Sun*
Located on Fleetinsel, this light-filled restaurant has become a popular post-work meeting place for people in the media. Potato gnocchi and lentil-and-spinach soup are especially popular.

Matsumi
Japanese   €€   **Map** 9 C1
Colonnaden 96, 20354
Tel *34 31 25*
This is the oldest Japanese restaurant in Hamburg. The cold green-tea noodles with a sour dip are bold and popular with regulars; the fried eel and prawn dumplings with lotus root are no less exotic. Japanese beer and a huge choice of sakes.

Shalimar
Indian   €€   **Map** 9 C2
ABC-Straße 46 – 47, 20354
Tel *44 24 84*
Here, Indian cuisine, from mild to devilishly hot, is served between golden columns. Dishes include chicken fillet in yoghurt sauce, vegetable curry with rice and fillet of lamb in ginger sauce.

Die Bank
European   €€€   **Map** 9 C2
Hohe Bleichen 17, 20354
Tel *238 00 30*
The menu of this brasserie in a former bank opens to reveal "bank secrets" such as the gold hamburger with goose liver and truffle sauce. A chickpea stew with wild shrimp is another classic.

[m]eatery
American   €€€   **Map** 9 C2
Drehbahn 49, 20354
Tel *30 99 95 95*
Steaks are the speciality of this restaurant in the designer hotel SIDE *(see p177)*. The meat is sourced from Argentina, the US and Schleswig-Holstein.

DK Choice

La Mirabelle
French   €€€   **Map** 7 A3
Bundesstraße 15, 20146
Tel *410 75 85*   **Closed** *Sun*
"Where wine and cuisine are married" is the motto at this French restaurant where the proprietor often helps guests choose the perfect wine to accompany their meal. One of the top palate pleasers is baby goat – the leg is simmered, the saddle roasted. The cheese selection is unsurpassable.

Old Commercial Room
Traditional   €€€   **Map** 9 A4
Englische Planke 10, 20459
Tel *36 63 19*
Most patrons of this traditional Hamburg restaurant come from outside the city. Plaice Büsum-style with saltwater shrimp, beef roulade with red cabbage and potato dumplings, eel soup and *Labskaus* (seaman's stew with beetroot) are the menu's hits.

Rialto
Mediterranean   €€€   **Map** 9 C4
Michaelisbrücke 3, 20459
Tel *36 43 42*
Come here for light Mediterranean cuisine, such as red snapper wrapped in a banana leaf with spinach salad, or goat's cheese on beetroot *carpaccio*. Elegant tables and subdued lighting create a cosy atmosphere. On warm days, the terrace gets busy.

Zu den alten Krameramtsstuben am Michel
Traditional   €€€   **Map** 9 B4
Krayenkamp 10, 20459
Tel *36 58 00*
In a narrow cul-de-sac at the foot of St Michaelis church is this unique 17th-century building complex *(see p72)*. "The Michel" serves traditional Hamburg fare beneath the wooden ceilings.

Port and Speicherstadt

Oberhafen Kantine
Traditional   €   **Map** 6 E4
Stockmeyerstraße 39, 20457
Tel *32 52 74 13*
This restaurant serves Hanseatic classics: *labskaus*, meatballs, eggs and bacon and beef goulash.

La Baracca
Italian   €€   **Map** 10 E5
Am Sandtorkai 44, 20459
Tel *284 673 733*
Upon entering La Baracca, you'll be handed a tablet computer where you'll find the menu and information on ordering the drinks and Italian food – pizza, pasta, soups, antipasti and desserts.

Schönes Leben
European   €€   **Map** 6 D4
Alter Wandrahm 15, 20457
Tel *180 48 26 80*
This restaurant serves breakfast from 10am, a buffet including a main course and side dishes at lunchtime, coffee and cakes in the afternoon, and pasta, meat, fish and vegetarian dishes for dinner.

Pierre Moissonnier, head chef at French restaurant, La Mirabelle

Stricker's KehrWiederSpitze
Traditional   €€   **Map** 9 B5
Am Sandtorkai 77, 20457
Tel *51 90 30 61*   **Closed** *Mon (Jan, Feb)*
Enjoy the fantastic view from the terrace of this restaurant, located at the westernmost edge of HafenCity. Good Hanseatic food at reasonable prices.

CARLS
European   €€€   **Map** 5 B5
Am Kaiserkai 69, 20457
Tel *300 32 24 00*
Brasserie, bistro and bar in one. This gastronomic outpost of the Louis C. Jacob hotel *(see p176)* with dark wooden floors and giant chandeliers is located beside the Elbphilharmonie *(see pp88–9)* and serves French-Hanseatic cuisine.

DK Choice

MEERWEIN
Traditional   €€€   **Map** 10 E5
Koreastr. 1 (Kaispeicher B), 20457
Tel *3008 7888*   **Closed** *Mon*
Located in the massive Kaispeicher B, a Neo-Gothic warehouse housing the Maritime Museum *(see pp 86–7)*, this restaurant has an excellent, lovingly maintained oyster bar. Head chef Gilbert von Hof and sommelier Gaillaume Boullay also offer wonderful seafood entrées and wine.

VLET
Traditional   €€€   **Map** 5 C4
Am Sandtorkai 23/24, 20457
Tel *334 75 37 50*   **Closed** *Sun*
Gourmet restaurant located in an old warehouse The pike-perch fillet, veal tenderloin and eel soup please even the most demanding palates. The cheese platters are sensational.

For more information on types of restaurant *see page183*

Wandrahm €€€
European **Map** 5 C5
Am Kaiserkai 13, 20457
Tel *31 81 22 00*
Elegant and chic, the Wandrahm
offers everything: mornings it's a
coffee- and tea-shop; at lunch it
is a place for a quick snack; the
afternoon is sweetened with
home-made cakes; and in the
evenings fine-dining meals.

St Pauli

Hamborger Veermaster €
Traditional **Map** 3 C4
Reeperbahn 162, 20359
Tel *31 65 44* **Closed** *Jan – Easter:*
Sun –Thu
The oldest and most atmospheric
restaurant on the Reeperbahn
offers shrimp soup, *Pannfisch* (a
dish of leftover fish in a mustard
sauce), and *Rote Grütt* (cooked
red berries with vanilla sauce).

Man Wah €
Chinese **Map** 4 D4
Spielbudenplatz 18, 20359
Tel *319 25 11*
This Chinese restaurant in the
Reeperbahn area is open until
4am and offers dumplings filled
with meat or vegetables.

Bullerei €€
International
Lagerstraße 34b, 20357
Tel *33 44 21 10*
Run by a TV-chef this restaurant
is cherished by aficionados of
hearty fare. Regulars keep returning for the stuffed black-feathe-
red chicken, lamb shoulder
cooked in milk and fillet steak.

Fischerhaus €€
Traditional **Map** 2 E48
St Pauli Fischmarkt 14, 20359
Tel *31 40 53*
Rustic atmosphere and North
German cuisine with classics
such as eel soup and *Labskaus*,
and specialities like ocean perch,
white halibut and giant prawns.

Luxor €€
International **Map** 2 F1
Max-Brauer-Allee 251, 22769
Tel *430 01 24* **Closed** *Mon*
Despite what the name might
lead you to expect, the food
here is International, and not
Egyptian. Instead, expect Viennese
Tafelspitz, Provençal fish soup and
Irish oysters.

Nil €€€
European **Map** 4 D2
Neuer Pferdemarkt 5/6, 20359
Tel *439 78 23* **Closed** *Tue*

The stylish interior of VLET, located in a refurbished warehouse *(see p189)*

The 1950s decor creates a unique
atmosphere over the restaurant's
three floors. Organic ingredients
are used in dishes such as chicory
stuffed with spinach and asparagus with ham and mushrooms.

Schauermann €€€
Mediterranean **Map** 3 C4
St Pauli Hafenstraße 136 – 138, 20359
Tel *31 79 46 60* **Closed** *Sun*
An oasis of minimalist style with
turquoise and black leather seats.
Lamb shank with beans, scallops
and crispy prawns are among the
dishes served here.

Altona

Altamira €
Spanish **Map** 1 C1
Bahrenfelder Straße 331, 22761
Tel *380 93 42*
Rumoured to have the best tapas
north of Barcelona, with 70 differ-
ent dishes each day including
many vegetarian options.

Bolero €
Mexican **Map** 1 C3
Bahrenfelder Straße 53, 22765
Tel *390 78 00*
Fajitas, enchiladas, nachos and
more – typical Mexican food that
will fill you up. Load up your
tortilla with meat and veg to your
liking. More than 100 cocktails.

DK Choice

Haifischbar €
Traditional **Map** 2 E4
Große Elbstraße 128, 22767
Tel *380 93 42*
The furniture is a bit dusty and
the menu only features
traditional favourites: *Matjes*,
plaice and *Labskaus*. But even
so, the Haifischbar is imbued
with the romance of seafaring
and is well loved by its guests.

German stars such as Hans
Albers, Freddy Quinn and Lale
Andersen frequented this bar
back in the day. Not to be
missed – a quintessential
Hamburg experience.

Zum Schellfischposten €
Traditional **Map** 2 E4
Carsten-Rehder-Straße 62, 22767
Tel *38 34 22*
Altona's oldest seaman's pub
serves up plain food such as fish
in a roll. The restaurant has been
used as a set for numerous TV
productions, including the
popular late-night show *Inas
Nacht* with German singer and
cabaret artist Ina Müller.

Breitengrad €€
Sri Lankan **Map** 2 E1
Gefionstraße 3, 22769
Tel *43 18 99 99*
Large portions of rice and mixed
salads are served with fiery hot
dishes (such as chicken curry and
lamb vindaloo). Sunday brunch
with live music.

Eisenstein €€
European **Map** 1 B2
Friedensallee 9, 22765
Tel *390 46 06*
Located in an old ship-propeller
factory, Eisenstein is a fine-dining
restaurant, breakfast place
and beer garden all rolled into
one. Try the scallops with sweet
potatoes, saddle of venison with
black salsify ragout, or perfect
thin and crisp wood-fired pizzas.

IndoChine €€
Southeast Asian **Map** 1 B5
Neumühlen 11, 22763
Tel *39 80 78 80*
The kitchen blends Southeast
Asian flavours with French notes
and they do this to perfection.
Prawns prepared Cambodian-style
or banana and coconut-rice
rolls with fruity dips are typical.

Lutter & Wegner €€
European **Map** 2 E4
Große Elbstraße 49, 22767
Tel 809 00 90 00
The speciality is Wiener Schnitzel, and here is one of the best, especially on the terrace, with the fresh breezes blowing off the Elbe.

Shikara €€
Indian **Map** 1 C2
Bahrenfelder Straße 241, 22765
Tel 39 90 66 96
Indian specialities coloured by an aray of spices are featured here. Along with tandoori dishes, there are also pakoras, dhall dishes and chicken tikka.

La Vela €€
Italian **Map** 2 E4
Große Elbstraße 27, 22767
Tel 38 60 93 93
Italian restaurant in a top location at the start of "gastronomy mile" between the Fischmarkt and Övelgönne. Lasagne and tagliatelle with asparagus tips are among the choices for mains.

Au Quai €€€
Mediterranean **Map** 2 D4
Große Elbstraße 145b – d, 22767
Tel 38 03 77 30 **Closed** Sun
Combining Mediterranean cuisine and Asian-influenced decor. The view of the Elbe is absolutely wonderful. From the terrace, you can watch the sun setting over Hamburg.

DK Choice

Fischereihafen €€€
Restaurant
International **Map** 2 D4
Große Elbstraße 143, 22767
Tel 38 18 16
Hamburg's celebrities love the exquisite fish cuisine served in this gastronomic institution belonging to the Kowalke family. Along with regional fish dishes of fresh turbot, flounder and eel, this restaurant also serves French oysters and Iranian caviar. This is an ideal place for pampered palates.

Henssler & Henssler €€€
Fusion **Map** 2 D4
Große Elbstraße 160, 22767
Tel 38 69 90 00 **Closed** Sun
The cuisine here is rich in contrasts, featuring classic Japanese culinary artistry with modern international influences. Try chicken skewers Yakitori or tuna sashimi with a selection of marinated vegetables. A perfect blend of flavours.

Rive €€€
European **Map** 2 D4
Van-der-Smissen-Str 1, 22767
Tel 380 59 19
This award-winning restaurant and oyster bar offers everything the ocean provides along with a wonderful river view. Delicacies include a seafood platter with oysters, langoustines and mussels amongst others.

Das Seepferdchen €€€
Traditional **Map** 2 D4
Große Elbstraße 212, 22767
Tel 38 61 67 49 **Closed** Sun
This restaurant is located in a former warehouse that was once used for storing fish. It is decorated in sand-coloured tones and offers a large variety of seafood, including fish burgers, grilled lobster, sautéed haddock and giant prawns.

Around the Alster

ALEX im Alsterpavillon €
European **Map** 10 D2
Jungfernstieg 54, 20354
Tel 350 18 70
Once a plush café, a permanent institution on the Jungfernstieg, has been bought up by a restaurant chain. The Alex is popular with a young crowd, particularly for brunch. The view out over the Binnenalster is phenomenal.

Max & Consorten €
European **Map** 6 E2
Spadenteich 1, 20099
Tel 280 22 28
This long-established restaurant in St Georg has the casual ambience of a pub. The menu features Hamburg classics such as pickled herring with sour cream, apples and onions, and pan-fried potatoes with a fried egg, as well as pasta dishes.

Brodersen €€
Traditional **Map** 7 B3
Rothenbaumchaussee 46, 20148
Tel 45 81 19
Appeals to aficionados of Hanseatic cuisine with its comfort food made from local ingredients, including *Büsumer Krabben* (crabs fished from the waters near the city of Büsum in Schleswig-Holstein), *Heidekartoffeln* (a local variety of potato) and meat obtained from Altes Land.

Kajüte €€
An der Alster 10A (Steg), 20099
Traditional **Map** 8 E4
Tel 24 30 37

Set on a private landing stage, which has berths for ships, the Kajüte is literally "on", not "by", the river Alster and has breathtaking views of the river and city, especially from its gorgeous sun deck and winter garden. Tasty, seasonal cuisine features on the small menu, which favours fish and seafood, and the occasional sushi dish.

Ristorante Galatea €€
Italian **Map** 10 E2
Am Ballindamm, 20095
Tel 33 72 27
Here, Hamburg gastronomy shows itself from a different side. This restaurant boat docked at the Binnenalster shore serves Italian food, along with a few regional specialities. As you might expect, the tables sway, but that only adds to the meal.

Suzy Wong €€
Chinese
Mittelweg 141, 20148 **Map** 7 C2
Tel 45 41 12
Suzy Wong pampers guests with refined dishes from the Far East, specializing in food from Shanghai. The most popular among the specialities on the menu are: beef-curry with coconut milk, roast duck with broccoli, prawns with bamboo shoots and steamed turbot with ginger.

Brasserie Flum €€€
French **Map** 7 B3
Rothenbaumchaussee 10, 20148
Tel 41 41 27 23
The brasserie at the Grand Elysée Hotel (*see p176*) has been designed with authentic Parisian flair by architect Max Flum and features a wonderful Art Nouveau ceiling. It serves classic French dishes such as *boulliabaisse*.

Restrained elegance in the dining room at Küchenwerkstatt (*see p192*)

For more information on types of restaurant *see page 183*

Cox €€€
European **Map** 6 E1
Lange Reihe 68, 20099
Tel *24 94 22*
Hip restaurant with a bistro feel.
Guests sit at small tables on red
leather banquettes and enjoy
stewed duck with apple and
horseradish sauce, gnocchi with
rosemary, and lamb stew with
olives and sun-dried tomatoes.
Special offers at lunchtime.

DK Choice

Haerlin €€€
International **Map** 10 D2
Neuer Jungfernstieg 9–14, 20354
Tel *34 94 33 10* **Closed** *Sun, Mon*
Upon surveying the majestic
restaurant in the Hotel Vier
Jahreszeiten *(see p125)*, and
studying the princely menu,
you might feel that anything
can be found here. However,
the primary focus of the kitchen
is French cuisine; enjoy spectacular dishes such as: the grilled
sea bass with a purée of fennel
and pesto froth.

Jahreszeiten Grill €€€
International **Map** 10 D2
Jungfernstieg 9–14, 20354
Tel *34 94 33 12*
Located in the Hotel Vier Jahreszeiten *(see p125)* takes guests
back to the 1920s with Art Deco
lamps, plaster ornamentation
and wood panelling. You
can choose your own side dishes
for some main courses (the *entre-
côte*, for example). Featuring
excellent options, the wine list
is a oenophile's delight.

DK Choice

Küchenwerkstatt €€€
International
Hans-Henny-Jahnn-Weg 1, 22085
Tel *22 92 75 88* **Closed** *Sun, Mon*

This is the real Hamburg:
authentic Delft tiles and
wooden carvings in the high,
lofty rooms of an old patrician
villa. In summer, the Alster ferry
stops directly in front of the
door. Rack of salt-meadow lamb
poached in goat's milk with a
purée of onions is a popular
main course. Fish dishes include
yellowtail amberjack with lime
and soy.

Piazza Romana €€€
Mediterranean **Map** 7 B3
Rothenbaumchaussee 10, 20148
Tel *41 41 27 34*
Housed in the Grand
Elysée Hotel *(see p176)*, sample
Mediterranean cuisine, with an
emphasis on Italian specialities.
Fillet of sea bass with Umbrian
truffle and calf's liver in sage but-
ter are two of the many culinary
delights. There is a fantastic
selection of Italian desserts, all of
which are great palate pleasers.

Raven €€€
International **Map** 7 C2
Mittelweg 161, 20148
Tel *41 42 45 50*
The Raven restaurant and lounge
takes its guests on a culinary tour
of the world. The specialities
range from steak and Italian
pasta dishes, to sushi and Persian
fare such as chicken in pomegra-
nate sauce.

Ristorante Portonovo €€€
Italian **Map** 7 C4
Alsterufer 2, 20354
Tel *41 35 66 16*
Here, Italian cuisine and lifestyle
can be enjoyed on a landing
stage at the Außenalster or – if
the weather is unfavourable – in
the dining room. The fish soup
portonovo, grilled king prawns
and linguine with scampi are the
most popular choices.

DK Choice

Turnhalle St Georg €€€
European **Map** 6 E1
Lange Reihe 107, 20099
Tel *28 00 84 80*
Located in the gymnasium of a
school built in 1889, the dining
room here has huge arched
windows. The beautiful space is
a restaurant, café and bar all in
one and the owners manage a
gastronomic balancing act between pizza and pasta, and *ent-
recôte* and *bouillabaisse*. Sunday
brunch (11am–2pm).

Further Afield

Strandperle €
Traditional
Övelgönne 60, 22605
Tel *880 11 12*
In summer, patrons can sit on
the terrace – or sprawl on the
sand. Enjoy the view of the harbour, while dining on snacks or
having a drink. A popular place
to meet, it can be reached by
taking the HADAG ferry no. 62.

Brücke €€
European
Innocentiastraße 82, 20144
Tel *422 55 25*
This is a small restaurant with few
frills, so it's a little surprising that
it's so popular with Hamburg's
in-crowd. Perhaps the fabulous
Wiener schnitzel with mashed
potatoes and cucumber salad
pulls them in. For its size and
taste, it is unbeatable.

Engel €€
European
Fähranleger Teufelsbrück, 22609
Tel *82 41 87*
This is a popular food destination
at the Teufelsbrück ferry stop,
bound to be a hit for a Sunday
brunch or a relaxed dinner.
Sautéed sea bass with Ligurian-
style lentils and *saltimbocca*
(veal topped with prosciutto
and sage and rolled).

Fischclub Blankenese €€
European
*Strandweg 30a, Blankeneser
Landungsbrücken, 22587*
Tel *86 99 62*
As the name suggests, fish –
both from the Mediterranean
and local waters – is served here.
Main courses such as North Sea
plaice and wild-mushroom
risotto with red mullet, taste

Stylish interior of the Turnhalle St Georg, with floor-to-ceiling windows

especially divine when you are sitting near the windows with premium views of passing ships.

Morellino €€
Italian
Eppendorfer Landstraße 36, 20249
Tel *480 22 16*
This Italian restaurant caters to the sophisticated clientele of Eppendorf. Along with classic dishes such as *carpaccio*, diners swear by the grilled calamari and the octopus salad. The *porchetta* (suckling pig) with rosemary roasted potatoes is to die for.

Das Neue Landhaus Walter €€
Traditional
Hindenburgstraße 2, 22303
Tel *27 50 54* **Closed** Winter: Mon
An unusual combination of northern German dining and Bavarian beer garden. Here, wicker beach chairs are placed beside wooden benches, and the menu lists fish dishes and pretzels. The Sunday morning live jazz sessions are very popular. When the weather turns get comfortable inside.

Sài gón €€
Vietnamese
Martinistr. 14, 20251
Tel *46 09 10 09*
Vietnamese fare such as pho (glass noodle soup with chicken and morels), and a variety of tofu dishes are eaten at large communal tables. You may be given a spoon, but if you would prefer to eat with chopsticks, just ask.

Witthüs Teestuben €€
Traditional
Elbchaussee 499a, 22587
Tel *86 01 73* **Closed** Mon
In this splendid thatched-roofed Neo-Classical villa in the middle of Blankenese's Hirschpark, patrons sit at tables covered with crisp white cloths and strewn with flowers. The café is especially popular with ladies in the afternoon. In the evenings, the café and tea-house turns into a restaurant serving dishes such as fish soup and veal tenderloin.

DK Choice

Zollenspieker Fährhaus €€
Traditional
Zollenspieker Hauptdeich 141, 21037
Tel *793 13 30*
Whether the sun is shining or the rain is falling, a trip to the Fährhaus is worthwhile. After all, herb-crusted fillet of turbot, roast beef with fried potatoes and

---

Pannfisch taste good whether eaten inside in the winter garden restaurant or outside in the beer garden. Kids enjoy dishes such as "Käpt'n Kuddl" – fish fingers with mashed potatoes.

Dal Fabbro €€€
Italian
Blankeneser Bahnhofstr. 10, 22587
Tel *86 89 41*
Many consider this to be the best Italian restaurant in Blankenese. Tuna tartar with sour cream and salmon caviar, or turbot in a crust of potato with truffled cream sauce feature on the menu. And who can say no to *limonensorbet con Prosecco* for dessert?

Jacobs Restaurant €€€
European
Elbchaussee 401 – 403, 22609
Tel *82 25 50*
Elegant and classic, Hanseatic to the tips of its napkins, and with hardly an equal for culinary variety. This restaurant has a terrace with old linden trees, belongs to the Louis C. Jacob hotel *(see p183)*. It is the darling of gourmands, who enjoy dining on dishes like lobster cannelloni.

Landhaus Scherrer €€€
Traditional **Map** 1 A4
Elbchaussee 130, 22763
Tel *883 07 00 30* **Closed** Sun
At the top of the Hamburg food scene, the head-chef Heinz Wehmann turns regional specialities into *haute cuisine*. His artistry is evident from a peek at the menu, which lists delicacies like saddle of Holstein fallow deer and fillet of beef with fava bean purée.

Sagebiels Fährhaus €€€
International
Blankeneser Hauptstraße 107, 22587
Tel *86 15 14* **Closed** Mon Oct – Mar

This half-timbered building appeals to those who set great store in a dignified atmosphere with a touch of the exotic. The latter is provided by several Chinese dishes that complement North German fish cuisine. A typical meal starts with shark-fin soup and continues with a Chang Dong seafood platter.

Seven Seas €€€
International
Süllbergsterrasse 12, 22587
Tel *866 25 20* **Closed** Mon, Tue
This traditional restaurant pulls out all the stops to please its demanding guests with the finest food. The culinary works of art come beautifully plated. The cuisine here is French classic with ingredients from the world's oceans.

Stock's €€€
Fischrestaurant
Traditional
An der Alsterschleife 3, 22399
Tel *611 36 20* **Closed** Mon
This country house with terrace is home to one of the finest fish restaurants in the Alstertal. *Bouillabaisse* is made from fresh North Sea fish and is served as a starter, sautéed red snapper or grouper is a popular choice for main and desserts change regularly. The cosy pub on the first floor has a warming fireplace.

Das Weiße Haus €€€
International **Map** 1 A5
Neumühlen 50, 22763
Tel *390 90 16* **Closed** Sun
At this former pilot station with views of the Museumshafen Övelgönne *(see p135)*, the head chef prepares exceptional creations influenced by French, Italian and Asian cuisine. The extensive set menu for evening diners comes with a choice of three or four courses.

Tea, coffee and cake at Witthüs Teestuben on a sunny afternoon

For more information on types of restaurant *see page 183*

Cafés and Snack Bars

When you are under way and suddenly need something to eat, Hamburg offers many choices. Booths selling tasty fish sandwiches or German sausages are plentiful. If you like to linger longer over your food, then try out a snack bar, bistro or sandwich shop. There are also many cosy cafés in Hamburg – there is practically one on every corner of the city. Whether you prefer latte macchiato, café au lait or that German classic – an individual small pot of strong coffee – your coffee will certainly taste good. Tea is also available, and you can take time to relax, people-watch, read the newspaper or leaf through your travel guide.

Cafés

The choice of cafés, in which young and old can eat a light snack or just simply drink a cup of coffee, is enormous. Some of these establishments have a terrace, although when the weather is good it might be hard to get a spot. Most cafés open around 9am and close in the mid or late evening. Breakfast is ordered either from a menu or selected from the buffet. At lunch, there is usually a choice of hot dishes and usually one dish or more is still available from the breakfast menu. But in every single café, no matter what time of day it is, the choice of cakes and pastries is extremely tempting.

Cafés with great atmospheres are spread out over the whole city, but none is more centrally located or more opulent than the **Café Paris**. It is not only perfectly located on the Rathausmarkt, but offers an enticing selection of snacks both small and large, as well as many different kinds of French speciality coffees.

Die Rösterei is a Viennese-style coffee house, complete with dark-red velvet curtains. One of the most elegant places for a cosy coffee break is the **Literaturhaus Café**, with its plaster ornamentation. It is worth stopping here for a break during a walk along the Alster. You can come here simply to soak in the atmosphere, or perhaps combine a visit with an event at the Literaturhaus. On a side arm of the Alster lakes you will find the **Café Canale**. This is a really practical

establishment for paddlers: you can place your order at the kitchen window and be served promptly. The guests of **Café Prüsse** have a premium seat overlooking the Alster. Here, too, patrons can relish one of the many types of salads, the prawn-skewers, or simply a pot of tea or coffee.

Among the favourites in the Ottensen district west of Altona is **Knuth** (a breakfast joint with many vegetarian spreads to put on your bread, among other fare) and the lovely **König** with its changing dishes (partly organic food).

Delicious cakes still warm from the oven can be sampled in the cosy living-room-like atmosphere of the **Petit Café**. Here, you will also find an especially large selection of teas, as well as specialty coffees. At first glance the three branches of **TH²** look a bit plain, but they are always well frequented. While they serve the usual kinds of breakfast foods, what's unique to this chain are the light Belgian snacks on the menu. Sweet temptations come in many forms here, but well worth trying are the Swedish almond tarts and Portuguese vanilla cakes. A wide range of food is offered by **Die Herren Simpel** – café and bar in one. The broad selection ranges from a "Sylt breakfast" to a hearty plate "for men".

Many students and artists are drawn to the **Café Koppel**, which is located in a former machine factory that has been nicely renovated. This café has become well known chiefly

because of its scrumptious cakes and its many vegetarian creations. Another example of a successful renovation is **Hadley's**. It is hard to believe that this was once an emergency room. The sterile hospital atmosphere has long been replaced by that of an urbane coffee house.

The **Eisenstein** (café and restaurant in one) pampers with delicious snacks like wood fired oven pizza – or just simply with a cup of coffee (see p190). For a Viennese-style breakfast in the Schanzenviertel, the **Café unter den Linden** is a good choice; it is frequented by students. Many types of breakfast are served in the **Funk-Eck** in the NDR's broadcasting headquarters (Rundfunkhaus).

Most museums also have cafés, and some of these are among the most beautiful in Hamburg. In **Café George Economou**, visitors to the Kunsthalle (see pp64–65) can muse about all the wonderful art they have just seen over a cup of coffee. Since history alone does not assuage hunger, **Café Fees** in the hamburgmuseum (see p73) takes care of this need. The elegant lighting (which includes bright chandeliers) creates a very special ambience. Landscape pictures dominate the warm decor of the **Café Destille** in the Museum für Kunst und Gewerbe (see pp130–31).

There is something unique about the **Speicherstadt Kaffeerösterei**. Here, you can watch as coffee is roasted in gas-fired drums several times during the day, and enjoy one of the many freshly roasted coffee specialities.

For a congenial atmosphere and large choice of savoury dishes, cakes and pastries, other cafés worth visiting include **Amphore**, **Beanie Bee**, **Bedford**, **Café Backwahn**, **Café Johanna**, **Café Klatsch**, **Café Smögen**, **Café Stenzel**, **Café SternChance**, **Café Tarifa**, **Caffèteria**, **Elbgold**, **Elia and Max**, **Kyti Voo**, **MAY** and **Westwind**.

Soup Bars

Especially on cold days, soup is an ideal snack if you are strolling about the city or out on a shopping trip. You are guaranteed to find a delicious and filling bowl of soup at branches of the **Soup City** chain. There are usually between eight and ten soups on offer – both classic and exotic, including standards such as potato or tomato soup as well as creations that change every day. Each bowl of soup comes with a bun and an apple.

A bowl of something hot and tasty is also on offer at **Soup & Friends**. Here, you can choose your own toppings which include cheese, herbs, crème fraîche and croutons to spice up minestrone, Indian lentil stew, Argentinian beef soup or carrot and orange soup. **Souperia** in the Schanzenviertel is also a paradise for soup lovers. The soups come with special breads such as ciabatta or moist sourdough bread, and with rice.

Sandwich Bars

Sourdough, baguettes, panini, bagels and other sandwiches are sold in the many shops that specialize in this quick snack. They are often quite inventive, and many are seriously substantial, making them not just a snack but a full meal. **Oh It's Fresh!** serves up sandwiches, bagels, panini and wraps with a huge variety of wholesome fillings. Salads come with a range of dressings to choose from – American ranch, balsamic vinegar or curry. Bircher muesli, antipasti and chicken or prawn skewers are also available.

Naturally, in Hamburg there are also branches of **Subway**, the world's largest sandwich chain. Their gigantic sandwiches, or "subs", are custom made. The choices are huge, from many kinds of meat, sausage and cheese, as well as a good many toppings and your dressing of choice.

From veggie to chicken, from tuna to "Santa Fe" (made with turkey) – branches of the **Bagel**

Brothers chain specialize in fresh bagels with many sweet or savoury toppings – among them unusual combinations. Especially popular is the Bagel Burger, a sesame bun with a minced beef patty, salad leaves, tomatoes, pickles and sauce.

The **Jahreszeiten Deli** in the Hotel Vier Jahreszeiten (*see p125*) serves more than 60 different kinds of sandwiches.

Gourmet Snack Bars

Visitors to Hamburg get the opportunity to enjoy an excellent kind of fast food: the quality of dishes offered by some of the city's snack stalls is on a par with restaurant fare. At **Curry Queen**, currywurst is prepared on a lava stone grill and handed out with a side salad instead of chips. You have a choice of six different levels of heat – from fragrantly mild to extremely spicy. **Döner Queen** has been awarded a quality seal. Here, the choice of dips is impressive: they range from avocado to sweet-and-sour. There are also many vegetarian options. **hin & veg** offers a range of vegetarian meals, including soya-based imitation scallops and burgers.

Cake and Chocolate

Discover the world of chocolate over a cup of coffee at **Stolle Pralinen**, where sweet sins such as marzipan confections, pralines and truffles are handmade by the owner herself. **Confiserie Paulsen**, which has been in business since 1928, stocks its own truffle-pralines and ginger chocolates, along with tempting products from internationally renowned chocolate-makers.

Lovers of the cacao bean cannot leave empty handed after walking in to **Schokovida**, a combination of café and chocolate shop. **Herr Max** offers many kinds of cakes and muffins. In the time-honoured dessert salon **Andersen**, the chef's creations include the finest of pralines and a range of tempting layer cakes. At the **Konditorei Lindtner** in Eppendorf, guests enjoy

Baumkuchen (a cake cooked in layers on a spit), *petit fours* and gateaux in nostalgic surroundings.

Coffee Bars

In recent years, the American-style coffee shop has also arrived in Hamburg. Are you in the mood for a speciality coffee, such as espresso con panna, vanilla latte or caramel macchiato? Then the place to go is a branch of Starbucks or **Balzac Coffee**. These chains combine classic coffee-house culture with the modern philosophy of takeaway coffee. There is a huge choice of syrups for flavouring coffees – In fact, they are seemingly limitless. The stores of **Campus Suite** offer a range of coffee specialities. Along with coffee, these coffee shops sell Italian and American baked goods, such as biscotti and cookies.

For a good cup of coffee, the cosy **Carlos Coffee** in Ottensen is a good choice. Speciality coffees and Portuguese snacks are what **Caravela** in St Georg is known for.

Tea Salons

After a stroll along the Elbe, a cup of tea in **Witthüs Teestuben** on the Elbchaussee in Blankenese is just the perfect thing. The atmosphere in this 200-year-old house is extremely cosy. Why not try Russian smoked tea over cherries marinated in rum with a piece of spiced black bread made in the tea house's own bakery? It is definitely "very British" in **Lühmanns Teestube**, which offers a wide selection of teas such as the Cornish Cream Tea, with home-made scones and clotted cream. The **Teeteria** which has a roofed-over tea garden, offers teas and "teemonades" – drinks made of tea with fresh fruit. In the new city district HafenCity **samova Tee-Lounge** is tearoom and shop in one. The range of accessories for a cosy tea ceremony is enormous. **Messmer Momentum** is famous for exceptional teas. The shop in this tea salon offers a great selection of teas.

DIRECTORY

Cafés

Amphore
St. Pauli Hafenstraße 140.
Map 4 D4.
Tel 31 79 38 80.
Open 10am–1am daily.

Beanie Bee
Lilienstr. 15.
Map 10 E3.
Tel 32 00 49 79.
Open 7am–7:30pm
Mon–Fri, 9am–9pm Sat,
10am–9pm Sun.

Bedford
Schulterblatt 72.
Map 3 C1.
Tel 43 18 83 32.
Open noon–1am Mon–
Wed, noon–2am Thu,
noon–3am Fri, 10am–3am
Sat, 10am–midnight Sun.

Café Backwahn
Grindelallee 148.
Map 7 A2.
Tel 410 61 41.
Open 8am–7pm Mon–Fri,
10am–7pm Sat, Sun.

Café Canale
Poelchaukamp 7.
Tel 270 01 01.
Open 10am–7pm daily.

Café Destille
Museum für Kunst und
Gewerbe, Steintorplatz 1.
Map 6 E2.
Tel 280 33 54.
Open 11am–5pm
Tue–Sun.

Café Fees
hamburgmuseum,
Holstenwall 24.
Map 9 A3.
Tel 317 47 66.
Open 10am–5pm Tue–
Sat, 9:30am–6pm Sun.

Café George Economou
Hamburger Kunsthalle,
Glockengießerwall 1.
Map 10 F3.
Tel 428 54 26 11.
Open 10am–8pm
Tue–Sun (Thu to 9pm).

Café Johanna
Venusberg 26.
Map 4 F4.
Tel 38 64 52 78. **Open**
8am–6pm Mon–Fri,
10am–6pm Sat.

Café Klatsch
Glashüttenstr. 17.
Map 4 E1.
Tel 439 04 43.
Open 10am–8pm daily.

Café Koppel
Lange Reihe 75.
Map 8 E4.
Tel 24 92 35.
Open 10am–11pm daily.

Café Paris
Rathausstr. 4.
Map 10 D3.
Tel 32 52 77 77.
Open 9am–11:30pm
Mon–Fri, 9:30am–11:30pm
Sat, Sun.

Café Prüsse
An der Alster 47a.
Map 8 E4.
Tel 24 60 58.
Open 11am–11pm,
Mon–Fri, 10am–11pm,
Sat, Sun.

Café Smögen
Klaus-Groth-Str. 28.
Tel 18 11 24 72.
Open 10am–6pm Mon,
10am–10pm Tue–Fri,
10am–2:30pm Sun.

Café Stenzel
Schulterblatt 61.
Map 3 C1.
Tel 43 43 64.
Open 7am–8pm
Mon–Sat, 8am–8pm Sun.

Café SternChance
Schröderstiftstr. 7.
Tel 430 11 68.
Open 11am–midnight
Mon–Fri, 10am–11pm
Sat.

Café Tarifa
Große Rainstr. 23.
Map 1 C3.
Tel 39 90 35 29.
Open 9am–midnight
Mon–Fri, 10am–midnight
Sat, Sun.

Café unter den Linden
Juliusstr. 16.
Map 3 C1.
Tel 43 81 40.
Open 9.30am–1am daily.

Caffèteria
Abendrothsweg 54.
Tel 46 77 75 33.
Open 10am–11pm Mon–
Fri, 10am–7pm Sat, Sun.

Eisenstein
Friedensallee 9.
Map 1 B2.
Tel 390 46 06.
Open 11am–1am daily.

Elbgold
Mühlenkamp 6a.
Tel 27 88 22 33..
Open 8am–7pm
Mon–Fri, 9am–7pm Sat,
10am–6pm Sun.

Elia und Max
Schulterblatt 98.
Map 3 C1. **Tel** 43 64 04.
Open 8am–11pm
Mon–Fri, 9am–10pm Sat,
10am–8pm Sun.

Funk-Eck
Rothenbaumchaussee 137.
Map 7 B1.
Tel 44 41 74.
Open 7:30am–9pm daily.

Hadley's
Beim Schlump 84a.
Map 7 A2.
Tel 450 50 75.
Open 10am–2am Mon–
Sat, 11am–2am Sun.

Die Herren Simpel
Schulterblatt 75.
Map 3 C1.
Tel 38 68 46 00.
Open 5pm–3am Mon–Fri,
2pm–1am Sat, 2–8pm Sun.

Knuth
Große Rainstr. 21.
Map 1 C3.
Tel 46 00 87 08.
Open 9am–midnight
Mon–Sat, 10am–8pm Sun.

König
Ottenser Hauptstr. 28.
Map 1 C3. **Tel** 41 35 88 77.
Open 8am–9pm
Mon–Fri, 9am–9pm Sat.

Kyti Voo
Lange Reihe 82.
Map 8 E4.
Tel 28 05 55 65.
Open 10am–midnight
Mon–Fri (Nov–Mar from
noon), 10am–midnight
Sat, Sun.

Literaturhaus Café
Schwanenwik 38.
Map 8 F2.
Tel 220 13 00.
Open 9am–midnight
Mon–Fri, 10am–
midnight Sat, Sun.

MAY
Lappenbergsallee 30.
Tel 32 03 81 62.
Open 8am–midnight
daily.

Petit Café
Hohe Bleichen 20.
Map 9 C2.
Tel 52 59 60 90.
Open 9am–7pm Mon–Fri,
10am–6pm Sat, Sun.

Die Rösterei
Mönckebergstr. 7.
Map 10 F3.
Tel 30 39 37 35.
Open 9am–9pm
Mon–Fri, 10am–8pm
Sat, Sun.

Speicherstadt Kaffeerösterei
Kehrwieder 5, in Kultur-
und Gewerbespeicher
Block D.
Map 9 C5.
Tel 31 81 61 61.
Open 10am–7pm daily.

TH²
Klosterallee 67.
Tel 42 10 79 44.
Open 9am–7:30pm
Mon–Fri, 9am–6pm Sat,
10am–6pm Sun.

Mittelweg 146.
Map 7 C2.
Tel 85 10 65 62.
Open 9am–8pm
Mon–Fri, 9am–6pm Sat,
10am–6pm Sun.

Mühlenkamp 59.
Tel 27 88 00 80.
Open 8am–8pm
Mon–Fri, 9am–6pm Sat,
10am–6pm Sun.

Westwind
Spadenteich 1.
Map 8 E5.
Tel 41 92 43 44.
Open 11am–midnight
Mon–Fri, 10am–
midnight Sat, Sun.

Soup Bars

Soup & Friends
Valentinskamp 18.
Map 9 C2.
Tel 34 10 78 10.
Open 11:30am–6pm
Mon–Fri, noon–4pm Sat.

DIRECTORY

Soup City
Am Sandtorkai 30 (in HafenCity InfoCenter).
Map 10 D5.
Tel 28 41 04 90.
Open 10am–6pm Tue–Sun (May–Sep until 8pm).

Neuer Wandrahm (Bei St. Annen).
Map 10 E5.
Tel 87 87 66 95.
Open 8am–4pm Mon–Fri.

Steinhöft 9.
Map 9 B5.
Tel 28 41 04 90.
Open 11:30am–3pm Mon–Fri.

Steinstr. 17a.
Map 10 E3.
Tel 32 87 38 87.
Open 10am–4pm Mon–Fri.

Souperia
Bartelsstr. 21.
Map 4 D3.
Tel 43 09 95 55.
Open 11am–8pm Mon–Fri, noon–5pm Sat.

Sandwich Bars

Bagel Brothers
Osterstr. 9.
Map 1 C3.
Tel 21 99 89 97.
Open 7:30am–8:30pm Mon–Fri, 8.30am–6.30pm Sat, 9am–6pm Sun.

Ottenser Hauptstr. 7.
Map 1 C3.
Tel 46 00 87 31.
Open 7:30am–8:30pm Mon–Fri, 8:30am–8:30pm Sat, 8:30am–6:30pm Sun.

Jahreszeiten Deli
Hotel Vier Jahreszeiten, Neuer Jungfernstieg 9–14.
Map 10 D2.
Tel 34 94 33 15.
Open 8am–6:30pm Mon–Fri, 10am–6pm Sat, Sun.

Oh It's Fresh!
Dilmar-Koel-Straß.
Map 9 B4.
Tel 36 09 68 45.
Open 7am–4pm Mon–Fri.

Burchardstraße 10.
Map 10 F4.
Tel 30 39 34 44.
Open 7am–7pm Mon–Thu, 7am–4pm Fri.

Am Sandtorkai 40.
Map 9 C5. **Tel** 37 80 30 25.
Open 7:30am–6pm Mon–Fri.

Subway
(Selected branches)
Gänsemarkt 36. **Map** 9 C2.
Tel 33 44 19 88.
Open 9am–11pm daily.

Glockengießerwall 8–10.
Map 10 E2.
Tel 46 86 68 85.
Open 6am–11pm daily.

Paul-Nevermann-Platz 15/16 (Bahnhof Altona).
Map 1 C3.
Tel 27 86 20 12.
Open 8.30am–10.30pm Mon–Sat, 10:30am–10:30pm Sun.

Ballindamm 38.
Map 9 D3.
Tel 41 11 22 60.
Open 9am–10pm Mon–Sat, 11am–9pm Sun.

Gourmet Snack Bars

Curry Queen
Erikastr. 50.
Tel 52 67 77 62.
Open 11:30am–10pm Tue–Sat.

Döner Queen
Jarrestr. 57.
Tel 60 00 89 05.
Open 10am–11pm daily.

Schlossmühlenstr. 7.
Tel 32 52 88 50.
Open 10am–2am daily.

hin & veg
Schulterblatt 16.
Map 4 D1.
Tel 59 45 34 02.
Open 11:30am–10:30pm Mon–Thu, 11:30am midnight Fri, Sat, 12:30pm–10pm Sun.

Cake and Chocolate

Andersen
Wandsbeker Marktstr. 153.
Tel 689 46 40.
Open 9am–7pm Mon–Sat, 9am–6:30pm Sun.

Confiserie Paulsen
Großs Bleichen 36.
Map 9 C3.
Tel 36 77 81.
Open 10am–7pm Mon–Fri, 10am–6pm Sat.

Herr Max
Schulterblatt 12.
Map 4 D1.
Tel 69 21 99 51.
Open 10am–9pm daily.

Konditorei Lindtner
Eppendorfer Landstraße 88.
Tel 480 60 00.
Open 8:30am–10pm Mon–Sat, 11am–9pm Sun.

Schokovida
Hegestr. 33.
Tel 87 87 08 08.
Open 10am–7pm Mon–Fri, 10am–4pm Sat.

Stolle Pralinen
Hoheluftchaussee 88.
Tel 50 74 54 88.
Open 10am–7pm Mon–Fri, 10am–4pm Sat.

Coffee Bars

Dalzac Coffee
Tel Main: 355 10 80.
(Selected branches)

Gustav-Mahler-Platz 1.
Map 9 C2.
Open 7am–8pm Mon–Fri, 8am–8pm Sat, 9am–8:30pm Sun.

Kurze Mühren 4.
Map 10 F3.
Open 6:30am–8.30pm Mon–Fri, 8am–8:30pm Sat, 9am–8pm Sun.

Lange Reihe/Danziger Str. 70.
Map 6 E1.
Open 6:30am–8pm Mon–Fri, 8am–8pm Sat, Sun.

Mittelweg 130.
Map 7 C2.
Open 6:30am–7:30pm Mon–Fri, 7:30am–7:30pm Sat, 8:30am–7pm Sun.

Rathausstr. 7.
Map 10 D3.
Open 7am–7pm Mon–Fri, 9am–7pm Sat, 11am–6:30pm Sun.

Steinstr. 25.
Map 10 E3.
Open 8:30am–4pm Mon–Fri.

Campus Suite
Tel Main: 23 85 83 80.
(Selected branches)
Großer Grasbrook 10.
Map 5 C5.
Open 7am–8pm Mon–Fri, 8am–8pm Sat, Sun.

Valentinskamp 91.
Map 9 C2.
Open 6:30am–8pm Mon–Fri, 8am–8pm Sat, 9am–6:30pm Sun.

Caravela
Lange Reihe 13.
Map 6 E2.
Tel 41 29 99.
Open 8am–8pm Mon–Fri, 9am–8pm Sat, Sun.

Carlos Coffee
Bahrenfelder Str. 169.
Map 1 C2.
Tel 39 90 99 90.
Open 6:30am–8pm Mon–Sa, 8:30am–8pm Sun.

Tea Salons

Lühmanns Teestube
Blankeneser Landstr. 29.
Tel 86 34 42.
Open 9am–11pm Mon–Fri, 9am–6pm Sat, 10am–11pm Sun.

Messmer Momentum
Am Kaiserkai 10.
Map 5 C5.
Tel 73 67 90 00
Open 11am–8pm daily

samova Teespeicher
Hongkongstr. 1.
Map 6 D4.
Tel 85 40 36 40.
Open 9am–6pm Mon–Fri, noon–6pm Sat.

Teeteria
Hellkamp 11–13.
Map 3 C1.
Tel 76 99 23 51.
Open 9am–6pm Tue–Sun.

Witthüs Teestuben
Elbchaussee 499a.
Tel 86 01 73.
Open 2pm–11pm Tue–Sat, 10am–11pm Sun.

SHOPPING IN HAMBURG

Hamburg is a true shopper's paradise. From fashion and jewellery to furniture and antiques, from interior design to arts and crafts – the spectrum of goods on offer ranges from the elegant and chic to the unique and unusual to the practical and proven. No one who strolls along Hamburg's streets can fail to be impressed as the city's shops reveal how international and stylish it is, explaining perhaps why it is considered Germany's shopping capital. The magnificent shopping areas in the best downtown locations offer consumers a world of experience. Whether you prefer large shopping centres, the glamorous passages or the countless small boutiques – shopping in Hamburg is an absolute pleasure.

Shopping Areas and Passages

In the past few years, Jung-fernstieg (see pp124 – 25) has been completely rebuilt and is now considered one of the most impressive boulevards in Europe. One of the main reasons is the glamorously restored **Alsterhaus**. Con-tributing to the refurbished splendour of this light-filled department store are a large lingerie department and a beauty department. The Neue Wall branches off from the Jungfernstieg. Here, flagship stores of well-known interna-tional labels (such as Armani, Joop, Cartier and Louis Vuitton) line this luxury shopping mile. But many Hanseatic stores also have a long tradition of offering luxury wares.

You can find great variety in a small amount of space in the Mönckebergstraße, which Hamburg residents fondly call "Mö". Here, between the Rathaus and the Hauptbahnhof, large department stores alternate with well-known local shops. In the Spitalerstraße, which branches off from the "Mö", the majority of the stores are branches of larger chains. There is a distinct Mediterranean atmosphere in the Alster Arcades (see p58), and you can shop without ever getting wet in the passages (see p76) between the Rathausmarkt and the Gänsemarkt. Bleichen-hof, Galleria, **Gänsemarkt-Passage**, **Hanse-Viertel**, and other covered shopping passages ensure the weather will not spoil your shopping fun. The largest shopping area is the 160-m (525-ft) long **Europa Passage** that runs between Jungfernstieg and Mönckebergstraße. It contains more than 120 shops on five floors.

In the Wandelhalle in the Hauptbahnhof (see p62), the shops are located on two levels. You can shop seven days a week here from 6am to 11pm. Most other stores and boutiques in Hamburg are open Monday to Saturday until 7 or 8pm. Many have extended hours (often until 10pm) on Thursday or Friday to attract more customers.

Fashion

Hamburg is trendy. Luxury labels such as Gucci, Joop, Prada, Louis Vuitton and René Lezard are represented by their own shops on the Jungfernstieg, Neue Wall or in the passages. Along with haute couture and prêt-à-porter from the fashion design elite,

Shopping in Alsterhaus, an upmarket department store

there are also more affordable labels, such as Benetton, H&M, Diesel and Tommy Hilfiger.

But Hamburg is not just a top shopping destination for international designer clothing. Elegant creations are also designed and tailored here, as demonstrated by Jil Sander. And too, the many smaller boutiques stock fashion for every taste. The two proprietors of **Hello** in Eimsbüttel have earned an excellent reputation for their Hello collection. It appeals with timelessly elegant clothes that encourage Hamburgers to be a bit less understated.

The philosophy behind **Anna Fuchs** is to provide appealing everyday wear for the sophisti-cated woman. Her recent designs have been characterized by bold blocks of colour.

Clothes with clean lines do not have to be boring, as witnessed by the collection designed by **DFM** on Alsterfleet; their own creations are supplemented by carefully selected trendy labels. **Prayed** has successfully blended, neatly tailored clothes with

A world of pampering lotions and massages awaits patrons of Nivea Haus (see p200)

playful details. Many of the one-off garments have unusual combinations of fabrics and colours, and each is elegant and yet casual at the same time. Restrained elegance is the focus of **Garment**. In this boutique the emphasis is on classic lines.

GuteJacke in HafenCity offers jackets for all tastes and kinds of weather. Sporty types are particularly well catered for with plenty of practical outerwear.

Second-hand

That second-hand does not have to mean second class is proved by the many shops of this kind found in Hamburg. One of the best examples is **Secondella**, which sells about 100 designer labels, and features brand new, elegant pieces from Armani, Gucci, Prada, Versace and Chanel's last collections. In **Classen Secondhand**, very reasonable no-name and designer clothes (such as Prada and Hermès) are sold. Bags and shoes complete the assortment. **Vintage & Rags** source their unusual, flashy wares from the USA – such as crocheted tops and hippie dresses.

Second-hand clothes of the finest British sort are found in the store of **Rudolf Beaufays**. With examples of the art of British tailoring and unusual collections in the classic British style, Beaufays cultivates the art of good taste – in which other German city would he be so successful?

Trendy bags designed by FREITAG-Taschen *(see p200)*

A large choice of furniture and accessories sold at stilwerk *(see p119)*

Furniture and Design

Hamburg is also renowned for its interior design and furnishings, and many pieces of furniture seen in glossy magazines come from the Elbe metropolis. Such seemingly mundane items as picture-frames or cups have been turned into design classics by **Toni Thiel**. It is not enough that something is practical; it must also be strikingly beautiful. There are, of course, matching carpets to go with the furniture and accessories; that wicker chair absolutely cries out to be placed on that futuristic-looking designer carpet.

All those who want to bring style from the four corners of the globe into their homes will find just the right thing at **Octopus**. Furniture from many countries, from Swedish sofas to Italian chests of drawers, can be found in the selection on offer. There is also Asian style furniture. **Die Wäscherei** is an ideal place for shoppers who delight in browsing for hours among furniture, lamps and fabrics in various styles.

Pottery lighthouses – a souvenir of the region

A more suitable place than **stilwerk** *(see p119)* could not be found to house a mecca for lovers of good taste, an exclusive centre for furniture, interior design and lifestyle accessories. A glass elevator brings customers from the spacious lobby to seven floors filled with stores with names such as ligne roset, bulthaup and Bang & Olufsen.

Those who are more budget minded often find something in

Yellow Möbel in Winterhude. Along with practical shelving systems and sleek modern furnishings, the collection also includes accessories. Flexibility is at the core of **BoConcept**. This Danish company sells modules made of various fabrics and colours which customers combine to create their dream interiors.

Jewellery and Watches

Montblanc has been in business since 1906 and now has over 360 boutiques in more than 70 countries – a few of them are in Hamburg, it being the home of the company's headquarters. Customers can choose from watches and accessories as well as exquisite jewellery. The Montblanc diamond has achieved cult status and can be set into cufflinks, for example. **Goldene Zeiten** is one of the oldest and best-known jewellers and watchmakers in Hamburg. Collectors can also purchase the requisite tiny tools to care for their horological treasures. Precious metals such as platinum, gold and silver are turned into unique treasures by **Ivar Kranz** in his jewellery store in the Schanzenviertel.

Wempe, headquartered in Hamburg, produces and sells deluxe jewellery and watches. The valuable nature of the products suits the location of the flagship store on the well-to-do shopping street Jungfernstieg, next to other luxury outlets.

Food

There are many shops in Hamburg selling delicious specialities either produced in-house or gathered from around the world that are guaranteed to please the most discerning palates. The number of fine food shops is enormous. The time-honoured **Hummer Pedersen** has been a purveyor of ocean delicacies since 1879. Along with lobsters, there are ocean crabs, crayfish, oysters and many other kinds of bivalves for sale. But there is some very unusual seafood here, too, and parrotfish and scorpionfish also find their takers.

Lovers of fine wines have no trouble indulging in their passion in the North German metropolis. A small shop with a large selection is **La Vigna**, which has a wide-ranging assortment of wines from many different corners of the globe in all price ranges. It has a reputation throughout the city for the regular wine seminars it holds. **Käse, Wein & mehr** not only sells a large selection of cheeses, sausages and antipasti specialities, but also carefully chosen wines, first-class olive oil, various types of pesto they make themselves, sweet and savoury Italian baked goods and much more.

Aficionados of fine coffee must make a pilgrimage to the **Kaffeerösterei Burg**, where a genuine treasure-trove awaits them. Among the specialities from different parts of the world are Ethiopian mocca, Hawai'i Kona and Jamaica Blue Mountain as the most expensive ones. The assortment of teas from Darjeeling, Assam, South Africa and other regions is also extensive.

Chocoholics feel they've died and gone to heaven in **Sweet Dreams Confiserie**. But buyer beware: the huge choice of exquisite chocolates, pralines, cookies and cakes will throw even the most determined dieter off-track – which is just as the shop's owner likes it. After all, his motto is "A balanced diet is a chocolate in each hand".

Books

In recent years bookshops in Hamburg have started to turn into complete book-buying experiences, with cosy reading nooks and large CD- departments for audio books and music. All large bookshops have a good selection of English books on offer. The **Thalia** group oversees twelve branches in Hamburg, the one in the Spitalerstraße 8 covers 3,200 sq m (35,000 sq ft). It is the largest bookshop in the city. The branch in the Europa Passage on Ballindamm has the largest selection of English books. A further centrally located Thalia branch is on Große Bleichen.

Heymann, with its 15 locations, is one of the leading bookshop chains in the greater Hamburg area. They also organize a series of literary events that include readings and exhibitions.

Opposite the university, the **Heinrich Heine Buchhandlung** offers an excellent selection of literature and all kinds of scientific books.

In Germany's largest bookshop devoted to travel, **Dr. Götze Land & Karte**, there are 70000 maps, travel guides, globes, navigation systems and all sorts of literature related to travel.

Beauty and Lingerie

Perfumes and incense, Ayurvedic and Feng-Shui items, natural cosmetics and lines of body-care products, massages and treatments – **Secret Emotion** offers wellness for body and soul. **Lush** has a large assortment of handmade cosmetics, including bath-balls in every conceivable fragrance.

Beiersdorf AG, a company headquartered in Eimsbüttel, a district in Hamburg, opened a lovely oasis for regeneration and relaxation in its home town. Here, in **Nivea Haus**, beauticians pamper their clients from head to toe with massages and cosmetics, and provide advice. Of course, all products used in this huge spa are from the NIVEA label – from body lotion to sunscreen lotion.

In **Palmers**, the clothing ranges from cotton nightgowns to lace body-stockings. This fashion giant sets the latest trends in lingerie.

Braviange offers bespoke lingerie – the perfect fit compensates the dearness.

Many late-night shoppers looking for that extra-special piece of lingerie end up in the **Boutique Bizarre** (open daily to 2am), which is located – where else – on the Reeperbahn.

Specialist Shops

Precious woods such as mahogany and rosewood are turned into exquisite writing instruments by **Stefan Fink**. His fountain pens and sketching pencils are small works of art. A few important state documents have been signed by these unique creations. Photo albums and diaries, wrapping paper and postcards can all be found in **Druckwerkstatt Ottensen**.

"There is a hat suited to everyone" insists hat-maker Birke Breckwoldt, owner of the hat shop **Behütet**. From corduroy cap to an artfully made feather hat – even those who are not hat-friendly will find something they like here.

From high heels to ballerina slippers and pumps to boots, **Catwalk** stocks the latest models and fashion trends and is a darling of fashionistas. There are also matching accessories such as handbags and belts.

Patrons of Atelier für Frottier feel as though they are back in the 1970s. Choosing between bathrobes, pillow covers and even key-rings – all made out of terry cloth – the dream of a fluffy and soft world comes closer.

Pappnase & Co. is a place of wonder for children small and large. The brightly coloured shop astounds and pleases with exciting items from the theatre and circus worlds, among them many masks and equipment for making magic.

In **FREITAG-Taschen**, the bags and accessories made of used materials like bicycle inner tubes and airbags come in every colour and design.

DIRECTORY

Shopping Areas and Passages

Alsterhaus
Jungfernstieg 16 – 20.
Map 10 D2.
Tel 35 90 12 18.

Europa Passage
Ballindamm 40.
Map 10 D3.
Tel 30 09 26 40.

Gänsemarkt-Passage
Gänsemarkt 50. **Map** 9 C2.
Tel 350 16 80.

Hanse-Viertel
Große Bleichen 30.
Map 9 C3.
Tel 348 09 30.

Fashion

Anna Fuchs
Karolinenstr. 27. **Map** 9 A2.
Tel 40 18 54 08.
w annafuchs.de

DFM
Stubbenhuk 38.
Map 9 B4.
Tel 374 27 12.
w dfm-hamburg.de

Garment
Marktstr. 26. **Map** 4 E1.
Tel 410 84 03.
w garment-online.de

GuteJacke
Überseeboulevard 2.
Map 5 C4.
Tel 76 75 34 44.
w gutejacke.de

Hello
Weidenstieg 11.
Tel 40 39 89.
w hello-mode.de

Prayed
Glashüttenstr. 3.
Map 4 E1.
Tel 40 18 78 16.
w prayed.de

Second-hand

Classen Secondhand
Grillparzerstraße 2b.
Tel 227 32 31.
w classen-secondhand.de

Rudolf Beaufays
Büschstr. 9.
Map 9 C2.
Tel 35 71 59 77.
w rudolf-beaufays.de

Secondella
Hohe Bleichen 5.
Map 9 C3.
Tel 35 29 31.
w secondella.de

Vintage & Rags
Kurze Mühren 6.
Map 10 F3.
Tel 33 01 07.
w vintage-rags.de

Furniture and Design

BoConcept
Große Elbstr. 39.
Map 2 E4.
Tel 380 87 60.
w boconcept.com

Octopus
Lehmweg 10b.
Tel 420 11 00.
w octopus-versand.de

stilwerk
Große Elbstr. 68.
Map 2 E4. **Tel** 30 62 11 00.
w stilwerk.de

Toni Thiel
Hoheluftchaussee 39.
Tel 42 93 87 97.
w toni-thiel.com

Die Wäscherei
Mexikoring 27 – 29.
Tel 271 50 70.
w die-waescherei.de

Yellow Möbel
Gertigstr. 24.
Tel 27 07 59 09.
w yellow-moebel.de

Jewellery and Watches

Goldene Zeiten
Gerhofstr. 40.
Tel 35 71 23 30.
w goldenezeiten.net

Ivar Kranz
Schulterblatt 78.
Map 3 C1.
Tel 43 18 87 49.
w reingold-schmuck.de

Montblanc
Neuer Wall 18.
Map 10 D3. **Tel** 35 11 75.
w montblanc.de

Wempe
Jungfernstieg 8.
Map 10 D3.
Tel 33 44 88 24.
w wempe.de

Food

Hummer Pedersen
Große Elbstr. 152.
Map 2 D4.
Tel 52 29 93 90.

Kaffeerösterei Burg
Eppendorfer Weg 252.
Tel 422 11 72.

Käse, Wein & mehr
Erikastr. 58.
Tel 46 24 25.

Rob & Stephen's little cake Co.
Lehmweg 41.
Tel 46 88 10 45.

La Vigna
Beim Schlump 10 – 12.
Map 7 A2.
Tel 45 20 91.

Books

Dr. Götze Land & Karte
Alstertor 14 – 18.
Map 10 E3.
Tel 357 46 30.
w mapshop-hamburg.de

Felix Jud Buchhandlung
Neuer Wall 13.
Map 10 D3.
Tel 34 34 09.
w felix-jud.de

Heymann
Eppendorfer Baum 27.
Tel 48 09 30.
w heymann-buch.de
One of 15 branches.

Thalia
Spitalerstr. 8.
Map 10 F3.
Tel 48 50 10.
w service.thalia.de
One of 12 branches.

Beauty and Lingerie

Boutique Bizarre
Reeperbahn 35.
Map 4 D4.
Tel 31 76 96 90.
w boutique-bizarre.de

Braviange
Bernstorffstr. 153.
Map 3 C1.
Tel 67 38 28 27.
w braviange.de

Lush
Spitalerstr. 7 – 9.
Map 10 F3.
Tel 40 18 57 84.
w lush.com

Nivea Haus
Jungfernstieg 51.
Map 7 C5.
Tel 82 22 47 40.
w nivea.de

Palmers
Neuer Wall 17.
Map 10 D3.
Tel 35 71 07 41.
w palmers.de

Secret Emotion
Berglusstraße 3.
Map 1 B3.
Tel 390 29 30.
w secret-emotion.de

Specialist Shops

The art of Hamburg
Ditmar-Koel-Str. 19. **Map** 9 A5. **Tel** 41 42 44 19.
w the-art-of-hamburg.de

Behütet
Weidenstieg 16.
Tel 51 31 02 03.
w birkebreckwoldt.de

Catwalk
Eppendorfer Baum 34.
Tel 54 80 38 87.
w catwalkhamburg.de

Cucinaria
Straßenbahnring 12.
Tel 80 60 99 90.
w cucinaria.de

Druckwerkstatt Ottensen
Ottenser Hauptstr. 44 – 48.
Map 1 C3. **Tel** 398 63 60.
w druckwerkstatt-ottensen.de

FREITAG-Taschen
Klosterwall 9. **Map** 10 F4.
Tel 328 70 20.
w freitag.ch

Pappnase & Co
Grindelallee 92. **Map** 7 A3. **Tel** 44 97 39.
w pappnase-hamburg.de

Stefan Fink
Koppel 66. **Map** 8 E4.
Tel 24 71 51.
w stefanfink.de

ENTERTAINMENT IN HAMBURG

The image of Hamburgers as cool and reserved Northerners proves to be just another stereotype when you look at the variety of entertainment offered here. Whether you are interested in mainstream culture or looking for something different, there is plenty to do in the city. You can spend an evening experiencing unforgettable musicals and plays at the many theatres, both large and small, or be amused by vaudeville and cabaret.

Without a doubt the district of St Pauli is the launching pad for up and coming trends. It was here, in the Star-Club, that the Beatles enjoyed their first big breakthrough. The adjoining Schanzenviertel is also a centre for cutting-edge culture and experimentation, with a thriving alternative scene.

Information

Hamburg's Tourist Information offices are always happy to provide you with an overview of the events taking place in the city. They have several outlets, and all offer extensive information about the city's cultural events. Daily newspapers, as well as smaller local papers like OXMOX and PRINZ, provide listings for events such as concerts, plays, films and shows.

On the Hamburg Tourismus GmbH website (www. hamburg-travel.com) you can download the Happy Hamburg Reisen catalogue. It contains great deals for musicals, boat trips and cultural events, as well as attractive package and hotel deals for your trip. The online magazine www.hamburg-magazin.de is also a good source of entertainment information on events ranging from museum exhibitions to film screenings

Colourful and cosy lobby of Schmidts Tivoli *(see p204)*

Poster for the Rolling Stones Hamburg show

Tickets

You can buy tickets at the venues themselves, order them over the telephone, or purchase them online. The addresses and telephone numbers of many of the best-known venues are provided on pages 205 and 209. Ticket sales for some events begin several months in advance, and tickets can go quickly. For the big, popular musicals, tickets can sell out fast, so it is essential to book early; on the evening of the show itself there are usually no tickets available.

However, if you have not been successful in getting a ticket in advance, you can try your luck at the box office an hour or so before the show is scheduled to begin, even if it is officially sold out. Sometimes pre-ordered tickets are not picked up. And you might be in luck and be given a ticket by someone whose "date" has not turned up.

Many tour operators offer tickets for events from culture to sports in combination with package trips to the city. These special deals can be found in newspapers and on the Internet, on the websites of trusted operators.

Kasino Reeperbahn – a magnet for gamblers

Tickets are also available at branches of the **Tourist Information** office. **Hamburg Tourismus GmbH** also has blocks of tickets for a wide range of events. If it is more convenient, you can also purchase tickets by phone or online from one of the many ticket agencies such as **hamburg-ticket** or **funke-ticket**.

Disabled Travellers

Many event venues have special seating places for patrons in wheelchairs and those with other mobility issues, and special equipment for the hearing impaired. Parking spots, entrances and toilets that are wheelchair accessible are clearly marked. Make sure to telephone the box office prior to booking to find out what facilities are available. A download of "Ratgeber Hamburg" can be found at www.handicap-info.de, a German-language website with valuable information for disabled visitors run by

Shuttle-boat bringing patrons to Theater im Hamburger Hafen *(see p209)* for a performance of *The Lion King*

Behinderten-Ratgeber. At www. tagh-hamburg.de, the facilities for disabled visitors in each venue, as well as in cafés and restaurants, are described in detail in the "Hamburger Stadtführer für Rollstuhlfahrer" (wheelchair guide to Hamburg). You can download the guide. It is in German, but the symbols used are easy to understand.

Outdoor Events

Hamburg offers many open air events, especially during spring and summer. In Planten un Blomen (see pp78–9), water-light-concerts are held daily at 10pm from May to the end of August, and at 9pm from September until mid-October. On the park's lake, coloured lights illuminate spouting jets of water to the beat of classical music, jazz and film soundtracks. From May to September, jazz, pop and other concerts are hosted in the

Stadtpark *(see p134)*. In early May, Hamburg celebrates the birthday of its port *(see p85)* with a variety of harbour-based events, such as ship parades. "The arts, culture and the culinary arts" are the themes of a ten-day festival on Fleetinsel *(see p76)*. In late summer, a two-day dragon boat festival is held on the Binnenalster, with a fair lasting several days more – the Alstervergnügen *(see p45)*. The Hamburger Dom – fairs lasting several weeks and offering great fun to young and old – are held three times a year on Heiligengeistfeld *(see pp44–6)*. Treats are in store for film buffs at the outdoor summer film festival in Sternschanzenpark *(see p45)* and, in autumn, at Filmfest Hamburg *(see p46)*. The high-point of Pride Week in late July or early August is the joyful and celebratory CSD (Christopher Street Day) parade that begins in St Georg.

DIRECTORY

Ticket Sales

funke-ticket
Tel 450 11 86 76.
W funke-ticket.de

hamburg-ticket
Tel 68 85 55.
W hamburg-ticket.de

Hamburg Tourismus GmbH
Postfach 102249.
Tel 30 05 17 01.
W hamburg-travel.com

**Tourist Information
at the Hauptbahnhof**
Hauptausgang Kirchenallee.
Map 6 E2.
Open 9am–7pm Mon–Sat,
10am–6pm Sun.

**Tourist Information
am Hafen (at the Port)**
St. Pauli Landungsbrücken
(between quays 4 and 5).
Map 4 D5.
Open Apr–Oct: 8am–6pm daily;
Nov–Mar: 10am–6pm daily.

**Tourist Information
Airport Office**
Hamburg Airport, Airport
Plaza (between terminal 1 and 2).
Open 6am–11pm daily.

The shanty choir *De Tampentrekker* giving a concert in HafenCity

Music, Theatre and Cinema

Hamburg has much to offer lovers of the performing arts. With its many stages, shows and other events, the city prides itself on a more varied cultural life than that of many other European centres. From serious to modern music, classical to alternative theatre, cabaret to film – the range of performing art offerings in the Hanseatic city is enormous. The names of some of its venues, among them the Staatsoper, resound throughout the world. When it opens in 2016, the Elbphil-harmonie will certainly add to Hamburg's illustriousness. Some of the city's approximately 40 theatres look back on a long tradition. Fans of cabaret and comedy find many theatres squeezed into a small area of St Pauli. Clubs with live music are listed on pages 206–207; musical theatres are on page 209.

Opera and Classical Music

The **Hamburgische Staatsoper** *(see p77)*, founded in 1678, was Germany's first opera house and has long been considered one of the most renowned opera houses in Europe. Under the direction of the Australian conductor Simone Youn since 2005, its repertoire encompasses 400 years of music history – from Baroque opera to modern music theatre. The Staatsoper is also the venue for performances of the Hamburg Ballet under the direction of John Neumeier.

In the **Laeiszhalle** *(see p73)*, concerts by the Hamburg Symphony, the NDR (North German Radio) Symphony Orchestra and the Hamburg Philharmonic are performed. Guest performances by international orchestras and soloists round out the programme. Along with small operas, the **Junges Forum Musik + Theater** of the Hochschule für Musik und Theater Hamburg presents interesting works by and concerts of its students on a regular basis.

Theatre

The **Deutsches Schauspielhaus** *(see p129)* is not only the largest, but is considered by many professionals to be the most beautiful stage in the country for drama. Its repertory includes the classics as well as contemporary

plays. It achieved its great reputation partly under the direction of Gustaf Gründgens (1955 – 63), a famous German actor. The Junges Schauspielhaus mounts experimental plays and produces matinées in the Malersaal.

Although the **Thalia Theater** *(see p59)* is considered to be Hamburg's "second theatre" after the Schauspielhaus, it is currently presenting exciting productions, and it is no coincidence that it was again voted "Theatre of the Year" in 2007. Typical for the Thalia is demanding drama, including modern classics.

Kampnagel is well-known as a forum for innovative contemporary theatre and dance theatre. Housed in a former machine factory, this cultural institution is a meeting place for first-class ensembles from around the world. Each August, Kampnagel mounts the very famous International Summer Festival.

The **Hamburger Kammerspiele,** a renowned private theatre, presents great shows on a small stage – and with a top-notch cast each time. Along with critical dramas, the theatre holds readings and *Lieder* (song) evenings.

With its 744 seats, the **Ernst Deutsch Theater** is the largest private theatre in Germany. It has been a firm presence on the Hamburg theatre scene since 1951. Its programme focuses on the rich offerings between traditional and modern plays. The theatre

established a young company called by the name of "Plattform".

Productions of plays by British authors performed in the original English are presented by the **English Theatre**, *the* address for Anglophile theatre lovers. The actors are not only professionals, they are also native speakers; for most performances, they are flown in from England. The programme mainly features contemporary plays that are rather conventionally directed.

The **Altonaer Theater** has the character of a municipal theatre; its repertory encompasses mystery comedies as well as adaptations of films such as *Die Feuerzangenbowle* and literary musical evenings. If you want to really test your German, there is folk theatre performed in Low German (*plattdeutsch*) in the **Ohnsorg-Theater** *(see p 129)*, known to many Germans due to television broadcasts. The **Komödie Winterhuder Fähr-haus** stages classic boulevard theatre and comedies from harmless fun to black humour.

In summer, there is also open-air theatre in Hamburg. One classic is *Hamburger Jedermann*, which is performed on eight weekends (Fri – Sun) in July and August in the **Theater in der Speicherstadt**.

Cabaret

There has always been alternative theatre in Hamburg, especially in the district of St Pauli, and much of it today is found around the recently renovated Spielbudenplatz. The **St. Pauli Theater,** a theatre steeped in tradition, features well-known actors and cabaret stars. It mounts original shows as well as international musicals, cabaret and comedy. Musical theatre, comedy and vaudeville of the highest quality can be seen in the **Schmidt Theater**. Next door is **Schmidts Tivoli** *(for both see p104)*, a stage for smaller musicals and one of the most beautiful theatres in the city. It is also one of the Reeperbahn's attractions. Both theatres are run by Corny

Littmann, a St Pauli celebrity. The experimental stage **fools garden** has a loyal following. This is the place to watch a variety of artists such as stand-up-comedians and cabaret artists as well as magicians and improvisation artists. Many talented performers have used this supportive theatre as a springboard to larger stages or to television.

The **Alma Hoppes Lustspielhaus** is run by the two members of the Alma Hoppe company – Nils Loenicker and Jan-Peter Petersen. Most of the headliners (such as Henning Venske and Martin Buchholz) specialize in political cabaret, just like the theatre's two

founders. Since 1975, the first sea-worthy theatre in Europe has been moored at Nikolaifleet: **Das Schiff** presents literary political cabaret, often based on texts by authors such as Kurt Tucholsky or Joachim Ringelnatz.

Cinema

Given the wide range of films screened in Hamburg, from art films to the latest Hollywood blockbusters, film buffs do not have to fear missing a classic. Although large companies such as **CinemaxX** (which owns many multiplex cinemas in Hamburg) dominate the film scene, independent cinema is alive and well. Many artistically

demanding films premiere in the two art house cinemas: the **Abaton**, Germany's oldest independent cinema, and the **Zeise Kinos**, located in a former ship's screw factory in Altona. They also screen many film series and have a children's programme in the afternoons. **B-Movie** in St Pauli is also known for its curated film series. The speciality of **Metropolis**, which screens films in an historic movie house, are the milestones of movie history. This cinema screens a range of films including silent movies with piano accompaniment.

An engaging programme of documentaries is presented at **3001 Kino**.

DIRECTORY

Opera and Classical Music

Hamburgische Staatsoper
Große Theaterstr. 25.
Map 9 C2.
Tel 35 68 68.
W hamburgische-staatsoper.de

Junges Forum Musik + Theater
Harvestehuder Weg 12.
Map 8 D2.
Tel 428 48 24 00.
W hfmt-hamburg.de

Laeiszhalle
Johannes-Brahms-Platz.
Map 9 B2.
Tel 357 66 60.
W elbphilharmonie.de/laeiszhalle

Theatre

Altonaer Theater
Museumstr. 17.
Map 1 C4.
Tel 39 90 58 70.
W altonaer-theater.de

Deutsches Schauspielhaus
Kirchenallee 39.
Map 6 E2. Tel 24 87 10.
W schauspielhaus.de

English Theatre
Lerchenfeld 14.
Tel 227 70 89.
W englishtheatre.de

Ernst Deutsch Theater
Friedrich-Schütter-Platz 1.
Tel 22 70 14 20.
W ernst-deutsch-theater.de

Hamburger Kammerspiele
Hartungstr. 9–11.
Map 7 B2.
Tel 413 34 40.
W hamburger-kammerspiele.de

Kampnagel
Jarrestr. 20.
Tel 270 94 90.
W kampnagel.de

Komödie Winterhuder Fährhaus
Hudtwalckerstr. 13.
Tel 48 06 80 80.
W komoedie-hamburg.de

Ohnsorg-Theater
Heidi-Kabel-Platz 1.
Map 10 F2. Tel 350 80 30.
W ohnsorg.de

Thalia Theater
Alstertor 1.
Map 10 E3.
Tel 32 81 40.
W thalia-theater.de

Theater in der Speicherstadt
Auf dem Sande 1.
Map 5 C4. Tel 369 62 37.
W speicherstadt.net/jedermann.html

Cabaret

Alma Hoppes Lustspielhaus
Ludolfstr. 53.
Tel 55 56 55 56.
W almahoppe.de

fools garden
Lerchenstr. 113.
Map 1 D1. Tel 43 65 82.
W foolsgarden-theater.de

Das Schiff
Nikolaifleet/Holzbrücke 2.
Map 9 C4.
Tel 69 65 05 80.
W theaterschiff.de

Schmidt Theater und Schmidts Tivoli
Spielbudenplatz 24–25 und 27–28.
Map 4 D4.
Tel 31 77 88 99.
W tivoli.de

St. Pauli Theater
Spielbudenplatz 29–30.
Map 4 D4.
Tel 47 11 06 66.
W st-pauli-theater.de

Cinema

3001 Kino
Schanzenstr. 75.
Tel 43 76 79.
W 3001-kino.de

Abaton
Allendeplatz 3.
Map 7 A2. Tel 41 32 03 20.
W abaton.de

B-Movie
Brigittenstr. 5.
Map 3 C2. Tel 430 58 67.
W b-movie.de

CinemaxX Hamburg Dammtor
Dammtordamm 1.
Map 5 C1.
Tel 80 80 69 69.
W cinemaxx.de

Metropolis
Kleine Theaterstr. 10.
Tel 34 23 53. W metropolis-hamburg.de

Zeise Kinos
Friedensallee 7–9.
Map 1 B2.
Tel 390 87 70.
W zeise.de

Bars, Clubs and Live Music

The night life in Hamburg is as full of contrasts as the city itself. There is a great deal for night owls to do, from settling into cocktail bars to discuss the day's events with friends, to dancing the night away at trendy clubs. Every kind of taste in music is gratified – there is no scene which is not represented in the city. However, it's hard to pin down the latest places to see and be seen since they change as frequently as the Hamburg weather. And as some older clubs close, new ones are constantly opening. The pulsing heart of Hamburg's night life is St Pauli, where the famous (or infamous) Reeperbahn is located. The fun really only starts to peak here after midnight. But in the "Schanze", as locals call the Schanzenviertel, a well-established pub and club scene has also arisen.

Bars

Bar Hamburg in St Georg is stylish down to the last detail. It is divided into various lounges and impresses not only with its large selection of cocktails and whiskies, but also with its exclusive interior design. No less popular is the **Bar Rossi** in the Schanzenviertel. With its excellent cocktails, friendly staff and live DJs, it attracts a chicer crowd.

3Freunde is known for mixing the best cocktails; in Smoker's Bar smokers can relax as they imbibe. The **Komet Bar** is located in the most "sinful" corner of the Reeperbahn. This small bar is very cosy although rock music is often played here. **Bar Cabana** exudes an enticing caribbean flair. The range of cocktails and cigars is exuberant. Your search for the perfect cocktail might end at **Christiansen's**, where bartender Uwe Christiansen has received awards for his mouth-watering drinks.

In the **Indochine Ice Bar** – Germany's first ice bar – the temperature is maintained at a chilly –5 ° C (23 ° F), just right for keeping the drinks served there frosty; there are parkas at the ready to keep guests warm.

In the Hafen Hamburg hotel (see p179), the **Tower Bar** offers fantastic views over the bustling port from the 12th floor at a height of 62 m (203 ft). **Skybar 20up** also has amazing views, from the 20th floor of the Empire Riverside Hotel (see p177).

Clubs

A Hamburg institution, with the charm of a temporary structure that is now permanent, is the **Astra-Stube**. Cool beer and expensive champagnes are the beverages of choice here. Lovers of indie, reggae and techno music frequent this club. **Große Freiheit 36** is one of the oldest clubs in St Pauli – and not only because it's at the address of the Star-Club from where the Beatles shot to fame. Themed nights such as Rock 36, Return to the 80s and 90s Reloaded pull in huge crowds.

Great soul, funk, pop and rock are performed live at **Angie's Nightclub**. Another good venue is **Waagenbau**, where a series of DJs play drum'n'bass, techno and hip-hop. **Floryaclub** is one of Hamburg's most popular clubs entertaining an eclectic crowd with extraordinary laser shows and a range of international DJs.

Grüner Jäger, located in a small cottage on a public green space at Neuer Pferdemarkt, is considered one of the best clubs in the Schanzenviertel.

The **Golden Pudel Club** at the Fish Market, with its nose for underground trends, is a good counter to the increasing chicness of the area. Club-goers happily queue in line for up to two hours to get into **China Lounge**. The DJs spin R'n'B, hip-hop, house and electro.

Live Music

Along with large venues such as the open-air theatre in Stadtpark (see p134) and the **O2 World Hamburg**, there are also many smaller venues in Hamburg that feature live music. They keep alive the tradition of the legendary Star-Club (which was located at Große Freiheit 39 from 1962–69), in which the Beatles began their unparalleled international success.

Jazz lovers head to the **Cotton Club**, Hamburg's oldest Jazz cellar, where, from Monday to Saturday, everything revolves around jazz- and jam-sessions and swing. Other popular jazz venues include **Birdland**, Das Feuerschiff (see p89), Jazzclub Bergedorf and **Jazzclub im Stellwerk**. Blues legends take to the stage at the **Downtown Bluesclub**.
International soul, funk, jazz, rock and pop stars perform at the **Stage Club** in the Neue Flora. Many famous interpreters of World Music, as well as rock

Udo Lindenberg – German Rock Star

Even though he is from Westphalia, Udo Lindenberg (born on 17 May 1946) is linked with Hamburg's music scene like none other. After arriving in Hamburg in 1968, he played the city clubs with various bands before forming his own, the Panikorchester. He was one of the first German musicians to popularize rock music with German lyrics. Commercial success was achieved by Lindenberg with his album *Andrea Doria*, which he recorded with the Panikorchester in 1973. Trademarks of this musician and songwriter are his ironic lyrics about personal relationships and his characteristic talking-singing style of delivery. Lindenberg, who has always been socially engaged, still goes on tour. When he is in Hamburg, he stays in the Atlantic Kempinski hotel (see p128). On his 50th birthday, Udo Lindenberg was honoured with his own star – modelled on Hollywood's Walk of Fame – which was set into the sidewalk in front of Café Keese on the Reeperbahn (see pp102–03).

musicians and jazz players, grace the stage of the **Fabrik**. Artists like Mikis Theodorakis, Ten Years After and Miles Davis performed here.

"Rock 'n' Roll since 1974" – this is the motto of the long-established club **Logo**, where live music is played exclusively. Rock music is also king at **Molotow** on the Spielbudenplatz. The venue's concert programme encompasses practically every type of rock there is – The White Stripes, Billy Talent and Die Toten Hosen amongst many others. Bands playing indie rock can be seen live on stage in **Knust**. The clubs **Uebel & Gefährlich** and **Prinzen bar** attract music fans with indie pop and other modern music.

Beach Clubs

The first beach bar on the Elbe river opened in 2003 and was an instant hit with Hamburgers. Palms, large beach umbrellas, deck chairs, and hammocks created a somewhat Mediterranean ambience. None of this is diminished by the view of the bustling port. On the contrary, looking out over the sparkling Elbe river with a cocktail in your hand, it's easy to forget that you are actually in a large city. DJs play chill-out music to enhance the mood. Popular locations are **Hamburg City Beach Club**, **Hamburg del mar** and StrandPauli (*see p 109*).

Gay and Lesbian Bars and Clubs

Hamburg's gay scene is concentrated in the St Georg district. Some of the most popular meeting spots are located on Lange Reihe. Among them are **Café Gnosa**, which is the best-known gay and lesbian café in Hamburg, and **Generation Bar**, a stylishly lit cocktail bar with a fantastic party atmosphere.

WunderBar – which is located in the district of St Pauli – is a classic gay bar decorated in rich red plush. The **Frauencafé Endlich**, which is strictly for women only, is in the New Town.

DIRECTORY

Bars

3Freunde
Clemens-Schultz-Str. 66.
Map 3 C3.
Tel 53 26 26 39.

Bar Cabana
Fischmarkt 6.
Map 3 B5.
Tel 80 00 71 14.

Bar Hamburg
Rautenbergstr. 6–8.
Map 8 D5.
Tel 28 05 48 80.

Bar Rossi
Max-Brauer-Allee 279.
Tel 43 34 21.

Christiansen's
Pinnasberg 60.
Map 2 F4.
Tel 317 28 63.

Indochine Ice Bar
Neumühlen 11.
Map 1 B4.
Tel 39 80 78 80.

Komet Bar
Erichstr. 11.
Map 3 C4.
Tel 27 86 86 86.

Skybar 20up
Bernhard-Nocht-Str. 97.
Map 4 D4.
Tel 31 11 97 04 70.

Tower Bar
Seewartenstr. 9.
Map 4 E4.
Tel 31 11 37 04 50.

Clubs

Angie's Nightclub
Spielbudenplatz 27.
Map 4 D4.
Tel 31 77 88 11.

Astra-Stube
Max-Brauer-Allee 200.
Map 2 F1.
Tel 319 75 55 13.

China Lounge
Nobistor 14.
Map 3 C4.
Tel 31 97 66 22.

Floryaclub
Holstenstr. 73.
Map 3 B2.
Tel 0172 207 00 50.

Golden Pudel Club
St. Pauli Fischmarkt 27.
Map 3 B5.
Tel 31 97 99 30.

Große Freiheit 36
Große Freiheit 36.
Map 4 C3.
Tel 31 77 78 10.

Grüner Jäger
Neuer Pferdemarkt 36.
Map 4 D2.
Tel 31 81 46 17.

Waagenbau
Max-Brauer-Allee 204.
Map 2 E1.
Tel 24 42 05 09.

Live Music

Birdland
Gärtnerstr. 122.
Tel 40 52 77.

Cotton Club
Alter Steinweg 10.
Map 9 B3.
Tel 34 38 78.

Downtown Bluesclub
Hindenburgstr. 2.
Tel 01805 57 00 00.

Fabrik
Barnerstr. 36.
Map 1 C2.
Tel 39 10 70.

Jazzclub im Stellwerk
In Fernbahnhof Harburg over tracks 3 and 4,
Hannoversche Str. 85
Tel 30 09 69 48.

Knust
Neuer Kamp 30.
Map 4 D2.
Tel 87 97 62 30.

Logo
Grindelallee 5.
Map 7 B2.
Tel 410 56 58.

Molotow
Spielbudenplatz 5.
Map 4 D4.
Tel 430 11 10.

O2 World Hamburg
Sylvesterallee 10.
Tel 040-80 60 20 80.
🌐 o2world-hamburg.de

Prinzenbar
Spielbudenplatz 19.
Map 4 D4. **Tel** 317 88 30.

Stage Club
Stresemannstr. 159a.
Map 2 E1.
Tel 43 16 54 60.

Uebel & Gefährlich
Feldstr. 66.
Map 4 E2.
Tel 0157 38 27 64 69.

Beach Clubs

Hamburg City Beach Club
Bei den St. Pauli Landungsbrücken 7.

Hamburg del mar
Bei den St. Pauli Landungsbrücken 3.

Gay and Lesbian Bars and Clubs

Café Gnosa
Lange Reihe 93.
Map 8 E1.
Tel 24 30 34.

Frauencafé Endlich
Dragonerstall 11.
Map 9 B2. **Tel** 34 13 45.

Generation Bar
Lange Reihe 81.
Map 8 E1.
Tel 28 00 46 90.

WunderBar
Talstr. 14–18.
Map 3 C3.
Tel 317 44 44.

Musicals

Hamburg is Germany's musical theatre capital. In a survey of the most important musical theatre centres in the world it took a respectable third place after New York and London. No other German city stages more musicals. With an amazing 15-year run (1986 – 2001), *Cats* was the country's longest-running musical. Anyone who loves colourful shows, catchy tunes, exciting entertainment, songs with feeling, perfect choreography and riveting plot-lines is in exactly the right place here in the Elbe metropolis. For many German visitors to the city, the chance to see one of these world-famous productions is the sole reason for their trip. On the following pages, you will find information on the development of Hamburg's musical industry, the city's theatres and major productions *(see pp210–11)*. All productions are in German; plays in English are staged at the English Theatre *(see p204)*.

Hamburg Becomes a Musical Theatre Capital

Hamburg's rise to become a musical theatre mecca started on 18 April 1986 with the German premiere of *Cats*. This Andrew Lloyd Webber production was already pulling in the crowds at Broadway theatres in New York and West End venues in London – the unrivalled eldorados for musical theatre fans. The *Cats* premiere in the Hamburger Operettenhaus (since 2007 **TUI Operettenhaus**, *see p105, p210*), which up to that point had not been used in years, marked the start of the era of commercial musical theatre in Germany.

From the beginning, the plan was to run the production over an extended period of time in one single theatre. It ran day in, day out, and twice a day at weekends without a single break. This approach had been successfully tested beforehand in the US and Great Britain, but was greeted with great scepticism in Germany. However, the show was a huge success and the producers proved that their risky approach was the right one – *Cats*, a touching story performed by singers /actors dressed up as cats, ran for no less than 15 years. When the final curtain fell after about 6,100 performances, more than six million people had seen this success story.

The foundation for Hamburg's development into a musical theatre centre with an international reputation had been laid. The Operettenhaus still prides itself on its status as the birthplace of musical theatre in Germany.

The Rise of Musicals

The success of *Cats* set free energy and resources: new venues for large productions were created in order to solidify Hamburg's status as Germany's musical theatre capital and to keep the stream of visitors into the city flowing. Two new venues were built for the performances of the German versions of *Phantom of the Opera* and *Buddy – The Musical*: the **Neue Flora** *(see p119, pp210 – 11)*, built in 1989 – 90, and the **Theater im Hafen Hamburg** *(see p92, p211)*, which opened in 1994. Both were designed for the sole purpose of staging musical productions.

These theatres are run by **Stage Entertainment**. Founded in the Netherlands in 1989, this live entertainment company owns and licenses productions worldwide. In 2011, it also took over the TUI Operettenhaus. Stage Entertainment attends to the production and marketing of musicals as well as to the theatres themselves. Currently, it is overseeing around 70 productions.

Musicals in Hamburg

Over many years, other successful musicals have livened up Hamburg's cultural scene. Early classics were followed by *Tanz der Vampire (Dance of the Vampires)*, *Mamma Mia!*, *Der König der Löwen (The Lion Kong)*, *Dirty Dancing*, *Ich war noch niemals in New York (I Have Never Been to New York)*, *Tarzan*, and *Sister Act*. *Rocky* debuted in 2012 and is the first German musical production that will also be staged on Broadway in New York City beginning in spring 2014. This export to the United States, the birth place of musical theatre, strengthens Hamburg's international reputation as a bastion of musical theatre even further.

The fact that some early productions flopped at the box office and were closed down after just a few months *(see p211)* did not impede the success of musical theatre in Hamburg; rather, it provided valuable lessons.

Importance of Musicals for the City

Other German cities that tried to promote musicals enjoyed only mixed success. In Hamburg, the genre had not only become an important part of the city's entertainment offerings, it had become a key aspect of Hamburg's cultural image, and the high bar set by *Cats* was subsequently met. With some musicals, such as *Mamma Mia!*, almost every performance was sold out, and very few of any musical performance suffered from empty seats. Hamburg managed to avoid many of the problems other German cities had when attempting to develop a musical industry. Today, the musicals staged in Hamburg are enjoyed by almost two million people from around the world each year.

Parallel to the growing enthusiasm for musicals and the rise in the number of tourists and overnight guests, the number of hotels in

Hamburg grew. New hotels were built and old ones were thoroughly modernized. Hamburg owes its importance as a travel destination in large part to these spectacular shows – for many visitors to Hamburg, musicals are the reason for (or at least a highlight of) their stay. Musical theatre tourism is now well-established as a sector of the tourism industry. There are many agencies that not only organize a visit to a glamorous stage production but also offer package deals which include the journey to Hamburg and the hotel stay. Since many of the spectacular productions also appeal to children, the package deals are immensely popular with families.

The musical boom brought many creative people to the Elbe metropolis. Directors, choreographers, musicians, actors, dancers and many other artists who are involved in the shows live and work in Hamburg, greatly enhancing the city's cultural life.

Upcoming Developments

As in other cities, the market for musical theatre productions seems far from being saturated. Big thinking prevails in the musical theatre industry, and new venues and shows are planned. The **Stage Musical Theatre**, scheduled to open in the harbour area in autumn 2014, is considered to be the cornerstone of future development. The productions staged at this new venue will be another highlight among the city's entertainment offerings.

Tips for Visitors

Large venues (see pp210–11) present eight shows a week, with two performances on Saturdays and Sundays. Theatres are closed on Mondays. The shows last for about three hours, with one intermission.

Since the shows often sell out months in advance, you should make sure to plan your visit to a musical early. If you organize your visit to Hamburg

well in advance, you are more likely to obtain tickets for your favourite show in the price category that suits you best. For popular musicals in particular, the demand is very high.

On the other hand, visitors who decide on the spot may get hold of unsold tickets (sometimes at reduced prices) on the day of the performance. To check availability, call the Stage Entertainment ticket hotline. Box offices open one hour before performances begin, tickets must be collected at least 30 minutes prior to the show.

If you're planning to see *Rocky*, consider purchasing a Golden Circle Ticket (Price Category 0). Holders of these tickets are entitled to change seats for the last act. As soon as the boxing ring is pulled into the auditorium, you can grab a spot right beside the boxing ring. Just like VIPs at a title fight, you'll experience the energy and excitement of the final fight at close quarters. As the ring-side seats are up a flight of steps, they are not accessible to those with reduced mobility.

Backstage Tours

The **TUI Operettenhaus**, the **Neue Flora** and the **Theater im Hafen Hamburg** – the large venues in Hamburg – give visitors the opportunity to look behind the scenes. Backstage tours provide insight into the complexity of a performance and the interplay of sets, sound and lighting. Visitors also get to tread the boards seeing the stage from the actors' perspective. Markings on the stage floor indicate where actors need to position themselves – especially important for action scenes and the carefully timed acrobatics of *Tarzan*.

Backstage tours cost €18.25, and last between 45 minutes and an hour. Tours do not run every day, so do call the relevant theatre to find out tour times. Unfortunately, none of the backstage tours are wheelchair accessible.

DIRECTORY

Major Venues

Neue Flora
Stresemannstraße 159a.
Map 2 E1.
Tel 43 16 50.
W **neueflora.de**

Stage Musical Theatre
For information on the new theatre contact Stage Entertainment.
Tel 0180 544 44.

Theater im Hafen Hamburg
Norderelbstraße 6.
Tel 42 10 00.
W **loewenkoenig.de**

TUI Operettenhaus
Spielbudenplatz 1.
Map 4 D4.
Tel 31 11 70.
W **tuioperettenhaus.de**

Other Venues

Delphi Showpalast
Eimsbütteler Chaussee 5.
Tel 431 86 00.
W **delphi-showpalast.de**

Schmidts Tivoli
Spielbudenplatz 27–28.
Map 4 D4.
Tel 31 77 88 99.
W **tivoli.de**

Tickets

Since there is great demand for tickets to Hamburg musicals, it is recommended that you book your tickets as far in advance of the shows as possible. Many theatre-goers purchase their tickets as part of a package deal, which often includes travel. Tickets for musicals produced by Stage Entertainment should be booked well ahead of time, ideally by calling the ticket hotline (see below). Other venues should be contacted directly.

Stage Entertainment ticket hotline
Tel 0180 544 44 (14 cents a min. from a German landline / 42 cents a min. via mobile phones).
W **stage-entertainment.de**

Large Venues

There are three renowned musical theatres in Hamburg: the **TUI Operettenhaus**, the **Neue Flora** and the **Theater im Hafen Hamburg**. They present world-famous productions, and each of them is equipped with state-of-the-art stage machinery, lighting and sound technology. Views of the stage from the seats in the well-designed auditoria are excellent, and the theatres' foyers are impressive.

The theatres, each of which has its own individual flair, are located in different parts of the city. There are restaurants and bars in each venue and food is offered before and after the show.

TUI Operettenhaus

The TUI Operettenhaus on Spielbudenplatz seats approximately 1400 (see p105). The epoch of the "great" musical theatre hits in Hamburg began here in 1986 with **Cats**. Previously, operettas, plays and revues were performed in the theatre. After the last performance of that long-running hit in 2001, no one knew whether or not the shows that followed would be as successful as their predecessor. Two musicals were taken off the programme after only six months, but then along came **Mamma Mia!** much to the producers' relief. After its premiere in late 2002 all doubts were laid to rest. The musical brought the biggest hits of the Swedish group ABBA to the stage, and the varied audience danced in the aisles to the songs of their youth (or of their parents' youth). Memories of the golden age of sky-blue eyeshadow and bell-bottoms came alive once again.

In December 2007, **Ich war noch niemals in New York (I Have Never Been to New York)** premiered at the TUI Operettenhaus, a turbulent yet very romantic musical featuring 23 of Udo Jürgens' greatest hits – from Merci Chérie to Mit 66 Jahren to Griechischer Wein. The musical's title is also taken from the work of the Austrian composer and pop singer. Jürgens' songs have been woven into a story that covers three generations, telling of unfulfilled dreams, homesickness, and the joy of living and of love. Appropriately for a Hamburg production, part of the story takes place on the high seas, and there is an exciting chase scene on the deck of a cruise ship. **Ich war noch niemals in New York** is a story of a life's dream (to travel to America just once!), and it certainly touched the hearts of those lucky enough to see it.

Sister Act, which premiered in December 2010, tells the story of a night club singer who is threatened by gangsters, is forced into hiding and ends up in a Catholic convent. With her particular charm, she revives the nuns' choir. The swinging songs for this musical were composed by the Academy Award winner Alan Menken.

Since November 2012, the musical **Rocky** has been running at the TUI Operettenhaus. The story of the boxer Rocky Balboa is modelled on the film of the same name, which starred Sylvester Stallone in the leading role. Here, the fascination of a musical theatre performance is enriched by the excitement of sport. To grant authenticity to the fights, the world champions Vitali and Wladimir Klitschko were involved in the production. Interwoven with the dramatic rise of Balboa in the boxing world is a moving love story. The stagecraft is spectacular: in the final act, the boxing ring – the setting for turbulent scenes and heavy fighting – is pulled into the auditorium, while the song Eye of the Tiger is played. This production was awarded the Live Entertainment Award (LEA) 2013, a much coveted accolade in the musical theatre industry, for the Best Musical in Germany.

Neue Flora

Due to the success of **Cats**, the Neue Flora (see p119) was built in 1989–90. It was designed in 1920s style, its shape reminiscent of a ship's hull. Today, the Neue Flora is firmly rooted in the city's cultural life. This theatre, which seats 2,000, opened in June 1990 with the musical **Das Phantom der Oper (The Phantom of the Opera)**, which ran until June 2001. This show, which transports the audience into the world of the Paris Opera, became a huge hit – it was performed approximately 4,400 times in front of some seven million people.

The subsequent productions at the Neue Flora were shorter lived; **Mozart!** and **Titanic** only ran for about ten months each. Thankfully a run of successful musicals followed. In December 2003, **Tanz der Vampire (Dance of the Vampires)**, modelled on Roman Polański's film (1967) of the same name, premiered. **Dirty Dancing** was brought to the stage in March 2006. This music and dance show was based on the 1987 film of the same name and had its European premiere in Hamburg. Woven into the moving story are 51 songs from the 1960s to the 1980s.

In October 2008, the fourth Disney musical produced by Stage Entertainment, **Tarzan**, celebrated its premiere in the Neue Flora. It tells the tale of a young man looking for his roots who ends up finding romantic love. Breathtaking acrobatics with approximately 300 stunts high above the heads of the audience, ingenious sets, colourful costumes, evocative sounds (such as the reverberating rhythm of jungle drums and the squawking of exotic birds); and the music of Phil Collins are the key ingredients of this multi-faceted and fast-paced show about friendship, finding one's identity and determination. For the performance of **Tarzan**, the theatre is transformed into a spectacular and lively jungle landscape. Some of the performers, who came from 16 different countries, were chosen on a talent show broadcast on SAT.1, a German television channel. The musical ran until autumn 2013.

Das Phantom der Oper (The Phantom of The Opera) returned to the Neue Flora in the autumn of 2013, the first time a musical has returned to Hamburg. This production, with its famous songs written by Andrew Lloyd Webber, is one of the best attended musicals in the world.

Theater im Hafen Hamburg

The third and newest of the Hanseatic city's large musical theatre venues is the Theater im Hafen Hamburg (see p92), which seats more than 2000. Housed in a permanent yellow tent on the south shore of the Elbe, this theatre has been attracting attention since 1995. Visitors to *Buddy – The Musical*, which premiered right after the completion of the theatre, took a trip back in time to the 1950s. The musical is dedicated to Buddy Holly, one of the early pioneers of rock 'n' roll.

In 2001, *Buddy* was replaced by *Der König der Löwen (The Lion King)*, an inspiring African-themed theatrical experience. Fabulous costumes, inventive masks and wonderful songs written by Elton John – a mix of African rhythms and western pop – are the framework for the Walt Disney story of the young lion Simba, who fights to take his place as the king and has to prove his courage many times. Since its premier, this spectacular show has broken every record in visitor numbers, and continues to do so, even though it has been running for more than a decade.

At the Theater im Hafen Hamburg, the experience starts for most audience members with the trip to the show. In just a few minutes, the free

shuttle boat takes theatre-goers from the Landungs-brücken to the venue. After sunset, passengers enjoy a fantatstic view of Hamburg's skyline. The last shuttle boat back to the Landungsbrücken departs 90 minutes after the end of the show.

Other Venues

There are several other theatres in Hamburg that mount their own smaller productions. **Schmidts Tivoli** (see p104) on the Reeperbahn practically has a cult following. After the audience hit *Fifty-Fifty*, the show *Heiße Ecke – Das St. Pauli Musical (Hot Corner – The St Pauli Musical)* was brought to the stage. The show is set in a snack bar called Heiße Ecke and brings the St Pauli district to life with song and dance. It is a fast-paced musical revue full of wit and surprises. The production, with its nine actors, singers and dancers playing over 50 roles, is directed by Corny Littmann. The portrayal of St Pauli is authentic – everyone is represented, from the neighbourhood's mavericks and failures, to those "normal" characters going about their day-to-day business. It is also typical of St Pauli that many members of the audience drink beer or eat a currywurst during the performance. Littmann also directs the follow-up production *Oh Alpenglühn! (Oh Alpen Glow!)*. This enchanting performance is all about glamour, fun and song. The actors embark on a mountain trek accompanied by a selection of varied tunes.

The **Delphi Showpalast** also produces rousing shows. This musical venue stages several different shows a week. The pop-musical *Westerland*, packed with Top 20 chart hits and infectious oldies, was a box office success. The entertaining love story *Mandy in Love* takes place on a riversteamer and includes pop favourites by Elvis Presley and Take That. The musical *Starcut*

told the hilarious story of a hairdresser's rise to the top – a very entertaining performance. *Paul & Paula*, with a funfair serving as scenery, celebrated its premier in September 2012. The following September, the musical *Hüttenzauber – Die Show (Mountain Magic – The Show)* was performed for the first time. This production portrays the social life of skiers and winter-sports enthusiasts, revolving around the flirtatious après-ski scene.

MUSICALS

TUI Operettenhaus

Cats
(Apr 1986 – Jan 2001)

Fosse – Die Show (Fosse – The Show)
(Jun – Dec 2001)

Oh, What a Night!
(Jan – Jun 2002)

Mamma Mia!
(Nov 2002 – Sep 2007)

Ich war noch niemals in New York (I Have Never Been to New York)
(Dec 2007 – Sep 2010)

Sister Act
(Dec 2010 – Aug 2012)

Rocky
(running since Nov 2012)

Neue Flora

Das Phantom der Oper (The Phantom of the Opera)
(Jun 1990 – Jun 2001)

Mozart!
(Sep 2001 – Jun 2002)

Titanic
(Dec 2002 – Oct 2003)

Tanz der Vampire (Dance of the Vampires)
(Dec 2003 – Jan 2006)

Dirty Dancing
(Mar 2006 – Jun 2008)

Tarzan
(Oct 2008 – Oct 2013)

Das Phantom der Oper (The Phantom of the Opera)
(running since Dec 2013)

Theater im Hafen Hamburg

Buddy – The Musical
(Dec 1994 – Jun 2001)

Der König der Löwen (The Lion King)
(running since Dec 2001)

Puppets on set, *König der Löwen (The Lion King)* ▶

Sports and Outdoor Activities

Whether you play just for fun or are a serious competitive athlete, the range of activities in Hamburg is huge. After all, it is a city of sports lovers, and about 500,000 Hamburgers belong to one of the 800 sport associations. And, since Hamburg lies on the water, there are countless opportunities to take part in water sports.

But you can also have fun as a spectator. Hamburg is a venue for many well-known events, from cycling to tennis and equestrian events. Real crowd-pleasers are the Hamburg City Man (a triathlon) and the Hamburg Marathon, in which not only world-class athletes compete but anyone wanting to test their mettle can run, urged on by hundreds of thousands of spectators.

Running

Casual joggers and ambitious marathon runners alike can choose from several routes through varied terrain. One of the most popular is the 7.6-km (4.7-mile) long circuit around the Außenalster. The scenic route takes you along the Alster shore and through expanses of parkland, and there are only a few short sections that are on a city street. Since the route is well lit, it can be used day and night, and in every season. A further magnet for joggers is the Stadtpark, where you can select your preferred route for distance and terrain. The Elbuferweg – a lovely path running along the Elbe between Neumühlen and Blankenese – is well used. For those with stamina, the **Hamburg Marathon** every year in April is an ideal challenge; approximately 20,000 participants run in this marathon each year.

Cycling

Since there are not too many steep hills in Hamburg, it is an ideal city to explore by bicycle. In Hamburg and its environs, there are some lovely routes, for example along the Elbe and the Alster. Unfortunately, many cycling paths in the city are in bad shape, being either too uneven or too narrow.

Some bicycle shops rent out bicycles by the day or the week. You are allowed to take your bicycle on ferries as well as on the U-Bahn and S-Bahn. The **Allgemeiner Deutscher Fahrradclub (ADFC)** provides suggestions for cycling trips as well as useful tips and information.

The high point of the cycling sport season are the **Vattenfall Cyclassics**. Here, the world's best cyclists are joined by thousands of amateurs at the starting line. The latter can choose between three distances – 55 km (34 miles), 100 km (63 miles) or 155 km (96 miles). The number of participants is limited to 20,000.

Swimming

There is bathing fun for everyone in the waters of the Alster at **Naturbad Stadtparksee** in the eastern part of the Stadtpark. The swimming pool is truly gigantic at 124 m (407 ft) long by 107 m (351 ft) wide. There is a separate area for non-swimmers, and numerous pools. The **Alster-schwimmhalle** offers special attractions such as an outdoor pool that is open all year round, a 10-m (33-ft) high diving platform, a 76-m (250-ft) long slide and the spacious sauna world (800 sq m/8,600 sq ft).

Housed in a protected building, the **Holthusen Spa** attracts visitors with an astonishing array of fitness and wellness offerings, such as a stone sauna, a Finnish sauna, massages and a beauty bath. Pure relaxation is on offer at the **Bartholomäus-Therme** with its Ottoman bath.

The **MidSommerland** on Außenmühlenteich is considered by many Hamburgers to be the most beautiful baths in the city. Designed in Scandinavian style with a great deal of wood and granite, the complex offers its patrons every kind of facility to promote health and wellness – from a relaxing midnight sauna to an action-packed wild-water canal.

Sailing, Rowing and Paddling

It is no secret that Hamburg's citizens consider water their element. When a stiff breeze blows, many Hamburgers can hardly wait to take to their boats. After all, the Elbe flows past the front door, and the Außenalster, a very large inland lake, is located in the heart of the city. But no matter whether you sail the Elbe towards the North Sea or stay on the Alster – hoisting the sails is a wonderful leisure time activity. If you have never sailed, then try it out at least once at one of the many sailing clubs around the Alster and at City-Sporthafen. All are run by professionals.

You can hire boats along the Alster, and take out a boat for a leisurely paddle. To hire a more sporty boat such as a single, double or eight-oared racing shell, you must be a member of a rowing club.

Hamburg's network of canals and narrow channels can be easily explored by canoe or kayak. Boats can be rented from 20 Euros a day from **Gadermann** – a perfect way to get to know the "Venice of the North" from one of its most attractive sides.

Triathlon

Over land, by water and on a bicycle – the triathlon event of the Hamburg City Man, held in July, allows anyone who feels fit enough to participate in the race. There are two competitions: the shorter sprint on Saturday – 0.5 km (0.3 mile) swim, 22 km (14 mile) bike, and 5 km (3 mile) run, and the

Olympic challenge on Sunday – 1.5 km (0.9 mile) swim, 40 km (25 mile) bike, and 10 km run.

In-line Skating

In-line skating is very popular in Hamburg. In the spring and summer, several events open up routes to recreational rollers exclusively. Every now and then the streets around the Außenalster are blocked off to traffic for the Alsterrunde. The route is approximately 8 km (5 miles) long. **Stadttours** runs in-line skating tours, including a circular route through Old and New Town – no booking necessary. You can find out more about in-line skating on the websites of **Interline-skating Hamburg** and the **Hamburg Inline-Skating Club**.

Other Sports

Along with several golf courses, Hamburg also has a golf centre for beginners and professionals – the **Golf Lounge**. It offers ideal training conditions year-round.

Skiers, too, can indulge in their passion not too far from Hamburg. Kletterzentrum Hamburg offers an indoor and outdoor area with routes for all levels. The downhill run in **alpincenter** InHamburg-Wittenburg is 300-m (984-ft) long. The facility is a 30-min drive from Hamburg.

Spectator Sports

Hamburg has two football (soccer) clubs: the **Hamburger SV** (HSV) *(see p134)* and **FC St. Pauli** *(see pp110–11)*. While HSV tries to add to its roster of past successes, FC St. Pauli has often fought valiantly just to stay alive and, in 2010, fans celebrated as it moved up into German Bundesliga.

It feels like a party during ice-hockey games of the **Hamburg Freezers** in the O2 World Hamburg *(see p207)*. The HSV football club also has a handball team (2013 winners of the Champions League), that, along with the Freezers is the long-standing hit in this large venue.

Top tennis players compete annually at the tennis complex **Tennisanlage am Rothenbaum** *(see p45)*. The Deutsches Spring- and Dressurderby at **Derbyplatz Klein Flottbek** is famous. The **Deutsches Derby** is the crowning end to a week of races at Galopprennbahn Horn.

DIRECTORY

Running

Hamburg Marathon
Ⓦmarathon-hamburg.de

Cycling

ADFC Hamburg
Koppel 34–36.
Map 8 E4.
Tel 39 39 33.
Ⓦhamburg.adfc.de

Fahrradladen Altona
Barnerstr. 28.
Map 1 C2
Tel 390 38 24.

Fahrradladen St. Georg
Schmilinskystr. 6.
Tel 24 39 08.

Vattenfall Cyclassics
Ⓦvattenfall-cyclassics.de

Swimming

Alster-Schwimmhalle
Ifflandstr. 21.
Map 8 F4.

Bartholomäus-Therme
Bartholomäusstr. 95.

Holthusen Spa
Goernestr. 21.

MidSommerland
Gotthelfweg 2.

Naturbad Stadtparksee
Südring 5b.

Sailing, Rowing and Paddling

Bobby Reich
Fernsicht 2.
Tel 48 78 24.
Ⓦbobbyreich.de

Bootshaus Silwar
Eppendorfer Landstr. 148b.
Tel 47 62 07.
Ⓦbootshaus-silwar.com

Bootsverleih Goldfisch
Isekai 1.
Tel 41 35 75 75.
Ⓦgoldfisch.de/bootsverleih

Gadermann
Hummelbütteler Steindamm 70.
Tel 52 98 30 06.
Ⓦgadermann.de

Segelschule Pieper
An der Alster / Atlanticsteg.
Map 8 D4.
Tel 24 75 78.
Ⓦsegelschule-pieper.de

Triathlon

Hamburg Triathlon
Ⓦhamburg.triathlon.org

In-line Skating

Hamburg Inline-Skating Club
Ⓦskating-hamburg.de

Inlineskating Hamburg
Ⓦinlineskating-hamburg.de

Stadttour Hamburg
Ⓦstadttour-hamburg.de

Other Sports

alpincenter Hamburg-Wittenburg
Zur Winterwelt 1,
19243 Wittenburg.
Tel 038 852 23 41 91.
Ⓦalpincenter.com

Golf Lounge
Billwerder Neuer Deich 40.
Tel 81 97 87 90.
Ⓦgolflounge.info

Kletterzentrum Hamburg
Döhrnstr. 4.
Tel 60 08 88 66.
Ⓦkletterzentrum-hamburg.de

Spectator Sports

Derbyplatz Klein Flottbek
Hemmingstedter Weg 2.
Tel 82 81 82.
Ⓦnfr-hamburg.de

FC St. Pauli
Heiligengeistfeld 1.
Map 4 D/E2.
Tel 31 78 74 21.
Ⓦfcstpauli.com

Galopprennbahn Horn
Rennbahnstr. 96.
Tel 651 82 29.
Ⓦgalopp-hamburg.de

Hamburg Freezers
Hellgrundweg 50.
Tel 380 83 50.
Ⓦhamburg-freezers.de

Hamburger SV (Fußball)
Sylvesterallee 7. **Tel** 41 55 18 87. Ⓦhsv.de

Hamburger SV (Handball)
Hellgrundweg 50.
Tel 309 87 60.
Ⓦhsvhandball.com

Tennisanlage am Rothenbaum
Hallerstr. 89. **Map** 7 B1.
Tel 238 80 44 44.
Ⓦgerman-open-hamburg.de

CHILDREN'S HAMBURG

Hamburg is a good destination for families with children, and given the wealth of activities on offer they certainly will never get bored. Many of the great things to do in the city – such as taking a boat tour of the harbour, visiting the zoo, Tierpark Hagenbeck, or enjoying the water and sand on an Elbe beach – are fun for the entire family. There are also loads of attractions designed specifically to appeal to children. Some of the city's renowned museums have created exciting sections aimed at young visitors. The Planetarium has a special children's programme, and the larger parks have well-equipped adventure playgrounds and provide lovely settings for picnics.

A round of mini-golf, always a popular choice with families

Practical Advice

Hamburg's information offices like **Hamburg Tourismus GmbH** can provide you with ideas about how to best plan your stay with children. Organizations such as **Kinder Hamburg** and **Kindernetz Hamburg** will also supply you with information. Many sights and attractions offer child reductions, and there are also discounts on public transit.

Parks and Zoos

Hamburg has a great number of parks that offer more than just lovely walking paths. A visit to the **Stadtpark** *(see p134)* is fun for the entire family. In **Planten un Blomen** *(see pp78 – 9)*, there are also amusements for children such as mini-golf, pony-rides and much more. Magicians do their best to confound their young audiences, clowns put smiles on their faces and puppets delight the kids at the outdoor children's stage, which is open only during the summer.

Which child does not dream of feeding a giraffe, petting a goat, riding an elephant or admiring colourful parrots? At **Tierpark Hagenbeck** *(see pp136 – 37)* all this is possible. Among the zoo's attractions are its large outdoor enclosures, in which the animals are kept in their natural habitats. It is easy to spend a whole day here without anyone becoming bored.

PLANTEN un BLOMEN ROLLSCHUHBAHN

Sign for the roller-skating track at Planten un Blomen park

Museums

It was not too long ago that children dragged their heels on museum visits. Thankfully, this has all changed, and "hands-on", is the new museum mantra. In the **Deichtorhallen** *(see pp62 – 3)*, children are invited into a painting studio; in the **Museum für Völkerkunde** *(see p128)*, they experience the rituals of other peoples. There are also museums tailored especially to children: in **Klick Kindermuseum**, the little ones get to explore a construction site; indeed, they are urged to enter it. Another exhibit, "Treffpunkt Körper" (meet your body), lets them play at being dentists. With its copies of famous paintings made by children, a walk through the **KinderKunstMuseum** is a stroll through art history. **Miniatur Wunderland's** *(see p84)* claim to fame is the largest computer-controlled model railway in the world, which covers 1,150 sq m (12,400 sq ft). Visitors can have fun switching the points themselves, getting the trains running along different sections of the 13 km (8 miles) of track. Children's hearts also beat faster when they go on board to explore the museum ships **Cap San Diego** *(see pp98 – 99)* and **Rickmer Rickmers** *(see pp94 – 95)*.

Theatre

In Hamburg, there are many theatres for children and youth whose shows generally do not exceed an hour. They are usually suitable for those aged four years and up. One of the best theatres is the Fundus Theater,

Fun to be had at the Hamburg City Beach Club

Many exciting details to discover in Miniatur Wunderland

which combines theatre with puppet shows in a spectacular way. The **Theater für Kinder** is the oldest children's theatre in Germany. Along with performances, **Hamburger Puppentheater** offers two-hour workshops on making hand puppets for puppet fans large and small. The **Theaterschiff Batavia** in Wedel offers a rich and varied programme. The **Junges**

Musiktheater specializes in opera and operetta for both children and adults.

Sports

Children get very enthusiastic at the thought of playing beside, in or on the water. A boat trip through Hamburg's canals is a great way to explore the city. Of course, you can also rent a paddle-boat or row boat and tour the Alster under your own steam. Hamburg has many outdoor and indoor pools perfect for bathing fun. **Bäderland Hamburg** provides information. In summer, older children can let off steam on the roller-skating track in Planten un Blomen (see pp78–9). From November to March, there's an outdoor ice rink – the **Eisarena Planten un Blomen** is one of the world's largest. Skate rental is available..

Hamburg Dungeon In the Speicherstadt

Other Amusements

Visitors to the **Hamburg Dungeon** (see p85) take a trip back in time to the grisliest scenes in Hamburg's history. In the **Planetarium** (see p134) every Sunday afternoon it is time for "Sun, Moon and Stars", a show created for children aged five to nine. Great fun for all is to be had at the **Hamburger Dom** (see pp44–46) on the Heiligengeistfeld. This series of folk fairs, featuring a giant Ferris wheel, carousels, vendors and much more, is held three times a year. The indoor arena in **SchwarzLICHTviertel** is lit up ultraviolet. Here, you can play a round of mingolf. You soar 150 m (492 ft) up on the **HighFlyer Hamburg** (see pp62–3), a fixed hot-air balloon that rises up into the air in front of the Deichtorhallen.

DIRECTORY

Practical Advice

Hamburg Tourismus GmbH
Tel 30 05 17 01.
w hamburg-travel.com

Kinder Hamburg
w kinder-hamburg.de

Kindernetz Hamburg
w kindernetz-hamburg.de

Parks and Zoos

Planten un Blomen
Klosterwall 8.
Map 5 A–B1.
w plantenunblomen.de

Stadtpark
w hamburg-stadtpark.de

Tierpark Hagenbeck
Lokstedter Grenzstr. 2.
Tel 530 03 30.
w hagenbeck.de

Museums

Kinder-KunstMuseum
Bovestr. 10 -12. Tel 732 79 86. w kinderkunst-museum.de

Klick Kindermuseum
Achtern Born 127.
Tel 41 09 97 77.
w kindermuseum-hamburg.de

Miniatur Wunderland
Kehrwieder 2,
Block D.
Map 9 C5.
Tel 300 68 00.
w miniatur-wunderland.de

Theatre

Fundus Theater
Hasselbrookstr. 25.
Tel 250 72 70.
w fundus-theater.de

Hamburger Puppentheater
Bramfelder Str. 9.
Tel 23 93 45 44.
w hamburger puppentheater.de

Opernloft
Fuhlentwiete 7.
Map 9 C2
Tel 25 49 10 40.
w opernloft.de

Theater für Kinder
Max-Brauer-Allee 76.
Map 2 D2.
Tel 38 25 38.
w theater-tuer-kinder.de

Theaterschiff Batavia
Brooksdamm, 22880
Wedel.
Tel (04103) 858 36.
w batavia-wedel.de

Sports

Bäderland Hamburg
Tel 18 88 90.
w baederland.de

Eisarena Planten un Blomen
Holstenwall 30.
Map 9 A3.
Tel 319 35 46.
w eisarena-hamburg.de

Other Amusements

Hamburg Dungeon
Kehrwieder 2, Block D.
Map 9 C5.
Tel 36 00 55 20.
w the-dungeons.de

Hamburger Dom
Heiligengeistfeld.
Map 4 E2.
w hamburg.de/dom

HighFlyer Hamburg
Vor den Deichtorhallen.
Map 10 F4.
Tel 30 08 69 69.
w highflyer-hamburg.de

Planetarium
Hindenburgstr. 1b.
Tel 42 88 65 20.
w planetarium-hamburg.de

SchwarzLICHTviertel
Kieler Str. 571.
Tel 219 01 91 50.
w schwarzlichtviertel.de

SURVIVAL GUIDE

Practical Information   220 – 229
Getting to Hamburg   230 – 233
Getting Around Hamburg   234 – 241
Hamburg Street Finder   242 – 257

PRACTICAL INFORMATION

Hamburg is a city that has always welcomed the world, and there is something to please every visitor among the rich variety of cultural sights and attractions here. A trip to the Elbe metropolis is delightful in all seasons. Its excellent infrastructure and tourism facilities ensure that your stay will go smoothly. Telephones and ATMs are easy to find, and parking is well sign-posted. Going on a bus tour is one of the best ways to orientate yourself and gather an initial impression of Hamburg, but perhaps more essential is a boat tour of the port – the very heart of the city. Before coming to Hamburg, check out the events that will be on during your visit and book tickets well in advance.

Information

You can gather a great deal of information about Hamburg before your trip. Contact **Hamburg Tourismus GmbH** to request that they send you material to help plan your visit. This tourist office also helps visitors find hotel rooms and organizes various package deals. Tickets to various events in the city are also available here.

The Internet gateway www.gohamburg.de offers tips for your trip under the heading "Explore Hamburg", as well as suggestions on how to put together a perfect weekend trip that takes in the top sights. Another reliable source of information is the online magazine www.hamburg-magazin.de. It provides details about all there is to see and do in the city, as well as lots of useful information about the city itself.

Once you have arrived in Hamburg, you can get information at one of the branches of **Tourist Information** (see p203) located in the Haupt-bahnhof, at the port or at the airport. Along with maps of the city, there are all kinds of brochures and souvenirs, tickets for tours and plays, musicals and sports events. The Hamburg CARD (see Hamburg on a Budget, p223) is also available at tourist offices.

Immigration

Citizens of European Union member countries need a valid identity document (a national identity card or a passport). Citizens of non-European Union countries need a valid passport; for a stay of more than 90 days, a visa is also required. Contact the German consulate or German embassy in your country to find out current entry requirements.

City Tours and Sightseeing Flights

Visitors to Hamburg can get an ideal overview of the city from land, on the water or in the air. You can enjoy one of the many harbour tours (see pp240–41), take a bus tour, or even a flight over the city. These are all good ways to find your bearings. **Hamburg City Tour** offers tours in a double-decker bus with an open top (when the weather permits). Tours last 2 hours and start at the Landungsbrücken. Your ticket allows you to get off at 15 attractions and continue your tour on a later bus. It is valid for a full day, so you can take your time, stopping at the sights that appeal most to you.

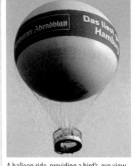

A balloon ride, providing a bird's-eye view of the city

On a tour with the **Rote Doppeldecker** visitors also have the advantage of pursuing their exploratory trip according to their particular interests.

Hamburg's oldest bus company **Hansa Rundfahrt GmbH** offers two options – the shorter City-Tour and the longer Gala-Tour, which includes, among other attractions, a drive over the Köhlbrandbrücke (see p135). Visitors might also want to treat themselves to the "Anbend-Tour" – an evening excursion which covers, among other areas, the spectacularly illuminated Speicherstadt as well as the area around the harbour.

Air Hamburg offers flights in four-seater Cessnas. The bird's-eye view of Hamburg is wonderful. Window seats are, of course, guaranteed. Flights last either 35 minutes, covering the city centre, or 50 minutes,

Lifesaving ring on *Rickmer Rickmers*

A double-decker bus for

◄ The east side of the Hamburg Hauptbahnhof (see p62)

Sign advertising the many different harbour tours on offer

going further afield. **Hanse-ballon** or the **aero ballooning company** offer an opportunity to float effortlessly over the roofs and canals of the Hanseatic city.

Segways also provide a convenient way to explore the city. These electric scooters run at a maximum speed of 12 mph (20 km/h). **Mindways Segway Citytour Hamburg** offers tours.

Guided Tours

The history of Hamburg, and stories that illustrate it, are the focus of guided tours, some of which have a specific theme **Hempel's Beatles Tour** takes you on a walk to the place where it all began for the Fab Four from Liverpool, with their moptop haircuts. A stroll past the traditional office buildings of Hanseatic merchants is equally fascinating as a guided tour through HafenCity, Hamburg's newest district. The **Rotlichttour** (red-light district tour) offers a behind-the-scenes look at prostitution in Hamburg.

Tour guide operators are plentiful, but **k3 Stadt-führungen** counts among the best. Its art tour, which takes visitors to many artistic treasures off the beaten path, is very popular.

As an alternative to a set tour, you can hire a private tour guide and see the things in Hamburg that interest you the most. Try **Hamburg-Lotse** who run personalized tours.

Museums in Hamburg

Hamburg and the surrounding area have a lively museum scene with over 300 museums covering a broad range of subjects. In addition to their ongoing displays, many regularly mount temporary exhibitions. New cultural institutions are opening up all the time. Among the newest are BallinStadt – Auswandererwelt Hamburg (see p93), Prototyp Museum (see p89), and the St Pauli Museum (see p105). Some museums are being given new homes, including the Maritime Museum, which in June 2008 moved into the renovated Kaispeicher B in the Speicherstadt (see pp86 – 7).

This travel guide provides information on the city's most interesting museums, as well as on a series of smaller museums that are equally rewarding. More detailed information about specific museums and their current exhibits can be obtained from **Museumsverband Hamburg e.V.** The **Museumsdienst Hamburg** also provides information about additional activities at the museums in Hamburg. Most Hamburg museums are open from Tuesdays to Sundays between 10am and 5 or 6pm. The museum ships docked at the Landungsbrücken can also be visited on Mondays.

Once a year (usually in April) about 50 Hamburg museums are open until 2am for the "Lange Nacht der Museen" ("Long Night of the-Museums"). You can visit such renowned cultural institutions as the Kunsthalle, the Deichtorhallen or the Altonaer Museum, as well as smaller ones such as the Freie Akademie der Künste on Klosterwall. Hamburg public transit (HVV) provides special buses to help ferry visitors between the various museums. The fare is included in the admission price.

Statue on the harbour promenade

DIRECTORY

Information

Hamburg Tourismus GmbH
Postfach 102249.
Tel 30 05 17 01.
w hamburg-travel.com

City Tours and Sightseeing Flights

aero ballooning company
Vogelweide 9. **Tel** 20 00 47 41.
w aeroballooning.de

Air Hamburg
Kleine Bahnstr. 8. **Tel** 70 70 88 90.
w air-hamburg.de

Hamburg City Tour
Starting point: Landungsbrücken.
Map 4 D4. **Tel** 32 31 85 90.
w hamburg-city-tour.eu

Hansa Rundfahrt GmbH
Hegholt 57. **Tel** 641 37 31.
w hansa-rundfahrt.de

Hanseballon
Im Dorf 48, 21256 Handeloh.
Tel (04187) 78 99.
w hanseballon.de

Mindways Segway Citytour Hamburg
Großer Burstah 44.
Tel 4/ 11 33 00.
w segway-citytour.de

Die Roten Doppeldecker
Starting point: Hauptbahnhof bzw. Landungsbrücken.
Map 6 E2 bzw. 4 D4.
Tel 30 39 36 77.
w die-roten-doppeldecker.de

Guided Tours

Hamburg-Lotse
w hamburg-lotse.de

Hempel's Beatles Tour
w hempels-musictour.com

k3 Stadtführungen
Tel 22 88 72 99.
w stadtfuehrungen-in-hamburg.de

Rotlichttour
w rotlicht-tour.de

Museums in Hamburg

Museumsdienst Hamburg
Glockengießerwall 5a. **Map** 6 D2.
Tel 428 13 10. **w** museumsdienst- hamburg.de

Museumsverband Hamburg e.V.
w museen-in-hamburg.de

A HADAG ship – a popular way to see the port

The Port

It is no surprise that the port is one of Hamburg's top attractions. Most visitors are drawn to the water at least once a day. The port is the heart of the city, whether your destination is HafenCity or Speicherstadt, a museum ship or a tour of the harbour, the Alte Elbtunnel or the Landungsbrücken, the Fischmarkt or the Hamburg City Beach Club. A boat tour of the port is even more special if your boat passes close to one of the big ocean-going ships either when it is on the water or in dry dock. A trip on HADAG-ferry no. 62 (see p135) from the Landungsbrücken to Finkenwerder is also a wonderful thing to do.

Every year in early May, when the port's birthday (see p85) is celebrated, the maritime flair of the city is wonderfully accentuated. If you wish to attend the celebrations, make sure to book accommodation well in advance. With a bit of luck, you might get to witness the arrival of a large cruise ship such as the Queen Mary 2. Thousands of spectators flock to the shores of the Elbe for an opportunity to see a luxury cruise ship as it sails into the harbour and to watch it dock. Information on cruises starting from Hamburg, departure and arrival times for the large cruise ships, as well as facts and figures on individual ships, can be found at www. hamburgcruise.de

Senior Citizens

On a visit to Hamburg, senior citizens will find the cosy, relaxed side of the Hanseatic city very enjoyable. The pretty districts, the well-tended parks, and the river banks are ideally suited for undertaking refreshing and inspiring walks. Whether you are strolling through the elegant district of Blankenese (see p138), sauntering through the extensive greenery of Planten un Blomen (see pp78–9), or taking a walk along the Elbe river – one of the typical elegant but cosy cafés or characteristic tea salons (see p195) is always within easy reach. Senior citizens are also entitled to various reductions. In many traditional and musical theatres – from the Schmidt Theater to the Neue Flora – senior citizens aged 65 and older are entitled to discounts on a particular day of the week or for particular events.

Reduced fares for the public transport system are only available when purchasing a monthly pass. Even though there is no reduction on the Hamburg CARD (see p223) specifically for seniors, the pass does still offer very good value.

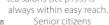

Rubbish bin to keep the city clean

Green Travel

In Hamburg, environmental awareness is taken very seriously. That is why the city has been nominated European Green Capital (Umwelthauptstadt Europas) of the year 2011 by the European Commission (Hamburg is the second city after Stockholm (2010) to be awarded this title). The accolade emphazises Hamburg's status as an attractive as well as environmentally friendly city.

The city offers numerous advantages to ecologically minded visitors and the public transport system, which includes the harbour ferries, is extraordinarily efficient.

Hamburg is an extremely bicycle friendly city. Bicycles can be hired at many different places throughout the city (see p235). You can take your bicycle with you free of charge on U-Bahns and S-Bahns, as well as on the harbour ferries and onto many buses during off-peak hours.

In the city centre, Fahrrad-Taxis (see p237) are an interesting alternative. Solar-powered boats have been introduced on the Alster, allowing visitors to cruise on the lake noiselessly with zero emissions and not a single drop of oil used.

Visitors preferring wholefood nutrition can choose between many restaurants, cafés and shops offering suitable products (also from organic farming). Ottensen in particular offers a broad range of options.

StadtRAD – environmentally friendly transport

Hamburg on a Budget

If you purchase a **Hamburg CARD** you get a range of discounts. This card entitles you to unlimited public transport in the Greater Hamburg Area and as much as a 40 per cent discount for more than 150 Hamburg museums and other attractions, such as Tierpark Hagenbeck, Hamburg Dungeon, Miniatur Wunderland or the Rathaus. Also included are reduced prices for city and harbour tours, boat tours of the Alster lakes and a number of guided tours. You can also get reductions for performances in numerous theatres and musical theatres (such as Hamburgische Staatsoper, Altonaer Theater, Thalia Theater and Neue Flora), as well as in some restaurants and shops. An overview of the whole range of reductions is published on the website of **Hamburg Tourismus GmbH**.

The Hamburg CARD is available at Tourist Information branches, in many hotels and at ticket vending machines. Passes are valid for either one, three or five days. For a single adult travelling with up to three children 15 years and under, it costs 8.90, 21.90 or 37.50 Euros, respectively. A group ticket for up to five people of any age costs 14.90, 38.90 or 63.90 Euros.

The **Hamburg CARD – plus Region** offers good value to visitors who wish to explore the many attractions in the Greater Hamburg Area. It is valid for the HVV total network. In addition to the discounts offered by the Hamburg CARD, this pass offers further discounts in the Hamburg region, such as for a visit to the Deutsches Salzmuseum (German salt museum) in Lüneburg, an excursion to the bat caves in Bad Segeberg, and the Industriemuseum Elmshorn (museum of industry in Elmshorn) or a trip to the

Hamburg – »European Green Capital« 2011

adventure park Erlebnisbahn Ratzeburg. A one-day pass costs 19.90 Euros for one adult with up to three children 15 years and under. Groups of up to five people of any age can purchase the Hamburg CARD – plus Region for 28.50 Euros.

Tips for Students

In a city with about 40,000 students, there quite naturally is a huge selection of popular pubs and trendy shops. Much of student life takes place in the university district to the west of the Außenalster; one of the main arteries is the Grindelallee with its down-to-earth cafés and bars. Another alternative area is the Schanzenviertel with its multicultural atmosphere and a large number of witty shops. The Beach Clubs (see p207) on the Elbe river are popular places to unwind.

Students with valid ID cards benefit from discounts at many attractions and events, such as at movie houses and theatres.

There are a number of agencies in Hamburg called Mitwohnbörsen that help students find budget lodgings. These companies arrange flat-sharing in private homes around the city. Some of these accomodation services (such as www.studenten-eg.de) do not charge commission.

Drinking water dispenser

Information for Night Owls

In many Hamburg clubs and discos, it is not unusual for patrons to celebrate the night away, especially on weekends.

For some all-night revellers, a visit to the Fish Market (see p108) on Sunday mornings is the finale of a Saturday night out. The action in the Fish Auction Hall (Fischauktions-halle) continues all morning – it is especially full after the gong has been struck at 9:30am and the market closes. Nothing is better after an all-nighter than a traditional Fish Market buffet. For those who do not feel like fish, a pot of coffee helps to while away the time while waiting for your energy to return.

Hamburg Time

Hamburg is one hour ahead of Greenwich Mean Time (GMT), Summer time in Germany is from the end of March to the end of October, as in all European countries.

DIRECTORY

Embassies and Consulates

American Embassy
Flughafenallee 18, 28199 Bremen.
Tel 0421 301 58 60.
W germany.usembassy.gov

British Embassy
Wilhelmstr. 70, 10117 Berlin.
Tel 030 20 45 70.
W gov.uk/government/world/germany

Canadian Embassy
Leipziger Platz 17, 10117 Berlin.
Tel 030 20 31 24 70.
W canadainternational.gc.ca/germany-allemagne

Hamburg on a Budget

Hamburg CARD & Hamburg CARD – plus Region
Tel 30 05 17 01.
W hamburg-travel.com

Personal Security and Health

With its long tradition as a port and trading city, Hamburg is a cosmopolitan metropolis, open and tolerant. In comparison to many other large European cities, it is relatively safe, even though there are sometimes thefts in popular tourist areas. However, if you observe the usual precautions, there is not much to worry about. There are many pharmacies, and it is worth seeking initial advice from a pharmacist for minor health problems. For more serious medical help, you can contact one of the emergency numbers listed on the opposite page for assistance.

The Davidwache, Hamburg's best-known police station

Personal Security

Violent crime is rare in Hamburg, but even so, you should not walk down poorly lit streets at night or frequent large parks or other isolated areas. In the St Pauli district, especially in the Reeperbahn area, the occasional act of violence has been known to occur and tourists have sometimes been hurt, even though this is the district with the highest concentration of police in the city. By taking a few sensible precautions, you can significantly reduce the risks.

As in any large city, pickpockets do operate and will target anyone who looks like a tourist. Be especially vigilant if a stranger tries to distract you by engaging you in a discussion, or spilling food or a beverage on you; pickpockets often work in pairs or groups, with one distracting you while the other steals your belongings. Places to exercise extra caution are the Fish Market, large fairs such as the Hamburger Dom, the Port's Birthday celebration, and at bus stops, public transit, railway carriages and stations, and department stores. Police regularly patrol the tourist areas, but it is still advisable to prepare the day's itinerary in advance, use common sense and stay alert. Try not to

International
pharmacy sign

advertise that you are a tourist; study your map before you set off, avoid wearing expensive jewellery, and carry your camera securely. Carry small amounts of cash; credit and debit cards, or even travellers' cheques are a more secure option. Keep these close to your body in a money belt or inside pocket.

Make use of the hotel safe for valuable items and important documents. When you are out and about, keep a close eye on your valuables, especially in crowds, and never leave your luggage unattended at the airport or train station. In cafés and bars keep shoulder bags on your lap and avoid hanging them on the back of your chair.

Just as in many other cities, Hamburg's U-Bahn and S-Bahn stations and platforms are not very inviting, especially late at night. Security patrols are frequent, and they will come to your aid in an emergency. If it is necessary, you can use one of the emergency buttons found on every platform to summon help.

If, despite all your precautions, you are a victim of a crime, go immediately to a police station and report it. In the case of theft, make sure to obtain a copy of the police statement with a list of the stolen items to give to your insurance company.

The Wasserschutzpolizei Hamburg – the police force protecting the city on water and land

Lost Property

In Hamburg's Central Lost and Found (Zentrales Fundbüro der Freien und Hansestadt Hamburg) unclaimed items are stored for up to six months.

If you have lost something at the Hamburg airport, contact the Airport Office for help. If you have left something behind in the airplane or your luggage has not turned up, go directly to the counter of whichever airline you travelled on.

Items left behind on the S-Bahn are the responsibility of the Deutsche Bahn (German railway); contact their Lost and Found (Fund-Service) for assistance in finding your property. If you have any idea of the area where you might have misplaced an item, you will have a better chance of tracing it.

Medical Assistance

It is advisable to carry proof of health insurance with you. If you have an EHIC card (European Health Insurance Card), bring it with you. Doctors can be found in telephone books in the Yellow Pages. In the case of serious illness, you will have to call an Emergency Doctor (Ärztlicher Notfalldienst). The Hamburg hospitals that have emergency departments are shown on the Street Finder maps *(see pp242–57)*.

There are a large number of pharmacies in Hamburg that keep the same hours as shops. At night and on Sundays, pharmacies hang in their doorway the address of the nearest open pharmacy. This

Old pharmacy sign

information is also published in the daily newspapers. If you take prescription medication, bring an adequate supply with you and carry a prescription in case you need an emergency refill. Should you need the urgent services of a dentist, you can call the Emergency Dental Care Service (Zahnärztlicher Notfalldienst). Hamburg also has a Drug Hotline (Drogen-Hotline).

If you live outside Germany, it is a good idea to carry insurance that will pay any expenses you have incurred and the cost of your return to your home country in case of an emergency.

DIRECTORY

Emergency Services

**Emergency
(Police, fire and ambulances)**
Tel 112.

Emergency Doctor
Tel 116 117

**Emergency Dental
Care Service**
Tel 0180 505 05 18.

Red Cross
Tel 55 42 00.

**Children's and Youth
Helpline**
Tel 0800 111 03 33.

Drug Hotline
Tel 01805 31 30 31.

Spiritual Advice
Tel 0800 111 01 11.

Lost Property

**Central Lost and Found of
Hamburg**
Bahrenfelder Str. 254–260.
Tel 428 11 35 01.

Airport Office
Hamburg Airport,
Terminal 1 and 2,
Arrivals area.
Tel 50 75 10 10.

**Deutsche Bahn
Lost and Found**
Tel 0900 199 05 99.

Hamburg police car

Hamburg fire engine

Ambulance

Banking and Local Currency

Hamburg is the second most important banking city in Germany, after Frankfurt am Main. There are about 130 banks here, and over 30 of them have their headquarters in the city. One of these is the Hamburger Sparkasse (Haspa), which is one of Germany's largest banks. Cash machines (ATMs) are located throughout the city centre and beyond in great numbers. Debit and credit cards are widely accepted and a convenient method of paying for accommodation, meals and purchases from shops.

Banking and currency exchange

If you are coming from a country that has the Euro as its currency, you will not have to exchange any currency. Otherwise, you should use banks to exchange currencies, since they offer a better exchange rate than bureaux de change or hotels. It is a good idea to exchange larger amounts at one time, since you have to pay a fee each time.

Most banks open at 9am and close between 4 and 6pm; only a few (among them, branches of the Postbank) are open on Saturday mornings. Bureaux de change can be found at the Hauptbahnhof, at Bahnhof Dammtor, at the airport and near tourist attractions. They have longer hours of operation, including most Sundays. The convenient ATMs (cash machines) allow you to withdraw cash around the clock – as much as your daily limit permits.

Deutsche Bank

Logo of the Deutsche Bank, one of Germany's largest banks

2-Euro coin with St Michaelis

Credit cards and Debit Cards

Since credit cards are widely accepted throughout Hamburg, you do not have to bring large sums of money with you when you travel here. Signs displaying the logos of credit cards that will be accepted are displayed at the entrances to hotels, restaurants and shops.
MasterCard and **Visa** are the most widely accepted, **American Express** and **Diners Club** less frequently. If you have one, you can also pay with a **girocard** (formerly Maestro-/EC-Card).

Traveller's cheques are another secure method of payment. However, few hotels and restaurants accept them anymore, so they are useful simply as a supplement to cash and credit cards.

Directory

Banks and Bureaux de Change

Hamburger Sparkasse
Adolphsplatz/Großer Burstah.
Tel 35 79-0.
ⓦ **haspa.de**

HSH Nordbank
Gerhart-Hauptmann-Platz 50.
Tel 33 33-0.

International Exchange
Kirchenallee 57.
Tel 280 36 31.

Postbank
Alter Wall 38.
Tel 01802 33 33.
ⓦ **postbank.de**

ReiseBank
Hachmannplatz 10.
Tel 32 34 83.

Lost Credit Cards

General Emergency Number
Tel 116 116.
ⓦ **116116.eu**

American Express
Tel (069) 97 97 20 00.

Diners Club
Tel (07531) 363 31 11.

girocard
Tel (069) 74 09 87.

MasterCard
Tel 0800 819 10 40.

Visa
Tel 0800 811 84 40.

The branch of the Hamburger Sparkasse located at the Rathaus

Currency

The common currency Euro (€) is used by 17 members of the European Union: Austria, Belgium, Estonia Finland, France, Germany, Greece, Ireland, Italy, Luxembourg, Malta, Netherlands, Portugal, the Republic of Cyprus, Slovakia, Slovenia and Spain. The Deutschmark, Germany's former currency, is no longer legal tender, but notes and coins can be changed at the Bundesbank (www.bundes-bank.de). While Euro notes share a common design, the backs of the coins are minted individually by every country. Every year, member states may utter commemorative 2-Euro coins. A coin showing Hamburg's St Michaelis church was brought into circulation in 2008, and in 2010 a coin depicting Bremen Rathaus was minted.

Euro Bank Notes

Euro bank notes have seven denominations (5, 10, 20, 50, 100, 200 and 500 €). Designed by the Austrian Robert Kalina, the notes vary in size, and show architectural elements and styles of different eras, as well as a map of Europe and the flag of the European Union with its twelve stars.

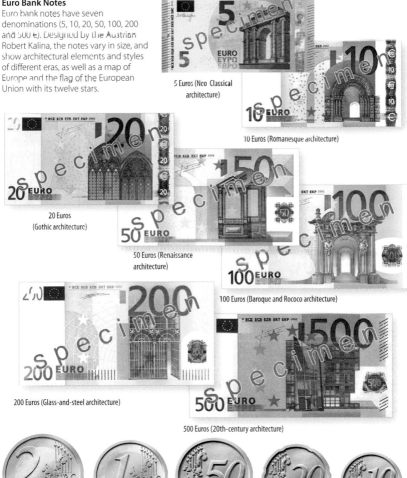

5 Euros (Neo Classical architecture)

10 Euros (Romanesque architecture)

20 Euros (Gothic architecture)

50 Euros (Renaissance architecture)

100 Euros (Baroque and Rococo architecture)

200 Euros (Glass-and-steel architecture)

500 Euros (20th-century architecture)

2 Euros

1 Euro

50 cents

20 cents

10 cents

Coins

The Euro has eight coin denominations: 2 €, 1 €; 50, 20, 10, 5, 2 cents and 1 cent. Their standardized fronts were designed by the Belgian Luc Luycx. On the reverse side, German coins show the federal eagle, the Brandenburg Gate, and an oak-leaf cluster.

5 cents

2 cents

1 cent

Communications

Germany's telecommunications and postal services function extremely efficiently. Letters and postcards are usually delivered the next working day within the country. The distinctive yellow postboxes are common. There is a phone booth on practically every corner in Hamburg, and many restaurants and cafés have a coin-operated public telephone. Mobile telephones work well, and there are many shops selling hand sets. Most hotels have Internet access, although some do charge for the service, Internet cafés are common and the number of Wi-Fi hotspots is growing constantly.

Post-box in Hamburg

Historic stamp (1973) with Hamburg's towers and churches.

Letters and Postcards

Postal rates are based on the weight and size of your letter or parcel. The price of a standard letter up to 20g (0.7 oz) is 58 cents within Germany, 75 cents within Europe and 1.70 Euros to other continents. Postcards cost 45 cents within Germany, and 75 cents internationally. There are fixed rates for special services such as express delivery, registered letters or COD.

Postage stamps are available at post offices, from stamp machines and at kiosks selling postcards. Only German-Euro stamps can be used. There are a large number of post-boxes in Hamburg. Collection times are displayed on the post-boxes. You can also use an international courier service

such as **DHL** to send letters and parcels to your home country.

Post Offices

Post offices are usually open Mondays to Fridays from 8 or 9am to 6 or 6:30pm, and on Saturdays they are open until noon. Airport and railway station branches usually have longer opening hours. Along with general counter service, post offices have public telephones, and at most you can send faxes, make photocopies and buy telephone cards as well as stationery supplies such as letter-writing paper, envelopes and boxes. You can also send post to post offices (*poste restante*).

DHL
delivery van

Public Telephone

Hamburg has an excellent public telephone network. You will need coins for the coin-operated telephones, which accept 10-cent to 2-Euro coins.

If you have overpaid, any unused coins will be returned at the end of your call. It is far more convenient to use a telephone card, which can be purchased at post offices, T-Punkt shops and many kiosks. An illuminated display beside the telephone receiver shows the amount of credit left on the card. In the past few years, more and more telephone booths in Germany have been turned into starker "base stations". There is no booth and no lighting, just a freestanding column with a telephone that only accepts credit cards or a prepaid calling card (such as a T-card), which are activated after you key in your PIN.

T-cards can be purchased in all branches of the Deutsche Post, T-Punkt shops and in the Deutsche Bahn Reisezentrum (travel centre), and most kiosks sell a range of calling cards. T-cards and calling cards can be used in traditional telephone booths as well.

Depending on the time and day, and the distance, different tariffs apply. Usually, the highest rates are charged weekdays between 8am and 6pm. You should avoid calling from your hotel room, since these calls will be much more expensive than those made from public telephone booths.

Mobile Telephones

There are no gaps in the mobile telephone network, and all GSM mobile telephones

Ruler for measuring the size of letters

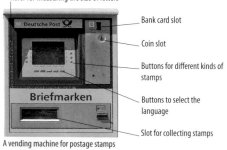

Bank card slot

Coin slot

Buttons for different kinds of stamps

Buttons to select the language

Slot for collecting stamps

A vending machine for postage stamps

function properly. In 2007, the European Union regulated roaming prices for subscribers travelling within member states. As of July 2013 the price caps, excluding VAT, are 20p (from July 1st 2014 15p) a minute to make a call; 6p (from July 1st 2014 4p) a minute to receive a call; 7p (from July 1st 2014 5p) to send a text message; and 38p (from July 1st 2014 16p) a megabyte to download data or browse the internet. Roaming charges may end in July 2015.

Internet and E-Mail

Most hotels offer their guests computers with a WLAN, a local wireless network, often free of charge. Hamburg has many Internet cafés; most of them are open daily between 10am and 10pm. You can access local websites *(see p 220)* for the latest information about events in the city.

Newspapers and Magazines

Hamburg is Germany's most important media centre – especially for print media. Many of the country's most successful newspapers and magazines are produced in the publishing houses located in the Hanseatic city. The largest subscriber-based newspaper in the Greater Hamburg Area is the *Hamburger Abendblatt*, with a circulation of about 240,000 copies. The *Hamburger Morgenpost* ("Mopo") is seen as

a local alternative to *Bild*. Published by Springer, this tabloid sells about three million copies, making it Germany's best-selling daily newspaper. Other national newspapers originating in Hamburg are the *Financial Times Deutschland* (FTD), *Die Welt* and the Hamburg edition of the *taz*.

DIE ZEIT, Germany's most renowned weekly newspaper, has been published by the Zeitverlag Gerd Bucerius in Hamburg since the first edition appeared on 21 February 1946. Spiegel Verlag's chief publication is *DER SPIEGEL*; it has the largest circulation of any news magazine in Europe. The publishing house Gruner + Jahr, which is the source of such magazines as *stern*, *GEO*, *Brigitte*, *P.M. Magazin* and *Gala*, is the biggest magazine publisher in Europe *(see pp40–41)*.

Television and Radio

The Norddeutsche Rundfunk (NDR) counts among the biggest public television broadcasters in Germany. The *Tagesschau* is one of its most important programmes. The regional broadcasting station NDR Fernsehen is also based in Hamburg. The ZDF also maintains a regional studio in Hamburg. The regional television broadcasting station Hamburg 1 is renowned for its in-house productions.

In addition to public radio stations such as NDR Info (News), NDR Kultur and the station N-JOY which focuses on young listeners private stations

NDR ①
Logo of the television station NDR

addressing various target groups like Hamburg, Klassik Radio or Oldie 95 also are very popular.

Hamburg daily newspapers

Mobile phone – essential for people who travel

GETTING TO HAMBURG

Hamburg is one of Europe's central routing points. No matter what mode of transport you choose, Hamburg is easy to reach. Many international airline carriers fly into Hamburg Airport, which lies just outside the city. Four long-distance railway stations serve Hamburg, and they are well-integrated into the ICE and IC train networks that cross Germany and Europe. Since many motorways meet in Hamburg, the city is easy to reach by bus or car. Of course, the most authentic way of arriving in this port city is by ship. Many visitors enjoy sailing into the impressive harbour in style on an equally impressive cruise ship.

Information counter at the Hamburg Airport

Arriving by Air

From Hamburg, you can fly non-stop to and from about 13 national and international destinations. Flights into the second-largest German city are offered by more than 70 airlines, among them **Lufthansa**, **British Airways**, **Air Canada**, **American Airlines**, **Delta Airlines** and **Qantas** as well as Air France, Aer Lingus, KLM, SAS and Emirates. Budget travel airlines are also well represented by carriers such as **easyJet**. Information about flights to Hamburg and destinations that can be reached via Hamburg is available from the respective airlines or directly from the airport. Hamburg Airport maintains an up-to-date website which provides the departure and arrival information for all flights.

If you are planning to fly to Hamburg, then it is a good idea to compare prices before you book. Due to stiff competition between airlines, there are occasionally flights on sale at sensationally low prices. These usually must be reserved and paid for several weeks in advance, there are travel restrictions, and you will pay a penalty if you change your flight. Very often, the ticket prices do not include taxes, such as security taxes and airport taxes. A charter flight or a package tour can be a reasonable alternative. The latter generally includes airport transfers and accommodation in Hamburg, and sometimes admission to an event or a tour of the city. Before you book, check the location of your hotel to make sure it is not too far outside the city.

Hamburg Airport

In comparison with numerous other national and international

Destination boards and automatic check-in machines

Hamburg Airport

The completion of the second terminal allowed the airport to increase its capacity enormously. The Airport Plaza links the two terminals.

KEY

- ▪ Administration
- ▪ Indoor parking
- Ⓢ S-Bahn station
- 🏢 Police station
- 🚕 Taxi
- 🚌 Bus stop
- 𝒊 Information
- 🅿 Parking
- 🍴 Restaurant
- ☕ Café
- 🛍 Shop
- ♿ Wheelchair access

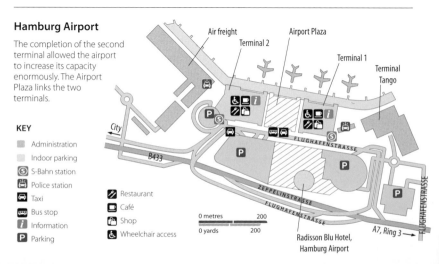

Air freight
Terminal 2
Airport Plaza
Terminal 1
Terminal Tango
City
B433
FLUGHAFENSTRASSE
ZEPPELINSTRASSE
FLUGHAFENSTRASSE
A7, Ring 3 →
FLUGHAFENSTRASSE
Radisson Blu Hotel, Hamburg Airport

0 metres   200
0 yards   200

The main hall in Hamburg Airport

airports, Hamburg Airport is relatively close to the city, and travellers find the short trip to the city centre convenient.

During the course of an ambitious expansion project called HAM 21, the airport has been undergoing major changes over the past few years. Among the key components of this gigantic investment in the airport's future have been the installation of a guided parking system, the completion of the Airport Plaza, and the construction of a second terminal.

The airport offers every convenience that travellers would expect from a modern airport. The duty-free shop alone, the largest retail outlet in Airport Plaza, covers an area of 1,400 sq m (15,000 sq ft). Some of the other amenities are travel agencies, car hire agencies, many kinds of restaurants and snack bars, long-term parking, conference rooms and modern business services, as well as post office and bank services (which include a number of ATMs). There are also medical services on hand.

The Airport Offices in the arrivals area of each terminal are an important source of information for visitors to the city. Here, you can pick up brochures about Hamburg, book a hotel, buy a Hamburg CARD (see p221) or tickets to events. From the observation terraces of the restaurants in terminals 1 and 2, there are excellent views of take-offs and landings.

For travellers with limited mobility and those in wheelchairs, the airport offers wide-ranging assistance with transport and luggage. Toilets for the disabled are well sign-posted and easy to find in the terminals.

Getting from the Airport to the City

The centre of the city is easy to reach using public transport from Hamburg Airport. The airport is linked to the S-Bahn system, and by taking the S1 line, you can reach the centre of Hamburg in just 25 minutes. The train departs every 10 minutes. The S-Bahn-station Hamburg Airport is in front of both terminals accessible by lifts, escalators and stairs.

Buses operated by Jasper offer a non-stop connection between the airport and the Hauptbahnhof (main train station). The price for a single journey is 5 Euros, a return ticket costs 8 Euros.

Of course, there are plentiful taxis lined up at the airport, too. Taxi ranks can be found at terminal 1 and terminal 2. The journey from the airport to downtown costs about 20 Euros and takes approximately 20 minutes (longer during heavy traffic).

DIRECTORY

Hamburg Airport

Airport Office
Terminal 2, arrivals area.
Tel 50 75 10 10.

Flight Information
Tel 507 50. W ham.airport.de

Airlines

Air Canada
Tel 069 27 11 51 11.
W aircanada.com

American Airlines
Tel 069 29 99 32 34.
W aa.com

British Airways
Tel 0421 557 57 58.
W britishairways.com

easyJet
Tel 0871 246 00 00 (UK)
0900 116 05 00 (German only).
W easyjet.com

Delta Airlines
Tel 01805 80 58 72.
W delta.com

Lufthansa
Tel 069 86 79 97 99.
W lufthansa.com

Qantas
Tel 0421 69 64 11 00.
W qantas.com

Europcar – just one of the many car hire agencies at the airport

Arriving by Rail

Travelling to Hamburg by train makes for a very comfortable trip, but it is often more expensive than flying. The city is well connected by rail to the German and European railway network, with direct connections to many large cities in Germany and throughout Europe.

If you are travelling from Great Britain, a combination of ferries and trains makes for an interesting journey. You can take a ferry from Dover to Oostende in Belgium, and travel on to Hamburg by train from there. This route is, naturally, somewhat time-consuming.

Hamburg has four long-distance railway stations: the Hauptbahnhof, Hamburg Dammtor, Hamburg-Altona and Hamburg-Harburg. Most long-distance trains stop at the Hauptbahnhof, but do not terminate here. From here, they continue to Bahnhof Dammtor before terminating at Bahnhof Altona.

Check the city map before you get off to find out which station is best for you. Bahnhof Hamburg Dammtor, where ICE (Inter-City Express trains) stop, is the best station for trade fair attendees. Hamburg-Harburg is the most important railway station for areas of the city south of the Elbe river. Destinations in Hamburg are easily reached on public transportation from any of the four railway stations.

DB

Deutsche Bahn
sign

Trains run by the **Deutsche Bahn** (German railway) are safe and offer many comforts. Keep in mind that, especially in peak travel times, tickets can sell out quickly, so book well in advance. It pays to book early in more ways than one. The earlier you make your purchase and select the date of travel by reserving a seat, the cheaper the trip will be. Deutsche Bahn offers a range of attractive ticket deals, which change frequently. Their website (www. bahn.de) provides information about prices and special offers. It also contains a large number of attractive package deals for trips to Hamburg, some of which include accommodation and the option of buying tickets for cultural events.

If you are coming from a great distance, a trip on a **City Night Line** is the best option. These modern overnight trains offer a number of comforts. You can relax as you stretch out in a sleeping car or couchette car, though regular seats are also available. The advantages of using the overnight train are that you do not lose any time and you arrive at your destination wide-awake and ready to see the sights. Wake-up calls are available at your request. For guests in sleeping cars, breakfast is included in the price for the overnight train.

A view over the tracks in the Hamburg Hauptbahnhof

ZOB – Bus-Port Hamburg
in St Georg

Arriving by Bus

Hamburg is not only an important rail hub, but is also the most important motorway hub in Northern Germany. You can travel to Hamburg by road via several different motorways: the A7 (North-South motorway), the A1 (Bremen – Lübeck), the A24 (Berlin – Hamburg) and the A23 (from Schleswig-Holstein). These motorways are so well constructed that usually a bus trip to Hamburg does not take much longer than a trip on the train.

Coach travel in Hamburg has increased since the industry was liberalized in 2013. There are a number of private operators, such as: FlixBus, city2city and MeinFernbus. ADAC run a nationwide route network between many cities. The most direct and economical routes can be found by consulting the useful German website **busliniensuche**.

Travelling by bus can be much cheaper than travelling by train. However, there is less freedom of movement on board a bus. Many long-distance coaches entertain passengers with films shown on DVD. Some also offer reclining seats on overnight journeys. Drinks and frequently snacks, too, can be purchased on board.

Long-distance buses arrive from many countries at **ZOB – Bus-Port Hamburg**, which is conveniently located just down the street from the Hauptbahnhof. It bustles with travellers practically around the clock. The service area, whose amenities include an Internet café, a fast food restaurant and car hire agencies, is open daily from 5am to 10pm (on Wednesdays and Fridays to midnight). Bus trips can be booked at one of the travel agencies in ZOB.

Due to its striking, huge glass roof, which measures 300 sq m (3,300 sq ft) and curves out in a sickle-shape 11 m (36 ft) over the bus bays, the Hamburg bus station can be seen from quite a distance away. More than three million passengers arrive at or depart from ZOB every year. The buses travel to all large German cities, and to large cities in almost 30 other European countries.

The new bus network of ADAC Postbusserves also Hamburg

Arriving by Car

If you drive into Hamburg from the south, you will end up going through the Elbtunnel to get to the north shore of the Elbe. There are often traffic jams here, especially in rush hour, but attempting to find another route if you are unfamiliar with the city is not recommended.

If you are going to the trade fair, take the Hamburg-Volkspark exit if you are coming from the north, northwest, west or southwest. Take the Hamburg-Centrum exit if you are coming from the south or southeast. Take the Hamburg-Horn exit if you are coming from the east or northeast. No matter which exit you take, once you're off the motorway follow the signs to the trade fair, which read "Messe/CCH".

To drive in Germany, you have to carry a valid driving licence as well as your vehicle's registration document. By law the car must also carry a red triangle in case of a breakdown, and a pro-

Motorway sign to Hamburg on the A7

perly stocked first-aid kit; a safety vest is recommended.

To hire a car in Germany, you need a valid driver's licence, country ID card or passport, and a credit card. In Hamburg, there are many car hire agencies with branches in the city centre, including at the Hauptbahnhof.

Arriving by Ship

Although the heart of Hamburg is its port, and most visitors spend some time visiting sights on the water, most travellers do not arrive in Hamburg via the water. However, many tourists do go on a boat trip during their visit. The kinds of tours available range from harbour round trips of varying duration, to tours along the Elbe and trips to Helgoland on high-speed catamarans. Information about such excursions on the water is found on pages 240–41. The most elegant way of arriving in Hamburg is as a passenger on a cruise ship. These huge vessels dock at the **Hamburg Cruise Center** (Kreuzfahrtterminal; see p88). Terminal 1 was expanded in 2006, when a second hall was built. A new terminal in Altona opened in 2010. Thousands of

spectators come to the port to watch asone of these giant ocean liners docks or departs.

Hamburg Cruise Center, where the ocean liners dock

DIRECTORY

Trains

Deutsche Bahn (Train Information)
Tel 0180 699 66 33. (Main service number for the German railway).
Tel 08001 50 70 90 (Recorded announcements. Free call).
[w] bahn.de

City Night Line
In Germany:
Tel 0180 699 66 33.
[w] dbnachtzug.de

Buses

busliniensuche
[w] busliniensuche.de

ZOB – Bus-Port Hamburg
Adenauerallee 78.
Tel 24 75 76.
[w] zob-hamburg.de

Ships

Hamburg Cruise Center (Kreuzfahrtterminal)
Großer Grasbrook 19.
Tel 30 05 13 93.
[w] hamburgcruisecenter.eu

A Deutsche Bahn Inter-City Express – ICE

GETTING AROUND HAMBURG

Although the city is large, the distances between the main sights and attractions of Hamburg are actually quite short. The best way to explore the centre is on foot. The different districts of the city and the surrounding area can be reached easily using public transport. This includes the U-Bahns, S-Bahns and buses as well as a range of boats and ships. Bicycles are another excellent way of getting around Hamburg, especially since the city is rather flat, allowing for easy and relaxed transport. A network of cycling paths extends all the way to the outer city districts. Driving a car gives you flexibility, but in rush hour especially, traffic can move very slowly and parking fees in the city centre are relatively high. Taxis are plentiful and easy to find.

Pedestrian signals with digital displays

Walking in Hamburg

Even though Hamburg is spread out over a large area, the city centre is compact. Distances between the individual sights and attractions are usually agreeably short, and there is hardly any destination that requires going a great distance out of your way. With a bit of planning, visitors can get to sights just by walking to them. One of the favourite walking (and jogging) routes in the city is around the Alster lakes. The route not only follows the water's edge, but it also dips into some of the most elegant districts in the Hanseatic city. There are many inviting cafés with terraces and other lovely places to stop for a break along the way.

Gorgeous views of the Elbe river and the port can be enjoyed from the Hamburger Balkon, which stretches between the Landungsbrücken and the Altonaer Balkon, a lovely park which also offers a fabulous view (see p117). An excellent way of learning about the city, including its many hidden charms, is to take one of the walking tours (see p221) led by guides who are knowledgeable about the various areas of the city. The walks are usually organized around a theme, such as history, art, culture or architecture.

Driving in Hamburg

Germans drive on the right side of the road. A car can come in handy for visiting some attractions outside Hamburg. There are many car hire agencies in the city. The best-known ones – such as **AVIS**, **Europcar**, **Hertz** and **Sixt** – have branches at the airport, at the Hauptbahnhof and in other locations. To hire a car, you will need a valid licence, country ID card or passport, and, usually, a credit card. If your car breaks down, the German automobile club, **ADAC**, offers emergency roadside assistance. Speed traps are often set up at the exits and entrances to motorways, and there are a good number of red-light cameras at intersections in Hamburg. They capture the licence plates of cars that go through red lights.

In Germany, the permitted blood alcohol level is 0.5, although it is 0.0 for the first two years after acquiring a driving license, and for those younger than 18 years of age.

Sign showing distances and direction

The three parking divisions in the city centre

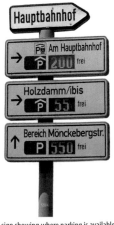

A sign showing where parking is available in the city centre

Parking Ticket Vending Machine

Parking ticket vending machines can be found on most city streets. Parking fees usually apply weekdays from 8am to 6 or 8pm. The longest you can park is either 60 minutes or 120 minutes.

Coin slot

Date and time display

Information about the hourly rate

Ticket dispenser

Parking

Thanks to an automated guided parking system, finding a parking spot in the centre of Hamburg is fairly easy. The city is divided into three parking areas: red (Mönckebergstraße), yellow (Jungfernstieg) and green (Port/St Michaelis). Well before you reach the centre of the city, signs inform you about the parking system.

Indoor parking in the city centre accommodates over 11,000 cars. About 250 digital displays, which change each minute, show drivers how many parking spots are left in each lot. Fees for using indoor parking lots are usually two Euros per hour. The maximum amount is about ten to 15 Euros. Fees can be paid by mobile phone or on the web (www.mobil-parken.de).

Cycling

Hamburg is extremely bicycle friendly. Many city streets have dedicated bike lanes, some of which go from the city centre all the way to the outer districts. Popular routes follow along the Alster or the Elbe.

Hiring a bicycle is easy. You can hire for a single day or for longer periods of time; most hire agencies offer reduced rates for a weekly rental. You usually only have to reserve your bicycle the day before you will need it.

If you would like a specially equipped bicycle, it would be wise to book earlier. **Hamburg anders erfahren** delivers your bicycle directly to your hotel.

Fahrradverleih Altona offers a large selection of bicycles.

Call a Bike is a subsidiary of DB Rent, which is owned by the German railway. To hire a bicycle, you first need to register with Call a Bike and you will be assigned a customer number. This serves as a direct withdrawal billing number, and will also allow you to unlock a bike at the train station. Displays show which of the silver and red bicycles are still available. From **StadtRAD Hamburg**, bicycles can be ordered around the clock via telephone or at one of the 70 stations.

Cyclists will find the Hamburg-Atlas published by **ADFC Hamburg**, Hamburg's cycling association, very useful. As you would in all other big cities, lock up your bicycle when you cannot keep an eye on it.

Advertisement for StadtRAD Hamburg

StadtRAD Hamburg – an environmentally friendly alternative

Boating

Given the enormous importance of the Elbe and port to Hamburg, and the great number of canals criss-crossing the city, there is a great deal of boat traffic on the waterways in the city centre. Information about taking a boat trip on the harbour, the Elbe, the canals, and the Alster lakes as well as information about longer excursions is provided on pages 240–41. There's also a free shuttle boat service to the Theater im Hafen Hamburg (see p92). .

is provided on pages 240–41. There's also a free shuttle boat service to the Theater im Hafen Hamburg (see p92). .

DIRECTORY

Car Hire

AVIS
Tel 0180 621 77 02.
W avis.de

Europcar
Tel 520 18 80 00.
W europcar.de

Hertz
Tel 0180 633 35 35.
W hertz.de

Sixt
Tel 0180 625 25 25.
W sixt.de

Roadside Assistance

ADAC
Tel 0180 222 22 22.

Bicycle Hire

ADFC Hamburg
Koppel 34–36.
Tel 39 39 33.
W hamburg.adfc.de

Call a Bike
Tel (069) 42 72 77 22.
W callbike-interaktiv.de

Fahrradverleih Altona
Thadenstr. 90.
Tel 439 20 12.
W fahrradverleih-altona.de

Hamburg anders erfahren
Peutestr. 16–18.
Tel 0178 640 18 00.
W hamburg-anders-erfahren.de

StadtRAD Hamburg
Scharrenstr. 10.
Tel 822 18 81 00.
W stadtrad.hamburg.de

Travelling by City Buses and Taxis

Hamburg's well-run public transportation system, HVV, makes it very easy to travel on public transit. You can switch between an HVV bus, an S-Bahn or U-Bahn and ferries, without ever having to purchase a new ticket. One of the cheapest ways to travel on the transit system is to purchase a day pass, which pays for itself after just two trips. The bus network includes many types of buses, from express buses to night buses. Taxis are a much more comfortable and convenient mode of transport, but also considerably more expensive.

MetroBus – a fast way to travel, often in a dedicated lane

HVV

In many large cities, trying to understand how the public transport system works is a seemingly impossible task. But this is not the case in Hamburg, whose transit system, founded in 1965, has yet to find its equal.

The **HVV** (Hamburger Verkehrsverbund) includes more than 30 different transport companies that run various kinds of buses, railways and harbour ferries. One incalculable advantage of the HVV is that its fare system is divided into easy-to-understand zones, and the same ticket can be used on different kinds of city transport.

Hamburg's public transit system covers not only the Free and Hanseatic City of Hamburg, but also extends into the adjacent regions of Schleswig-Holstein and Lower Saxony. The network covers approximately 8,700 sq km (3,360 sq miles). There are about two-million HVV passengers living in these three German states. Statistics show that about two-thirds of all passenger traffic in the inner-city area is on HVV transportation.

HVV Ticket Vending Machine

Ticket vending machines are found in all U-Bahn and S-Bahn stations, as well as at centrally located bus stops. These machines dispense single-use tickets, day-passes and three-day-passes.

A chart showing the different kinds of tickets and prices

Coin slot

Touch-screen

Slot for card payment

Bank note slot

Tray into which the ticket and change are dispensed by the machine

Tickets

One ticket is valid on all HVV transit, whether you are travelling by bus, rail or on a harbour ferry. Tickets for one-way trips and day-passes (available for either one or three consecutive days) can be purchased from ticket vending machines as well as from bus drivers. Unlike in many other cities, the tickets do not have to be validated or stamped when you use them. If you are staying in Hamburg for a while, it pays to buy a weekly pass. Anyone with a Hamburg CARD *(see p221)* can use public transit in the Greater Hamburg area free of charge.

Day passes can be used for unlimited travel on the day of purchase until 6am the following day. The price is determined by the zones. The cheapest day pass (one to two zones) is available for 7.10 Euros. Even cheaper is the day pass that starts after 9am, which costs 5.80 Euros. It is valid from 9am until 6am the following day. Children five years and under travel on the HVV network for free. A day pass is valid for up to three children (13 and under) and two adults.

If you're travelling with friends or colleagues consider purchasing a 9-Uhr-Gruppen-karte (9 O'clock Group Card) which can be very good value. To cover up to five people travelling in zones 1 and 2 costing just 10.40 Euros. Even if it's only two of you travelling, a Group Card can still be good value, particularly as it is valid until 6am the next morning.

Buses

HVV buses include the StadtBus, MetroBus, SchnellBus, EilBus and NachtBus. A StadtBus (which usually has a three-digit number) brings passengers to the S-Bahn stations and regional transit stations. A MetroBus links destinations within the central area (lines 1 to 15) and outside the central area (lines 20 to 27). A SchnellBus (lines 31 to 39) travels to the outer districts right from the centre of the city. These buses offer extra comfort, have a large number of seats and cost more. Minibuses (lines 48 and 49) ride through the narrow lanes of Blankenese. An EilBus (which has an "E" in front of the bus number) links parts of the city that do not have an S-Bahn station with the nearest U-Bahn or S-Bahn station. This type of bus only runs during rush hour. In the mornings, it brings passengers from stops in residential areas to the closest S-Bahn station, in the afternoons,

A typical ivory-coloured German taxi

it reverses its journey. A NachtBus (night bus on lines 600 to 688) operates after the U-Bahn and S-Bahn have stopped running every 30 to 60 minutes from Sundays to Thursday all over Hamburg. On weekends, the MetroBus and StadtBus (as well as the U-Bahns and S-Bahns; see pp238–39) run around the clock.

Buses used in the greater Hamburg area are mostly low-floor-buses and do not have steps. People who use wheelchairs get into this type of bus with the help of a short ramp. On the HVV website (www.hvv.de/en), you can find excellent information about barrier-free access in the public transport system, along with route, schedule and ticket information.

Taxis

For visitors to Hamburg, taxis provide a comfortable, if relatively expensive, way to travel. More than 3,500 taxis are licensed to operate in the Hanseatic city. Since taxis are allowed to use dedicated bus lanes, they travel along at a good clip even in rush hour. At night, taxis are often the only option available, especially when a NachtBus has just pulled away right in front of you.

You can hail a taxi on the street, or order one by telephone (for telephone numbers see box), or pick up one at one of the many taxi ranks located strategically across the city.

The basic fare is 2.90 Euros; the per-kilometer price for the first four km (2.5 miles) is 2 Euros, from 5 to 10 km (3 to 6 miles) the cost is 1.90 Euros, for each additional kilometre travelled, there is a 1.40 Euro charge.

Perhaps you would enjoy a trip in a different kind of taxi – a Fahrrad-Taxi (bicycle taxi)? These unusual vehicles carry passengers between the Alster docks, the Rathausmarkt, the Hauptbahnhof, the Landungs-brücken and HafenCity. In this fun vehicle, the driver not only is transporting you in a way that is environmentally friendly, but will also provide you with interesting bits of information about the sights and attractions you pass en route.

StadtBus operated by the Hamburger Hochbahn (www.hochbahn.de)

Bus stop "Auf dem Sande", with signs for MetroBuses and city tours

U-Bahn and S-Bahn

The excellent network of "Schnellbahn" (S-Bahn) lines in the HVV area *(see back inside cover)* gives travellers a fast way to travel, independently of traffic. On weekends, as well as the night before a public holiday, trains on the three U-Bahn lines and the six S-Bahn lines roll through the night every 20 minutes. Tickets for both forms of transport are also valid for other types of transit (buses and some harbour ferries). Lines converge not just at the big railway stations, but at many stops, which makes switching to another line easy. It is also easy to purchase tickets from a vending machine.

U-Bahn sign showing the destination station of the train

The U-Bahn, which often travels above ground

U-Bahn

Hamburg's U-Bahn (underground train) network consists of four lines, which together travel more than 100 km (62 miles) of tracks. As part of the gigantic HafenCity complex *(see pp90–91)*, a new fourth U-Bahn line (U4) opened in 2013.

Most U-Bahn trains run from 4:30am to midnight every five to ten minutes. During peak times, they run every two to three minutes, and in the slower times (early morning and late evening hours) they operate at 20-minute intervals. The U-Bahn operates all night long on Fridays and Saturdays within the Hamburg area, with trains every 20 minutes.

A feature of Hamburg's U-Bahn network is that it often travels above ground. One of the highlights of a visit to Hamburg, which you should definitely take advantage of if you have the time, is to ride the U3 line on the section where it surfaces above ground. If you take the U3 line towards Barmbek, the train surfaces shortly after Rathaus station and travels past the Landungsbrücken on a portion

of the track known as the Hafen-Hochbahn *(see p92)*. You will have a wonderful panoramic view of the harbour from the train, but make sure to sit on the left-hand side in the direction of travel. This stretch is considered one of the loveliest trips you can take on public transportation in Hamburg. You can also travel this section in the opposite direction.

S-Bahn

While the U-Bahn runs exclusively in the city, the S-Bahn links Hamburg with the outlying areas. Each day, trains make about 1,000 trips.

The network covers about 140 km (87 miles), has 68 stations and on weekdays transports about 700,000 commuters. With these numbers, it is clear why the S-Bahn is considered the "backbone" of public regional transit in the Hanseatic city.

Trains operate daily between 4:30am and 1am, with service every 10 to 20 minutes. On weekends, the trains run around the clock. Since many lines share the same tracks, waiting times are short in the city centre.

For travellers arriving by air, the Hamburg Airport Station *(see pp230–31)*, is an important stop. It takes just 25 minutes to get from the airport to the centre of the city on the S-Bahn.

The S-Bahn network will be greatly expanded in the coming years, and more lines are being planned.

Bicycles

You can take your bicycle with you free of charge on U-Bahns and S-Bahns – as well as on many buses and on the harbour ferries. There is room for one bike just to the side of each door. There are some restrictions: you cannot take bicycles with you on the S-Bahn or on buses during peak times (6 to 9am and 4 to 6pm) from Mondays to Fridays. On weekends and public holidays, there are no

A platform in an S-Bahn station

restrictions. You can also take your bicycle on harbour ferries at any time, any day.

U-Bahn and S-Bahn Stations

U-Bahn and S-Bahn stations are clearly marked by signs. A square sign with a white "U" on a dark blue background stands for the U-Bahn, a round sign, with a white "S" on a green background stands for the S-Bahn. You can purchase a ticket at any station (see p236). It is a good idea to have small change and small bills with you for the ticket vending machines. Information displayed at the stations will tell you how much your trip will cost. If you are going to take several trips in one day, it pays to buy a day pass. For a longer visit, consider a weekly pass.

Electronic displays suspended over the platforms show the line number, and the final destination for each train that is pulling in. At each stop, and in each U-Bahn and S-Bahn car, there is a map of the HVV-transit network. The lines are marked in different colours, making them easy to distinguish. Also helpful are the maps which hang in every S-Bahn and

A joint U-Bahn and S-Bahn station, where you can transfer between lines

U-Bahn station. These provide information about the area around the station, including exits, entrances and bus stops.

Disabled Travellers

Many U-Bahn and S-Bahn stations are barrier free. Either they have wheel-chair accessible ramps or an elevator wide enough to accommodate a wheelchair. In the newest U-Bahn and S-Bahn trains, the distance between the platform and the car is a maximum of 6 cm (2.3 in), making it easy to get on and off the cars. On older trains, the distance is greater, but this does not usually pose a problem.

On maps depicting the HVV network that hang in every station, it is easy to see those stations that can be used by people in wheelchairs, since they are marked with a symbol. Detailed information about station entrances and exits for S-Bahn and U-Bahn stations, as well as the location of the toilets, is available online at www.hvv.de.

As a special free service for the blind and seeing impaired, the HVV will create on demand a schedule and list of the stops tailored to an individual's needs. You can order this specially prepared information by telephoning (040) 194 49.

Tickets for use anywhere on the HVV

Security

On every U-Bahn and S-Bahn platform there are emergency intercoms, which you can use to summon help if needed. As well as making regular patrols, security personnel use cameras to watch over the stations. If there are no incidents, the recording is erased after 24 hours.

When a passenger has pulled the emergency brake because there has been an incident, the U-Bahn or S-Bahn train will continue on to the next station before stopping. It is easier to provide help (which can also be summoned more quickly) at a station. Every tunnel has clearly marked emergency exits, should passengers be asked to exit the train.

HVV prices and destinations in the local and regional Hamburg area

Station name

Line

Pedestrian tunnel

The entrance to a U-Bahn station with various signs

Travelling by Boat

Hamburg's harbour is as much a part of this Hanseatic city as the Reeperbahn and St Michelis church. A tour by boat will be one of the high-lights of your visit – even if your vessel does not pass close to a luxury cruise ship. Taking a boat such as a HADAG ferry is a lovely way to travel the Elbe river. There are many special boat tours offered during the Port's Birthday Bash *(see p85)*. Boat tours of the Binnenalster, Außenalster and the canals are also available. You can get to the Altes Land and Helgoland from Hamburg quite easily by water, but to reach the island of Sylt it is better to go by rail, car or by plane.

Sign for
harbour tours

A large choice of harbour tours are available to visitors

Harbour Tours

Taking a harbour tour is a good way to get to know Hamburg from another perspective *(see pp48 – 49)*, and sightseeing from the water has its own special charm. If you depart from the city centre to Altona, you will pass by HafenCity, the Speicherstadt and the modern buildings lining the water's edge like pearls in a necklace.

Many tour companies tout their boat trips on the Landungsbrücken. The routes are all very similar. Choose the boat that suits you best.

Tours of the harbour take place all year round. Some have a special theme such as "Treasures and Sacks of Peppercorns",

Advertisement for boating on
the Alster

which focuses on Hamburg's importance as a maritime trading centre, or "The Port and Its Whores", concentrating on the history of prostitution. In summer, boat tours of the Speicherstadt at night are highly recommended, when its impressive red-brick buildings are beautifully lit up. Most round trips of the harbour last from one to two hours. If you are lucky, you will be able to see a large ocean liner up close.

Elbe Boat Tours

A fairly inexpensive way of seeing Hamburg from the water is to take one of the **HADAG** ferries. The most interesting ferry routes are plied by No. 61, from the Landungsbrücken to Waltershof; No. 62 *(see p135)*, from Landungsbrücken to Finkenwerder via Neumühlen, with its ship museums in Museumshafen Övelgönne; and No. 64 from Finken-werder to Teufels-brück. The cost for a HADAG ferry is the same as for any other form of public transport offered by the HVV. This means you do not have to buy an extra ticket if you have already been on public transit and are transferring, or if you have a day pass *(see p236)*.

You can travel from the Landungsbrücken to Altes Land *(see p138)* via Blankenese and Willkommhöft *(see p139)* on a HADAG ship run by the **Elbe Erlebnistörns GmbH**. They run on weekends and public holidays from Easter to the beginning of October, and also accept bicycles.

Alster Boat Tours

Excursions on the Binnenalster and Außenalster are popular with tourists and locals alike. Whoever experiences the metropolis from these lakes quickly discovers that Hamburg does not only have the most bridges of any city in Europe (apparently there are 2653!), but also ranks among the greenest cities. You glide by parks, overgrown shorelines and villas with lovely gardens.

Alster-Touristik GmbH offers mini "cruises" from March to early

Harbour tours – enjoyed by locals and visitors alike

A boat trip on the Alster – a relaxing way to see the sights

october. They depart from the Jungfernstieg and cross the Alster to the Winter-huder Fährhaus. You can get on and off at any of the stops as often as you like. This company also offers a tour of the Alster from November to March as a "Punschfahrt" (with mulled red wine, coffee and hot chocolate) in a heated cabin. Taking a trip between Jungfernstieg and Harvestehude in the evening could not be more romantic.

But the Alster is at its most idyllic when you cross it on a gondola with **La Gondola**.

Ticket booth for round trips of the harbour, including Speicherstadt

Canal Tours

What would Hamburg be without its many canals that course through some of the city's loveliest areas? One of the most popular canal boat tour companies is **Barkassen-Centrale**. On their boats, which are decorated in 1920s style, you glide through narrow waterways and pass under some of the oldest bridges

in Hamburg to the impressive Speicherstadt *(see pp82–83)*. Informative historic tours of the canals are also offered by the company **Kapitän Prüsse**.

Helgoland and Neuwerk

Getting to Helgoland *(see p159)*, Germany's largest sea island, is quite simple by water. The *Halunder Jet*, run by **FRS Helgoline GmbH**, sails from Hamburg to Helgoland starting in April through to October. The boat leaves daily from Landungsbrücke 3 or 4 *(see p93)*, and reaches the island in just four hours, stopping at Wedel and Cuxhaven along the way. You do not have to make any transfers. Tickets for this trip can be purchased daily from 7:30am at the Landungs-brücken. Prices vary, depending on the season and class you choose. You can sail to Helgoland from Cuxhaven throughout the year aboard MS *Atlantis*.

Also head to Cuxhaven if you'd like to reach the beautiful island of Neuwerk in the

Water-level indicator based on the mean sea level in Amsterdam (NN)

Hamburg Wadden Sea National Park *(see pp140–41)* at low tide on foot or in a horse-drawn wagon. When the tide is high, a ship run by **Reederei Cassen Eils** will transport you there.

DIRECTORY

Elbe Boat Tours

Elbe Erlebnistörns GmbH
Tel 219 46 27.
W elbe-erlebnistoerns.de

HADAG Seetouristik und Fährdienst AG
Tel 311 70 70.
W hadag.de

Alster Boat Tours

Alster-Touristik GmbH
Tel 357 42 40.
W alstertouristik.de

La Gondola
Tel 490 09 31.
W gondel.de

Canal Tours

Barkassen-Centrale
Tel 319 91 61 70.
W barkassen-centrale.de

Kapitän Prüsse
Tel 31 31 30.
W kapitaen-pruesse.de

Helgoland and Neuwerk

FRS Helgoline GmbH
Tel 0461 864 44.
W helgoline.de

Reederei Cassen Eils
Tel 0180 522 86 61.
W cassen-eils.de/ihre-faehre-nach-helgoland

HAMBURG STREET FINDER

The map references given with all sights, hotels, restaurants, shops and entertainment venues described in this book refer to the maps in this section. A complete index of street names and all the places of interest marked on the maps can be found on the following pages. The key map below shows the areas of Hamburg covered by the *Street Finder* maps. These are: Altona, 1– 2; St Pauli, 3 – 4; Port and Speicherstadt, 5 – 6; Around the Alster, 7 – 8; and New Town and Old Town, 9 –10. In addition to the six coloured city areas, other areas are also shown on these maps. The symbols used to represent sights and useful information are listed below in the key.

View of the Elbe with St Michaelis church (centre), Cap San Diego (right) and a boat-shuttle (front)

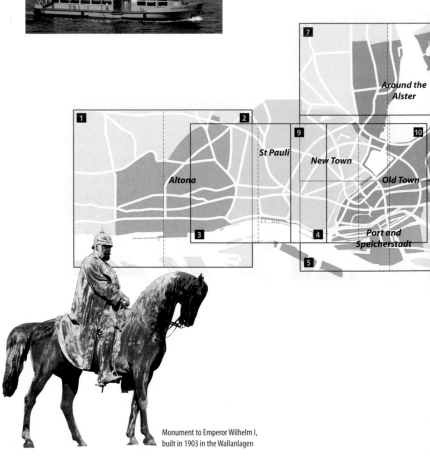

7

Around the Alster

1

2

9

St Pauli

New Town

10

Altona

Old Town

3

4

Port and Speicherstadt

5

Monument to Emperor Wilhelm I, built in 1903 in the Wallanlagen

How the Map References Work

The first figure tells you which *Street Finder* map to turn to.

⓱ Cap San Diego

Museum ship *Cap San Diego*,
Überseebrücke. **Map** 9 A5.
Tel 36 42 09. **U** Baumwall.
S Landungsbrücken.
Open 10am–6pm daily.
W capsandiego.de

The letter and number give the grid reference. Letters go across the map's top and bottom, figures on its sides.

The map continues on map 5 of the *Street Finder*.

KEY

- Major sight
- Other sight
- **S** S-Bahn station
- **U** U-Bahn station
- Railway station
- Bus terminal
- Ferry service
- Boat boarding point
- **i** Information
- Hospital with casualty department
- Police station
- Church
- Railway
- Pedestrian street
- Passage
- Ferry route

Scale of Maps 1–2 and 5–6

| 0 metres | 300 |
| 0 yards | 300 |

1:14 000

Scale of Maps 3–4 and 9–10

| 0 metres | 300 |
| 0 yards | 300 |

1:10 500

Scale of Maps 7–8

| 0 metres | 300 |
| 0 yards | 300 |

1:12,500

Huge container ship docked at Burchardkai

Street Finder Index

A

Abbestraße	1 C2–3
ABC-Straße	5 B2
	7 B5
	9 C2
Ackermannstraße	8 F3–4
Adenauerallee	6 E–F2
Admiralitätstraße	5 B3–4
	9 B4
Adolphsbrücke	5 B–C3
	9 C3
Adolphsplatz	9–10 C–D3
Afghanisches Museum	5 B4
	9 C5
Albertstraße	6 F3
Alexanderstraße	6 F2
	8 F5
Allgemeines Krankenhaus	
St. Georg	6 F1
	8 F4
Alsenstraße	2 E1
Alsterarkaden	10 D3
Alsterchaussee	7 C1
Alsterglacis	5 C1
	7 C4
	10 D1
Alsterpavillon	5 C2
	7 C5
	9 D2–3
Alsterterrasse	5 C1
	7 C4
	10 D1
Alstertor	5 C2–3
	10 E3
Alstertwiete	6 E2
	8 E4–5
	10 F2
Alsterufer	5 C1
	7–8 C3–4, D3
Alstervorland	8 D1
Alte Königstraße	2 D4
Alte Post	5 B2, C3
	9 C3
Alte Rabenstraße	7–8 C3, D2
Alter Botanischer Garten	5 B1
	7 B4
	9 C1
Alter Elbpark	4 E4
	9 A4
Alter Elbtunnel	4 D5
Alter Fischmarkt	5 C3
	10 D–E4
Alter Steinweg	5 A–B3
	9 B3
Alter Wall	5 B–C3
	9–10 C3–4, D3
Alter Wandrahm	6 D4
	10 E4
Altmannbrücke	6 E3
Altonaer Balkon	2 D4
Altonaer Poststraße	2 D3
Altstädter Straße	6 D3
	10 E–F4
Am Born	1 B3
Am Brunnenhof	2 F2–3
	3 C2–3
Am Dalmannkai	5 C5
Am Elbpark	4 E4
Am Elbpavillon	4 E4
	9 A4
Am Felde	1 C3
Am Kaiserkai	5 B–C5
Am Rathenaupark	1 A3
Am Sandtorkai	5 C4
	10 D–E5
Am Sandtorpark	5 C4–5
Am Sood	1 C2–3
Amsinck-Palais	5 C2
	7 C5
	10 D1

Amsinckstraße	6 F3–4
Amtsgericht	5 B2
	7 B5
	9 C2
Amundsenstraße	2 E4
	3 A4
An der Alster	6 D–E1
	8 D–E4
	10 F1
An der Verbindungsbahn	
	7 A–B3
Annenstraße	4 D3
Antonistraße	3 C4
Armgartstraße	8 F3
Arndtstraße	8 F1
Arnoldstraße	1 B4, C3
Auf dem Sande	9 C5
Augustenpassage	4 D1
August-Lütgens-Park	2 E2
	3 A2
Auguststraße	8 E2
Außenalster	6 D1
	8 D1–E4
	10 E–F1
Averhoffstraße	8 F2
Axel-Springer-Platz	5 B3
	9 C3

B

Bäckerbreitergang	5 A2
	7 A5
	9 B2
Badestraße	7–8 C–D3
Bahrenfelder Kirchenweg	
	1 A1–2
Bahrenfelder Steindamm	
	1 B1
Bahrenfelder Straße	1 C2–4
Balduinstraße	2 F4
	3 C4
Ballindamm	5–6 C–D2
	7–8 C–D5
	10 D3, E2
Banksstraße	6 E–F4
Barcastraße	8 F3–4
Barnerstraße	1 B–C2
Baumeisterstraße	6 E2
	8 E5
Baumwall	5 B4
	9 B5
Beatles-Platz	2 F3
	3 C3–4
Beckstraße	4 D1
Behnstraße	2 D3–4
Behringstraße	1 A3, B2
Bei den Kirchhöfen	5 A1
	7 A4
	9 B1
Bei den Mühren	5 C4
	9–10 C–D5
Bei den St. Pauli Landungs-	
brücken	4 D4, D–E5
Bei der Rolandsmühle	1 A3
Bei Sankt Annen	5 C4
	10 E5
Beim Grünen Jäger	4 D2
Beim Schlump	7 A2
Bergiusstraße	1 B3
Bergstraße	5 C3
	10 D3
Berliner Tor	6 F2
	8 F4–5
Bernadottestraße	1 A–B4
Bernhard-Nocht-Straße	
	3–4 C–D4
Bernstorffstraße	2 F1–3
	3 C1–2
Bertha-von-Suttner-Park	2 E1
	3 A1

Bieberstraße	7 B2
Bielfeldtstraße	1 A3
Biernatzkistraße	2 D3–4
Billrothstraße	2 D–E3
	3 A–B3
Binderstraße	7 B–C2
Binnenalster	5 C2
	7 C5
	10 D–E2
Bismarck-Denkmal	4 E4
	9 A4
Bleichenbrücke	5 B3
	9 C3
Bleichenhof	5 B3
	5 C3
Bleicherstraße	2 F2–3
	3 C2–3
Bleickenallee	1 A–B3
Blücherstraße	2 E3
	3 A3–4
Böckmannstraße	6 F2
	8 F5
Bodenstedtstraße	2 D2
Bogenallee	7 A1
Bogenstraße	7 A1–2
Böhmersweg	7 C1
Böhmkenstraße	4 F4
	5 A4
	9 A4
Boninstraße	1 B–C4
Bornstraße	7 A2
Börse	5 C3
	9 D3
Borselstraße	1 B2
Börsenbrücke	10 D4
Botanisches Institut	5 B1
	7 B4
	9 B1
Brahmsallee	7 A1
Brandenburger Hafen	4 F5
	5 A4
	9 A–B5
Brandsende	6 D2
	8 D5
	10 E2
Brandstwiete	5 C3–4
	10 E4
Brauerknechtgraben	4 F4–5
	9 A4
Breite Straße	2 E4
	3 A–B4
Breiter Gang	9 B3
Brennerstraße	6 E–F2, F1
	8 E–F5, F4
Brodersweg	7 A1
Brodschrangen	10 D4
Brook	5 C4
	10 D5
Brooktorkai	6 D4
	10 E5
Brüderstraße	9 B3
Brunnenhofstraße	3 C2
Buchtstraße	8 F3
Budapester Straße	4 D2–3
Bugdahnstraße	2 D3
Bugenhagenstraße	10 E–F3
Bülaustraße	6 F1
	8 F4
Bülowstieg	1 A3
Bülowstraße	1 A3
Bundesstraße	7 A2–3
Bundesweg	7 B3
Burchardstraße	6 D3
	10 E3–4
Büschstraße	5 B2
	7 B5
	9 C2
Buttstraße	2 E4
	3 B5

C

Café Keese	4 D3
Caffamacherreihe	5 B2
	7 B5
	9 B–C2
Cap San Diego	4 F5
	5 A4
	9 A5
Carsten-Rehder-Straße	2 E4
	3 A–B5
Celsiusweg	1 B1
Chemnitzstraße	2 D–E2
	3 A–B2
Chilehaus	6 D3
	10 E–F4
City-Sportboot-Hafen	4 F5
	5 A4
	9 B5
Clemens-Schultz-Straße	
	3–4 C–D3
Colonnaden	5 C1–2
	7 C4–5
	9–10 C1–2, D2
Congress Centrum Hamburg	
	5 B1
	7 B4
	9 C1
Cremon	5 B4
	9 C4–5

D

Daimlerstraße	1 B1–2
Dammtordamm	5 B–C1
	7 B–C4
	9 C1
Dammtorstraße	5 B2
	7 B4–5
	9 C2
Dammtorwall	5 B2
	7 B4–5
	9 C1–2
Danziger Straße	6 E1–2, F2
	8 E4–5, F5
Davidstraße	4 D4
Davidwache	4 D4
Deichstraße	5 B4
	9 C4–5
Deichtorhallen	6 D–E4
	10 F4
Deichtorplatz	6 D–E3
	10 F4
Deichtorstraße	6 D–E4
	10 F4
Detlev-Bremer-Straße	4 D3
Deutsches Schauspielhaus	6 E2
	8 E5
	10 F2
Deutsches Zollmuseum	
	5–6 C–D4
De-Voß-Straße	3 B5
Dialog im Dunkeln	6 D4
	10 E4
Dienerreihe	6 D4
	10 E4–5
Dillstraße	7 A2
Ditmar-Koel-Straße	4 E5, F4
	5 A4
	9 A4–5
Dockland	1–2 C–D5
Domstraße	5 C3
	10 D4
Donnerspark	1 B4
Donnerstraße	1 B3
Dosestraße	2 E4
	3 B4
Dovenfleet	6 D4
	10 D4

Drehbahn	5 B2
	7 B5
	9 C2
Düppelstraße	2 E1
Durchschnitt	7 A3
Duschweg	2 F2
Düsternstraße	5 B3
	9 C3

E

Edmund-Siemers-Allee	7 B3–4
Eggersallee	1 B4
Eggerstedtstraße	2 E1–2
	3 A1
Ehrenbergstraße	2 D3
Eichholz	4 L4
	9 A4
Ekhofstraße	6 F1
	8 F4
Elbchaussee	1 A–B4
Elbphilharmonie	5 B5
Elbtunnel	1 A–B5
Enckeplatz	4 F3
	5 A3
	9 A3
Englische Kirche	4 E4
	9 A4
Englische Planke	4 F4
	5 A3
	9 A–B4
Erdmannstraße	1 B3
Erichstraße	3 C4
Ericusbrücke	6 D4
	10 F5
Erlenkamp	8 F2
Ernst-Merck-Straße	6 D–E2
	8 D–E5
	10 F2
Erste Brunnenstraße	5 A3
	9 B3–4
Erzbergerstraße	1 C3
Eschelsweg	3 A3–4
Esmarchstraße	2 D–E2
	3 A2
Esplanade	5 C1
	7 C4
	9–10 C–D1
Eulenstraße	1 B–C3

F

Fachhochschule	8 F3
Fährdamm	8 D1
Fährhausstraße	8 E1
Feenteich	8 E1
Fehlandtstraße	10 D2
Feldbrunnenstraße	7 C2–3
Feldstraße	4 D–E2
	9 A2
Ferdinandstor	6 D2
	8 D4–5
	10 E2
Ferdinandstraße	5–6 C2–3, D2
	10 E2–3
Das Feuerschiff	4 F5
	5 A4
	9 B5
Finkenstraße	2 F3–4
	3 B–C4
Fischauktionshalle	2 E–F4
	3 B5
Fischers Allee	1 B3–4
Fischmarkt	2 E–F4
	3 B5
Fontenay	7 C3
Friedensallee	1 A–B2
Friedrich-Ebert-Hof	1 A2
Friedrichstraße	3 C4

Fuhlentwiete	5 B2–3
	9 C2–3
Funkstraße	3 A3–4

G

Gählerstraße	2 E2
	3 B2
Galleria	5 B2–3
	9 C3
Gänsemarkt	5 B2
	7 B5
	9 C2
Gasstraße	1 A1
Gaußstraße	1 B–C2
Gerberstraße	3 A3
Gerhart-Hauptmann-Platz	6 D2
	10 E3
Gerhofstraße	9 C2
Gerichtstraße	2 D2
Germerring	1 A2
Gerritstraße	2 F2
	3 B–C2
Gerstäcker Straße	4 F4
	5 A3
	9 A4
Gertrudenstraße	6 D2
	10 E3
Gilbertstraße	2 F2
	3 B–C2
Glacischaussee	4 E2–3
	9 A2–3
Glashüttenstraße	4 E1–2
	9 A1–2
Glockengießerwall	6 D2
	8 D5
	10 E 1–2
Goetheallee	2 D2
Goethestraße	2 D3
Gorch-Fock-Wall	5 A–B2, B1
	7 A5, B4
	9 B2, C1
Grabenstraße	4 E1
	9 A1
Grasbrook-Park	5 C5
Graskeller	5 B3
	9 C4
Graumannsweg	8 F3
Greifswalder Straße	6 E2
	8 E4–5
Grimm	5 C4
	10 D4
Grindelallee	7 A2–3, B3
Grindelberg	7 A1
Grindelhof	7 A–B2
Grindelweg	7 A3
Große Bergstraße	2 D–E3
	3 A3
Große Bleichen	5 B2–3, C2
	7 B–C5
	9 C3
Große Brunnenstraße	1 B2–4
Große Elbstraße	1–2 C–E4
	3 A–B5
Große Freiheit	2 F3
	3 C3–4
Große Rainstraße	1 C3
Große Wallanlagen	4 E–F3
	9A3
Großer Burstah	5 B–C3
	9 C4
Großer Grasbrook	5 C5
	10 D5
Großmarkthalle	6 F4–5
Großneumarkt	5 A3
	9 B3
Grünebergstraße	1 A2–3
Gurlittstraße	6 E1
	8 E4

Gustav-Mahler-Park	5 C1
	7 C4
	10 D1
Gustav Mahler-Platz	5 B–C2
	7 B–C5
	9–10 C–D2

H

Hachmannplatz	6 E2
	8 E5
	10 F2–3
HafenCity InfoCenter	5 C4
	10 D5
Hafenstraße	4 D4
Hafentor	4 E4
	9 A4
Hahnenkamp	1 C3
Hallerplatz	7 B1–2
Hallerstraße	7 A–C1
Hamburg Dungeon	5 B4
	9 C5
Hamburg Port Authority	5 C5
Hamburger Berg	3 C3
Hamburger Hochstraße	2 F4
	3 B4
Hamburger Kunsthalle	6 D2
	8 D5
	10 E–F2
Hamburgische Staatsoper	5 B2
	7 B5
	9 C2
hamburgmuseum	4 E3
	9 A3
Handelskammer	5 C3
	10 D3
Hans-Albers-Platz	3 C4
Hansaplatz	6 E2
	8 E5
Hansastraße	7 A–C1
Hanse-Viertel	9 C2–3
Harkortstraße	2 D1–3
Harmsenstraße	1 A2
Harry's Hafenbasar	2 F4
	3 C4
Hartungstraße	7 B2
Hartwicusstraße	8 F3
Harvestehuder Weg	8 D1–2
Haubachstraße	2 D1–2, E1
	3 A1
Heiligengeistfeld	4 E2–3
Heimhuder Straße	7 C2–3
Heine-Haus	1 C4
Heine-Haus	5 B–C2
	7 C5
	9 C2
Hein-Hoyer-Straße	4 D3
Hein-Köllisch-Platz	2 F4
	3 C4
Heinrich-Barth-Straße	7 A2
Heinrich-Hertz-Straße	8 F1
Heinrich-Hertz-Turm	7 A3
Helenenstraße	2 E2
	3 A1–2
Helgoländer Allee	4 E4
Helmholtzstraße	1 B2
Herbertstraße	3–4 C–D4
Herbert-Weichmann-Straße	8 E1–2, F2
Hermann-Behn-Weg	7 B2
Hermannstraße	5 C3
	10 D3
Herrengraben	5 A–B4, B3
	9 B4
Herrenweide	2 F3–4
	3 C4
Herrlichkeit	5 B4
	9 B–C4
Heuberg	9 C3
Hexenberg	2 F4
	3 B4
Hochallee	7 B1

Hochschule für Musik und Theater	7–8 C–D2
Hofweg	8 E–F1, F2
Högerdamm	6 E–F4
Hohe Bleichen	5 B2–3
	9 C2–3
Hohe Brücke	5 B4
	9 C5
Hohenesch	1 C2–3
Hohenzollernring	1 A2–4
Hohler Weg	4 F4
	9 A–B4
Holländische Reihe	1 B–C4
Holstenglacis	4 F1–2
	5 A1
	7 A4
	9 A–B1
Holstenplatz	2 E1
	3 A1
Holstenring	1 B3
Holstenstraße	2 E1–2, F3
	3 A1, B2–3
Holstentwiete	1 B3
Holstenwall	4 E3, F2–3
	5 A2–3
	9 A2–3
Holtystraße	8 F1
Holzbrücke	5 B4
	9 C4
Holzdamm	6 D2
	8 D4–5
	10 F2
Hongkongstraße	6 D4–5
Hopfensack	6 D3
	10 E4
Hopfenstraße	4 D4
Hospitalstraße	2 E2–3
	3 A2–3
Hotel Atlantic Kempinski	6 D1–2
	8 D4
	10 F1–2
Hotel Vier Jahreszeiten	5 C2
	7 C5
	10 D2
Hübenerstraße	5 C5
Hütten	4 F3
	9 A3

I

Ifflandstraße	8 F3–4
Imam-Ali-Moschee	8 E1
Immenhof	8 F2
Institut für Physik	5 A1
	7 A4
	9 B1

J

Jakobstraße	4 F4
	5 A4
	9 A4
Jessenstraße	2 D–E3
	3 A3
Johannes-Brahms-Museum	4 F3
	5 A3
	9 A3
Johannes-Brahms-Platz	4 F2
	5 A2
	7 A5
	9 B2
Johannisbollwerk	4 E–F5
	9 A5
Johanniswall	6 D3
	10 F3–4
Johnsallee	7 B–C3
Julius-Leber-Straße	2 D2
Juliusstraße	3 C1

Jungfernstieg 5 C2
7 C5
9-10 C-D2
Jungiusstraße 5 B1
7 B4
9 B1

K

Kaiser-Wilhelm-Denkmal 4 F2
9 A-B2
Kaiser-Wilhelm-Straße 5 A-B2
7 A-B5
9 B2-3
Kaistraße 1 C4
Kajen 9 C5
Kalkhof 5 B2
7 B5
9 C2
Kaltenkircher Platz 2 D1
Kampstraße 4 D1
Kanalstraße 8 F1
Karlstraße 8 E1
Karl-Theodor-Straße 1 C4
Karl-Wolff-Straße 2 E2
Karolinenstraße 4 F1-2
5 A1
7 A4
9 A1-2
Karpfangerstraße 4 F5
5 A4
9 A5
Kasino Reeperbahn 3 C4
Kastanienallee 4 D4
Katharinenfleet 5 C4
9-10 C-D5
Katharinenstraße 5 C4
9-10 C-D4
Katzenstieg 1 A4
Kehrwieder 5 B4
9 C5
Kennedybrücke 5-6 C-D1
7-8 C-D4
10 D-E1
Keplerstraße 1 B3
Kibbelsteg 5 C4
10 D5
Kieler Straße 2 E1
Kirchenallee 6 E2
8 E5
10 F2-3
Kirchenstraße 2 E4
3 A-B4
Kirchentwiete 1 C4
Kirchenweg 6 E2
8 E5
Klausstraße 1 C3
Klein Fontenay 7 C3
Kleine Bergstraße 3 A3
Kleine Freiheit 2 F3
3 C3
Kleine Marienstraße 3 B3
Kleine Rainstraße 1 C3
Kleine Reichenstraße 5-6 C-D3
10 E4
Kleine Wallanlagen 5 A-B1, A2
7 A-B4, A5
9 B1-2
Kleiner Burstah 9 C4
Klopstockplatz 1 C4
Klopstockstraße 1 C4
Klosterstieg 7 C1
Klosterwall 10 F3-4
Kohlentwiete 1 C1
Kohlhöfen 5 A2-3
9 B3
Koldingstraße 2 E1
Königstraße 2 D-E4, E5
3 A-B4

Koppel 6 E1-2
8 E4-5
9-10 C-D2
Koreastraße 6 D4
10 E5
Kornträgergang 5 B2-3
9 B3
Krameramtswohnungen 9 B4
Krayenkamp 4 F4
5 A3
9 B4
Kreuzfahrtterminal Altona 2 D5
Kreuzfahrtterminal HafenCity 5 C5
Kreuzweg 6 E2
8 E5
Kurt-Schumacher-Allee 6 F2-3
Kurze Mühren 6 D2
10 E-F3
Kurze Straße 4 F3
5 A3
9 B3

L

Laeiszhalle 4 F2
5 A2
7 A5
9 B2
Laeiszstraße 4 E1
Lamp'lweg 2 D3
Landesbank 6 D3
10 E3
Landeszentralbank 9 C4
Landungsbrücken 4 D5
Lange Mühren 6 D3
10 F3
Lange Reihe 6 E1-2
8 E4-5
Lange Straße 2 F4
3 B-C4
Langenfelder Straße 2 F2
Laufgraben 7 A3
Lawaetzweg 2 D3
Lerchenstraße 3 C1-2
Lessers Passage 2 D3-4
Lilienstraße 6 D2-3
10 E3
Lincolnstraße 2 F3-4
3 C4
Lindenplatz 6 F2
Lindenstraße 6 F2, 8 F5
Lippeltstraße 6 E-F4
Lippmannstraße 3 C1
Lisztstraße 1 A3
Lobuschstraße 1 C3
Löfflerstraße 2 D2
Lohmühlenstraße 6 E-F1
8 E-F4
Lohseplatz 6 D4
10 F5
Lombardsbrücke 5-6 C-D2
7-8 C4-5, D5
10 D-E2
Lornsenstraße 2 D3
Louise-Schroeder-Straße 2 E-F3
3 A-B3
Ludwig-Erhard-Straße 4 F4
5 A-B3
9 A-C4
Ludwigstraße 4 D1

M

Magdalenenstraße 7 C2
Magdeburger Straße 6 D4-5
Magellan-Terrassen 5 C4-5
10 D5
Mahnmal St. Nikolai 5 C3-4
10 D4
Marco-Polo-Terrassen 5 C5

Maritimes Museum 6 D4
10 E5
Marktstraße 4 E1
Markusstraße 4 F3
5 A3
9 B3
Marseiller Straße 5 B1
7 B4
9 B-C1
Martin-Luther-Straße 5 A3-4
9 B4
Mattentwiete 5 B4
9 C4-5
Max-Brauer-Allee 2 D2-4, E1-2, F1
3 A1-2, B1
Medienbunker 4 E2
Mendelssohnstraße 1 A1
Messegelände 4 F1
5 A1
7 A4
9 A-B1
Michaelisbrücke 5 B3
9 B-C4
Michaelispassage 5 B3
9 B3-4
Michaelisstraße 5 A-B3
9 B4
Milchstraße 7 C-D2
Millerntordamm 4 E3
Millerntorplatz 4 E3
Millerntor-Stadion 4 D2
Miniatur Wunderland 5 B4
9 C5
Missundestraße 2 E1
Mittelweg 7 C1-4
Mollerstraße 7 C2
Mönckebergstraße 5-6 C-D3
10 E3
Mönkedamm 5 B-C3
9 C4
Moorweide 7 C3-4
Moorweidenstraße 7 B-C3
Mörkenstraße 2 D-E3
3 A4
Mottenburger Straße 1 C3
Mumsenstraße 2 E2
3 B1-2
Mundsburger Damm 8 F2-3
Münzplatz 6 E3
Münzstraße 6 E3
Museum für Kunst
und Gewerbe 6 E3
Museum für Völkerkunde 7 B2
Museumshafen Övelgönne 1 A5
Museumstraße 1 C3-4

N

Nagelsweg 6 F3-5
NDR Funkhaus Hamburg 7 B1
Neanderstraße 4 F3-4
5 A3
9 A3-4
Nernstweg 1 C2
Neß 10 D4
Neue ABC-Straße 5 B2
9 C2
Neue Flora 2 E1
Neue Große Bergstraße 2 D3
Neue Rabenstraße 5 C1
7 C4-5
Neuer Jungfernstieg 5 C1-2
7 C4-5
10 D1-2
Neuer Kamp 4 D2
Neuer Pferdemarkt 4 D2
Neuer Steinweg 4 F3
5 A3
9 A-B3

Neuer Wall 5 B-C3
9-10 C-D3
Neuer Wandrahm 10 D-E5
Neumayerstraße 4 E4
Neumühlen 1 A-B4
Neustädter Neuer Weg
4 F4-5
5 A4
9 B4-5
Neustädter Straße 5 A-B2
9 B3
New-Orleans-Straße 6 D5
Niederbaumbrücke 5 B4
9 B5
Niedernstraße 6 D3
10 E4
Nivea Haus 5 C2
Nobistor 2 E-F3
3 B3
Nöltingstraße 1 B-C3
Norderhof 6 F3
Norderreihe 2 E-F2
3 B2
Norderstraße 6 E-F3
Nordkanalbrücke 6 E3
Nordkanalstraße 6 F3
Nordreihe 9 A2

O

Oberbaumbrücke 6 D4
10 F4
Oberhafenstraße 6 E4
Oberlandesgericht 4 F2
9 A2
Oelkersallee 2 F1
Oeverseestraße 2 D1
Ohnsorg-Theater 6 D2
8 D5
10 F2
Olbersweg 2 D4
3 A5
Osakaallee 6 D4-5
10 E5
Otawiweg 1 A2
Ottenser Hauptstraße 1 B-C3
Ottenser Marktplatz 1 C4
Otzenstraße 2 F2
3 C2
Overbeckstraße 8 F2

P

Palmaille 2 D4
Panoptikum 4 D4
Papendamm 7 A3
Papenhuder Straße 8 F2-3
Parkallee 7 B1
Paul-Gerhardt-Kirche 1 B1
Paulinenplatz 4 D2
Paulinenstraße 4 D2
Paul-Nevermann-Platz 1 C3
Paul-Roosen-Straße 2 F3
3 B-C3
Paulsenplatz 2 F1
3 C1
Paulstraße 5 C3
10 D-E3
Pepermölenbek 2 F3-4
3 B4
Peterstraße 4 F3
9 A3
Petkumstraße 8 F2
Philosophenweg 1 A4
Pickhuben 5 C4
10 D5
Pilatuspool 4 F2
5 A2
9 B2
Pinnasberg 2 F4
3 B-C4
Plan 5 C3
10 D3
Planckstraße 1 B2
Planten un Blomen 5 B1
7 B4
Platz der Republik 1 C3

Poggenmühle	10 E4–5	Schmarjestraße	2 D3	Steinhöft	5 B4	Vasco-da-Gama-Platz	5 C5

Poggenmühle 10 E4–5
Poolstraße 4 F2–3
  5 A2
  7 A5
  9 B2
Pöseldorfer Weg 7 C1–2
Poststraße 5 B2
  7 B5
  9 C2–3
Präsident-Krahn-Straße
  2 D2–3
Prototyp Museum 6 D4
Pulverteich 6 E–F2
  8 E–F5
Pumpen 6 D3
  10 F4

R
Raboisen 6 D2
  10 E2–3
Radermachergang 9 B3
Rambachstraße 4 F5
  5 A4
  9 A5
Rappstraße 7 A–B2
Rathaus 5 C3
  10 D3
Rathaus Altona 1 C4
Rathausstraße 5 C3
  10 D3
Rathenaupark 1 A3
Reeperbahn 2 F3
  3–4 C–D4
Reesendamm 5 C3
  10 D3
Rehhoffstraße 5 A–B4
  9 B4
Reimarusstraße 4 F4–5
  5 A4
Reimerstwiete 10 D4–5
Reinfeldstraße 7 A3
Rentzelstraße 7 A3
Repsoldstraße 6 E2
Richterstraße 8 F1
Rickmer Rickmers 4 E5
  9 A5
Rödingsmarkt 5 B4, 9 C4
Röhrigstraße 1 A2
Rolandswoort 1 A3
Rosenallee 6 E–F3
Rosengarten 1 A–B4
Rosenstraße 6 D2
  10 E3
Rostocker Straße 6 E–F2, F1
  8 F5, F4
Rothenbaumchaussee 7 B1–3
Rothesoodstraße 4 E–F4
  9 A4
Rothestraße 1 B3, C4
Ruhrstraße 1 B1
Rulantweg 1 A4
Rütgerweg 1 A3
Rutschbahn 7 A2

S
Sandtor-Park 5 C5
San-Francisco-Straße 5 C5
Sankt Annenufer 10 D–E5
Schaarsteinweg 5 A4
  9 B4
Schaartor 5 B4
  9 B4–5
Schauenburgerstraße 5 C3
  10 D3–4
Scheel-Plessen-Straße 1 C2–3
Scheplerstraße 2 F2
Schillerstraße 2 D3–4
Schleepark 2 D4
  3 A4
Schleestraße 3 A4
Schleusenbrücke 5 C3
Schlüterstraße 7 B2–3

Schmarjestraße 2 D3
Schmidt Theater 4 D4
Schmidt-Rottluff-Weg 2 F2
  3 C2
Schmidts Tivoli 4 D4
Schmilinskystraße 6 E1
  8 E4
Schmuckstraße 2 F3
  3 C3
Schnellstraße 2 D2
Schomburgstraße 2 D–E3
  3 A–B3
Schöne Aussicht 8 E1–2
Schopenhauerweg 1 B–C4
Schopenstehl 5–6 C–D3
  10 E4
Schottweg 8 F3
Schulterblatt 3–4 C–D1
Schultzweg 6 E3
Schumacherstraße 2 D2–3
Schützenstraße 1 C1
Schwanenwik 8 E3, F2–3
Schweimlerstraße 6 F1
  8 F4
Sechslingspforte 6 F1
  8 F4
Sedanstraße 7 A2
Seewartenstraße 4 E4
Seilerstraße 4 D3
Shanghaiallee 6 D4–5
Sievekingplatz 4 F2
  9 A2
Silbersackstraße 3 C4
Silbersacktwiete 2 F4
  3 C4
Simon-Utrecht-Straße 3 C–D3
Singapurstraße 5 C4
Sommerhuder Straße 2 E–F1
Sonninstraße 6 F3–4
Sophienterrasse 7 C1
Spaldingstraße 6 F3
Speckstraße 5 B2
  7 D5
  9 B2
Speersort 5–6 C–D3
  10 E3
Speicherstadtmuseum 5 C4
  10 D5
Spicy's Gewürzmuseum 5 B4
  9 C5
Spielbudenplatz 4 D4
Spitalerstraße 6 D2–3
  10 E–F3
Springeltwiete 10 F3–4
St. Ansgarkirche 9 B4
St. Georg 6 E2
  8 E4–5
  10 F2
St. Jacobikirche 6 D3
  10 E3
St. Katharinenkirche 5 C4
  10 D4
St. Michaeliskirche 4 F4
  9 B4
St. Nikolaikirche 5 C3–4
  10 D4
St. Pauli Fischmarkt 2 F4
  3 B–C5, C4
St. Pauli Hafenstraße 4 D4
St. Petersburger Straße 5 A1
  7 A3–4
  9 B1
St. Petrikirche 10 E3
Staatsanwaltschaft 5 A–B2
  7 A–B4
  9 B2
Stadtdeich 6 E4, F5
Stadthausbrücke 5 B3
  9 C3
Stahltwiete 1 B1
Steindamm 6 E–F2
  8 E–F5, F4
Steinheimplatz 2 E2
  3 A–B2

Steinhöft 5 B4
  9 B5
Steinschanze 6 D4
  10 F5
Steinstraße 6 D3
  10 E–F3
Steintorplatz 6 E2–3
Steintorwall 6 D–E3
  10 F3
Steintwiete 9 C4
Steintwietenhof 5 B4
  9 C4–5
Steinwegpassage 5 B3
  9 B3
Stephansplatz 5 B1
  7 B4
  9 C1
Sternstraße 4 D1
Stiftstraße 6 F1–2
  8 F4–5
Stockmeyerstraße 6 D–E4
  10 F5
Stresemannstraße 1–2 B–F1
  3 C1
Struenseestraße 2 D–E4
  3 A4
Stubbenhuk 5 A4
  9 B5
Stuhlmannplatz 2 E3
Susettestraße 1 B4
Suttnerstraße 2 E1
  3 A–B1

T
Talstraße 2 F3
  3 C3
Teilfeld 5 A–B3
  9 B4
Tennisanlage Rothenbaum 7 B–C1
Tesdorpfstraße 7 C3
Thadenstraße 2 E–F2
  3 B–D2
Thalia Theater 6 D3
  10 E3
Thedestraße 2 E3
  3 A3, B2
Theodor-Heuss-Platz 5 B–C1
  7 B–C4
Theresienstieg 8 E–F2
Thielbek 9 B3
Thomasstraße 1 B1
Tiergartenstraße 7 A–B3, B4
Tokiostraße 5 C4–5
Tönsfeldtstraße 1 B3–4
Trommelstraße 2 F3–4
  3 B–C4
Trostbrücke 5 C3
  10 D4
TUI Operettenhaus 4 D4
Turmweg 7 B–C2

U
U-434 2 F4
  3 B5
Überseeallee 5–6 C–D5
Überseebrücke 4 F5
  5 A4
  9 A5
Uhlenhorster Weg 8 F2
Universität 5 A1
  7 A–B4, B3
  9 B1
Unzerstraße 2 E3
  3 B3

V
Valentinskamp 5 B2
  7 B5
  9 B–C2
Van-der-Smissen-Straße 2 D4

Vasco-da-Gama-Platz 5 C5
Venusberg 4 E–F4
  9 A4
Versmannstraße 6 D–F5
Virchowstraße 2 E3
  3 A2–4
Völckersstraße 1 B2
Vor dem Holstentor 4 F1–2
  5 A1–2
  7 A4–5
  9 A1–2
Vorsetzen 4 F5
  5 A4
  9 B5
Vorwerkstraße 4 E1

W
Walter-Möller-Park 3 E–F2
  3 B3
Walther-Kunze-Straße 2 D–E2
  3 A1
Warburgstraße 5 C1
  7 C3–4
  10 D1
Warnholtzstraße 3 A2
Werderstraße 7 A–C1
Wexstraße 5 B3
  9 B3
Willebrandtstraße 2 D2–3
Willy-Brandt-Straße
  5–6 C4, D3
  9–10 C–E5
Wincklerstraße 4 F4
  5 A3
  9 B4
Windhukstraße 1 A2
Winklers Platz 2 F2
  3 C2
Winterstraße 1 C3
Wohlers Allee 2 F1–2
  3 B1–2
Wohlerspark 2 E–F2
Wohlwillstraße
  3–4 C3, D2
Wolfgangsweg 4 F5
  9 A5
Woltmanstraße 6 E3–4
Woyrschweg 1 A1

Z
Zeiseweg 2 E1–2
  3 A1
Zeißstraße 1 C2
Zeughausmarkt 4 E4
  5 A3
  9 A4
Zeughausstraße 4 E4
  9 A4
Zimmerstraße 8 F1
Zippelhaus 5 C4
  10 D4–5
Zirkusweg 4 D4–5
Ziviljustizgebäude 4 F2
  5 A2
  9 A2
Zollamt 5 B2
  7 B4
  9 C1–2

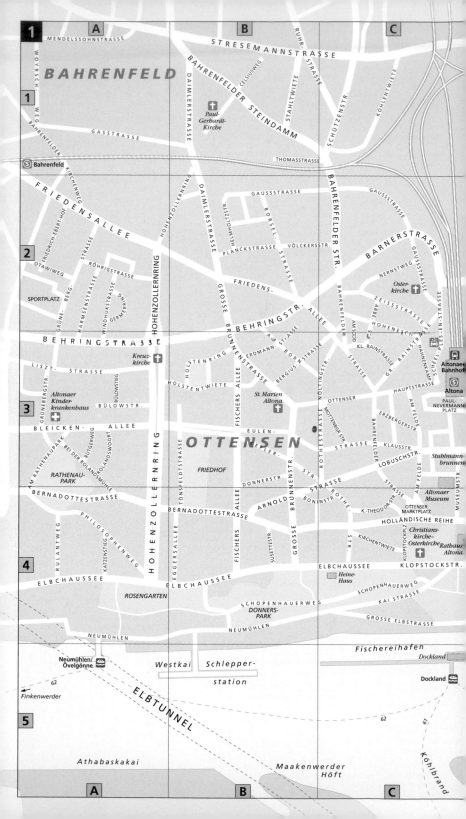

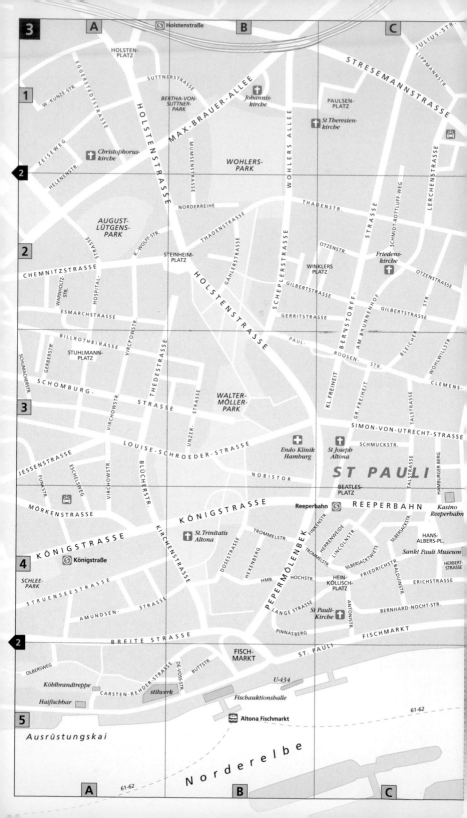

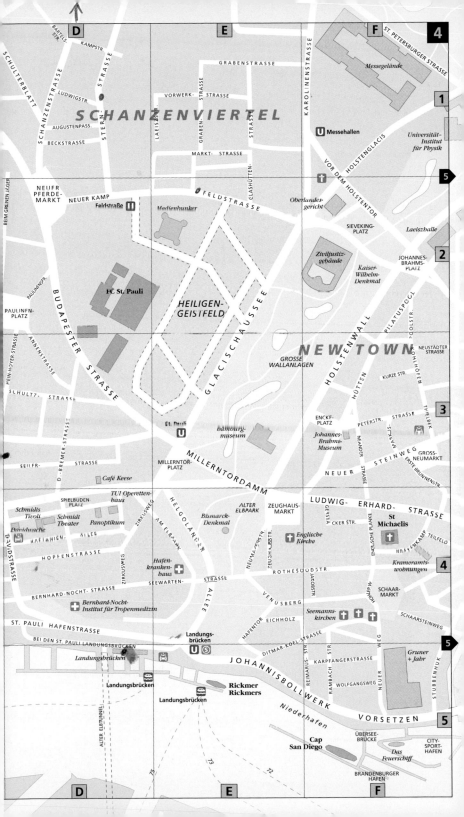

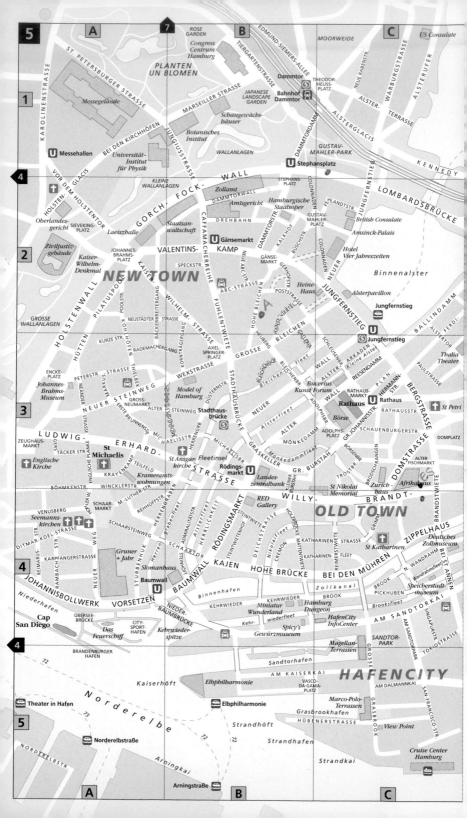

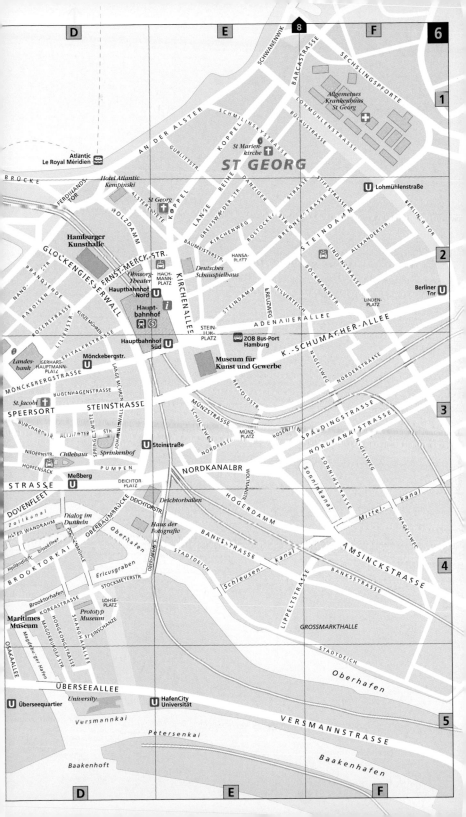

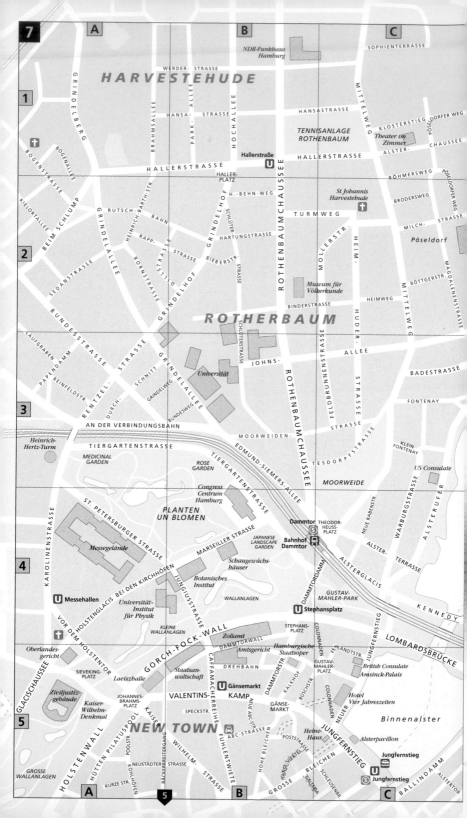

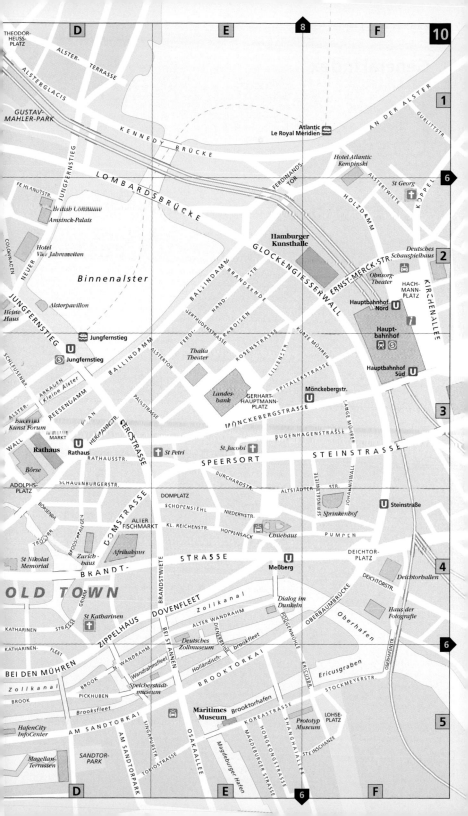

General Index

3Freunde (bar) 206, 207
25 Hours Hotel No. 1 181
3001 Kino (cinema) 205

A

A&O Hamburg Reeperbahn 181
A&O Hostel Hamburg 174, 175
Abaton (movie theatre) 205
ABBA 105, 210
Abtei (hotel) 176
Actors 43
ADAC (Allgemeiner Deutscher
   Automobilclub) 234, 235
Adalbrand (Archbishop) 22
Adaldag (Archbishop) 21
ADFC (Allgemeiner Deutscher
   Fahrradclub) 214, 215, 235
Adolf I, Count of Schauenburg 22
Adolf II, Count of Schauenburg 22
Adolf III, Count of Schauenburg 22,
   145
Adolf IV, Count of Schauenburg 22,
   23
Advance ticket sales 202
Aero ballooning company 221
Afghanisches Museum 33, 147
Afrikahaus 145
AIDAvita (cruise ship) 49
Air Berlin 230, 231
Air Canada 230, 231
Air Hamburg 49, 221, 222
air travel 230–31
Airbnb (agency) 174, 175
Airbus-Werk 48
Airport Office 225, 231
Airport transfers 231, 238
Albers, Hans 42, 43
   birth house 129
ALEX im Alsterpavillon (restaurant)
   124, 191
Allgemeiner Deutscher
   Automobilclub (ADAC) 234, 235
Allgemeiner Deutscher Fahrradclub
   (ADFC) 214, 215
Alma Hoppe Lustspielhaus 205
alpincenter 215
Alster see Around the Alster
Alster Arcades 5, 12, 18, 36, 57, 58,
   121, 198
Alster boat tours 11, 240–41
Alster-Schwimmhalle 214, 215
Alster-Touristik GmbH 241
Alsterarkaden see Alster Arcades
Alsterburg 22
Alsterfleet 56, 67
Alsterfontäne 122, 124
Alsterhaus 10, 124, 198, 201
Alsterpavillon 11, 122, 124
Alstervergnügen (festival) 45, 203
Alstervorland 39, 128
Alt Hamburger Aalspeicher
   (restaurant) 145, 188
Altamira (restaurant) 190
Alter Botanischer Garten 69
Alter Elbtunnel 37, 50, 93, 148
Alter Leuchtturm (Borkum) 160
Altes Land 133, 138

Altona 112–19
   area map 113
   boutique hotels 177–8
   budget hotels 181
   business hotels 181
   getting there 113
   Landungsbrücken to Altonaer
      Balkon (walk) 148–9
   restaurants 190–91
   Street-by-Street map 114–15
Altonaer Balkon 13, 114, 115, 117,
   149
Altonaer Museum 30, 32, 115, 116–
   17
Altonaer Theater 115, 204, 205
Altonale 45
American Express 226
Amphore (café) 194, 196
Amrum 158
Amsinck, Gustav 123
Amsinck-Palais 123
Amsterdam im Dammtorpalais
   (hotel) 178
Andersen (cake shop) 195, 197
Andersen, Lale 161
Andrea Doria (Lindenberg) 206
Andreaskirche (Verden) 167
Angie's Nightclub 206–7
Anna Fuchs (clothing shop) 198,
   201
Ansgar (Bishop) 4, 21, 59, 145
AQUAFÖHR (wave pool) 158
Architects 42
Architecture 34–7
Arcotel Onyx Hamburg 177
Around the Alster 120–31
   area map 121
   boutique hotels 178
   business hotels 181
   character hotels 179
   getting there 121
   luxury hotels 176
   Museum für Kunst und Gewerbe
      130–31
   restaurants 191–2
   Street-by-Street map 122–3
The art of Hamburg (speciality
   shop) 200, 201
Astra (beer) 186
Astra-Stube (club) 206, 207
Athletes 43
Atlantic Kempinski (hotel) 121, 128,
   172, 176
ATMs 226
Au Quai (restaurant) 191
Auf der Reeperbahn nachts um halb
   eins (song) 105
Augstein, Rudolf 43
Aussen Alster (hotel) 178
Außenalster 11, 13, 121, 128
Austrian (airline) 230, 231
Authors 42
Autobahnen 232, 233
Automobile hire 233, 234, 235
Automobiles
   driving in Hamburg 234–5
   driving to Hamburg 233

Automobiles (cont.)
   hire cars 233, 234, 235
   parking 235
AVIS (car hire) 234, 235
Axel-Springer-Verlag 40, 229

B

B-Movie (movie theatre) 205
Bach, Carl Philipp Emanuel 42
Bach, Johann Sebastian 42, 62
Dat Backhus 185
Bäderland Hamburg 217
Bagel Brothers (sandwich shop) 195,
   197
Bahre, Ricardo 122
Ballin, Albert 26, 43, 93
BallinStadt - Auswandererwelt
   Hamburg 27, 33, 43, 93, 221
Baltrum 160
Balzac Coffee (coffee bar) 195, 197
Die Bank (restaurant) 183, 189
Banking Machines 226
Banks 226
Bar Cabana 206, 207
Bär Hamburg 206, 207
Bar Rossi 206, 207
Barbarossa, Emperor 22, 85
Barceló Hamburg 181
Bardowicker Speicher 67
Barkassen Meyer 49
Barkassen-Centrale 49, 241
Barlach, Ernst 43, 57, 117, 138
Bars 206–7
Bartholomäus-Therme 214, 215
Baseler Hof (hotel) 179
Baurs Park 138
Bavaria-Brauerei 106–7, 186
Beach Clubs 207
Beanie Bee 194, 196
The Beatles 26, 206, 221
Beauty salons 200–201
bed & breakfast (agency) 174, 175
Bedford 194, 196
Bedroomforyou 174, 175
Beer 186
Behütet (hat shop) 200, 201
Benedict V, Pope 23
Behinderten-Ratgebar 174, 175, 203
Bensersiel (ferry terminal) 161
Bentheim, Lüder von 164, 165
Bentz, Johann Wilhelm 67
Bergedorfer Schifffahrtslinie 49
Berliner Bogen 37, 42
Bernhard II 22
Bertram see Meister Bertram
Best Western Plus Hotel St Raphael
   180
Beust, Ole von 27
Beylingstift 36, 73
Beyond Hamburg 150–69
   Bremen 162–7
   East Frisian Islands 160–61
   Helgoland 159
   Kiel Canal 161
   Museumsdorf Cloppenburg
      168–9
   North Frisian Islands 158

Beyond Hamburg (cont.)
  regional map 154–5
  Sylt **156–7**
Bicycling 214, 215, 235
  bicycle hire 214, 215, 235
  bicycle taxis 237
  bicycles on trains 238
Biikebrennen 158
Bild (newspaper) 229
Bildhauer 43
Billunger (dynasty) 22
Binnenalster 5, 11, 12, 13, 19, 38, 120, 121, 123, **124**, 126–7
Birdland (jazz club) 207
Bischofsburg 59, 144
Bismarck, Otto von 72
Bismarck-Denkmal 72
Bispingen 215
Bistum Hamburg 21
Black Form - Dedicated to the Missing Jews (monument by Sol LeWitt) 115, **117**
Blankenese 13, 113, 118, **139**
Blasendes Mädchen im Birkenwald (Modersohn-Becker) 167
Bleichenhof 76, 198
Block House (steakhouse chain) 182
Blohm + Voss 50, 118
Blücher-Altona, Conrad Daniel, Duke of (monument) 115
Blumfeld, Hotel-Pension von 181
Boat hire 214, 215
Boat tour 75
Boat travel 235, **240–41**
  A River View of Hamburg **48–51**
  arriving by boat 233
Bobby Reich (boat hire) 215
BoConcept (furniture shop) 199, 201
Boerner, Carl 83
Bolero (restaurant) 190
Bookstores 200, 201
Bootshaus Silwar 215
Bootsverleih Goldfisch 215
Borchert, Wolfgang 42
Borkum 154, 160
Börse see Stock Exchange
Boston Hamburg (hotel) 177
Bothe, Richter und Teherani 37
Böttcherstraße (Bremen) 166
Boulevard Hotel 176
Boutique Bizarre (lingerie) 200, 201
Boutique hotels 176–80
Braderup see Wenningstedt-Braderup
Brahms, Johannes 42, 73
Brandes, Gerhard 115, 117
Brandt, Emil 117
Brasserie Flum 191
Braviange (lingerie shop) 200, 201
Breckwoldt, Birke 200
Breitengrad (restaurant) 190
Bremen **162–7**
  map 163
  Rathaus 153, **164–5**
Bremen Town Musicians 154, 162
Bremer Landesmuseum für Kunst- und Kulturgeschichte see Focke-Museum

Bremerhaven 154, 162, 167
Bridges 18, 240
Brigitte (magazine) 229
Brix, Joseph 117
Brockes, Barthold Heinrich 42
Brodersen (restaurant) 191
Brücke (restaurant) 192
Brunsbüttel 160
Bucerius, Gerd 43
Bucerius Kunst Forum 32, 34, 36, 37, 57, **58**, 59
Buddy - The Musical 208, **211**
Budge Palace 131
Budget hotels 181
Bullerei (restaurant) 190
Burchardkai 243
Bureaux de Change 226
Bürgerschaft election 27
The burning of St Nicolai church during the night of 5 6 May 1842 8–9
Buses **232–3**, 236, **237**
Business hotels 180 81
busliniensuche 232, 233

C

Cabaret **204–5**
Café Backwahn 194, 196
Café Canale 194, 196
Café Destille 194, 196
Café Fees 194, 196
Café George Economou 65, 194, 196
Café Gnosa 207
Café Johanna 194, 196
Café Keese (club) 107
Café Klatsch 194, 196
Café Koppel 194, 196
Café Paris 182, **188**, 194, 196
Café Prüsse 194, 196
Café Smögen 194, 196
Café Stenzel 194, 196
Café SternChance 194, 196
Café Tarifa 194, 196
Café unter den Linden 194, 196
Cafés and Snack Bars **194–7**
Caffèteria 194, 196
Cake shops 195, 197
Call a Bike 235
Camping 175
Campus Suite (coffee bar) 195, 197
CANAIR Luftfahrtunternehmen 49
Canoe and kayak hire 214, 215
Cap San Diego 33, 51, **98–9**, 146, 173, 216
Caravela (coffee bar) 195, 197
Card telephones 228
Carlos Coffee (coffee bar) 195, 197
CARLS (restaurant) 189
Casino see Kasino Reeperbahn
Cats (musical) 105, 208, **210**, 211
Catwalk (shoe shop) 200, 201
CDU 27
Cell phones see Mobile telephones
Centrum Hotel Königshof 180
Character hotels 179–80
Charlemagne 21, 164

Charter 22–3
Chateauneuf, Alexis de 57, 58
Chéri Maurice 59
Cherry Blossom Festival 44
Children 216–17
  A Family Day 11
  in hotels 174
  information 216, 217
  museums 216
  parks and zoos 216
  in restaurants 183
  sports 217
  theatre 216–17
Chilehaus 35, 37, 42, **63**, 144
China Lounge (club) 206, 207
Cholera epidemic (1892) 25, 56
Christiansen, Uwe 206
Christiansen's (bar) 206, 207
Christmas market 47
Christopher Street Day 203
Churches
  Andreaskirche (Verden) 167
  Johanniskirche (Bremen) 166
  Johanniskirche (Verden) 167
  Mariendom 62
  Nikolaikirche (Helgoland) 159
  Pfarrkirche Unser Lieben Frauen (Bremen) 162
  St Jacobi 36, **62**
  St Johannis (Bremen) 166
  St Katharinen 36, **63**
  St Michaelis 10, 12, 13, 15, 18, 29, 34 36, 46, 69, 70, **74–5**
  St Nikolai (memorial) 36, **66**
  St Petri 36, **58–9**
  St-Petri-Dom (Bremen) 163
  St Salvator (Pellworm) 158
Cinema 128, 205
  Filmfest Hamburg 46, 203
  Sommerkino im Sternschanzenpark 45
CinemaxX (movie theatre) **205**
City House (hotel) 176–7
City Night Line 232, 233
City tours 220, 221
City-Sporthafen 51, 89, 214
Classen Secondhand 199, 201
Claudius, Mathias 42
Claus D. (tug boat) 135
Cloppenburg see Museumsdorf Cloppenburg
Clüver, Segebade 163
coffee bars 195, 197
Coin telephones 228
Collins, Phil 119
Colonnaden **76**
Color Line Arena see O2 World Hamburg
Columbus Haus 51, 84
Communications **228–9**
Confiserie Paulsen 195, 197
Constitution, first 25
Consulates 223
Container port 48
Continental (hotel) 179
The Continental System 25
Cotton Club (jazz club) 207

Cox (restaurant) 192
Credit cards 224, 226
  emergency numbers 226
Crowne Plaza Hamburg-City Alster
  181
Cruise Center see Hamburg Cruise
  Center
Cruises 233
Crusade, third 22
Cucinaria (speciality shop) 200, 201
Currency 226–7
Curry Queen (snack bar) 195, 197
Customs 220
Cycling 214, 215, 235

D

Dagebüll (ferry terminal) 158
Daily newspapers 223
Dal Fabbro (restaurant) 193
Dalmannkai 90
Dammtor 125
Daniel Wischer (restaurant) 188
Darboven, Albert 43
Daubner, Susanne 41
Davidwache 42, 103, **105**, 224
DB Rent 235
Deichgraf (restaurant) 145, **188**
Deichstraße 36, 55, **67**, 145
Deichtorcenter 37, 40, 42
Deichtorhallen 10, 12, 13, 30, 32, 37,
  62–3, 216
Delicatessens 200–201
Delphi Showpalast 209, **211**
Denmark 23, 25
DER SPIEGEL 41, 229
Derbyplatz Klein Flottbek 215
Design 199, 201
DesignLabor 131
Deutsche Bahn 232, 233
Deutsche Bank 226
Deutsche Presse-Agentur 40
Deutscher Bund 25
Deutscher Zollverein 25
Deutsches Derby (horse race) 215
Deutsches Pferdemuseum (Verden)
  167
Deutsches Salzmuseum (Lüneburg)
  223
Deutsches Schauspielhaus **129**,
  204, 205
Deutsches Schifffahrtsmuseum
  (Bremerhaven) 167
Deutsches Spring- und
  Dressurderby 215
Deutsches Zollmuseum 13, 33, 83,
  88, 147
Deutschlandhaus 77
DFM 198–9, 201
DHL 228
Dialog im Dunkeln 33, 83, **89**, 147
Diners Club 226
Dirty Dancing (musical) 119, 208, 211
Disabled Travellers
  buses 237
  entertainment 202–3
  hotels 174
  restaurants 183
  U- und S-Bahn 239
Dockland 12, 13, 27, **34**, 37, 42, 115,
  149

Dohnanyi, Klaus von 27
Dom (folk festival) see Hamburger
  Dom
Domherrenhaus (Verden) 167
Domingo, Plácido 77
Domplatz **59**, 144
Döner Queen (snack bar) 195, 197
Downtown Bluesclub 206
dpa see Deutsche Presse-Agentur
Dr. Götze - Land & Karte (bookshop)
  200, 201
Drachenboot-Festival 45, 203
Dragon boat races 85
Draußen vor der Tür (Borchert) 42
Drinks **186–7**
Druckwerkstatt Ottensen 200, 201
Drug hotline 225
Dschungelnächte (Jungle Nights)
  44
Duckstein Festival see Fleetinsel
  Festival
Dungeon see Hamburg Dungeon

E

E-mail 229
East Frisian Islands (Ostfriesische
  Inseln) 153, 154, **160–61**
East (hotel) 173, **177**
easyJet 230, 231
Eberlein, Gustav 117
EC/Maestro cards see girocard
EHIC card 225
Ehre, Ida 43
Ein Genius geleitet das Stadt-schiff
  (Barlach, Garbers) 117
Eisarena Planten un Blomen 217
Eisenstein (café/restaurant) **190**,
  194, 196
Eismeer (Friedrich) 64
Elba (restaurant) 149
Elbchaussee 12, 13, **118**
Elbe
  Alter Elbtunnel 26, 37, 50, **93**, 148
  HADAG ferries 49, 240–41
  Hamburg by boat **48–51**
  Neuer Elbtunnel 27, 37, 233
  Port and Speicherstadt **80–99**
Elbe 3 (lightship) 135
Elbe Erlebnistörns 49, 240, 241
Elbgold (café) 194, 196
Elbjazz Festival 44
Elbpark 69
Elbphilharmonie 12, 13, 27, 35, 37,
  51, 81, **88–9**, 90, 204
Elbtunnel see Alter Elbtunnel
Elbuferweg 113, 117
Eleazar Novum (hotel) 180
Elfriede (Ewer) 135
Elia und Max (café) 194, 196
Ellerntorsbrücke 28–9
Elton John 211
Emden (ferry terminal) 161
Emergencies 224–5
Emergency numbers 225
Empire Riverside Hotel 177
Ende, Hans am 167
Engel (restaurant) 192
English Theatre 204, 205
Enter the Dragon see Drachenboot-
  Festival

Entertainment **202–15**
  bars 206–7
  cabaret 204–5
  children 217
  clubs 206–7
  disabled travellers 202–3
  information 202, 203
  live music **206–7**
  movie theatres **205**
  music **204–5**
  musicals **208–11**
  opera and classical music **204–5**
  outdoor events 203
  sports **214–15**
  theatres **204–5**
  tickets 202, 203
Entrepreneurs 43
Entry requirements 222
Ernst Barlach Haus 32, 42, 138
Ernst Deutsch Theater 204, 205
Der Erzengel Michael im Kampf mit
  dem Drachen, Relief (Bremen) 166
Euro 227
Eurolines 233
Europa Passage 198, 201
Europäischer Hof (hotel) 179
Europcar (car hire) 231, 234, 235

F

Fabrik (live music) 207
Fachhochschule Bergedorf 47
Faerber, Friedrich Hermann 104
Fahrradladen Altona 215
Fahrradladen St. Georg 215
Fahrradverleih Altona 235
Fairmont Hotels & Resorts 125
Fall in Hamburg 46
Famous Hamburgers **42–3**
Fare system 236
Fashion shops 198–9, 201
Faust (Goethe) 129
FC St. Pauli **110–11**, 215
Fernsehturm see Heinrich-Hertz-
  Turm
Festivals **44–7**
Das Feuerschiff 51, **89**, 146, 173, 207
Fifty-Fifty (musical) 104, 211
Fillet of Soul (restaurant) 188
Financial Times Deutschland 229
Fink (hotel) 179
Fire brigade 225
Fischauktionshalle see Fish Auction
  Hall
Fischclub Blankenese (restaurant)
  192–3
Fischereihafen Restaurant 191
Fischerhaus (restaurant) 182, **190**
Fischmarkt see St Pauli Fish Market
Fish Auction Hall 36, 50, 108, 112,
  118–19, 148, 223
Flavours of Hamburg 184–5
Fleetfahrten 82, 241
Fleetinsel 76
Fleetinsel Festival 45, 76, 203
Flight information 231
Flights over Hamburg 49, 220, 221
Flimm, Jürgen 59
Flood (1962) 26
Floryaclub 206, 207

Flower of Uruguay (amethyst) 67
Focke-Museum (Bremen) 166
Föhr 158
Food and drink
  cafés and snack bars **194–7**
  cakes and chocolates 195, 197
  coffee bars and tea salons 195,
   197
  drinks 186–7
  Flavours of Hamburg 184–5
  restaurants **182–97**
  sandwich bars 195, 197
  soup bars 195–7
  What to drink **186–7**
fools garden (theatre) 204, 205
Football 110–11, 134, 215
Forsmann, Franz Gustav 36, 42, 66,
  123
Fosse – Die Show (musical) 211
Franks 21, 59
Frauencafé Endlich 207
Free Imperial City 24, 25
Freedom of the Seas 88
Freie Akademie der Künste 220
FREITAG-Taschen (speciality shop)
  199, 200, 201
Fresena im Dammtorpalais (hotel)
  179
Friedhof Ohlsdorf 38, 39, **134–5**
Friedrich, Caspar David 32, 64
Fritz Hotel 179
FRS Helgoline GmbH 241
Frühlingsdom 44
Fundus Theater 217
Funk Eck 194, 196
funke-ticket 202, 203
Furniture shops 199, 201
Further Afield **132–41**
  boutique hotels 178
  business hotels 181
  character hotels 180
  Hamburg Wadden Sea National
   Park **140–41**
  luxury hotels 176
  map 133
  restaurants 192–3
  Tierpark Hagenbeck **136–7**
Furtwängler, Maria 41

G

Gadermann (canoe and kayak hire)
  214, 215
Gala (magazine) 229
Galerie der Gegenwart *see*
  Hamburger Kunsthalle
Galerie Hotel Petersen 179
Galleria 76, 198
Galopprennbahn Horn 215
Gänsemarkt 19, **77**
Gänsemarkt-Passage 76, 198, 201
Garbers, Karl 117
Gardens *see* Parks and gardens
Garment (clothing shop) 199, 201
Gastwerk Hotel Hamburg 178
Gays 207
Generation Bar 207
Generator Hostel Hamburg 181
GEO (magazine) 40
The George Hotel 176

Gerd Bucerius Bibliothek 131
Gerhardt-Hauptmann-Platz 45
German Blade Challenge 215
German Reich 25
Getting Around Hamburg **234–41**
Getting to Hamburg 220, **230–33**
Gewürzmuseum *see* Spicy's
  Gewürzmuseum
Gezeitenland (wellness and
  adventure complex, Borkum) 160
girocard 226
Goethe, Johann Wolfgang von 129
Golden Cut (restaurant) 188
Golden Pudel Club 206, 207
Golf 215
Golf Lounge 215
Goßlers Park 138
Grabower Altar (Meister Bertram) 43
Graf Moltke (hotel) 179
Grand Élysée (hotel) 176
Great Days in Hamburg **10–13**
  3 Days in Hamburg 12
  5 Days in Hamburg 13
  48 Hours in Hamburg 12
  A Day on the Water 11
  A Family Day 11
  History and Culture 10
  Shopping in Style 10–11
Great fire (1842) 25, 57, 58, 67, 115
Green Party 27
Greenhouses 79
Gresham Carat Hotel 177
Grindel (Viertel) 18, 121, 223
Grönland (ship) 160
Groß-Hamburg-Gesetz 26
Große Bleichen 10
Große Elbstraße 148–9
Große Freiheit 36 (club) 206, 207
Große Kunstschau Worpswede 167
Großes Kaap (Borkum) 160
Großneumarkt 70, 71, 72
Großstadtrevier (TV series) 105
Gründgens, Gustaf 42, 129, 204
Gruner + Jahr 35, 37, 40, 68, 143,
  146, 229
Grüner Jäger (club) 206, 207
Guhr, Andreas 67
Guided tours 221, 234
GuteJacke (clothes shop) 199, 201

H

Haake Farmstead (Museumsdorf
  Cloppenburg) 168
HADAG ferries 49, 135, 222, 240, 241
Hadley's (café) 194, 196
Haerlin (restaurant) 192
Haerlin, Friedrich 123, 125
Hafen Hamburg (hotel) 179
Hafen-Hochbahn 12, 50, **92**, 238
HafenCity 12, 13, 27, 29, 32, 37, 81,
  90–91
HafenCity InfoCenter 11, 13, 32,
  90–91, 147
Hafenmuseum 135
Hafenstraße 108–9
Hagenbeck, Carl 43, 136, 137
Hagenbecks Tierpark *see* Tierpark
  Hagenbeck
Haifischbar 149, **190**

Haller, Martin 37, 42
Halligen 158
HAM 21 231
Hamann, Evelyn 43
Hamborger Veermaster (restaurant)
  190
Hamburg Airport 27, 230–31
Hamburg anders erfahren (bicycle
  hire) 235
Hamburg atlas 235
Hamburg CARD 223, 236
Hamburg City Beach Club 207
Hamburg City Man 214, 215
Hamburg City Tour 220, 221
Hamburg Cruise Center
  Altona 88, 114, 149, 233
  Hafen City 49, **88**, 147, 233
Hamburg Cruise Days 45
Hamburg cuisine 184–5
Hamburg del Mar (beach club) 207
Hamburg Dungeon 11, 82, 85, 147,
  217
Hamburg Freezers 215
Hamburg Inline-Skating Club 215
Hamburg kleine Hotels 173, 175
Hamburg-Lotse 221
Hamburg Marathon 44, 214, 215
hamburg-ticket 202, 203
Hamburg Tourismus GmbH 173,
  174, 175, 202, 216, 217, 220, 221
Hamburg Wadden Sea National
  Park **140–41**, 154
Hamburgbaum 78
Hamburger Abendblatt (newspaper)
  229
Hamburger Balkon 234
Hamburger Dom 11, 44, 45, 46, 203,
  217
Hamburger Jedermann 204, 205
Hamburger Kammerspiele 43, 204,
  205
Hamburger Krimifestival 46
Hamburger Kunsthalle 10, 12, 13,
  29, 30, 32, **64–5**
Hamburger Marlendom 62
Hamburger Morgenpost 229
Hamburger Pride Week 203
Hamburger Puppentheater 217
Hamburger Sparkasse 226
Hamburger Surffestival 44
Hamburger SV 110, 134, 215
Hamburger Theater Festival 46, 59
Hamburger Theaternacht 46
Hamburger Verkehrsverbund (HVV)
  236–7
Hamburgische Staatsoper **77**, 204,
  205
Hamburgisches Wattenmeer
  (national park) *see* Hamburg
  Wadden Sea National Park
hamburgmuseum 10, 12, 13, 21, 32,
  37, 42, 72, **73**
Hamburg's Best
  Architecture **34–7**
  Famous Residents **42–3**
  Media City **40–41**
  Museums and Galleries **30–33**
  Parks and Gardens **38–9**
Hammaburg 21, 22, 59, 73, 145
Handball 215

Hannah and Simeon in the Temple (Rembrandt) 64
Hans Albers Statue 103
Hans-Albers-Platz 103
Hansa Rundfahrt GmbH 220, 221
Hanse-Viertel 76, 198, 201
Hanseatic Helicopter Service 49
Hanseatic League 24–5
Hanseatic Trade Center 51, 147
Hanseballon 221
Hanseboot 46
Hansekogge 167
Hansen, Christian Frederik 118
HAPAG (Reederei) 25, 93, 124
Happy Hamburg Reisen 174, 202
Harbour ferries 49, 135, 222, 240, 241
Harbour Front Literaturfestival 46
Harbour tours 11, 48, 49, 222, 240
Harburg 24
Harlesiel (ferry terminal) 161
Harmstorf, Raimund 43
Harry's Hafenbasar 105
Haubach, Theodor 42
Hauke Drube - Schmuck und Uhren 199, 201
Hauptbahnhof 12, 35, 37, **62**, 218–19
  Wandelhalle 62, 198, 201
Haus Bernstein 141
Haus der Bürgerschaft (Bremen) 162
Health insurance 225
Heiligengeistfeld 109
Heimatmuseum (Langeoog) 161
Heine, Salomon 38, 122
Heine-Haus 122
Heine-Park 38
Heinrich Heine Buchhandlung (bookshop) 200, 201
Heinrich-Heine-Denkmal 55
Heinrich-Hertz-Turm 37, 42, **77**, 78
Heiße Ecke - Das St Pauli Musical 104, 211
Helgoland **159**, 241
Hello (clothing shop) 198, 201
Helms-Museum für Archäologie 59
Hempel's Beatles Tour 221
Henri Hotel 176
Henssler & Henssler (restaurant) 191
Herr Max (cake shop) 195, 197
Die Herren Simpel (café) 194, 196
Hertz (car hire) 234, 235
Hertz, Heinrich 77
Herzblut St. Pauli (restaurant) 103
Herzog & de Meuron 37, 88–9
Hessepark 138
Heymann (bookshop) 200, 201
HighFlyer Hamburg 12, 13, **63**, 217, 221
hin & veg (snack bar) 195, 197
Historisches Museum - Domherrenhaus (Verden) 167
History of Hamburg 20–27
Hochschule für Musik und Theater 125, 204–5
Hoetger, Bernhard 166, 167
Höger, Fritz 37, 42, 63, 144
Holiday apartments 174
Holiday Inn Hamburg 181
Holidays 47

Holsten-Brauerei 186
Holthusen Spa 214, 215
Horn, Galopprennbahn 215
Horn racetrack *see* Galopprennbahn Horn
Hörnum 156–7
Hosaeus, Herman 83
Hospitals 225
Hotel am Elbufer 179
Hotels **172–81**
  Altona 177–8, 181
  Around the Alster 176, 178, 179, 181
  boutique 176–8
  budget 181
  business 180–81
  camping 175
  character 179–80
  children 174
  disabled travellers 174
  einfach Hamburg (agency) 173, 175
  Further Afield 176, 178, 180, 181
  hotel categories 172
  hotel chains 173
  list of hotels **176–81**
  luxury 176
  New Town 177, 179, 180
  Old Town 176–7, 179, 180, 181
  package deals 173
  Port and Speicherstadt 177, 181
  private rooms 174
  reservations 173, 182
  St Pauli 177, 179, 181
  self-catering flats 174
  ship hotels 173
  youth hostels 175
Hours of sunshine 45
HSV *see* Hamburger SV
HSV-Arena (Volksparkstadion) 27, 38, 84, **134**
HSV-Museum 33, **134**
Hummel, Wasserträger **67**
Hummelfest *see* Sommerdom
Hummer Pedersen (fine food shop) 200, 201
Husmann, Carsten 163
Hüttenzauber – Die Show (musical) 211
HVV 236–7
  map *see* back inside cover
Hygieia-Brunnen 56, 61

Ibis budget Hamburg Altona 181
Ice hockey 215
Ice-skating 47
Ich war noch niemals in New York (musical) 105, 208, **210**, 211
Imam Ali Mosque 129
Immendorf, Jörg 102
Immigration 220
Imtech-Arena *see* HSV-Arena
In-line skating 215
IndoChine (restaurant) 190
Indochine Ice Bar 206, 207
Inhabitants 14
Inlineskating Hamburg 215
InterCity Hotel Hamburg Altona 181
InterCity Hotel Hamburg Hauptbahnhof 180

InterCityExpress 233
International Exchange 226
International Maritime Museum Hamburg *see* Maritime Museum
International Summer Festival 45, 204
Internationale Musikfest Hamburg 44
Internationales Haus der Fotografie 62
Internet cafés 229
Iphigenie auf Tauris (Goethe) 129
Islamisches Zentrum Hamburg 129
Itineraries **10–13**
  3 Days in Hamburg 12
  5 Days in Hamburg 13
  48 Hours in Hamburg 12
  A Day on the Water 11
  A Family Day 11
  History and Culture 10
  Shopping in Style 10–11
Ivar Kranz (jewellery shop) 199, 201

J

Jacobikirche **62**
Jacobs Restaurant 193
Jahreszeiten Deli (sandwich shop) 195, 197
Jahreszeiten Grill (restaurant) 192
Japanese Cherry-Blossom Festival 44
Japanese Garden with Teahouse 79
Jazzclub Bergedorf 207
Jazzclub im Stellwerk 207
Jedermann see Hamburger Jedermann
Jenisch, Martin Johann von 138
Jenisch Haus 32, 42, 138
Jenischpark 13, 32, 38, **138**
Jewellery shops 199, 201
Jewish cemetery 115
Jewish communities 117
Jews in Hamburg, Black Form - Dedicated to the Missing Jews (monument by Sol LeWitt) 114, **117**
Johannes-Brahms-Museum 33, **73**
Johanniskirche (Bremen) 166
Johanniskirche (Verden) 167
Juist **160**
Juister Musikfestival 160
Jung, Holger 40
Jung von Matt (ad agency) 40
Junges Forum Musik + Theater 204, 205
Junges Hotel 177
Junges Schauspielhaus 204
Jungfernstieg 10, 12, 13, 120, 121, 122, **125–6**
Jürgens, Udo 105, 210

K

k3 Stadtführungen 221
Kabel, Heidi 43, 129
Kaffeerösterei Burg 200, 201
Kaiser-Wilhelm-Kanal *see* Nord-Ostsee-Kanal
Kaispeicher B 91, 221
Kajüte (restaurant) 191
Kammerspiele *see* Hamburger Kammerspiele

Kampen 156
Kampnagel 204, 205
Kamtschatka-Bären 137
Kapitän Prüsse (ferry service) 241
Kartoffelkeller (restaurant) 145
Käse, Wein & mehr (fine food shop)
  200, 201
Kasino Reeperbahn 202
Kehrwieder (theatre) 147
Kehrwiederspitze 19, 37, 51, **84**, 147
Kesselhaus see HafenCity InfoCenter
Kiel Canal 14, 153, 160, **161**
KinderKunstMuseum 216, 217
Kindernetz Hamburg 216, 217
Konditorei Lindtner (cake shop) 195,
  197
Kirchner, Ernst Ludwig 65
Kleine Alster 56
Kletterzentrum Hamburg 215
Klick Kindermuseum 216–17
Klimahaus Bremerhaven 8°Ost 167
Klopstock, Friedrich Gottlieb 42
Klose, Hans-Ulrich 27
Knust (live music) 207
Knuth (café) 194, 196
Köhlbrand 135
Köhlbrandbrücke 27, 34, 37, 49, 117,
  133, **135**, 220
Köhlbrandtreppe 118, 142, 149
Kolumbus statue (Boerner) 83
Komet Bar 206, 207
Komödie Winterhuder Fährhaus
  204, 205
König (café) 194, 196
Der König der Löwen (The Lion
  King) 93, 208, **211**, 212–13
Königliche Eisenbahndirektion 118
Kontorhaus district 26, 37, **63**, 144
Koppel 66 129
Kornhausbrücke 83
Krameramtsstuben (restaurant) see
  Zu den alten Krameramtsstuben
  am Michel
Krameramtswohnungen 10, 32, 36,
  70, **72**
Kreuzfahrtterminal see Hamburg
  Cruise Center
Kuchenwerkstatt (restaurant) 192
Kunsthalle see Hamburger
  Kunsthalle
Kunsthalle Bremen **166**
Kunsthandwerk 32
Kyti Voo (café) 194, 196

L

La Baracca (restaurant) 189
La Gondola 241
La Mirabelle (restaurant) 189
La Vela (restaurant) 191
La Vigna (wine shop) 200, 201
Labskaus 185
Laeiszhalle 37, 42, **73**, 204, 205
Landhaus Flottbek (hotel) 180
Landhaus Scherrer (restaurant) 193
Landungsbrücken 11, 12, 13, 29, 34,
  37, 50, 80, **93**, 146, 148
Lange Anna (Helgoland) 155, 159
Lange Nacht der Museen 30, 44,
  221
Langeoog 160–61

Laufen 214, 215
Le Plat du Jour (restaurant) 188
Le Royal Méridien (hotel) 174, **176**
Lederer, Hugo 72
Lenz, Siegfried 42
Lesbians 207
Lessing, Gotthold Ephraim 77
Lessingstatue 19, 69, 77
LeWitt, Sol 114, 117
Der Lichtbringer (Hoetger) 166
Liebermann, Max 118
Liegendes Mädchen am Rasenhang
  (Pissarro) 166
LiLaBe (festival) 47
Lindenberg, Udo 77, 42, **206**
Lindner Park-Hotel Hagenbeck 178
Lingerie shops 200–201
List 156–7
Literaturhaus 46, **129**
Literaturhaus Café 194, 196
Littmann, Corny 104, 204, 211
Live music **206–7**
Lloyd Webber, Andrew 211
Loch Rannoch (tanker) 96–7
Loenicker, Nils 205
Logo (live music) 207
Long-distance buses 232
Lost and found (Deutsche Bahn)
  225
Lost and Found of Hamburg,
  Central 225
Louis C. Jacob (hotel) 118, **176**
Louis the German 21
Louis the Pious 21, 22
Lufthansa 230, 231
Lühmanns Teestube 195, 197
Lush (beauty shop) 200, 201
Lutter & Wegner (restaurant) 191
Luxor (restaurant) 190
Luxury hotels 176

M

Mackensen, Fritz 167
Mädchen auf der Brücke (Munch) 65
Madison Hamburg 177
Maestro card see girocard
Magdeburger harbour 91
Magellan-Terrassen 89, 91
Magic Flute (Mozart) 77
Mama (restaurant) 188
Mamma Mia (musical) 105, 208,
  210, 211
Man Wah (restaurant) 190
Mandy in Love (musical) 211
Manet, Édouard 65
Maps
  Altona 113
  architecture 34–5
  Around the Alster 121, 122–3
  Bremen 163
  Central Hamburg 18–19
  Europe 15
  excursions 154–5
  From the Alter Elbtunnel to
    HafenCity 50–51
  Germany 14–15
  Greater Hamburg 16–17
  HafenCity 90–91
  Hamburg Airport 230
  Hamburg by boat 48–9

Maps (cont.)
  Hamburg Wadden Sea National
    Park 140–41
  Helgoland 159
  Kiel Canal 161
  media 40–41
  museums and galleries 30–31
  Museumsdorf Cloppenburg 168
  New Town 69, 70–71
  Nord-Ostsee-Kanal see Kiel Canal
  Old Town 55, 56–7
  parks and gardens 38–9
  Planten un Blomen **78–9**
  Port and Speicherstadt 81
  Rathaus and Alster Arcades 56–7
  Reeperbahn 102–3
  St Pauli 101
  Speicherstadt 82–3
  Street finder maps **242–57**
  Sylt **156–7**
  Tierpark Hagenbeck 136–7
  Walk: Harbour promenade and
    Speicherstadt 146–7
  Walk: Landungsbrücken to
    Altonaer Balkon 148–9
  Walk: Old Town 144–5
  Walking tours: overview 143
Marblau (restaurant) 188
Marcks, Gerhard 162
Mariendom 59, 62
Marinehof (restaurant) 189
Maritim (Brandes) 115, 117
Maritim Hotel Reichshof 173, **177**
Maritime distress observation
  station (Langeoog) 161
Maritime Museum 12, 13, 33, **86–7**,
  91, 221
Markt der Völker 128
Marktplatz (Bremen) 162
Maskenzauber an der Alster 47
MasterCard 226
Matsumi (restaurant) 189
Matt, Jean-Remy von 40
Max & Consorten (restaurant) 183,
  191
Max Jens GmbH 49
MAY (café) 194, 196
[m]eatery (restaurant) 190
Media **40–41**
Medical care 225
Medical emergency 225
Meerwein (restaurant) 189
Meister Bertram 43, 64
Mendelssohn Bartholdy, Felix 42
Menken, Alan 210
Merchant guilds 23
Mercure Hotel Hamburg Mitte 180
Meßberg 145
Meßberghof (office building) 63
Der Messias (Klopstock) 42
Messmer Momentum (tea salon)
  195, 197
Metropolis 205
Michaeliskirche see St Michaelis
Michel see St Michaelis
Middle Stone Age 21
MidSommerland Harburg 214, 215
Millerntor-Stadion 45, 110, 111
Mindways Segway Citytour
  Hamburg 221

Mini-golf 79, 216
Miniatur Wunderland (model-railway) 11, 12, 13, 33, 82, **84**, 147, 216, 217
Mobile telephones 229
Model of Hamburg 72
Model railway (Miniatur Wunderland) 84
Modersohn, Otto 167
Modersohn-Becker, Paula 166, **167**
Modersohn-Becker-Museum (Bremen) 166
Molotow (live music) 207
Mönckebergstraße 19, 57, 198
Moneypenny 200
Montanhof (office building) 63
Montblanc (jewellery shop) 199, 201
Monuments and statues
 Bishop's Tower 59
 Bismarck-Denkmal 72
 Black Form - Dedicated to the Missing Jews (monument by Sol LeWitt) 114, 117
 Emperor Wilhelm I 79, 114, 117, 242
 Hammaburg 59
 St Nikolai (memorial) 66
Moorwerder 24
Morellino (restaurant) 193
Der Morgen (Runge) 64
Mövenpick Hotel Hamburg 109, 177
Mozart! (musical) 210, 211
Müller, Ina 71
Müller, Johanne Henriette Marie (Zironenjette) 71
Munch, Edvard 65
Museum Altes Land 138
Museum der Arbeit 30, 33, 132, **135**
Museum für Hamburgische Geschichte *see* hamburgmuseum
Museum für Kunst und Gewerbe 10, 12, 13, 30, 32, **130–31**
Museum für Völkerkunde 13, 30, **128**, 216
Museum mile 10, 32
Museum SteinZeiten *see* RED Gallery
Museums and Galleries
 exploring **30–33**
 for children 216
 practical information **221**
 Afghanisches Museum 33, 147
 Altonaer Museum 30, 32, 115, **116–17**
 BallinStadt – Auswanderer-welt Hamburg 33, **93**, 221
 Bucerius Kunst Forum 32, 34, 36, 37, 57, **58**
 Cap San Diego 24, 33, **98–9**
 Deichtorhallen 30, 32, **62–3**, 216
 Deutsches Pferdemuseum (Verden) 167
 Deutsches Salzmuseum (Lüneburg) 223
 Deutsches Schifffahrtsmuseum (Bremerhaven) 167
 Deutsches Zollmuseum 13, 33, 83, **88**, 147
 Dialog im Dunkeln 33, **89**, 147

Museums and Galleries (cont.)
 Domherrenhaus (Verden) 167
 Ernst Barlach Haus 32, 42, **138**
 Das Feuerschiff (lightship) 89
 Focke-Museum (Bremen) 166
 Große Kunstschau Worpswede 167
 Hamburger Kunsthalle 10, 12, 13, 30, 32, **64–5**
 hamburgmuseum 10, 12, 13, 30, 32, 37, 42, 72, **73**
 Harry's Hafenbasar **105**
 Haus Bernstein (Neuwerk island) 141
 Historisches Museum – Domherrenhaus (Verden) 167
 HSV-Museum 33, **134**
 Internationales Haus der Fotografie 62
 Jenisch Haus 32, 42, **138**
 Johannes-Brahms-Museum 33, **73**
 KinderKunstMuseum 216, 217
 Klick Kindermuseum 216, 217
 Klimahaus Bremerhaven 8°Ost 167
 Kunsthalle Bremen 166
 Lange Nacht der Museen 30, 44, 221
 Maritime Museum 12, 13, 33, **86–7**, 91, 221
 Museum Altes Land 138
 Museum der Arbeit 30, 33, 132, **135**
 Museum für Hamburgische Geschichte *see* hamburgmuseum
 Museum für Kunst und Gewerbe 10, 12, 13, 30, 32, **130–31**
 Museum für Völkerkunde 13, 30, **128**, 216
 Museumsdorf Cloppenburg 154, **168–9**
 Museumshafen Övelgönne 13, 33, **135**, 143, 149
 Panoptikum 12, 13, 33, **104**
 Paula-Modersohn-Becker-Museum (Bremen) 166
 Prototyp Museum **89**, 221
 RED Gallery 33, **67**
 Rickmer Rickmers 11, 12, 13, 30, 33, **94–5**, 221
 Roselius-Haus (Bremen) 166
 St. Pauli Museum 102, 105, 221
 Speicherstadtmuseum 13, 30, 32, 83, **85**, 135, 147
 Spicy's Gewürzmuseum 33, **84**, 147
 Spiekerooger Muschelmuseum 161
 Spielzeugmuseum im Schnoor (Bremen) 166
 Telemann-Museum 73
 U-434 13, 33, **108**
 Überseemuseum (Bremen) 166
 Universum Science Center (Bremen) **166**
 Worpsweder Kunsthalle 167
Museumsdienst Hamburg 221
Museumsdorf Cloppenburg 154, **168–9**
Museumshafen Övelgönne 13, 33, **135**, 143, 149

Museumsverband Hamburg e.V. 221
Music **204–5**
 Hamburgische Staatsoper 77, 204, 205
 Laeiszhalle **73**, 204, 205
 live music **206–7**
 musicals **208–11**
 Neue Flora **119**
 Schleswig-Holstein Musik Festival 45
 Schmidts Tivoli **104**
 Theater im Hafen Hamburg **92**
 TUI Operettenhaus **105**
Music halls *see* Laeiszhalle
Musical-Express 49
Musicals **208–11**
 behind-the-scenes tours 209
 Buddy - The Musical 208, **211**
 Cats 105, 208, **210**, 211
 Delphi Showpalast 209, **211**
 Dirty Dancing 119, 208, 211
 Fifty Fifty 104, 211
 Fosse – Die Show 211
 Heiße Ecke – Das St Pauli Musical 211
 Hüttenzauber – Die Show 211
 Ich war noch niemals in New York 105, 208, **210**, 211
 Der König der Löwen (The Lion King) 93, 208, **211**, 212–13
 Mamma Mia 105, 208, **210**, 211
 Mandy in Love 211
 Mozart! 210, 211
 Neue Flora **119**, 208, 209, **210–11**
 Oh Alpenglühn! 211
 Oh, What a Night! 211
 Paul & Paula 211
 Phantom der Oper 119, 208, 210, **211**
 Rocky 209, **210**, 211
 Schmidts Tivoli **104**, 209, **211**
 Sister Act 105, 208, **210**, 211
 Starcut 211
 Tanz der Vampire 208, 211
 Tarzan 119, 208, 209, **210–11**
 Theater im Hafen Hamburg **92**, 208, 209, 210, **211**
 tickets 209
 Titanic 119, 210, 211
 TUI Operettenhaus **105**, 208, 209, **210**, 211
 venues 209, **210–11**
 Westerland 211
Musicians 42

N

Nana (Manet) 65
Nannen, Henri 43
Napoleon's rule 25
Nationalpark Hamburgisches Wattenmeer *see* Hamburg Wadden Sea National Park
Nationalpark Niedersächsisches Wattenmeer *see* Wadden Sea National Park of Lower Saxony
Nationalpark Schleswig-Holsteinisches Wattenmeer *see* Wadden Sea National Park of Schleswig-Holstein
Nationalpark-Haus (Wangerooge) 161

Naturbad Stadtparksee 214, 215
NDR *see* Norddeutscher Rundfunk
Neßmersiel (ferry terminal) 161
Neue Flora **119**, 208, 209, **210–11**
Das Neue Landhaus Walter
   (restaurant) 193
Neue Nikolaikirche 66
Neuer Jungfernstieg 5, 125
Neuer Leuchtturm (Borkum) 160
Neuer Wall 10, 13, 198
Neuharlingersiel (ferry terminal) 161
Neumeier, John 77, 204
Neuwerk island 139, 141, 241
New Town **68–79**
   area map 69
   boutique hotels 177
   business hotels 180
   character hotels 179
   getting there 69
   Planten un Blomen **78–9**
   restaurants 188–9
   St Michaelis **74–5**
   Street-by-Street map 70–71
New Year's Eve 47
Newspapers and magazines 40, 229
NH Hamburg-Horn (hotel) 181
Nicolas I, Pope 59
Niebüll 155
Niedersächsisches Wattenmeer
   (national park) *see* Waddden Sea
   National Park of Lower Saxony
Nige Hus (hotel) 180
Nigehörn 141
Night clubs **206–7**
Nikolaikirche (Helgoland) 159
Nikolaikirche (memorial) 56, **66**
Nil (restaurant) 190
Nippon (hotel) **178**
Nivea Haus 123, 124, 198, 200, 201
Nord-Ostsee-Kanal *see* Kiel Canal
Norddeich (ferry terminal) 161
Norddeutscher Rundfunk 40–41
Norderney 160
Nordfriesische Inseln *see* North
   Frisian Islands
Nordstrand 158
North Frisian Islands (Nord-
   friesische Inseln) 154, **158**
Nossack, Hans Erich 42
Novum Hotel am Holstenwall
   175, **180**

O

O2 World Hamburg 206, 207, 215
Oberhafen Kantine (restaurant) 189
Oberland (Helgoland) 159
Obodrites 21
Octopus (furniture shop) 199, 201
Oevelgönne *see* Museumshafen
   Övelgönne
Oh Alpenglühn! (musical) 211
Oh It's Fresh! (sandwich bar) 195,
   197
Oh, What a Night! (musical) 211
Ohnsorg-Theater 43, **129**, 204, 205
Old Commercial Room (restaurant)
   189
Old Town **54–67**
   area map 55
   boutique hotels 176–7

Old Town (cont.)
   budget hotels 181
   business hotels 180
   character hotels 179
   getting there 55
   Hamburger Kunsthalle **64–5**
   luxury hotels 176
   Rathaus **60–1**
   restaurants 188
   Street-by-Street map 56–7
   walk **144–5**
Oldenburg (Coast Guard cutter) 86
Opera **204**, 205
   Hamburgische Staatsoper 77, 204,
      205
   Junges Forum Musik + Theater
      204, 205
   Laeiszhalle **76**, 204, 205
Operettenhaus *see* TUI
   Operettenhaus
Opernloft 217
Orang-utans 137
Ordeelbook 23
Osterfeuer 44
Ostfriesische Inseln *see* East Frisian
   Islands
Ottensen, Stadtcafé 194, 196
Otto V, Duke of Holstein-
   Schaumburg 118
Otto, Waldemar 56
Outdoor activities 203
Övelgönne *see* Museumshafen
   Övelgönne
Overbeck, Fritz 167
OXMOX (local newspaper) 202

P

Package tours 174, 202, 220, 230,
   232
Paddling 214, 215
Painters and sculptors 43
Palmaille 12, 13, 36, **118**
Palmers (lingerie shop) 200, 201
Panoptikum 12, 13, 33, 102, **104**
Pappnase & Co (speciality shop)
   200, 201
Park Hyatt Hamburg (hotel) 176
Parking 235
Parks and gardens
   Alstervorland 39, 128
   Baurs Park 138
   exploring **38–9**
   Friedhof Ohlsdorf 39, 134
   Goßlers Park 138
   Heine-Park 38
   Hessepark 138
   Jenischpark 13, 38, **138**
   Planten un Blomen 12, 13, 29, 39,
      45, **78–9**, 203, 216, 217
   Rhododendron-Park (Bremen) 166
   Stadtpark 11, 39, 134, 139, 216,
      217
   Sternschanzenpark 13, **109**, 203
   Tierpark Hagenbeck 38, 136–7
   Volkspark 38
Passages 12, 13, 37, **76**, 198
Paul & Paula (musical) 211
Paula-Modersohn-Becker-Museum
   (Bremen) 166
Paving stones 143

Pellworm 158
Persienhaus 147
Perthes, Friedrich Christoph 43
Petersen, Jan-Peter 205
Petit Café 194, 196
Pfarrkirche Unser Lieben Frauen
   (Bremen) 162
Pferdesport 215
Phantom der Oper (musical) 119,
   208, 210, **211**
Pharmacies 224, 225
   Pelikan-Apotheke 70
Philharmonisches Staats-orchester
   Hamburg 77
Piazza Romana (restaurant) 192
Pinnau, César 99
Pirates 24, 43
Pissarro, Camille 166
Plague epidemic (1350) 24
Planetarium 11, 134, 217
Planten un Blomen 12, 13, 29, 39,
   45, **78–9**, 203, 216, 217
Platz der Republik 13, 115, **116**, 149
Police 225
Politicians 42
Polizeirevier Davidwache (film) 105
Pony rides 216
Port and Speicherstadt 12, 13, 29,
   36, 47, 48, **80–99**
   area map 80–81
   boutique hotels 177
   business hotels 181
   Cap San Diego **98–9**
   character hotels 179
   getting there 81
   HafenCity **90–91**
   Harbour promenade and
      Speicherstadt (walk) 146–7
   Landungsbrücken to the Altonaer
      Balkon (walk) 148–9
   restaurants 189–90
   Rickmer Rickmers **94–5**
   Street-by-Street map:
      Speicherstadt **82–3**
Port's Birthday 44, **85**, 203, 222
Portugiesenviertel 182
Pöseldorf 121, **125**
Post offices 228
Postbank 226
Prayed (clothing shop) 199, 201
Precipitation 46
Pride Week 203
Principal churches 36
PRINZ (local newspaper) 202
Prinzenbar 207
Private rooms 174
Prototyp Museum **89**, 221
Public holidays 47
Publishing houses 40–41

Q

Quality Hotel Ambassador 180
Quatsch Comedy Club 102
Queen Mary II 88
Quinn, Freddy 42

R

Radio 229
Radisson Blu Hotel 180

Railway stations
Bahnhof Altona **116**, 232
Bahnhof Dammtor 37, **125**, 232
Bahnhof Harburg 232
Hauptbahnhof **62**, 232
Rathaus 5, 10, 12, 13, 18, 20, 25, 29, 35, 36, 42, 54, 56, 57, **60–61**, 144
Rathaus Altona 36, 114, **117**, 149
Rathaus Bremen 153, 162, **164–5**
Rathausmarkt 57, 144
Raven (Restaurant) 192
Red cliffs (Sylt) 156
RED Gallery 33, **67**
Red-light district tour see Rotlichttour
Red-brick architecture 63
Reederei Cassen Eils 139, 241
Reederei Sloman 147
Reederei Woermann 145
Reemtsma, Hermann 138
Reeperbahn 12, 13, 29, **102–3**, 104
Reeperbahn Festival 46
Reichsbank building, former 58
Reinhard, Ernie 104
ReiseBank 226
Reisen Hamburg (Messe) 47
Reisechecks 226
Reiterhof Ohlenhoff (hotel) 100
Rembrandt 64
Renaissance Hotel Hamburg 180
Restaurants **182–97**
Altona 190–91
Around the Alster 191–2
Cafés and snackbars **194–7**
children 183
disabled travellers 183
drinks 186–7
Flavours of Hamburg **184–5**
Further Afield 192–3
list of restaurants **188–93**
New Town 188–9
Old Town 188
Port and Speicherstadt 189–90
prices 183
reservations 182
St Pauli 190
smoking 183
tips and tipping 183
vegetarian dishes 183
What to drink **186–7**
Rhododendron-Park (Bremen) 166
Rialto (restaurant) 183, **189**
Rickmer Rickmers 11, 12, 13, 29, 30, 33, 50, **94–5**, 146, 216
The Rilano Hotel Hamburg 177
Rilke, Rainer Maria 167
Ristorante Galatea 191
Ristorante Portonovo 192
Rive (restaurant) 191
Riverkasematten (restaurant) 149
Rob & Stephen's little cake Co. (cake shop) 200, 201
Rocky (musical) 209, **210**, 211
Rödingsmarkt 144
Roland statue (Bremen) 162
Rollschuhbahn (Planten un Blomen) 79, 217
Romantik-N ächte 45
Roselius, Ludwig 166
Roselius-Haus (Bremen) 166

Rosenberg, Harry 105
Rosenberg, Karin 105
Die Rösterei (café) 194, 196
Die Roten Doppeldecker (agency) 220, 221
Rotlichttour 221
Rowing 214, 215
Rudolf Beaufays (second-hand shop) 199, 201
Runde, Ortwin 27
Runge, Philipp Otto 43, 64
Running 214, 215
Ruwoldt, Hans Martin 43

S
S-Bahn 238–9
Sagebiels Fährhaus (restaurant) 193
Sâi gón (restaurant) 193
Sailing 214, 215
St Annen (hotel) 181
St Georg (city district) 12, 18, **129**, 206, 207
St George the Dragon-Slayer 22, 66
St Jacobi 36, **62**, 144
St Johannis (Bremen) 166
St Katharinen 36, **63**
St-Lukas-Altar (St Jacobi) 62
St Michaelis 10, 12, 13, 15, 18, 29, 34, 36, 46, 69, 70, **74–5**
St Nikolai Memorial 10, 18, 32, 36, **66**, 144
St Pauli **100–111**
area map 101
boutique hotels 177
budget hotels 181
character hotels 179
FC St. Pauli **110–11**
getting there 101
restaurants 190
Street-by-Street map 102–3
Walk: Landungsbrücken to Altonaer Balkon 148–9
St Pauli Fish Market 12, 13, 29, **108**, 223
St Pauli Museum 102, 105, 221
St Pauli Theater 204, 205
St Petri 36, **58–9**, 144
Hochaltar (Meister Bertram) 64
St-Petri-Altar (St Jacobi) 62
St-Petri-Dom (Bremen) 163
Bibelgarten 163
Bleikeller 163
Dom-Museum 163
Thronender Christus 163
St Salvator (Pellworm) 158
Saliba Alsterarkaden (restaurant) 188
Salomonisches Urteil (Bremer Rathaus) 165
Samova Teespeicher 195, 197
Sander, Jil 125, 198
Sandtorhafen 12, 13, **90**
Sandwich bars 195, 197
Schaartorschleuse 67
Schanzenstern Altona (hotel) 181
Schanzenviertel 13, **109**, 199–200, 206, 207, 223
Schaper, Fritz 77
Scharhörn 141
Scharoun, Hans 167

Schaudt, Emil 72
Schauenburg, Dukes of 22–3
Schauermann (restaurant) 190
Schauspielhaus see Deutsches Schauspielhaus
Das Schiff (caberet stage) 205
Schifffahrtsmuseum (Langeoog) 161
Schinkel, Karl Friedrich 138
Schlepperballett 44, 85
Schleswig-Holstein Musik Festival 45
Schleswig-Holsteinisches Wattenmeer (national park) see Wadden Sea National Park of Schleswig-Holstein
Schleusenbrücke 56, 58, 67
Schmeling, Max 43
Schmidt, Helmut 26, 27, 42
Schmidt Show 104
Schmidt Theater 103, **104**, 204, 205
Schmidts Tivoli 103, **104**, 202, 204, 205, 209, **211**
Schnitger, Arp 62
Schnoorviertel (Bremen) 166
Schokovida (café) 195, 197
Scholz, Olaf 27
Schönes Leben (restaurant) 189
Schumacher, Fritz 37, 42, 73, 105
Schütting (Bremen) 162, 163
Schwanenwik (hotel) 174, **179**
Schwartzenberger, Charles Maurice 59
SchwarzLICHTviertel 217
Sculptors 43
Seaman's shanty choir De Tampentrekker 203
Secondella (second-hand shop) 199, 201
Secondhand shops 199, 201
Secret Emotion (beauty shop) 200, 201
Security **224–5**, 239
Seeler, Uwe 27, 43
Seemannshöft (pilot station) 48
Das Seepferdchen (restaurant) 191
Der Seewolf (TV movie) 43
Segelschule Pieper 215
Segways 221
Self-Portait with Model (Kirchner) 65
Senator (hotel) 179
Senatskoordinator für die Erleichterung behinderter Menschen der Freien und Hansestadt Hamburg 174, 175
Senioren 222
Seute Deern (ship) 167
Shalimar (restaurant) 189
Shikara (restaurant) 191
Ship hotels 173
Ships
Cap San Diego 13, **98–9**
Deutsches Schifffahrtsmuseum (Bremerhaven) 167
Das Feuerschiff 89
Grönland 167
Hansekogge 167
Rickmer Rickmers 11, 12, 13, **94–5**
Seute Deern 167
U-434 13, 33, **108**
Wilhelm Bauer 167

Shoe shops 200, 201
Shopping 58, **198–201**
  beauty and lingerie 200, 201
  books 200, 201
  fashion 198–9, 201
  fine foods 200, 201
  furniture and design 199, 201
  jewellery and watches 199, 201
  Passages 76, 198
  second-hand stores 199, 201
  shopping areas and passages 198, 201
  Shopping in Style 10–11
  specialist shops 200, 201
  stilwerk 119
SIDE 177
SindBad (Baltrum) 160
Sister Act (musical) 105, 208, **210**, 211
Sixt (car hire) 234, **235**
Skating on the Außenalster 47
Skiing 215
Skybar 20up 206, 207
Slevogt, Max 162
Sloman, Henry B. 63
Slomanhaus 146
Smolka (hotel) 178
Smuggling 86–7
Snack bars **194–7**
Sofitel Hamburg Alter Wall (hotel) 180
Sommerdom 45
Sonnin, Ernst Georg 42
Soup & Friends 195, 196
Soup bars 195, 196–7
Soup City 195, 197
Souperia 195, 197
SPD 27
Specialist shops 200–201
Spectator Sports 215
Speicherstadt see Port and Speicherstadt
Speicherstadt Kaffeerösterei 194, 196
Speicherstadtmuseum 13, 30, 32, 83, **85**, 135, 147
Spicy's Gewürzmuseum 33, 82, **84**, 147
Spiekeroog 161
Spiekerooger Muschelmuseum 161
Spielbudenplatz 102, 104, 105
Spielzeugmuseum im Schnoor (Bremen) 166
Spirits and liqueurs 187
Sport **214–15**
  children 217
Springer, Axel 43
Springtime in Hamburg 44
Sprinkenhof 63, 144
Staatsoper see Hamburgische Staatsoper
Stadtlagerhaus 148
Stadtpark 11, 39, **134**, 139, 216, 217
Stadtpark Revival 46
StadtRad Hamburg 235
Stadttour Hamburg 215
Stage Club 207
Stage Entertainment 208, 209
Stallone, Sylvester 210
Stamps 228

Star-Club 26, 202, 206
Starcut (musical) 211
Stefan Fink (speciality shop) 200, 201
Steigenberger Hotel Hamburg 176
Steigenberger Hotel Treudelberg 178
Stella Maris (hotel) 179
stern (magazine) 40, 41, 229
Sternschanze 109
Sternschanzenpark 13, **109**, 203
Stettin (ice breaker ship) 135
stilwerk 10, 11, 113, **119**, 148–9, 182, 199, 201
Stock Exchange 24, 25, 36, 56, **66**
Stock's Fischrestaurant 193
Stolle Pralinen (café) 195, 197
Stores see Shopping
Störtebeker, Klaus 24, 43, 85
Störtebeker Monument 91
Strandhotel Blankenese 178
Strandkai 90
StrandPauli (beach club) 109, 207
Strandperle (restaurant) 192
Street Finder maps **242–57**
Stricker's KehrWieder Spitze (restaurant) 189
Strucklahnungsh örn (ferry terminal) 158
Students 223
Stuhlmann, Günther Ludwig **116**
Stuhlmannbrunnen 115, 116
Subway (sandwich shop) 195, 197
Summer in Hamburg 45
Summer on Magellan-Terrassen (festival) 45
Superbude St Pauli 181
Surffestival 44
Suzy Wong 191
Swimming 214, 215
Swiss (airline) 230, 231
Sylt 152, **156–7**

T
Tabakhistorische Sammlung Reemtsma see Museum der Arbeit
Tagesschau 41
Tamm, Peter 88
De Tampentrekker (shanty choir) 203
Tanz der Vampire (musical) 119, 208, 211
Tanzende Türme 37, 42, 102
Tarzan (musical) 119, 208, 209, **210–11**
Tatort (TV series) 41
Taxis 231, 234
taz (daily newspaper) 229
Tea salons 195, 197
Teeteria (tea salon) 195, 197
Teherani, Hadi 42, 102
Tele-Michel see Heinrich-Hertz-Turm
Telemann, Georg Philipp 42, 73
Telephones **228–9**
Television **40–41**, 229
Temperature 47
Tennis 215
Tennisanlage am Rothenbaum 45, 215
Die Terrasse im Restaurant Jacob in Nienstedten (Liebermann) 118

Teufelsbrück 48
TH2 (café) 194, 196
Thalia (bookshop) 200, 201
Thalia Theater **59**, 204, 205, 223
Thälmann, Ernst 42
Thämers (bar) 70
Theater für Kinder 217
Theater im Hafen Hamburg 51, **92**, 203, 208, 209, 210, **211**, 235
Theater Kehrwieder 147
Theater of the Year 59, 129
Theaterfestival "Laokoon" 204
Theaterschiff Batavia 217
Theatres **204–5**
  Alma Hoppe Lustspielhaus 205
  Altonaer Theater 115, 204, 205
  Deutsches Schauspielhaus 129, 204, 205
  English Theatre 204, 205
  Ernst Deutsch Theater 204, 205
  fools garden 204, 205
  Fundus Theater 216, 217
  Hamburger Kammerspiele 204, 205
  Hamburger Puppentheater 217
  Junges Musiktheater 217
  Junges Schauspielhaus 204
  Kampnagel 204, 205
  Kehrwieder 147
  Komödie Winterhuder Fährhaus 204, 205
  Ohnsorg-Theater **129**, 204, 205
  Opernloft 217
  St Pauli Theater 204, 205
  Das Schiff 205
  Schmidt Theater **104**, 204, 205
  Schmidts Tivoli **104**, 204, 205, 209, **211**
  Thalia Theater 46, **59**, 204, 205
  Theater in der Speicherstadt 204, 205
  Theater für Kinder 217
  Theater im Hafen Hamburg 51, **92**, 203, **211**, 235
  Theater Kehrwieder 147
  Theaterschiff Batavia 217
Ti Breizh (restaurant) 188
Tickets
  entertainment and events 202, 209, 220
  travel 236–7
Tierpark Hagenbeck 11, 13, 38, 43, 133, **136–7**, 216, 217
Tiger (Dampfschlepper) 135
Time zone 223
Titanic 77
Titanic (musical) 119, 210, 211
Toni Thiel (furniture shop) 199, 201
Tourist information 202, 203, **220**, 221
Touristik Kontor 49
Tower Bar 206, 207
Trautwein, Fritz 37, 42
Travel
  city tours 220, 221
  flights over Hamburg 220, 221
  public transportation (HVV) **234–41**
  by boat **48–51**
  boat tours 240–41

Travel (cont.)
tickets and passes 236–7
see also inside back cover
Treaty of Gottorp 25
Treaty of Verdun 21
Treaty of Versailles 26
Triathlon 214, 215
Trimotion (bicycle taxis) 237
Trostbrücke 145
Tschebull (restaurant) 188
TUI Operettenhaus 102, **105**, 208, 209, **210**, 211
Turnhalle St Georg (restaurant) 192
Türpe, Paul 116

U

U-434 (museum ship) 13, 33, **108**
U-Bahn **238–9**
U-Boat museum *see U-434*
Überseemuseum (Bremen) 166
Überseequartier 91
Uebel & Gefährlich (club) 207
Ufa-Palast 77
Umweltbewusst reisen 222
Umwelthauptstadt Europas 27, 222
UNESCO world heritage sites 140, 153, 157, 162, 164
Ungers, Mathias 64
Universum Science Center (Bremen) 166
Der Untergang (Nossack) 42
Unterland (Helgoland) 159

V

Vasco-da-Gama-Standbild (Hosaeus) 83
Vattenfall Cyclassics 214, 215
Verden an der Aller 167
Verlagsgruppe Milchstraße 125
Verlagshaus Gruner + Jahr 35, 37, 40, 68, 143, 146, 229
Vier Jahreszeiten (hotel) 36, 121, 123, **125**, 172, **176**
View Point 11, 13, **88**, 147
Vikings 21, 59, 158
Village (hotel) 177
Vintage & Rags (second-hand shop) 199, 201
Visa (credit card) 226
Visas 220
Vitalienbrüder 43
VLET (restaurant) 189
Vogel, Hugo 60
Vogeler, Heinrich 165, 167
Voght, Johann Caspar 138

Volkspark 38
Volksparkstadion *see* HSV-Arena
Vorbach (hotel) 178
Voscherau, Henning 27

W

Waagenbau (club) 206, 207
Wachsfigurenkabinett *see* Panoptikum
Wadden Sea **140–41**
Wadden Sea National Park of Lower Saxony 153, 161
Wadden Sea National Park of Schleswig-Holstein 153, 158
Wagner, Hansjörg 91
Wagner im Dammtorpalais (hotel) 178
Walking tours
Harbour Promenade and Speicherstadt 146–7
Landungsbrücken to Altonaer Balkon 148–9
Old Town 144–5
Walking on the Watt 157
Wallanlagen 79, 121
Wallanlagen (Bremen) 162
Wandelhalle (in Hauptbahnhof) 62, 198
Wandrahm (restaurant) 190
Wandrahmsfleet 83
Wangerooge 161
Die Wäscherei (furniture shop) 199, 201
Waschk-Balz, Doris 71
Wasserschutzpolizei 224
Wasserträger Hummel 67
Watch shops 199, 201
Water Tower 109
Water-and-light concert 78
Wattenmeer **140–41**
Wattwagenfahrten Volker Griebel 139
Weather 45–7
Wedel 139
Wedina (hotel) 178
Das Weiße Haus (restaurant) 193
Die Welt (newspaper) 229
Weltbühne (restaurant) 188
Wempe (jeweller's shop) 199, 201
Wenningstedt-Braderup 156–7
Weser Renaissance 153, 164
Westerland (musical) 211, 1209
Westerland (Sylt) 156
Westwind (café) 194, 196
What to Drink 186–7

Wilhelm Bauer (U-Boot) 167
Wilhelm I, Emperor
equestrian statue (Altona) 114, 117
monument (Planten un Blumen) 79, 242
Wilhelm-Koch-Stadion *see* Millerntor-Stadion
Willkomm-Höft 13, 133, **139**
Wimmel, Carl Ludwig 36, 66
Winter in Hamburg 47
Winterdom 46, 47
Winterhuder Fährhaus 204, 205, 241
Wittdün (Amrum) 158
Wittenburg 215
Witthüs Teestuben **193**, 195, 197
World Music 207
World War
First 26
Second 26, 66
Worpswede 167
Worpsweder Kunsthalle 167
Wunderbar 207
Wyk (Föhr) 158

Y

Yellow Möbel 199, 201
YoHo (hotel) 179
Young, Simone 204
Youth hostels 175

Z

Zadek, Peter 59, 129
ZDF studio 40
Zeise Kinos 205
DIE ZEIT (newspaper) 41, 229
Zeit-Stiftung (Zeit foundation) 58, 129
Zeitgeschichte 32
Zentraler Omnibusbahnhof (ZOB) 37, 232, 233
Zentrales Fundbüro der Freien und Hansestadt Hamburg 225
Zimmer Frei Hamburg 174, 175
Zitronenjette 71
Zollenspieker Fährhaus (restaurant) 193
Zollmuseum *see* Deutsches Zollmuseum
Zu den alten Krameramtsstuben am Michel (restaurant) 10, 72, **189**
Zum Schellfischposten (restaurant) 190
Zürichhaus 145

Acknowledgments

Dorling Kindersley would like thank all the following people whose contributions and assistance have made the preparation of this book possible..

Autor

Gerhard Bruschke, Gerhard Bruschke has a degree in geography and has written Vis-à-Vis travel guide *Dresden*. He also edited the German editions of several Vis-à-Vis travel guides (such as *San Francisco, Moscow, India*) and was the consultant for the English editions of Dorling Kindersley Eyewitness Guides to *Germany, Austria, Switzerland* and *Munich & Bavaria*. Moreover Gerhard Bruschke has written for many travel guides, atlases and encyclopedias (print and digital media).

Publisher

Douglas Amrine

Publishing Director

Dr. Jörg Theilacker

Layout

Anja Richter

Photographers

Felix Fiedler, Susanne Gilges, Olaf Kalugin, Maik Thimm

Illustrators

Branimir Georgiev, Maria-Magdalena Renker, Eva Sixt, Bernhard Springer

Cartography

Anja Richter, Mare e Monte

Editor

Brigitte Maier, Konzept & Text

Picture Researcher, Editor & Co-Cartographer

Stefanie Franz

Consultant

Helen Townsend

Cover

Anja Richter, Kate Everson, Tessa Bindloss, Petra Kühner

Proofreader, Street Finder Index

Philip Anton

Fact-Checker

Renate Hirschberger

Special Assistance

Special thanks goes to the following individuals, without whose help this book would not have been possible: Andrew Phillips, Birgit Walter, Dr. Peter Lutz, Jane Ewart, Natasha Lu, Matthias Liesendahl, Barbara Narr,

Familie Schiefelbein, Joanna Jordan, Florian Steinert, Susanne Krammer, Andrea Rinck

Additional Cartography

Casper Morris, DK Cartography.

Revisions Team

Ashwin Adimari, Emma Anacootee, Mohammad Hassan, Mathew Kurien, Kathryn Lane, Carly Madden, Alison McGill, Azeem Siddiqui, Susanna Smith, Priyanka Thakur

Photography Permissions

Airport Hamburg (Tanja Bösche), Bremer Touristik-Zentrale, Gerhard Bruschke, Cap San Diego Betriebsgesellschaft mbH, Felix Fiedler, Branimir Georgiev, Susanne Gilges, Gruner + Jahr AG & Co KG (Maike Pelikan), Hamburger Verkehrsverbund GmbH (Herr Rahn), Heike Hensel, Herzog & de Meuron, IFA Bilderteam, Internationales Maritimes Museum Hamburg (IMMH), Dr. Klaus Jancke, Jung von Matt GmbH (Katja Weber), Olaf Kalugin, Kur- und Touristikservice Borkum (Monika Sauer), Museum für Hamburgische Geschichte (hamburgmuseum), Museum für Kunst und Gewerbe, Hamburg, NDR Presse und Information (Ralf Pleßmann), Anja Richter, Rickmer Rickmers, St. Michaelis Turm GmbH, Jürgen Scheunemann, Senat Hamburg, Pressestelle (Susanne Meinecke), SPIEGEL-Verlag (Wolfgang Ebert), stern (Daniela Geppert), Maik Thimm, DIE ZEIT (Silvie Rundel).

Picture Credits

a-above; b-below/bottom; c-centre; f-far; l-left; r-right; t-top.

Artothek/G. Westermann: 166bl.

Borkum, Kur- und Touristikservice 150–151 Doppelseite, 153b, 154br, 160tr.

Bremer Touristik-Zentrale 164clb, 165crb.

Bruschke, Gerhard 3c, 5cr, 12cl, 13tr, 17tr, 17cr, 20c, 20bl, 24bl, 25tr, 25tc, 29bl, 29bc, 30cl, 30br, 36tl, 38br, 39bl, 40cl, 41cbr, 46cr, 47bl, 48tc, 49tl, 49c, 56cla, 56clb, 58br, 59tl, 61bl, 66cr, 69tc, 70tr, 70cla, 71cra, 71bl, 71br, 78bl, 81tc, 82c, 90tl, 91tc, 92t, 102cr, 103cl, 103bl, 108br, 109b, 110cl, 110bl, 110br, 111tl, 111c, 113tc, 114cr, 114clb, 114tr, 115tl, 115c, 115bl, 116cr, 118tl, 121tc, 122tl, 122cla, 123tr, 124c, 125tc, 126–127, 128b, 144crb, 145tc, 145bl, 146tr, 149tr, 155tr, 156br, 157tc, 160tl, 160b, 161cl, 161cr, 161bl, 170–171, 172tc, 172cl, 173tl, 173bc, 174tl, 174c, 174br, 175tr, 184cl, 184br, 185tl, 186cl, 187tl, 187c, 187bl, 188cla, 188cra, 188bl, 189tr (3 photos), 189cla, 202tc, 202cr, 203tr, 203c, 203bl, 206tc, 206cra, 206clb, 206bl, 207t, 207c, 216cl, 216bl, 220tc, 220cr, 220cl, 220b, 221tl, 222c, 222br, 223tr, 223c, 224b, 225ca, 225b, 226tl, 226ca, 228tr, 228cl, 228bl, 229ca, 229bl, 230cr, 233cl, 234tc, 234bl, 234bc, 234br, 235cl, 235bl, 236bl, 237tr, 237cr, 237bl, 238tl, 238tr, 239br, 240tr, 240cl, 241t, 241cl, 241bc.

Deutsche Bundespost 228cl.

Europäische Zentralbank, Frankfurt am Main 226cb, 227.

Fiedler, Felix 8 – 9, 9c, 11tc, 11br, 16tr, 17bl, 18, 19bl, 19br, 20tl, 21c, 21bc, 21br, 22tl, 22bl, 22br, 23tc, 23cr, 23br, 24tl, 24br, 25bl, 25br, 29cc, 29trc, 29br, 31tr, 31br, 32br, 32cl, 33c, 34tr, 34clb, 35tr, 38tl, 38tr, 38cl, 38cr, 38bl, 39tr, 39cr, 42tr, 42bl, 43tr, 43br, 44tr, 44br, 45tr, 46tl, 48cr, 48bl, 49bl, 50cl, 51cra, 51bl, 53c, 60cla, 60clb, 60bl, 61tl, 61crb, 62bl, 70bl, 74tl, 74cl, 75tl, 75cra, 75crb, 75br, 78tr, 83tl, 84tr, 92br, 93br, 94tr, 94c, 94bl, 95tl, 95cra, 95crb, 95bc, 98tl, 98tr, 98bl, 98br, 98bc, 99tl, 99cra, 99crb, 99bl, 102tl, 111bl, 111crb, 117br, 118br, 119b, 130tl, 130tr, 130ca, 130cb, 131tl, 131cra, 131crb, 132, 133tc, 134tl, 134br, 135tl, 135br, 136tl, 136tr, 136c, 136br, 137tr, 137cra, 137bl, 138tr, 138bc, 139tr, 139b, 142, 143cl, 188crb, 221tl, 222tr, 242tl.

Franz, Stefanie 102bl, 109bl, 186cl

Georgiev, Branimir 40tl, 90tr, 90br, 102b, 103bl, 122tr.

Gilges, Susanne 5cl, 10tc, 10br, 16tl, 20br, 29tl, 29c, 31tl, 31cr, 31bl, 33tr, 33cb, 34tl, 34cla, 35bl, 36tr, 36cl, 36cr, 39tl, 39br, 41cla, 43cl, 44bl, 47tr, 48cl, 50tr, 50bl, 51tl, 51tr, 52 – 53, 54, 56tl, 56br, 57cr, 57bl, 58tl, 59br, 61cra, 63bl, 66tr, 66bl, 67tr, 67bc, 68, 70tl, 70br, 71tr, 72tc, 72bl, 73tl, 73bl, 73br, 76tl, 76br, 77tl, 77c, 77br, 78tl, 78cl, 78br, 79tl, 79tr, 79cra, 79crb, 79bl, 85tr, 85br, 88tr, 88bl, 89tr, 89bc, 93cr, 100, 101tc, 103cr, 104tr, 104cl, 105tr, 105bc, 108tr, 108c, 110tl, 110tr, 112, 114tl, 114b, 115cr, 116tl, 116bl, 117tl, 117c, 118c, 119tr, 120, 122clb, 122br, 123tc, 123br, 124t, 124b, 125b, 128t, 128c, 129tr, 129c, 144tr, 145cr, 147tl, 148tr, 148cl, 148bc, 149cc, 149bl, 216cr, 217c, 221c, 233cr, 242bl.

Gruner + Jahr 40bl, 40br, 40crb, 41bl, 41bcl.

Hamburg Airport 230tc.

Hamburger Verkehrsverbund 236tr, 238cl, 238br, 239tr, Hintere Umschlaginnenseiten HVV-Plan.

Hensel, Heike / Pelz, Andreas 230cl.

Herzog, de Meuron 25clb, 35br, 37c, 51crb, 90cl.

IMMH 86tl, 86tr (Michael Zapf), 86cla (Michael Zapf), 86clb (Michael Zapf), 86bc (Michael Zapf), 87tc, 87cra, 87bl (Michael Zapf), 87br (Michael Zapf).

Janke, Dr. Klaus 140cl, 140bl, 140br, 141tc, 141cr, 141bc, 154cl.

Jung von Matt 40tr, 40cr.

Kalugin, Olaf 2 – 3, 11cr, 16br, 29clb, 46bl, 84bl, 91bl, 93tr, 96 – 97, 102cl, 103br, 104br, 123tr, 146br, 217tl, 243bl.

KMJ@Wikipedia 232tr.

Moevenpick Hotel Hamburg 109tr.

NDR 41tl, 41tr, 41t.

Panzau, Thomas Umschlag Vorderseite, Hauptbild.

Renker, Maria-Magdalena 50 – 51 Artwork, 56 – 57 Detail, 70 – 71 Detail, 86 – 87 Artwork, 90 – 91 Artwork, 102 – 103 Detail, 114 – 115 Detail; Umschlag Vorderseite ur.

Richter, Anja 17tl, 23bl, 30tl, 30tr, 30bl, 43cr, 50br, 55tc, 94tl, 111cra, 145cl, 151c, 156tl, 171c, 184tc, 186c, 186c (3 photos), 187bc, 187br, 188tl, 188tr (5 photos), 188c,

188bl, 188bc, 188br, 189tr, 189cla (2 photos), 189clb (2 photos), 189br, 219c, 224cr, 226b, 229cr, 231tl, 231br, 239cl, 239cr, 240tl, 240bl, 240br, 242tc.

Rinck, Andrea 28, 137bcr.

Sixt, Eva 30 – 31 (9 Drawing), 34 – 35 (9 Drawing), 37u (5 Drawing), 38 – 39 (8 Drawing), 78 – 79 (4 Drawing), 122 – 123 Detail, 136 – 137 (7 Drawing), 140 – 141 (22 Drawing), 156 – 157 (6 Drawing), Umschlag Vorderseite ur

DER SPIEGEL 41cr.

Springer, Bernhard & Renker, Maria-Magdalena 5br, 60 – 61 Artwork, Umschlag Rückseite Mitte Artwork

Suhr, Christoffer und Peter@Wikipedia 21tl.

Theilacker, Dr. Jörg 4br, 5tl, 10cr, 24cl, 24cr, 26 – 27, 28, 4br, 45br, 80, 102c, 106 – 107, 123tl, 143tc, 143cr, 185tr, 185br, 202bl, 203bl, 207tl, 218 – 219, 224tl, 224cl, 225tr, 225c, 234cl, 234cr, 235tc, 239bl, Inside front cover 2br

Thimm, Maik 4tr, 19c, 57tl, 91br.

Westerland, Tourismus-Service 156cl, 156bl, 157cr.

DIE ZEIT 41cr, 41c, 144bl.

Front Endpaper

Left side: Felix Fiedler bc; Susanne Gilges tr, cl; DK Images bl. *Right side:* Susanne Gilges tc, tr, cr; Jörg Theilacker br.

Back Endpaper

Hamburger Verkehrsverbund.

Jacket

Front: Thomas Panzau, Hauptbild; Maria-Magdalena Renker br. *Back:* Felix Fiedler tl, clt, bl; Olaf Kalugin clb; Bernhard Springer, Maria-Magdalena Renker c. *Spine:* Thomas Panzau t; Susanne Gilges b.

All other images © Dorling Kindersley.

For further information see **www.dkimages.com**

Phrase Book

In an Emergency

Where is the telephone?	Wo ist das Telefon?	voh ist duss **tel**-e-fone?
Help!	Hilfe!	**hilf**-uh
Please call a doctor	Bitte rufen Sie einen Arzt	**bitt**-uh **roof**'n zee ine-en **artst**
Please call the police	Bitte rufen Sie die Polizei	**bitt**-uh **roof**'n zee dee poli-**tsy**
Please call the fire brigade	Bitte rufen Sie die Feuerwehr	**bitt**-uh roof'n zee dee **foyer**-vayr
Stop!	Halt!	hult

Communication Essentials

Yes	Ja	yah
No	Nein	nine
Please	Bitte	**bitt**-uh
Thank you	Danke	**dunk**-uh
Excuse me	Verzeihung	fair-**tsy**-hoong
Hello (good day)	Guten Tag	**goot**-en **tahk**
Goodbye	Auf Wiedersehen	owf-**veed**-er-zay-ern
Good evening	Guten Abend	**goot**'n **ahb**'nt
Good night	Gute Nacht	**goot**-uh **nukht**
Until tomorrow	Bis morgen	biss **morg**'n
See you	Tschüss	**chooss**
What is that?	Was ist das?	voss ist duss
Why?	Warum?	var-**room**
Where?	Wo?	voh
When?	Wann?	vunn
today	heute	**hoyt**-uh
tomorrow	morgen	**morg**'n
yesterday	gestern	**gest**'n
morning	Morgen	**morg**'n
afternoon	Nachmittag	**nahkh**-mit-tahk
evening	Abend	**ahb**'nt
night	Nacht	**nukht**
week	Woche	**vokh**-uh
month	Monat	**mohn**-aht
year	Jahr	yar
there	dort	dort
here	hier	hear

Useful Phrases

How are you?	Wie geht's?	vee **gayts**?
Fine, thanks	Danke, es geht mir gut	dunk-uh, es gayt meer goot
Pleased to meet you	Es freut mich, Sie kennenzulernen	ess **froyt** mish, zee **ken**'n-tsoo-lairn'n
Until later	Bis später	biss **shpay**-ter
Where is / are?	Wo ist / sind ...?	voh ist / sind
How far is it to ...?	Wie weit ist es ...?	vee **vite** ist ess
Which way to ...?	Wie komme ich zu ...?	vee **komm**-a ish tsoo...?
Do you speak English?	Sprechen Sie Englisch?	**shpresh**'n zee **eng**-glish?
I don't understand	Ich verstehe nicht	ish fair-**shtay**-uh nisht
Could you speak more slowly?	Könnten Sie langsamer sprechen?	**kurnt**-en zee lung-zam-er **shpresh**'n
I'm sorry	Es tut mir leid	es toot meer **lyte**

Useful Words

big	groß	**grohss**
small	klein	**kline**
hot	heiß	**hyce**
cold	kalt	**kult**
good	gut	**goot**
bad	schlecht	**shlesht**
enough	genug	**g'nook**
well	gut	**goot**
open	auf / offen	**owf / off**'n
closed	zu / geschlossen	**tsoo / g'shloss**'n
left	links	**links**
right	rechts	**reshts**
straight on	geradeaus	**g'rah**-der-**owss**
near	in der Nähe	in dair **nay**-er
far	weit	**vyte**
up	auf, oben	owf, **obe**'n
down	ab, unten	up, **oont**'n
early	früh	**froo**
late	spät	**shpate**
entrance	Eingang / Einfahrt	**ine**-gung / **ine**-fart
exit	Ausgang / Ausfahrt	**ows**-gung / **ows**-fart
toilet	WC / Toilette	vay-**say** / toy-**lett**-er
free / unoccupied	frei	**fry**
free / no charge	frei / gratis	fry/**grah**-tis

Making a Telephone Call

I'd like to make a phone call	Ich möchte telefonieren	ish mer-shtuh tel-e-fon-**eer**'n
I'll try again later	Ich versuche es später noch mal	es shpay-ter nokh es **zookh**-uh -mull
Can I leave a message?	Kann ich eine Nachricht hinterlassen?	kan ish **ine**-uh nakh-risht hint-er-**lahss**'n
answer phone	Anrufbeantworter	an-roof-be-**ahnt**-vort-er
telephone card	Telefonkarte	tel-e-**fohn**-kart-uh
receiver	Hörer	**hur**-er
mobile phone	Handy	han dee
engaged (busy)	besetzt	b'zetst
wrong number	falsche Verbindung	falsh-uh fair-**bin**-doong
long-distance call	Ferngespräch	**fairn**-g'shpresh

Staying in a Hotel

Do you have a vacant room?	Haben Sie ein Zimmer frei?	harb'n zee ine **tsimm**-er fry?
double room	Doppelzimmer	**dopp**'l-tsimm-er
with double bed	mit Doppelbett	mitt **dopp**'l-bet
single room	Einzelzimmer	**ine** ts'l tsimm er
room with a bath / shower	Zimmer mit Bad / Dusche	**tsimm**-er mitt bat / **doosh**-er
porter	Gepäckträger	g'**peck**-tray-ger
concierge	Concierge	kon-see-**airsh**
key	Schlüssel	**shloos**'l
I have a reservation for a room	Ich habe ein Zimmer reserviert	ish **harb**-er ine **tsimm**-er rezz-er-**veert**

Sightseeing

bus	Bus	**booss**
tram	Straßenbahn / Tram	**stra**-sen-barn, tram
train	Zug	**tsoog**
gallery	Galerie	gall-er-**ee**
bus station	Busbahnhof	**booss**-barn-hofe
train station	Bahnhof	**barn**-hofe
bus (tram) stop	Haltestelle	**hal**-te-shtel-er
palace / castle	Schloss, Burg	**shloss, boorg**
post office	Postamt	**pohs**-taamt
cathedral	Dom	**dome**
church	Kirche	**keersh**-er
garden	Garten, Park	**gart**'n, park
library	Bibliothek	bib-leo-**tek**
museum	Museum	moo-**zay**-oom
information	Information	in-for-mut-see-**on**
closed for public holiday	Feiertags geschlossen	**fire**-targz g'**shloss**'n
entrance ticket	Eintrittskarte	ine-**tritz**-kart-uh
cemetery	Friedhof	**freed**-hofe
place	Platz	plats
free admission	Eintritt frei	**ine**-tritt fry

Shopping

Do you have / Is there ...?	Gibt es ...?	geept ess
How much does it cost?	Was kostet das?	voss **kost**'t duss?
When do you open? close?	Wann öffnen Sie? schließen Sie?	vunn **off**'n zee **shlees**'n zee
Do you take credit cards?	Kann ich mit Kreditkarte bezahlen?	kunn ish mitt kred-**it**-**kar**-ter b'**tsahl**'n
this	das	duss
expensive	teuer	**toy**-er
cheap	preiswert	**price**-vurt
size	Größe	**gruhs**-uh
number	Nummer	**noom**-er
colour	Farbe	**farb**-uh
brown	braun	brown
black	schwarz	**shvarts**
red	rot	roht
blue	blau	blau
green	grün	**groon**
yellow	gelb	gelp

Types of Shop

antique shop	Antiquitäten-laden	un-tick-vi-**tayt**'n-lard'n
bakery	Bäckerei	beck-er-**eye**
bank	Bank	bunk

book shop	Buchladen /	**bookh**-*lard'n* /	Kalbfleisch	*kalb-flysh*	veal
	Buchhandlung	**bookh**-*hant-loong*	Kaninchen	*ka-**neensh**'n*	rabbit
butcher	Fleischerei	*fly-sher-**eye***	Karpfen	*karpf'n*	carp
cake shop	Konditorei	*kon-ditt-or-**eye***	Kartoffelpüree	*kar-**toff'l**-poor-ay*	mashed potatoes
chemist			Käse	*kayz-uh*	cheese
(for prescriptions)	Apotheke	*App-o-**tay**-ke*	Knoblauch	*k'nob-lowkh*	garlic
(for cosmetics)	Drogerie	*droog-er-**ree***	Knödel	*k'nerd'l*	dumpling
department store	Kaufhaus	*kauf-hows*	Kohl	*koal*	cabbage
delicatessen	Feinkost(laden)	*fine-kost(lahd'n)*	Kopfsalat	*kopf-zal-aat*	lettuce
fishmonger	Fischladen	*fish-lahd'n*	Krebs	*krayps*	crab
gift shop	Geschenke(laden)	*g'shenk-er(lahd'n)*	Kuchen	*kookh'n*	cake
greengrocer	Obst & Gemüse	*ohbst & g'**moozer***	Lachs	*lahkhs*	salmon
grocery	Lebensmittelladen	*layb'nz-mitt'l-ladn*	Leber	*lay-ber*	liver
hairdresser	Friseur / Frisör	*freezz-**er***	mariniert	*mari-neert*	marinated
market	Markt	*markt*	Marmelade	*marmer-**lard**-uh*	marmalade, jam
travel agent	Reisebüro	*rye-zer-boo-**roe***	Meerrettich	*may-re-tish*	horseradish
café	Café	*kaff-**ay***	Milch	*milsh*	milk
post office	Post	*posst*	Mineralwasser	*min-er-**arl**-vuss-er*	mineral water
boutique	Boutique	*boo-**teek**-uh*	Möhre	*mer-uh*	carrot
			Nuss	*nooss*	nut
			Öl	*erl*	oil
Eating Out			Petersilie	*payt-er-**zee**-li-uh*	parsley
			Pfeffer	*pfeff-er*	pepper
Have you got a table	Haben Sie einen	*harb'n zee ine'n tish*	Pommes frites	*pomm-**fritt***	French fries
for …?	Tisch für …?	*foor …?*	Radieschen	*ra-**deesh**'n*	radish
I want to reserve a	Ich möchte einen	*ish **mersh**-ter ine'n*	Rindfleisch	*rint-flysh*	beef
table	Tisch reservieren	*tish rese-**veer**'n*	Rippchen	*rip-sh'n*	cured pork rib
I am vegetarian	Ich bin Vegetarier	*ish bin vegg-er-**tah**-*	Rotkohl	*roht-koal*	red cabbage
		ree-er	Rührei	*rhoo-er-eye*	scrambled eggs
waiter	Herr Ober	*hair oh-bare*	Saft	*zuft*	juice
The bill please!	Zahlen, bitte!	*tsaarl'n **bitt**-er*	Salat	*zal-**aat***	salad
tip	Trinkgeld	*trink-gelt*	Salz	*zults*	salt
menu	Speisekarte	*shpize-er-kart-er*	Salzkartoffeln	*zults-kar-toff'l*	boiled potatoes
(fixed price) menu	Menü	*men-oo*	Sauerkraut	*zow-er-**krowt***	sauerkraut
cover charge	Couvert / Gedeck	*koo-vair / g'**deck***	Sekt	*zekt*	sparkling wine
wine list	Weinkarte	*vine-kart-er*	Senf	*zenf*	mustard
glass	Glas	*glars*	scharf	*sharf*	spicy
bottle	Flasche	*flush-er*	Schaschlik	*shash-lik*	kebab
cup	Tasse	*tass-uh*	Schlagsahne	*shlahgg-zarn-uh*	whipped cream
knife	Messer	*mess-er*	Schnittlauch	*shnit-lowkh*	chives
fork	Gabel	*garb'l*	Schnitzel	*shnitz'l*	veal or pork cutlet
spoon	Löffel	*lerff'l*	Schweinefleisch	*shvine-flysh*	pork
flatware, cutlery	Besteck	*be **shteck***	Spargel	*shparg'l*	asparagus
breakfast	Frühstück	*froo-shtook*	Spiegelei	*shpeeg'l-eye*	fried egg
lunch	Mittagessen	*mit-targ-ess'n*	Spinat	*shpin-art*	spinach
dinner	Abendessen	*arb'nt-ess'n*	Tee	*tay*	tea
main course	Hauptspeise	*howpt-shpize-er*	Tomate	*tom-art-uh*	tomato
starter, first course	Vorspeise	*for-shpize-er*	Wein	*vine*	wine
dish of the day	Tageskarte	*targ-erz-**kart**-e*	Weintrauben	*vine-trowb'n*	grapes
			Zander	*tsan-der*	pikeperch
Menu Decoder			Zitrone	*tsi-trohn-uh*	lemon
			Zucker	*tsook-er*	sugar
Aal	*arl*	eel	Zwieback	*tsvee-bak*	rusk
Apfel	**upf'l**	apple	Zwiebel	**tsveeb'l**	onion
Apfelschorle	**upf'l**-*shoorl-uh*	apple juice with			
		sparkling water	**Numbers**		
Apfelsine	**upf'l**-*seen-uh*	orange			
Artischocke	*arti-**shokh**-uh*	artichoke	0	**null**	*nool*
Aubergine	*or-ber-jeen-uh*	aubergine, eggplant	1	**eins**	*eye'ns*
Beefsteak	**beef**-*stayk*	steak	2	**zwei**	*tsvy*
Bier	*beer*	beer	3	**drei**	*dry*
Bockwurst	**bokh**-*voorst*	type of sausage	4	**vier**	*feer*
Bohnensuppe	*burn-en-zoop-uh*	bean soup	5	**fünf**	*foonf*
Branntwein	*brant-vine*	spirits	6	**sechs**	*zex*
Bratkartoffeln	*brat-kar-**toff**'ln*	fried potatoes	7	**sieben**	**zeeb**'n
Bratwurst	*brat-voorst*	fried sausage	8	**acht**	*uhkht*
Brötchen	**bret**-*tchen*	bread roll	9	**neun**	*noyn*
Brot	*brot*	bread	10	**zehn**	*tsayn*
Butter	**boot**-*ter*	butter	11	**elf**	*elf*
Champignon	**shum**-*pin-yong*	mushroom	12	**zwölf**	*tsverlf*
Currywurst	**kha**-*ree-voorst*	sausage with curry	13	**dreizehn**	**dry**-*tsayn*
Ei	*eye*	egg	20	**zwanzig**	**tsvunn**-*tsig*
Eis	*ice*	ice cream	21	**einundzwanzig**	**ine**-*oont-***tsvunn**-*tsig*
Ente	**ent**-*uh*	duck	30	**dreißig**	**dry**-*sig*
Erdbeeren	**ayrt**-*beer'n*	strawberries	40	**vierzig**	**feer**-*tsig*
Fisch	*fish*	fish	50	**fünfzig**	**foonf**-*tsig*
Forelle	*for-ell-uh*	trout	100	**(ein)hundert**	*(ine) hoond't*
Frikadelle	*Fri-ka-**dayl**-uh*	hamburger, meat ball	1,000	**(ein)tausend**	*(ine) towz'nt*
Gans	*ganns*	goose	1,000,000	**eine Million**	*ine-er mill-yohn*
Garnele	*gar-nayl-uh*	prawn / shrimp	1,000,000,000	**eine Milliarde**	*ine-er milli-arde*
gebraten	*g'**braat**'n*	fried			
gegrillt	*g'grilt*	grilled	**Time**		
gekocht	*g'kokht*	boiled			
geräuchert	*g'**rowk**-ert*	smoked	one minute	**eine Minute**	*ine-er min-**oot**-uh*
Geflügel	*g'**floog**'l*	poultry	one hour	**eine Stunde**	*ine-er **shtoond**-er*
Gemüse	*g'**mooz**-uh*	vegetables	half an hour	**halbe Stunde**	**hull**-*ber* **shtoond**-er
Gulasch	*goo-lush*	goulash	Monday	**Montag**	*mone-targ*
Gurke	**goork**-*uh*	gherkin	Tuesday	**Dienstag**	*deens-targ*
Hähnchen	*haynsh'n*	chicken	Wednesday	**Mittwoch**	*mitt-vokh*
Hering	**hair**-*ing*	herring	Thursday	**Donnerstag**	**donn**-*ers-targ*
Himbeeren	*him-beer'n*	raspberries	Friday	**Freitag**	**fry**-*targ*
Honig	**hoe**-*nikh*	honey	Saturday	**Samstag**	*zums-targ*
Kaffee	*kaf-**fay***	coffee	Sunday	**Sonntag**	*zon-targ*

Bruecke 10 - Landungs-
                    brucken
Estancia Stks
Grosser Reichenstrasse, 27
Groninger Braukeller
Willy-Brand 47
Oberhafenkantine
Stockmeyer St, 39
Argentum
    Hohe Bleichen, J

Clockers (bar)
Paul-Rossen, 27
Kong (wine, food)
    P-R, 35

Hamburg Public Transport Map